CRACKiNG KUBRiCK'S

CODE

THE SHiNiNG UnMASKED

P. MICHAEL HEFFRON

For

Mom

Anything will give up its secrets if you love it enough.

George Washington Carver

In every real man a child is hidden that wants to play.
The most spiritual men, as the strongest, find their happiness
where others would find their destruction: in the labyrinth,
in the hardness against themselves and others, in experiments.
Their joy is self-conquest;
difficult tasks are a privilege to them.

Fredric Nietzsche The Anti-Christ

Every great and deep difficulty bears in itself its own
solution. It forces us to change our thinking in order to find it.

Niels Bohr

Table of Contents

PROLOGUE

It is not the answer that enlightens, but the question
Eugene Ionesco

"Come and Play"
The Grady Twins

WHO ARE WE? Why are we here? Where do we come from and where are we going? What is truth? What does it mean to be human? What is freedom, and what is slavery? What does it all mean? What is "God"? And who gets to decide the answer to these questions: us, or someone else? And most importantly of all – why are we so afraid, of everything, of each other, and even ourselves? We're not born this way. So, what happened?

To be clear, this book is for anyone who has ever seriously wondered about the kinds of questions asked above just as much as it is for anyone who has ever wondered what *The Shining* by Stanley Kubrick is all about, and why Jack Torrance ultimately ends up where he does. More than that, however, it is also a book designed to convince you that Stanley Kubrick died with a secret about this film, and perhaps all of his films, which he never told to a single soul his whole life but confessed to everyone on the planet in *The Shining*. And no, this has nothing to do with the Apollo moon landing.

As it turns out, the answers Kubrick invites us to look for in *The Shining* can only be found by playing in the garden of curiosity that I have rolled out to the reader with the ball of questions at the top of this page. Why? Because, more than anything else, the infinite human capacity for curiosity and creativity was born to play in just such an Eden, "forever and ever and ever." In fact, curiosity is like the sunlight to the soul of learning and the oxygen of every thought we have. And while comparing life's biggest questions to the meaning of an old horror movie may at first sight look like comparing the sun to the tennis ball that rolls up to Danny in the 237 hallway, at "second sight" it turns out each is merely a reflection of the other, because both are the result of a meticulous orchestration of repeating patterns in a mirror, otherwise known as fractals. As we will see, Kubrick adorns every millimeter of his film with such fractals, all of which are trapped inside of his house of mirrors: just like all of us.

As for all of us, it has taken the universe 13.8 billion years to birth forth a species like our own, one capable of not only asking such questions but answering them as well, however we see fit. And there can be no greater form of blasphemy toward the miraculous process of chance that designed us with such remarkable abilities than to reject the responsibility of exercising the freedom we have to answer such questions, however we wish. Indeed, the fear that doing so may provoke the eternal ire of whatever designed us with such capacities is like being so afraid of angering whatever breathed life into us to begin with that we choose to suffocate ourselves to death rather than breathe.[1] In the hope

---

[1] An oft overlooked irony of this idea is that we are designed biologically with just as much of an ability, desire, and need to move and breathe as to question, all of which incentivize us to do so in order to forge new muscle fibers in our body and new synaptic connections in our brain. Christianity, however, claims that God literally killed himself in order to start a religion that could coerce homo sapiens into keeping their curiosity confined within the chastity belt of one specific brand of religious beliefs, of which – proving how threats and bribes from even God Himself are powerless to girdle the minds God had "intelligently

of being saved from such fears, and rewarded with a "happily ever after" for doing so, we embrace whatever promises to save us from the hell of our uncertainties, about this life and the next. To save us from the eternal sea of questions the mind is heir too, as a result, we decline the invitation from our ability to design our own meaning, and simply drop anchor and "believe" instead in the "meaning of life" sold to us by one brand of religion or another. That anchor of "belief" then becomes as much an umbilical cord as a sacred confirmation bias, coloring everything we think as if we are looking at the world through a stained-glass window.

But Houston, we have a problem. Here's the problem.

Upon our birth, we enter into a world shaped by the countless biases and beliefs of earlier generations. Yet we not only often fail to upgrade such beliefs, with beliefs in the morality of slavery and burning of witches lasting for centuries, we also learn to adopt and depend on, and to some degree even worship (since "work is prayer," as it says in Genesis 2:17) those biases and beliefs, for all our meaning, security, connection, and identity. As the underlying codes of the cultural paradigms we are born into, those biases and beliefs function as the operating system of a society. Like an invisible hand, that operating system serves to format all human consciousness born into its hungry embrace. Through an elaborate use of symbols and manipulation that are so ubiquitous and alluring that they constitute not only the bread of life itself, but also the water we drink and even the very oxygen we breathe, cultures designed by past generations feed like zombies on the minds of

---

designed" in the image and likeness of His own infinite 'creative' intelligence – there are over 42,000 different sub-brands today.

all who are born into their womb. And we either follow in the footsteps of those venerated ghosts, and often more out of fear of being rejected from the herd than love or respect for the ideas authored by those ghosts, or we muster the courage to "dare to go where no man has gone before," venture outside the barnyard of our various belief systems, and try something completely different.

Trying something new can feel as terrifying to some as it may feel exhilarating to others. One ingredient necessary for ensuring it feels more like the latter than the former comes from developing both a healthy balance between our biological needs for authenticity and attachment, and healthy boundaries around the permeable membrane of one's own mind. Creating such boundaries requires a level of self-awareness that allows us to discern the difference between our own consciousness, and who we think we are, and the lingering ideas that arose from other people's minds long since dead and gone, who have told us we are born flawed. One allows us to see we are born swans, simply put, while the other teaches us to believe we are born with the sin-stained souls of an ugly duckling. Today, the latter underwrites the cultural formatting that nurtures our brain to depend upon certain unquestioned assumptions about ourselves that science is increasingly demonstrating to be not only flawed or unfounded, but even toxic to our physical, emotional, and mental health, and simply false.

What does any of this have to do with *The Shining* by Stanley Kubrick? Everything. In simplest terms, *The Shining* is about the difference between a willingness to simply believe something out of fear or devotion, and the courage to ask questions, and whether a nature that designs us to seek the truth by questioning is better or worse than the religions that claim "truth" is something we must be conditioned and commanded to simply "believe." It is also about which leads to freedom, as we see with Danny and Wendy, and which to madness through a sacred process of mindless ritualized repetition, which is the very definition of insanity, just like Jack typing the same sentence over and over again; like a broken record; or a robot; or even a prayer repeated in pursuit of eternal life.

Like Danny in the Overlook hotel, I'd been riding these questions around in circles in my brain ever since Kubrick's film graced the silver screen some 42 years ago. It was those questions that led me behind the curtain of Kubrick's masquerade ball. The rolling of that ball began with my own need to try to "know thyself," as either a sinner or a misinformed swan. And to do that, I had to begin asking difficult questions about my own sacred and cherished religious beliefs, and why I held them to be so necessary for my survival, both in this life and the next.

◊◊

Nothing has fascinated me more in life than the contrast between how the world is and how people think. The former is as free and formless as water, the latter as rigid and brittle as ice. For Jesus, this was the same difference between the spirit and the letter of the law. While he saw the law as simply a tool for helping people navigate the travails of life, holding it up like a candle in the darkness, the religious leaders of his own day, much like the Catholic Church in the centuries that followed, used that same law as a chain to bind people to the stake of a sacred perspective with the threat of being burned at that stake like a witch or a heretic in this life, or a damned sinner in the next. One frees us from the dictates of a "brood of vipers," and the other nails us to a cross. And if ever there was a tool for helping me to understand the importance of seeing the difference it is *The Shining* by Stanley Kubrick.

Like nothing else, *The Shining* helped me to understand the difference between learning to trust my own mind and putting my faith in the brand of beliefs I had been conditioned to believe my own mind was required to wholly depend on in order to prevent me from devolving into a rabid serial sinner headed straight for hell. Why? Because it is a film designed to operate as a "games room" that illustrates just how much "unquestioned beliefs are the real authority in any culture," as Derek Jensen pointed out, and how those beliefs operate to prevent us from living a life we freely choose, even as they are also used to condemn us for using our "free will" to believe and think whatever we wish.

The Shining, in this respect, is a maze that invites us to free ourselves through the art of playing like a child. Doing so is the only way for us to not only enter Kubrick's Games Room, but to also "enter the kingdom of Heaven by becoming children again," for doing both requires relearning how to use our mind with the fearlessness we had as children. And we can do this, as simple as it may seem, by realizing just how important it is to question whether what we are watching in Kubrick's *Shining* is in fact being caused by forces of supernatural evil, as my Catholic perspective would have me believe, or whether such a "belief" is being used as a smokescreen to hide the truth from us instead.

Like a wizard operating behind the curtain of a silver screen, Kubrick hides in plain sight all the answers we seek, confident that our confirmation bias for our brands of beliefs will either blind us to noticing them or prevent us from understanding how to piece them together. And while the ultimate answer to *The Shining* may be of no real consequence either way when it comes to the film itself, no answer could be more important to the questions posed by the film when it comes to understanding the true nature of the world we are born into today; and especially important to the world we are born into tomorrow.

Unmasking Kubrick's film all began with the reading of a random article online that asked the same question about a movie that I was asking myself about life overall. And then I watched that movie, and noticed it was about a boy afraid of the future and a man stuck in the past, with one coming apart at the seams by acting like a robot, and the other finally unifying his conflicted halves into one by standing on his own two feet and thinking for himself, and that both were simply two sides of a mirror. And the mirror was me. And then I noticed a pattern, which formed a thread, which could be followed from one side of that mirror to the other, and from one ball to another. And before I knew it, I was playing a game of chess with a ghost, and following a bouncing ball, only to discover it was the same game I had been playing my whole life already. And then, in a flash of light, it all came together, and everything changed.

The article in question was written in May of 2020. Due to the ever-growing number of interpretations of Kubrick's adaptation, Scott Tobias wrote an article for The Guardian entitled, "The Shining 40 Years Later: will we ever fully understand what it all means?" At the time, I had no idea of just how much that question, and that movie, would change what I knew, or thought I knew, about everything, especially myself, and all the questions that had plagued me my whole life.

To understand any of this, however, we must first consider Tobias's question. Is fully understanding "what it all means" even possible, or did

Kubrick intentionally design his film to be a "mystery that no mortal man would ever solve," because it is simply a puzzle that could be deconstructed and reassembled in any infinite number of ways? Either way, Tobias's question opens the door to a flood of other questions, some of which it appears few if any have dared to ask about *The Shining*. Of all those questions, these three stand out:

1) Do we *really* want to know "what it *all* means," or do we want to simply confirm our "beliefs" about what we think it all means?
2) Just how far are we willing to go to find an answer to the first question? And, perhaps most importantly of all . . .
3) Do we have any duty to figure out what it all means, if only for ourselves, or is it all just a meaningless mind-game that was designed to be played "forever and ever and ever," and nothing more?

The answer to all three of these questions can be found in what follows, but only after we put Kubrick's film under a microscope. This means examining not only the film in great detail, pixel by pixel and error by error, but also the complexity and plasticity of the human mind. The curtain that hides the true face of Kubrick's masterpiece of modern horror, as such, are our "beliefs" in the supernatural, which blinds our brain from seeing just how much Kubrick created his film to be fully explainable by the psychological. To see this, we must tear open the curtain in the temple of our beliefs, much like the curtain in the temple is torn in two after Jesus dies. Like two sides of a mirror, one of those psychological explanations comes from looking into Jack's mind, and the other comes from putting together the jigsaw puzzle that Kubrick provides in every frame of his film. In fact, following these two threads is exactly what Kubrick was inviting us to try to do in the opening scene.

Consider first our brain, and how it makes us susceptible to such conditioning. On the one hand, that ball of meatloaf between our ears is wired to perceive reality in multiple yet seemingly contradictory ways simultaneously. Doing so allows it to endlessly expand its knowledge and understanding of itself and the universe it inhabits, for each is a mere reflection of the other. What impedes or corrupts this process, however, is the fact that, through systems of "beliefs" that teach us to prefer the old to the new, or to depend upon one perception of reality and fear or deny all the others, the mind can be conditioned to select a particular brand of "reality" from the buffet of possibilities we are hardwired to conceive. As a result, our capacity for infinite understanding is redirected toward the exercise of infinitely rationalizing why our own brands of "belief" reflects the most superior form of human understanding possible, while also rationalizing why everyone else's beliefs are either ridicules or naïve, or both. Through this process, our most cherished "beliefs" convince us to act like a cyclops: seeing things in only one way.

Consider next how we are conditioned to love one perspective and fear all others. For defending our sole perspective, as a brand of "belief" often requires, we expect no less than eternal reward, and eternal punishments for all those who use their brains to question everything, even though this is the only way for a brain to learn anything at all. Such expectations for the next life merely reflect how tightly one clings to their perspective and their brand of sacred "beliefs" in this one, for to question can lead to uncertainty. For some, uncertainty feels like freefalling into hell, for others, it feels like freedom. For those who feel the former, brands of religious "beliefs" feel like a protective womb, and every other perspective or "belief" feels like scourging or the fires of

hell. The point of installing such hopes and fears is that by doing so a person's curiosity, and thus their "free will" to be whoever they wish, is effectively collared or castrated; much like Jack in room 237.

What a thing is this brain of ours? Like the Overlook Hotel, it operates like a house of mirrors. On the one hand, our brain is wired to be incredibly dynamic, endowed with a magical ability to see a distinctively different reflection of ourselves in each and every mirror we happen to encounter in this Fun House we call reality. Each person we meet, as a result, has a different version of us inside their brain, much as the version we have of the people we know is unique to ourselves. Because of this, we so often feel like a different person around different people. Our brain thus operates like a radio or a TV that is capable of tuning into a limitless number of different channels, each with its own frequency and energy, and therefore programing and perspective.

Our brain is also incredibly malleable, making us vulnerable to being taught to depend upon "beliefs" that, like Narcissus, leads us to fall in love with an image of ourselves in one particular mirror or playing on one specific channel of perspective. Those "beliefs" also teach us to fear or loath all the other possible images we are capable of seeing of ourselves on other channels of perception. And *The Shining* shows us just how easy it is for us to be programmed to hate each other out of a love for the reflection we see of ourselves in the holy water of our most sacred and cherished "beliefs" of all.

Unlike anything else, Kubrick's *Shining* masterpiece provides the perfect lens through which to clearly see how a "belief" can use our emotions to color our perceptions with fear masquerading as love, without us even realizing it. While all art requires a degree of our

emotional vulnerability, and the highest arts are religions, freedom from emotional manipulation can be achieved through a process of careful consideration of the nature of reality, so we can understand how our brain is merely a mirror of that reality. If the latter illustrates how our rational brain was built to operate when given free reign unshackled from a fear of judgement and hell, the former illustrates how our emotional brain can be so easily manipulated, collared, and controlled, with threats of punishment and bribes of reward. And while both our emotional and our rational brains perceive the same uncertainty in life and the universe overall, the former cultivates pure gratitude by realizing such uncertainty is not to be feared, for it alone is what makes anything possible, while the latter sees that same uncertainty as something we must seek to safeguard ourselves against through a willingness to "believe" whatever alleviates our anxiety about such uncertainty. Anxiety about uncertainty in today's world, however, is often a result more of nurture than nature.

Simply put: our anxiety about the uncertainty of life is more unnatural to us than anything else. And the conditioning that instills this most unnatural response is simply a way of convincing beings who are born with all the apprehension of a god, as Hamlet remarked, into creatures who think their highest calling is to act like dogs for one brand of God or another. Hence, the "miracle" of faith that we are made in the image and likeness of a God who commands us to behave like a dog.

As the mental hardware we are born with, the rational and emotional parts of our brain are effectively formatted by culture to convince us we are relying on the former even when we are being manipulated through the latter. Understanding this difference is a necessary first step for understanding the difference between our true nature and what we are

nurtured to "believe" is our nature. And both are of critical importance for learning not only how to play Kubrick's *Shining* game, but more importantly, how to navigate the digital matrix of illusions being projected onto the walls of the cave of the digital cocoons we are born into.

To see reality in a whole new holistic way, Kubrick's game shines a light on the power we have to change our minds by first raising our awareness to that of a child, which child psychologist Alison Gopnik described as shining like the light of a lantern. This same heightened awareness occurs whenever we visit a new country. By doing so, Gopnik points out we see with new eyes, which allows us to see old things in new ways. The lens of *Uncle Tom's Cabin*, for example, gave America the ability to rethink the morality of slavery. As the eminent futurist and philosopher Alvin Toffler explained, "The illiterate of the 21st century will not be those who cannot read and write, but those who cannot learn, unlearn, and relearn." In fact, the ability to freely change our mind is the only thing that makes us different from a toaster-oven.

Our infinite capacity for change is, for many people, a truly terrifying idea to even consider, as if it is natural for the caterpillar to be either so terrified of becoming a butterfly, or hopeful of becoming one after it dies, that it devotes its whole life to rituals designed to avoid the one or obtain the other. And the genius of *The Shining* is how it is designed to function as a lens that allows us to see such an absurdity by holding up a mirror to our own perception. Doing so reveals how we are conditioned to perceive being afraid, which is the most unnatural thing of all to a child, as the most natural thing of all to an adult, thanks to the domesticating hand of contradictory religious beliefs that tell us "be not

afraid" on the one hand, even as the Bible tells us we must "work out our salvation in fear and trembling" (Philippians 2:12), on the other.

To illustrate this, each page that follows will slowly pull off the mask (or "pull back the curtain" if you prefer) on Kubrick's film to reveal how, more than being simply a movie, it is an incredibly elaborate tool, and game, one that Kubrick is inviting us to learn how to play, so we can see the invisible hand at work behind the shining shadows on the wall of the digital cave we are born into.

Playing *The Shining* game that Kubrick painstakingly designed for us not only provides definitive answers for all the questions that have been asked about this film, but it also explains a lot about how and why we have failed to find and decipher those answers until now. By showing us what is natural to our senses and our own intelligence, the film helps to reveal what we are merely conditioned to believe is natural to our senses and intelligence, which leads us to think it is natural for us to feel we need to be saved by one religion or another. All we have to do to see the difference between the two is embrace the willingness to become like a child again, for children have neither fear nor preconceptions of good and evil, and play this little game, a game which will allow us to crack Kubrick's code wide open. And to do that, we first must find the key that will open Kubrick's little box of horrors, so we can crack his code.

Is there more than one key to be found in Kubrick's maze? Yes. To begin to play this video-game, however, the first key to be found just happens to be the same one that led Charles Darwin to discover his theory of natural selection. As the core skill for learning by synthesizing information into a tapestry of understanding, that key comes in the form of the most natural thing of all for our brains: spotting patterns.

Pattern recognition is as natural to our brains as seeing is to our eyes, smelling flowers is to our nose, and hearing rhythms is to our ears. Those patterns, it turns out, are the sine qua non for not only learning anything, but also seeing what is really going on in *The Shining*. They serve as the road map that shows us how to start piecing together the answers that Tobias was asking about. To do that requires a painstaking examination of the insane level of detail and perfection that Kubrick included in every frame, and indeed every single second, of his film. To see this, we must put Kubrick's film under a microscope and consider the smallest and most overlooked of details in the film, especially what appear to be errors.

So, in short, yes: 42 years after the movie was released, we will finally know what it *all* means. But we can only do so if we are willing to consider all the incredibly intimate details that Kubrick labored so secretly and assiduously to include, all of which reveal why and how *The Shining* is unlike any other film ever made.

Then there is the second question: just how curious are we? Because to truly discover "what it all means," we must be willing to follow that maxim inscribed above the door of the Temple of Apollo at Delhi: "know thyself." According to Thales of Miletus, the pre-Socratic philosopher who paved the way for scientific skepticism, this is the hardest thing of all for us to do. Among many other reasons, this is why we happen to see Danny enter room 237 wearing an Apollo 11 sweater, with the "II" symbol seen on his sweater looking more like the Zodiac sign for the Gemini as he does. At that same moment, he is also looking into twin full length mirrored doors that stand like twin "shining" monoliths that open like legs into the "living" room of 237. Is it really just a meaningless coincidence that room 237 has gold wallpaper, while a singer on the Gold Room sign reminds us of Jim Morrison of The Doors, which in turn reminds us of the psychedelic experiences of Aldous Huxley under the influence of mescaline in May 1953? Like the doors to room 237 and the Gold Room, Huxley explored those experiences in his book *The Doors of Perception: Heaven and Hell*. Indeed, where the rational brain sees uncertainty as its Heaven, for there alone is anything possible, the emotional brain can be trained to see pure Hell.

Huxley's experiences are common to us all. In fact, even religion operates as a means of altering consciousness, only not always in the way "believers" often believe. As Michael Pollan pointed out in *The Botany of Desire* and *How To Change Your Mind*, our species has "a universal desire to change consciousness." And as Brian Muraresku details in his groundbreaking book *The Immortality Key*, this same desire may even have been the basis for the original Eucharist of the Catholic Church (and why female botanists and midwives were attacked as "witches" by the early Catholic "saints"). This desire to change consciousness led Ken Kesey, author of *One Flew Over the Cuckoo's Nest*, Jack Nicholson, and even Stanley Kubrick, to all follow Huxley through those doors.

By walking through the doors of perception that Kubrick opens for us into his games room, the investigation that follows will begin to reveal how all the pieces of Kubrick's puzzle can be fitted together, once the plank of our emotional smokescreen has been removed from our eye. This includes revealing how the disjointed design of the Overlook hotel itself can be stitched together into a pattern that, when the right perspective is applied, makes perfect sense. Stitched together, Kubrick's film reveals the scariest image I have ever seen before or since, and explains why, for most of my life, I preferred to have the plank of my religious beliefs stuck in my eyes rather than dare to remove it. And again, if there is any requirement from the reader for engaging in such an investigation it is simply this: a willingness to become as innocent as a child so we can learn to be brave enough to play again, especially with our ideas and our beliefs.

Why, you might ask, is it important to learn how to play again, let alone play Kubrick's *Shining* game? Because "we are never more fully alive, more completely ourselves, or more deeply engrossed in anything," as Charles Shaefer wrote, "than when we are at play." And nothing is more necessary for solving Kubrick's puzzle than a willingness to play with the images he splashes across our screen. Nor is it a coincidence that when the Grady twins invite Danny to "come and play with us," they are also staring directing at the audience.

In contrast to Shaefer's comment, as Jack eventually discovers, we are never more fully crucified then when we are "all work and no play." And if "work is a form of prayer," than prayer is a form of rigor mortis that grows from ritualized repetition that has lost all meaning, but the hope of avoiding the hell of uncertainty about "what it all means." And like no other film before or since, *The Shining* serves as a glaring invitation to know ourselves through doing what is most natural to us of all, but only if we have the courage to accept the invitation to "come and play."

If *The Shining* is a film that never prompted you to wonder "what does it all mean," and even if you think that getting to know yourself is a fool's errand, then the first question you may be asking yourself is "why should

I even care what it all means, let alone bother to read a book that claims to offer an answer to such a question?" Hell, two years ago, I was asking myself a similar question. I mean, really, who cares about what a 42-year-old movie may 'mean' anyway, especially if that meaning is completely subjective to everyone, as is the nature of all art? In fact, even what we decide to define as "art" is subjective. The answer to this question is that, once you understand what it all *really* means, you may come to the same conclusion that I did: that *The Shining* by Stanley Kubrick may be to motion pictures what the Bible is to the written word; or, if not the Bible, then at least *The Catcher in the Rye*.

So, what has contributed to why, for 42 years, we have failed to discover what it all means? More than anything else, what blinds us from seeing the truth, even as that truth has been staring back at us the whole time, is the plank in our own eye. That plank is comprised of our own beliefs, one of which is the belief that the "truth" of the film is that "it does not mean anything at all – it's just a friggen movie!" This explanation, which no doubt strikes those who offer it to be as insightful as Sir Isaac Newton blaming the apple that struck him upon the head on the dastardly designs of gravity, is nevertheless perfectly true, at least for those who prefer to see it that way. It *is* just a movie, after all. Yet such an answer has also often been used like a verbal club against anyone who has dared to speculate that the film may be about so much more than just a haunted hotel, or an unhinged father bent on killing his clairvoyant little boy. It is a plank, in other words, that is comprised of a trinity of essential threads which we weave into the security blanket of our comfort zone.

The trinity we rely on to feather our comfort zone consists of our confirmation bias for our preferred brands of beliefs, our dependence upon social connection and cohesion, and our preference for simple straightforward answers (which are often incorrect) over complex ones (which are often more correct). We wear this triumvirate like a crown, even as it often acts like a blinder that hides from the audience all the answers they are looking for. So confident that this crown would do just that, in fact, Kubrick even went so far as to place virtually all the answers generated by his little game in plain sight, just like "The Purloined Letter" by Edgar Allen Poe. Hell, Kubrick even sometimes shines a light directly on the very answers we are looking for. But, because those answers are obscured behind the mask of a Stephen King story about supernatural evil, the audience either fails to notice those answers, or fails to discover how the pieces they do happen to find all fit together like a puzzle. Being just a movie, people like to let it just wash over them like the blood rushing out of the elevators. Think too much about it, on the other hand, and you run the risk of ending up like Jack, and that bronze statute by Auguste Rodin.

This brings us to the third question I asked above: do we have any obligation, moral or otherwise, to figure out what it all means? The answer to that question really depends upon what you think is more important: defending a cherished "belief" as the only source of truth, or finding the truth, even at the expense of our most cherished "beliefs." The problem is that, on the one hand, we are taught it is a virtue to conflate our "beliefs" for truth, so that we can scarcely tell the difference between the two. On the other hand, while our "beliefs" tend to be a form of mental shorthand - otherwise known as "heuristics"- which we rely on the most for our sense of meaning, security, and social connection, anything that constitutes actual truth – which, because it requires far more mental energy and time, is often inefficient, and may challenge our meaning, security, and social connections – tends to be seen as only undermining our sense of certainty. Indeed, a culture that venerates its "beliefs" as the embodiment of the greatest truth, especially in a world where quick decisions are treated as superior to contemplative understanding, and that values certainty over uncertainty, will reflexively see anything that resembles actual truth as the enemy of such a "belief." Truth, in such an environment, always looks like a lie because of the threat is poses to the certainty offered by the "beliefs" we choose to define as "ultimate truth," even if they ain't. And we are as likely to believe a lie to be true as we are to believe a truth is a lie.

But think about it: shouldn't we use truth as the North Star that guides our beliefs, rather than looking through the stained glass of a "belief" to define what is true? And does not the former cultivate curiosity to the same degree the latter confines that curiosity to a coffin masquerading as a comfort zone? Where the discovery of the Higgs boson and landing a rover on Mars are examples of the laborious fruits borne of the former, slavery, human sacrifice (especially through war), and the labeling and burning of witches are only some of the stripes borne of the latter. In fact, fear, war, and violence are always proof that we have chosen to put more faith in our beliefs than in our ability to learn, evolve, and play well with others. No wonder uncertainty drives us to need our "beliefs," for our "beliefs" contribute to only adding to our uncertainty, what with a hell to be feared and a heaven to be lost, even though neither can be demonstrated to be any more real than Valhalla or Santa's workshop in the North Pole.

Far more than anything else, the veil that hides the true face of Kubrick's film is our willingness to be blinded by our sacred "beliefs," beliefs that allow us to see what we want to see rather than what is really staring back at us. As Thich Nhat Hagh observed, however, "for things to reveal themselves to us, we need to be ready to abandon our views about them." Failure to do so is what keeps the story room door to Kubrick's film securely locked. The key to unlocking that door, as such, comes in the form of our curiosity and the courage to be born again with a whole new way of seeing. To do that requires the courage to change the lens through which we perceive our beliefs about reality, from one in which those "beliefs" offer us simpler and more comforting answers, to one in which we become more comfortable with deeper truths, about both reality and ourselves, despite their complexity and the initial discomfort they may cause us by undermining our sense of certainty. After all, were the mind of a fetus conditioned with beliefs as frightful as our own about what comes next, it would live with as much terror of being born as we live with dying, for what could be more uncertain to such an infant than leaving the comfort and security of its mother's womb than the world we live in, especially as we have designed it to operate? Hope for salvation, as such, is simply born of a flower of fear, the seeds of which are planted in the soil of a child's innocence, to bear the fruit of spiritual dependence.

So, "what does it all mean," and why should anyone care anyway? More than anything else, *The Shining* is a film about two things. On its face, it is a murder mystery that prompts the audience to wonder who or what causes Jack to try to kill his family, then kill Dick, and then freeze to death in the hedge maze, only to end up in an old photograph dated 1921. Behind that face, however, is a much scarier story, and film, about the nature of human perception. That story reflects a truly terrifying reality about both human nature and the nature of the modern world. While everyone who has watched the film has seen the former, few have ever noticed, let alone fully appreciated or understood, the latter, even though the latter is what the film is mostly about.

It is necessary to see how Kubrick weaves these two faces together in order to create not only an incredibly elaborate game, but also a tool; one designed to teach the blind to see and the lame to walk, to make straight the crooked path and allow the confused to clearly understand. And maybe even, in a sense, raise a man from the dead, again and again and again, forever and ever. Sounds crazy, right? Yeah, I thought so too, at least at first.

In simplest terms, *The Shining* is a coded message that operates like an antidote, disguised as a game, wrapped in a riddle and hidden deep in the details of a movie adaptation of a Stephen King novel. But to show you what kind of antidote *The Shining* really is, we must take a "fantastic voyage," starting with an overlook of the film like Jack overlooking the model hedge maze table, and then a closer look at nearly every pixel of every frame of the movie. *Fantastic Voyage*, by the way, is a film from 1966 in which a submarine is shrunken down to a microscopic size and injected into the bloodstream of a scientist to save his life by repairing damage to his brain. And to unmask Kubrick's film so we can finally see the true face of "what it all means," we will have to take a similar voyage through both Kubrick's murder mystery and our own brain, like Jonah jumping into the mouth of the whale of his own beliefs in the ocean of ideas, in order to effectively do the same thing to our own brain.

◊◊

My own journey to repair my divided mind intersected with Kubrick's *Shining* at the point of a shadow standing in the parking lot outside of the Boulder apartment complex, where we first see Danny and Wendy eating lunch. The more attention I paid to that shadow, which I had never noticed before, the more it looked like one of the most important pieces, and clues, needed to finally begin decrypting Kubrick's code and assembling his puzzle. That shadow reminded me of similar shadows that I had seen before when I was no older than Danny, shadows which I likewise had to decrypt to overcome my fear of them and myself.

Like a pack of faceless gremlins, those shadows came stealing into my bedroom in the dead of night. One by one they filed through my bedroom door, huddled at the foot of my bed, and began clawing at the bedsheets. Terrified by such a spectacle, my first instinct was to pray like hell that God or my guardian angel would save me from such demon nightshades, all of which seemed to be eyeing my toes like French fries and ketchup. Having been raised a Roman Catholic, praying like hell was my automatic reflex to such night terrors, even though such prayers only seemed to guarantee the recurrence of such apparitions. After all, what was the point of a child's prayers, indeed what was the point of being Catholic at all, if not to defend one's toes from gangs of gnome-gobbling-gremlins that prowled about the earth looking to feast upon children's souls (and toes) in the middle of the night?

At the time, I was wholly unaware of how our perception of reality is shaped by the stories we tell ourselves, and especially the stories we are conditioned to cling to for our sense of community and security, identity and purpose, meaning and morality. As a Roman Catholic, I was raised to have a deep emotional and psychological dependence upon a Bible chalked full of magical demons and devils and various forms of massacres, genocides, and human sacrifice, with an unavoidable apocalyptic Armageddon to look forward to and an eternal damnation to lie awake worrying about, night after night. And all because God offers no feedback whatsoever on whether I'm passing His "test," or not. Like trauma, Carl Jung pointed out that such stories sink into our subconscious mind and there take on a life of their own, directing our thoughts and behaviors in ways that feel like we are making free choices, even when our choices are really being controlled by the "shadow" that forms within us from such ideas. Also like trauma, the only way for a person to free themself from the control of such an invisible hand, according to Jung, was "to make the unconscious conscious" or it would control our life and we would call it fate.

So, armed with nothing more than a brain addled with fear from being stewed in such stories, a brain that I not only had no idea how to operate but which would not fully form for another two decades, I had little choice but to hope to God that I wouldn't wake up in a pizza oven called purgatory if the gremlins prowling about my room ever managed to turn me into a late night snack. Since it was blasphemy to doubt the reality of demons prowling the world hungry for children's souls (and toes), and frowned upon to ask why a God that *could* fumigate the earth of such shadowy vermin choose instead to depend on them as His greatest form of motivation to obey his Catholic Church, praying like a madman to be saved from one supernatural force by another supernatural force became my wholly natural trauma response to anything that provoked such anxiety. This response I dutifully continued well into adulthood, even as all my other beliefs in imaginary beings all receded with the advance of puberty.

What prevented my religious beliefs in things like demonic gremlins from receding along with my beliefs in Santa Claus and tooth fairies? The fear of being not only ostracized from my religious community, which included my school and family, but losing the approval of my obsessively Roman Catholic parents, who so often conflated approval for love, much as their own parents had been raised to do.

For my Mom and Dad, being Catholic was not only the thing that mattered most in life, it was the thing that was far more important than even life itself. They may have been pro-life when it came to the fetus, as their religion required, but when it came to defending their eternal reward through an unquestioning devotion to their Catholic brand of faith, they were adamantly pro-martyr, as their religion also required. Life was sacred, as they saw it, but it wasn't nearly as important as your brand of religious beliefs, and it certainly wasn't worth losing eternity over; especially when hell awaited those who asked too many damn questions.

And so, to ensure my parents would not stop "loving" me (that is, approving of me for pretending to love Catholicism as much as they did) - since Matthew 5:30 commanded them to "cut off the hand" that offended their (beliefs in) "God" - I had no choice but to pray like my eternal soul, my little toes, and even the room and board a five-year old requires, all depended on it. Because the only "infallible truth" I knew at that point in my life was that they most definitely did.

Over time, the question such visions naturally raised was whether I was seeing the world for what it truly was or was I seeing simply a figment of my imagination born out of what I had been taught since circumcision to "believe" was the "truth" about the world around me. Was I really seeing "the truth" that operated behind the curtain of reality, as my religion taught me, nay required me, to believe, or was I simply seeing shadows cast on the wall of my room, as if to see the world through a sheepskin curtain that had been pulled over my eyes, and fashioned from a mechanized profession of my undying "beliefs" in the "lamb of God"?

Four decades later, after I had reclaimed some modicum of control of my own mind from the prolonged trauma of my childhood conditioning, I was able to finally begin answering that question for myself, rather than depending upon priests and nuns to answer it for me. From what I had gleamed from the insights of people like Carl Jung and many others, it appeared that, perhaps more than anything else, my Catholic beliefs about demons prowling the world in search of children's souls had only assured that such ideas were prowling about the wild imagination of a five-year-old boy in the middle of a dark and sleepless night. There, those ideas became the lens of faith through which I was taught to perceive reality.

Yet the more I learned about the diversity of perspectives offered not only within my own Catholicism – from mystics like Meister Eckhart to Mathew Fox – but from the universe of other religions and philosophers as well, the more I discovered that the "truth" I had been raised to depend on was simply one brand of beliefs in a global bazaar of ever evolving ideas. My own brand of beliefs, which were but one of countless versions available for purchase in the marketplace of self-improvement ideas, were simply the one my own family had found socially profitable to accept, adopt, and depend on. And because they did, those beliefs had been implanted in my mind like Leonardo DiCaprio implanting false memories in *Inception* (it's been scientifically proven that implanting such false memories is not only possible, but much easier to do than we think). There, such beliefs sank deep into my unconscious and, with some moisture from a few wet dreams, grew like mold spores of fear in the dark recesses of my previously fearless imagination. And after a few years of gestation, out popped the toe-gobbling gremlins that crept into my bedroom in the middle of the night looking to treat my toes like tator-tots. My gremlins, in other words, were like Calvin's stuffed tiger coming to life in the comic strip "Calvin & Hobbes." And because I was taught to see my own body as the sinful meat-puppet of my sacred soul, I was Hobbes and they were Calvin, which is like John Nash seeing his hallucinations as real, and himself as the hallucination.

What was I really seeing prowling about my room as a child in the middle of the night, which so often led me to pray to a God who had made both my soul and the very demons I had been taught to believe spent their nights prowling the planet looking to gobble up souls that, like Reagan MacNeil in *The Exorcist*, had not been properly LoJacked with the right religion? In my house, the only acceptable answer to such a question was that my religion had blessed me with spiritually bionic eyes, enabling to me to spy Satan's little helpers as they hurriedly raced about collecting souls like Pac-Man gobbling up little white dots. Since our eyes can see only a mere fraction of the total range of light frequency, my religion, which I was taught to believe was needed to improve the "imperfections" I was born with, must therefore be increasing that range beyond those of unbelievers (which explained why they didn't believe).

Another theory (hatched by yours truly) was that those images were the result of how I had been taught to interpret the imaginative fruits of my own perceptions (which, ironically enough, were probably the very same fruits that enabled Stephen King to write his novels). Simply put, what clawed away at the foot of my bed all those years ago were the product of my Catholic colored perceptions. They were, to be more specific, most likely the result of my eyes constantly adjusting to the dancing shadows that were being cast into my room from the headlights of passing cars and the streetlamp on the corner outside my house.

More than anything else, those shadows were the "burnt toast" of a picture Bible we read on a nightly basis, along with other religious art that often made "home" feel like a gothic monastery in the mountains of Transylvania. In fact, the art in our house made it feel like I was living inside the pages of my picture Bible, as if those pictures had crawled out of the pages of that Bible and into my room. Both were adorned with various images of demons and cherubim at play in a never-ending war for my soul. And for some disturbing reason I never understood, those cherubim were depicted as bird-winged naked infants swaddled in diapers. Like army ants in diapers, such pictures led me to imagine legions of naked babies crawling about on the topside of clouds, the white ones defending the gates of Heaven from the red ones, as if the spiritual battle for the universe was ultimately a game of cowboys and

Indians, the Milky Way galaxy a gridiron for a game between the Dallas Cowboys and the Washington Redskins. No wonder the gremlins that lurked about in my room looked like Chucky dressed like a Ninja.

While this theory of my childhood experiences amounted to armchair psychologizing at its finest, it nevertheless had more grounding in scientific facts than that the bowels of hell had farted inky oompa-loompas into my bedroom as a child. And if someone else's imaginings had sent me down a rabbit hole that only fostered in me an ever-deeper dependence upon a brand of beliefs through a fear of the unknown, I saw no reason why I couldn't trust my own mind to lead me back out of such a rabbit hole by befriending my fears and making them an ally.

Either I had to believe that God had designed me to think for myself, as any good parent would raise their child to do, or doubt myself, so I would depend upon others to do my thinking for me. Having been raised to believe the latter for most of my life, finding an ability to exercise my faith in the former took decades, and was largely rebuffed by a family that saw such an exercise as turning my back upon the religion they loved, cherished, and depended on to save them from the hell of uncertainty, in this life and the next: just like I had my whole life. Walking away from Catholicism, from such a perspective, was like crucifying Christ all over again, like Peter denying Christ, like I was daring God to start the apocalypse.

My slow crawl to freedom from the spiritual Shawshank of my religious beliefs began at an early age. By slowly weening myself off of the habit of trusting others, especially the priests which were always a staple around my home growing up, and the nuns who treated elementary school classrooms like the octagon in the UFC, I learned to trust and follow my curiosity in and out of any rabbit holes it found inviting. Those rabbit holes, which were often treated as "forbidden zones" from *The Planet of the Apes* by my religious superiors (which I guess made me Charlton Heston, and them a bunch of "damned dirty apes"), ranged from topics about history, theology, psychology, perception, consciousness, and the workings of my own brain. The animus for such skullduggery was a need to better understand what was going on inside my own skull, and my own bedroom, and why.

Again and again, all of those rabbit holes led me back to the shadows in my room, and left me to wonder whether I was seeing an objective truth about reality that others could not - a perspective my religion only encouraged and indeed helped to reinforce - or merely seeing the afterglow of what I had been taught to see by the stories of hellfire and human sacrifice I was force-fed on a nightly basis, and every Sunday, before an altar and under a 12 foot statue of a crucified victim. The subtext of such a crucifix, of course, was always understood to be "You did this to me!" And I was only "loved" for as long as I was willing to show up every seven days to beg forgiveness for it, and all in the hope that I wouldn't suffer a fate far worse in the afterlife for failing to dutifully do so, as I was commanded to do. And this, to me, was what true "love" was all about.

Unable to trust the answers offered by those who had taught me to define "love in such a way, and to "see" such visions in the first place, I was forced to allay the fears such visions generated by designing my own theories of what might be the source or the cause of such visitations. Although no Leonard McCoy, my best guess was that my night terrors were largely the result of the two hemispheres of my brain living in fear of each other, a kind of "cold war" between the two sides of my cerebellum. Put another way, it was a war between the ideals that my Catholicism had furnished my mind with, and the flawed bodily flesh of my own brain that my soul was crucified inside of, the former reflecting a perfection that could only be achieved after shuffling loose from the flawed and sinful nature of the latter. And I was seeing things not as they were, as Anais Nin put it, but as I had been conditioned to be.

Simply put, the darkness of my bedroom was merely a canvas that operated as a mirror. Like the spells being chanted around a cauldron by those witches in *Macbeth*, my religious stories and rituals were designed to conjure frightful images out of the left hemisphere of my brain, weaponizing the pareidolia – the habit we have of seeing shapes and patterns in random information – being committed by the right hemisphere of my brain. Shaped and colored by my Catholic ideals, my devotion to believing that the universe was a battleground between God and the devil, personifications of light and darkness, led me to interpret the patterns dancing around in my room as if they were devilish babies that had crawled out of the pages of my picture Bible to "take my soul before I wake." In short, I had been trained to depend upon the verbal and analytical part of my brain to defend me from my own non-verbal imaginative part of my brain.

To save myself from such night terrors, I had to stop fearing my talent for fashioning abstract shapes into creative creatures with a refined taste for children's toes. And I did so by not only doubting my fears about supernatural forces of evil, but by questioning why a supernatural God, one that claimed to have loved me so much he laid down his life for me, had decided to unleash such forces in the world for a child to live in perpetual fear of in the first place. In other words, I had to become a spiritual version of John Nash, and doubt my own scripturally induced schizophrenia.

Discovering that my mind had been colonized to see fearful forces prowling about the earth is what eventually led me to wonder if maybe the same thing had been going on with how people were interpreting *The Shining*. If so, then at the heart of Kubrick's mystery lay the famous question that Pontius Pilate asked Jesus, between having him flogged and having him crucified: "What is truth?" The answer to such a question could be found by realizing it was sandwiched between these two acts of violence. The flogging was the Roman equivalent of the Ludovico technique, while the crucifixion was the result of Jesus failing to accept that believed brands of "truth" have nothing to do with what is true, and everything to do with who gets to define what is true. For "all things are subject to interpretation," as Friedrich Nietzsche said, and "whichever interpretation prevails at a given time is "a function of power and not truth."

Like the Roman Catholic Pope, so the emperors of Rome were infallible in their proclamations. And they were because, since the time of Julius Caesar, the emperors of Rome were living gods. Both forms of violence inflicted upon Jesus were thus mere reflections of the tactics employed later by all those who claim to possess a divine authority to declare "what is truth" in God's stead. As with all inquisitions, the violence that was applied physically to those who challenged sacred beliefs illustrated how often "truth" is determined, not by using the highest functions of our own brains to engage in careful investigation and consideration, but by those who, like spiritual schoolyard bullies, possess the power to use violence and the threat of it, in this life or the next, to coerce people to override their own free will and accept what such spiritual bullies alone may seek to define as "truth."

Claiming a moral monopoly on violence has always been necessary for convincing "true believers" of the moral necessity of violence. It convinced the masses of the moral necessity of executing all those who dared to exercise their right to think for themselves, from Socrates and Jesus Christ to Hypatia and Giordano Bruno. To follow actual truth, however, requires applying such violence only to the answers offered by anyone claiming to possess a "God given authority" to define all truth "infallibly." For if God had given the human soul the power of skepticism, than it only followed that each of us was required to be at least as intellectually violent in our inquiry of claims to ultimate "truth" as the medieval Inquisitions had been physically violent to those who dared to question the authority of those Inquisitions; and especially the authority of those Inquisitions to use such violence to defend their claims that they alone had been given the sole authority to define what is true. All those who were tortured and killed by such Inquisitions, including Jesus himself, are the real saints and martyrs who died "for our God given right," and indeed our moral duty, to question all those who claim they have been given an authority by God to speak for "Truth;" an authority that, according to them, God had given to them and them alone, which that very same God, in accord with some divine plan, decided to withhold from everyone else.

What better way to rip to pieces the seamless garment of the human family than by teaching each member of that family a "belief" that they must love and obey above all else, in order to save themselves from eternal torture, and to do so even more than they may love one another or even their own children, or their own lives. Hell, doesn't just the threat of hell mean that the one doing the threatening is more evil than the devil, since not only did the devil not create hell, but hell is the same place the devil is being threatened to be thrown in as well? Aside from the fact that those beliefs require division in the name of love, they are also contrary to evidence and reason, and are in fact the very opposite of love. Indeed, so contrary to evidence, reason, and love are such "beliefs" that they require threats of torture and promises of eternal rewards, in both this life and the next, to be maintained. And the most unforgivable sin of all is having second thoughts about whether God would really pick a select minority to define "what is truth," and then task that minority with having to save themselves from hellfire by trying to convince all others on the planet to accept their claims. Worse, the only evidence such a "God" provides those who are required to save themselves by converting others is a license to use threats of torture and death, in this life and the next, and a conviction that their quest for spiritual perfection is really a sign of their "love" for their "God." Such a religion reduces the world to a dark, dank basement bathroom in the horror movie *Saw*, and casts a loving and benevolent God in the role of a serial killer interested in purifying souls through our willingness to show our gratitude for being alive by cutting off our foot with a hacksaw, with one commandment above all others: "Make your choice, and let the game begin."

Here, the patient reader may again be wondering "what the hell does any of this have to do with *The Shining* by Stanley Kubrick, ferchrisake?" Like my quest to reclaim my own mind from the tyranny of my sacred unquestionable beliefs, Kubrick's film operates as a macrocosm of this contest between those who assert their "beliefs" are infallibly true, and those who search for truth with the humility that can only come from accepting that such a claim is only evidence of one's insecurity, not divine authority or enlightenment. It does this by challenging the audience to consider not only what is really going on in the film, but whether rational beings have any moral obligation to try to answer three age old questions:

What is truth?

Who gets to decide?

And how can we really know the difference between what is true and what is simply a "belief" that some group or other commands all others to accept as the one and only "truth," even if it is the greatest lie ever told?

All three of these questions bring us to the questions of what is really going on in the Overlook, how we can determine truth from "truth," and who should be the ultimate authority in defining "what it all means"? Should the "truth" of the film be determined simply by those who believe it the most, and who are even willing to feed themselves (or "non-believers") to lions to prove how right they are, or those who offer evidence, and are humble enough to admit that, because they do not "commune" with an "infallible God," they are only human, and could therefore be wrong? Indeed, why would "God" design us with the ability to discern one kind of truth and then command us to save ourselves from hell by faithfully following the other?

It is assumed that, like in King's novel, the ultimate evil operating in Kubrick's *Shining* is supernatural. This appears to be confirmed when Jack escapes the locked storage room with the assistance of (we assume) the ghost of Delbert Grady. But there's a catch: if the ghost of Delbert Grady can open the bolt locks on the storage room door, then why can't he engage in other physical acts? Even more so, if it is ultimately just a ghost story, then why did Kubrick feel the need for such incredible secrecy and meticulousness in the filming of *The Shining*? Is he just a madman, or did he have something to hide?

The threshold of Kubrick's game is the realization that simply blaming everything that occurs in the film on "supernatural forces" not only makes for a very boring film - which would be the last thing we would expect from the likes of Stanley Kubrick - it also does little to fully explain why Kubrick felt the need for such secrecy in the making of this film, and why he included so many incredibly curious details and anomalies. So accepted is the "supernatural evil" interpretation of *The Shining* that we never even consider whether Jack both escaping the storage room *and* ending up in a photograph dated 1921 have explanations that, rather than being the result of supernatural forces, are the result of the same curious details and anomalies that Kubrick labored to include in the film.

Put another way, what if the hedge maze Kubrick is luring his audience into can only be navigated by first realizing how much our belief in supernatural forces is, in fact, the very thing that hides the thread that will allow us to not only navigate our way through Kubrick's maze, but also tie everything together with a single unified answer about "what it *all* means"?

Sure, on one level, *The Shining* really is "just a friggen movie." And those who insist that *The Shining* is just a movie based on a fictional novel about something that never really happened, are not altogether wrong, since the film is, ultimately, just a piece of art. And by design, art can be whatever the viewer wishes it to be. On another level, however, it is a work of art, and all art invites us to become artists, and imagine how art is just a mirror held up to the audience. Like Nietzsche's abyss, when we look into art, art also looks into us. It is a doorway that not only invites us into ourselves, it also teaches us about ourselves, by inviting us to come and play, to have an experience, and to question, both what we believe and how we perceive, and even why.

But if each individual viewer is the ultimate interpreter of any piece of art, then no one interpreter can claim the role of an "infallible" pope by trying to impose their own interpretation of that art on everyone else. And this is all the truer because, while *The Shining* may be just a movie, it is also the retelling of some of the oldest stories in history, stories that were designed to convey profound truths about human nature to future generations: namely, us. Like Jack "believing" he has a duty to murder his own family in order to receive his divine reward of eternal life from the Overlookers, so those stories function as both a lesson and a warning. That warning was explored in an essay written exactly one century before the novel Kubrick's film is based on was published.

In 1877, the inventor of geometric algebra, William K. Clifford, wrote an essay entitled, "The Ethics of Belief." In it, Clifford explored the moral hazards that can come from believing in something on insufficient evidence and the incredibly disastrous consequences that can result, especially when those beliefs are based mostly or purely on emotions like love and fear: two emotions that not only release the same endorphin in our brain, oxytocin, but because they do, so often operate in tandem like reflections in a mirror. This is why one's "love" of some*thing* is often always proportional to the "fear" they have of something else. A "love" of a particular brand of God, for example, was the mask of fear of a hell that convinced people of the need to burn all those "strange" people they branded as "witches." In fact, acting like the devil became for believers a moral necessity for securing the passage of their own souls away from the hell they feared and toward an eternal land of Shangri-La they craved, however distasteful such an exercise may have seemed for many of them, and however delicious it clearly was for others. And if they were wrong in the torture and murder they employed to defend their souls, as much from the devil as from their own God, they also "believed" that Jesus had taken away the sins of the world already anyway. And, since they knew that at least their hearts were in the right place in executing those who threatened their own salvation, they "believed" they could always just ask for forgiveness. Because they "believed" what they were commanded by God to believe, as such, they trusted that it was always better to commit evil for their belief in God, for which they could always be forgiven, than to commit the sin of omission by having doubts, which was the only sin God deemed to be wholly unforgivable. Salvation belonged to those who had the conviction and stomach for the former, and damnation for everyone else. "It is hard to imagine a more stupid or dangerous way of making decisions," as Thomas Sowell observed, "than by putting those decisions in the hands of people who pay no price for being wrong." And when a person can simply ask for forgiveness because they happen to believe the right story, their sins are always paid for in advance.

Thanks to Clifford's essay, I wondered if simply "believing" in the existence of evil "ghosts" in the Overlook hotel was like my willingness to believe in my own Roman Catholicism, which led me not to question my interpretation of the ghostly imps I'd imagined were stalking my toes all those years ago. And if so, was my love for a "savior" simply the mirrored reflection of my fear of all the things I felt I needed to be saved from: things like hell, demons, and perhaps most of all, my own sin-stained soul, even though I couldn't prove the existence in any of these things?

Like Pandora's box, other questions soon followed. Like, did I need God to "save me" from God's wrath for having been made by that God in such a way as to assure I would always anger that God, regardless of how many supernatural sacraments I ingested or partook of, and despite His divine incentives of hell and heaven to prevent me from doing so, and all because I was made in the image and likeness more of the devil than of God himself? And, if the "stain of original sin" meant that the most natural thing for me was to be a serial sinner, then didn't God have infinitely more "free will" to choose *not* to be angry at me for the sinful nature he designed me with than I have to stop triggering God's anger by engaging in the sin that is so natural to being born human? And if we are all born sinners, then isn't religion an attempt to force us to do what is wholly unnatural to what is most natural to our human nature? Questions like these, and plenty of others, all led me to wonder if, by failing to question what was really going on in the Overlook hotel, I was simply following the herd, and a wolf disguised as a shepherd, right off a cliff or into the chophouse.

While simply accepting an assumption of ghosts in the Overlook seemed to be a foregone conclusion, four problems nagged at me by doing so. First, simply accepting such an answer is like saying "the devil did it," which is like answering every question for which humanity has failed to find a better answer so far with "God did it, in the laboratory, with the candlestick." Second, such an answer requires the very least amount of thought and creativity possible. After all, if Delbert can open the pantry door, then is everything that moves around in the hotel and even the entire movie – changes that occur not only from scene to scene but even shot to shot – the result of such ghostly powers, or simply continuity errors on Kubrick's part? And if the former, why don't the ghosts use that power to kill Danny, Wendy, and Jack, rather than requiring Jack to do it for them? Third, to what extent was simply accepting the easier answers to Kubrick's film the very thing Kubrick was relying on the most to hide from his audience both the way out of his maze and the answer to "what does it all mean"? And lastly, again, why would Kubrick require such secrecy during the filming of *The Shining* if he had nothing to hide? Was it all to hide the fact that he really had nothing to hide in the first place?

I could see why Kubrick would construct such a game. If for no other reason, Kubrick - who King once described as a "visceral skeptic" - may have done so because he no doubt would have enjoyed watching people fumbling over themselves in their search for spiritual answers to a purely rational problem. But aside from whatever amusement he may have enjoyed from constructing such a game, much like the fun he pokes at nuclear annihilation in *Dr. Strangelove*, there was also a danger to simply accepting unfounded beliefs that a man like Kubrick could surely appreciate.

As Clifford explained, simply "believing" something without sufficient evidence opens the floodgates for the acceptance of falsehoods as facts through an act of "faith," especially in how "right" or even righteous we think we are. Like Danny out the window, accepting such "beliefs" can be a truly slippery slope, "for when one falsity has been let in," as Baruch Spinoza wrote, "infinite others follow." To believe one claim on insufficient evidence, as a result, primes us to accept virtually any belief on the same grounds, especially when the second unsubstantiated belief is presented as the natural consequence of the first unsubstantiated belief. Anti-Semitism, for example, has always depended on the "belief" that Jesus, who was a Jew, was killed by Jews, rather than those few who, having aligned themselves with Rome, saw Jesus as a threat to their status, affluence, and authority. Jesus was less a victim of Jews, in other words, than of a privileged class of "vipers" that drew all their power from the gullibility of true "believers." As Clifford explains:

If I let myself believe anything on insufficient evidence, there may be no great harm done by the mere belief; it may be true after all, or I may never have occasion to exhibit it in outward acts. But I cannot help doing this great wrong towards Man, that I make myself credulous. The danger to society is not merely that it should believe wrong things, though that is great enough; but that it should become credulous, and lose the habit of testing things and inquiring into them; for then it must sink back into savagery.

Is Jack not also "sinking back into savagery," and all because he fails to question the nature of his "beliefs" and what he sees dancing before him, seduced as he is with the apple of the "prosperity gospel" being dangled in front of him in the form of the Gold Room and the naked woman in the bathtub in room 237? Jack, after all, is only questioning the obedience of his family, and their willingness to accept what he appears to interpret as 'divine authority,' not his own beliefs about the Overlook or the fallible nature of his own mind.

Like Jack, the passion and devotion one has to *not* question the validity of their own beliefs is always mirrored in their devotion to denying the validity of all other beliefs. This double standard is exercised whenever we require all others to prove the legitimacy of their beliefs while knowing full well that the greatest evidence for our own beliefs, and perhaps even the only evidence, is that they can never be disproven; and mostly because every contradiction is simply attributed to that black box we call "the mystery of faith." And anyone who questions such a mystery is then seen to be asking questions that are above their paygrade, at least until they die anyway, and only if they've earned a promotion.

If questioning long held sacred assumptions that color our perceptions of reality and determine what we define as "truth" is a moral obligation for us to exercise as beings endowed with such God-like powers of discernment and reason, and not only out of respect for what designed us in such a way but also as the only means of exercising anything that qualifies as humility or free will, then anything which allows us to exercise such a virtue is well worth the effort to come and play. And Kubrick's film provides just such a sandbox to play in. The question is whether we have the courage to do so.

◊◊

Over the course of the last several years, Kubrick's film became a magic mirror in which the more I played with it, the more it left me scratching my head. Something clearly did not add up. Again, why would Kubrick exercise such secrecy and attention to detail for a film that was simply about ghosts? Even Jack talking to Delbert just before he escapes the pantry was insufficient evidence to support the belief that supernatural forces are at work in *The Shining*.

Such a belief suffered from the gravest of problems: it was too easy. If Kubrick really wanted the audience to accept that there were supernatural forces operating within the Overlook, even though it was just as likely that the voice of Delbert Grady heard in the pantry was all in Jack's head, meant that Kubrick wanted to watch his audience drive themselves crazy by rejecting the obvious answer he had provided by having Delbert open the pantry door. Conversely, the only way to open the door to Kubrick's Games Room was by assuming that Kubrick had not exercised such secrecy and precision simply to dupe his audience into rejecting the simplest and most obvious answer. If he had, then giving the film a 'second sight' is truly a waste of time. It also means that the notoriously brutal number of retakes Kubrick required during filming were, in fact, an even bigger waste of time. And *The Shining*, from this perspective, would simply be the cinematic equivalent of the Siren's Song.

Is Kubrick's *Shining* just a ghost story, as many insist, and nothing more? On its face it certainly appears to be. But we're not in Kansas anymore, we're in a film by Stanley Kubrick film. And in a Kubrick film, appearances are always deceiving. Indeed, for Kubrick, appearances are part of his deception. Given everything we know about Kubrick, therefore, and about the extreme secrecy surrounding the making of *The Shining* and the incredible amount of precision found within the film, which conclusion does such evidence more readily support: that Kubrick had merely wasted his own time in order to lure his audience into wasting theirs, or that Kubrick was hiding something? Of the two conclusions, in other words, which one does such evidence more readily support, and which "belief" is based on insufficient evidence?

And as Clifford warned, if we are wrong in our belief that Kubrick's film is just an exquisitely portrayed ghost story and nothing more, might our willingness to be so credulous only be opening a door that, just like Jack, only allows us to sink "back into savagery" by failing to use our higher powers of cognition? In fact, as Jack devolves into a wild animal out of a devotion to his belief in the powers of the Overlook, leading him into the belly of a maze and a black and white view of life, Wendy and Danny wonder, play, question, strategize, and shine on. As Clifford summed it up as a warning to future generations who followed in Jack's footsteps by failing to heed the lessons of history:

> It is wrong always, everywhere, and for anyone, to believe anything upon insufficient evidence. If a man, holding a belief which he was taught in childhood or persuaded of afterwards, keeps down and pushes away any doubts which arise about it in his mind, purposely avoids the reading of books and the company of men that call into question or discuss it, and regards as impious those questions which cannot easily be asked without disturbing it--the life of that man is one long sin against mankind.

Indeed, it is also one long sin against truth itself, and a form of blasphemy against both our spiritual and intellectual abilities, and whatever designed us with such abilities.

If allowing someone to dupe us into believing something on insufficient evidence - and the desire that something be true because it would make us feel bad or uncomfortable to accept that it is false, is the most insufficient evidence of all - constituted "one long sin against mankind," it also constituted a form of blasphemy against any and all truths that are founded on more sufficient evidence. If "God is Truth," then truth should be determined not by papal fiat that presumes we were designed to need someone to decide for us what is true, but by using our God-given abilities to weigh the sufficiency of the evidence for or against any given claim, untainted by emotional insecurity about what happens after we die. Coercing people into accepting truths proclaimed by a church, as such, amount to forms of spiritual terrorism, and treat stories like Sodom and Gomorrah as God's version of 9/11.

Beliefs based on the most insufficient evidence of all, as such, are simply a form of mutual hypnosis operating between the deceiver and the deceived. Worse still, by accepting the deception, each person, through their own failure to exercise a responsible degree of skepticism toward such charlatans, only empower all charlatans to enrich themselves by deceiving others. And whatever crimes such charlatans engage in as a result of people's willingness to "believe" in them is the true "original sin," because such "sins" always originate in the willingness to "believe" something that the use of higher reason would've exposed to be false.

With *The Shining*, Kubrick creates a game to exercise such skills by throwing down a gauntlet that challenges each member of his audience to question what they think they know just as much as what they "believe." By doing so, he also challenges his audience to see if we can determine whether our "beliefs" are showing us the truth, or only being used to hide that truth instead, out of a preference for our preferred brand of "beliefs."

Re-watching *The Shining* that fateful Halloween night suddenly transported me back to my bedroom in the middle of the night, and brought me face to face with such questions, which were the real gremlins prowling about my room, and my brain, in the middle of the night. It was as if the floor had opened beneath me, and I had dropped through a wormhole back into my five-year-old self, staring at gremlins that were now clawing at me from the other side of my screen, like the vampires clawing at the window in *Salem's Lot*. Like those gremlins, were my interpretations of Kubrick's film all being generated in my head and simply projected into the film? And if so, where did those "demons" really come from, and how did they get inside my head in the first place?

"No way," I whispered to myself as I watched the images on the screen slowing forming into repeating patterns, again and again and again, like birds murmuring in a blue and white sky; like blood pooling and spiraling down a shower drain; like mathematical fractals streamlining the secrets of symmetry that held the universe together: "no fuckin' way!"

A fractal, by the way, is a pattern that nature repeats at different scales. The simplest example of a fractal is called a Sierpinski triangle, many of which, as we shall see, Kubrick places strategically in the carpets of the Overlook Hotel. Other examples can be seen in the relationship between us and the world around us. Our lungs look like the roots and the branches of a tree, for example, from which we derive our oxygen. And in the same way we inhale the oxygen that trees exhale, so trees inhale the CO_2 we exhale. The true "tree of life" is not a cross, in this sense, but an actual living tree, whose divine breath breathes life into us, and every other species on this planet, just like it is our breath that breathes life into those trees. Mother Nature, in other words, is truly our mother, and to lose our connection to her is to cut down a tree and erect a cross. As so many Native American tribes knew only too well, and as science is discovering more and more, everything really is interconnected and interdependent: especially us.

The only thing that makes our own species special is that we may be alone in our ability to fully understand and appreciate the nature, and indeed the majesty, of such interdependence. And yet, we so often only use our incredible intelligence and perception to find ever more clever ways to logic-chop our way to an opposite "truth:" that we are special, and separate, and deserve to be treated by God infinitely better than we treat everything God created, including ourselves, each other, our planet, and every other species of life we encounter. And by doing so, we only "slide back into savagery." All of these truths, as we will see, operate like the invisible hand, and the tell-tale beating heart, of *The Shining*.

◊◊

The impetus for my wonder-lust about *The Shining*, began with another famous horror film (which I will discuss later) and a documentary I had watched several years earlier. That documentary was *Room 237*. In it, director Rodney Ascher presents interviews with several fans who each offered different theories about all the underlying symbolism to be found in *The Shining*. These were theories I had never heard of before, let alone ever thought to consider.

For me, *The Shining* was always just a movie, and not even a very scary one at that. But what I saw when I watched the movie one fateful evening seemed to go a great deal further than anything anyone else had ever shared publicly. It felt like a revelation, and something completely different from the theories explored in Ascher's documentary, or anywhere else. It was like seeing pieces of an incredibly elaborate puzzle that were suddenly dancing in unison along an invisible thread, coagulating into a single monolithic masterpiece which left me reeling for weeks, months, even years afterwards. But like the gremlins in my room, I had to wonder if I was simply seeing through the lens of the ideas those fans had presented in Ascher's documentary. Yet even as I doubted my own instincts as the burnt toast of that documentary, like staring at a piece of 3D art, a tapestry of synchronicities slowly began unveiling themselves, again and again.

As it turned out, unlocking Kubrick's puzzle came from following the advice of that heretical theologian, Peter Abelard, who said that "the key to wisdom comes from constant and frequent questioning, for only by doubting are we led to question, and by questioning we arrive at the truth." Not through faith in dogmas and obedience to priests of various institutions who define obedience to the groupthink they design as the greatest of virtues, but through the power of our inquisition into the nature of truth itself. Such a power is not only the very first instinct we possessed when we were born (while a "belief" in contrast is a construct of dead brains that possess us), it was the only thing our brain is born with that helps us stay alive. It was that power alone that we relied on to evolve into the species we are now, long before we became possessed by our beliefs and a terrible desire to hold on to them in order to protect our eternal souls from the threat of the greatest form of evil ever created: hell.

Only by re-engaging our curiosity, untainted as it was when we were first born by a fear of judgement and hell, are we able to "be born again."

For only by exiting the temple tomb of our sacred "beliefs" can we see the true face of *The Shining*, and only if we are willing to take a voyage that is as much about self-discovery as it is an invitation to question everything. And by so doing, we not only unmask Kubrick's film, but "perhaps a bit more, if I may be so bold." And this book is the story of that journey, and that discovery, and why it was the most important discovery of my whole life.

As a small child in Catholic school, where much of my own natural desire to question everything was systematically hobbled by nuns treating it like Kathy Bates treats James Caan's ankles in *Misery*, we would pass the last minutes of the school day engaging in what we called "show and tell." Anyone could get up and "show and tell" the rest of the class pretty much anything they cared to show or tell. Well, this book is my version of that, of not only what I did during the Covid pandemic to keep my mind occupied, but also, as embarrassing as it is to admit, what I've been doing my whole life: just trying to understand the thoughts in my head.

And if you, dear Reader, are daring enough to descend into the "boundless depth of midnight cavern," as H. P. Lovecraft once wrote, "where we tremble at what sightless Stygian worlds may lay beyond," I will show you the way into all of this, and, most importantly of all, how I found my way home again.

PREFACE

Curiosity is lying in wait for every secret.
Ralph Waldo Emmerson

All learning begins when our comfortable ideas turn out to be inadequate
John Dewey

I T WAS A DARK AND STORMY NIGHT the evening I sat down
to watch a horror classic I hadn't seen in four decades. Although I
had seen the film before, nothing prepared me for what I was about
to experience. In the darkness that enveloped me, with rain rapping on
my window lattice like Poe's nightmarish raven, what unmasked itself
before my eyes that night sent me spiraling down a series of rabbit holes
that turned the fabric of everything I believed into Swiss cheese. In short,
pushing the "play" button launched a nuclear bomb into the center of
everything I thought I knew. Then, the shattered pieces all began
reassembling themselves into a seamless web of sprawling connections,
drawing me deeper and deeper into one of the most famous mazes of the
20th century. Those connections began explaining everything as they
reached out in all directions like a spider wed; like a galaxy; like a
genome. And like an astronaut returning from the moon, that experience
would leave me reeling for weeks, even years, after. The film that did
all of this was *The Shining* by Stanley Kubrick. And the night that turned

my world upside down and inside out was All Hallows' Eve, the day before All Saints Day, otherwise known as Halloween: the same day the Torrances move into the Overlook Hotel. And that was only the beginning.

What flushed me into the heart of Kubrick's maze that night was a journey I began traveling in 1976 through a parallel universe, which began around the time of my First Confession and First Communion. In the Roman Catholic religion, you must confess your "sins" to a "God" to help facilitate your "soul's" ability to "commune" with said God, which is like saying you could only talk with the pope after you'd taken a bath, and all to avoid being thrown into a volcano for refusing to wash up. With such "communion," one is lure into believing their own ideals are as infallible as Catholicism itself claims to be, at least with regards to "faith and morals," which pretty much covers everything. Being only a child, however, the "infallibility" of my religion never helped me on school exams, or make new friends, and I had no idea what a "soul" was, let alone that my own was morally defective due to it being "stained" with a cancerous condition called "original sin," the chemo for which was the blood of an innocent man who also needed to be a god.

What lessened the shock of discovering that my soul suffered from this unsightly blemish were two things. The first was learning that, because it was caused by the first of our species some eons ago, everyone else had been born with the same defect as well, which someone made it okay. The second was that the God who had kindly given me such a defective soul in the first place also provided both a vaccine and incentives to take that vaccine to overcome the spiritual handicap of that sin-stained soul. That vaccine came with supernatural ingredients via the

Vatican in Rome and included a regimen of God infused sacraments that needed to be administered regularly over the course of my entire life. Born with spiritual diabetes, in other words, God was good enough to provide me with the insulin shots I needed to maintain a healthy soul through a spiritual syringe called "sacraments," and motivated me to take such sacraments with the threat of hellfire and promise of heavenly treats (which at that age I assumed was a pantry stuffed with an eternal supply of Ho-Hos and Devil Dogs). This was like having to be on chemotherapy for the rest of my life in order to keep my soul alive after my body finally gave up the ghost. But, according to my parents, since everyone else had been born with the same defective sin-stained soul, and God had provided us all with a course of chemo-Christianity to keep that "stain" from spreading (because everyone knows there's no money in curing anything), everything was going to be okay.

Only it wasn't okay. Why not? Because, as my parents and teachers would later assure me, the "God" I was said to be 'communing' with was threatening to roast me alive if I failed to work like hell to scrub out that stain before my untimely death. This was like being ordered by Amon Goth, the Nazi commandant of a Concentration Camp in Steven Spielberg's *Schindler's List* (played by Ralph Fiennes), to spend my life scrubbing out the stain in the bathtub of my own soul or be shot, every day, for eternity. The trouble was, because you could die at any moment, you were far more likely to find yourself suddenly standing before the Supreme Deity of the Universe with a sin-stained soul than that you would happen to drop dead immediately following a long hot bath in the confessional with a priest. I also had no idea what it meant to "commune" with a God who was said to have died as the only means of cleansing the sinful filth from my soul. And while he had forgiven me for my filthy soul, I still had to spend the rest of my life working to get the sin-stain out of it by apologizing for both the stain and its effects on the world. That stain, mind you, could only be "washed out" by drinking copious amounts of the blood of Christ, one stain replacing another, and only after the mortality that resulted from the former left me dead enough to inherent the fruits of the latter. And the only way to provide Jesus with the detergent he needed to finally wash out such a stain completely was to cannibalize Christ at least every seven days. It was as if Jesus only rose from the dead so he could come back and tell the whole world to "eat me," only his followers took it literally. Two thousand years later, and salvation was only promised to those who devoted their lives to living like vampires in the hope that they too could be raised from the dead like zombies. What a great plan!

Unbeknownst to me, the mental gymnastics required to maintain a belief in a religion as paradoxically macabre as Roman Catholicism turned out to be the precise mental training needed to play Kubrick's little game. And it did so by introducing me to the art of cultivating a "false face" and making it my own. And opening Kubrick's game required seeing the difference. Allow me to explain.

According to my Catholicism there are no guarantees to salvation. Instead, each of us must "work out our salvation in fear and trembling," as St. Paul assures us in his letter to the Philippians (2:12). Life, it turned out, was one long religion class, and either you passed it or were tortured mercilessly forever, and the teacher never gave you any feedback, nor did they let you know exactly how you'll be graded when it's all said and done. The only clear instructions to such a test was that we were required to make a weekly visitation to a large redbrick building that sat across the street from the school I was attending. This I had to do for the rest of my life while agreeing to fork over 10% if my annual income. It seemed God was a spiritual socialist, and priests were like God's parole officers, and they wore a collar that looked like the flea-collar my dog wore, which confirmed that demons were like fleas, as seen in *The Amityville Horror*.

Once inside that building, I then had to pretend that I really wanted to be there, rather than playing football or watching Godzilla or Abbott and Costello on TV. I also had to pretend that anything being said by the man behind the altar, whose flowing robes looked like curtains and the bedsheets we wore when we pretended to be ghosts on Halloween, made perfect sense, even when what he said didn't make any sense at all. And most importantly of all, I also had to promise that no matter what, I would accept the claims of my church as my only "infallible truth," so long as we both shall live.

Being shy and wanting desperately to "fit in," I followed the lead of everyone around me, starting with my Mom and Dad. And since they were all pretending these requirements were okay with them, I acted like they were okay with me too. And that's when I began having to act like two different people: one who outwardly acted like my religion made perfect sense, and one in which I inwardly suspected that my religion made no sense whatsoever. And with the splitting of the atom (Adam?) of my mind in half in this way, as if baptism is the initiation of a mental mitosis, I found myself cast into the maze that is the true "mystery of faith." And that's when my own game began.

My parents initiated me into this "mystery of faith" from birth. Being a "mystery" that only God himself could solve or make any sense of assures that all who enter it will have to "abandon all hope" of ever understanding it, even as we are required to "believe" we understand a God who is an even bigger mystery than such a confusing "faith." For 42 years, as a result, I had been pedaling around inside of that mystery-maze of branded "faith" trying to make sense of it all, but to no avail. Indeed, the more I tried to understand it in any objective sense, the more purely subjective my understanding of it necessarily became. Such is love, that to understand it proves it can't be love at all, because the beauty of its mystery has been plucked out, and to not understand it proves that love is all it could truly be, because the heart has reasons that the mind can never understand.

And whenever I encountered evidence or arguments that made me aware of this reality, fear led to anger that I would then direct toward whatever messenger had delivered such evidence or arguments. That fear led to a constant underlying sense of anxiety. Like a lifelog fever, that anxiety receded like my hairline as my need to be right about my religion waned with age. And as it did, I grew more comfortable with being honest about the fact that the bald truth of my own brand of religion was that it seemed to make no more sense than anyone else's. I was just so used to pretending that it did, and so dependent on being approved of by my parents by so pretending, that it became the pillar of my whole identity. In doing so, however, my religion had turned me into a scarecrow, leaning together with others in my pew, heads stuffed with straw-man arguments and a need to be right posing as a love of truth.

Noticing the difference between my true need for unconditional love and my conditioned need for approval and acceptance masquerading as love, awakened me to the fact I had been playing a game my whole life, one that required me to separate my true-self from my false-self. Like Danny sliding out the window, discovering that I had been playing such a game flushed me right into the heart of Kubrick's maze. Kubrick's mystery unmasked itself to me, in other words, when I discovered it was simply a mirror.

So, what game had I been playing when I sat down to watch Kubrick's *Shining*? It was a game with ideas, about whether to believe or not to believe, and why. Playing with those ideas allowed my atheism toward other gods and religions to begin eating away at my dependence on my own brand of god and religion, like a school of piranha made up of my own curiosity eating away at the whale that had swallowed me whole, from the inside out. Every human being is born an atheist and an agnostic, after all. As we grow up, we simply continue in these perspectives with regards to every other god but the brand we happen to find profitable to subscribe to at one time or another, whether emotionally or financially, or both. And whenever we convert from one monotheistic religion to another, we are simply changing our mind about which brand of "God" we are deciding no longer exists, and which brand we are choosing to believe had always existed all along, despite our misjudgment. My brand of the word "God," of course, was Roman Catholicism, and the devil came in the form of my doubts about such a God. What *The Shining* revealed to me was that the truth I had been looking for had been staring back at me the whole time, only I was looking at it the wrong way. My religion ordered me to obey, but the "God" I was taught to believe created me had designed me to play.

Despite my growing questions about Catholicism, I can only compare the experience of watching Kubrick's adaptation of King's novel that night to St. Paul's spiritual epiphany on the road to Damascus, which led him to fall off his horse and bump his head;[2] like that guy telling Wendy about the "great party." Like nothing before or after, the experience of that fateful night changed profoundly the way I have looked at everything ever since, including the infinite possible ways of defining the word "God." It especially changed the way I understand the true nature of the "religions" that all claim to be authorized by the word "God" to make the lives of anyone who happens to disagree with the definitions they provide pure hell on earth. (And they do this, much like I did for so many years, in large part because their religion convinces them that they can only demonstrate to their "God" that they are worthy of being saved from eternal torments in actual hell by doing so.)

As already mentioned, while I had seen the film before, and perhaps more than once, watching it that night left me reeling in more ways than I could have ever imagined. Now I finally understood why Kubrick had called it a "masterpiece of modern horror," and why it was one of the most analyzed films in history; with record numbers of takes per scene and countless numbers of different interpretations that were only multiplying with time, aping the evolution of what we call "religion."

---

[2] To the "believer" of Christianity, such an event was God's way of altering the course of Paul's life (effectively overriding Paul's "free will"), while to the "believer" of any other perspective, Paul falling off his horse was likely the result of a seizure of some sort. Hell, maybe he was drunk.

I also finally understood why the film has been interpreted in so many ways. It has been interpreted as being about everything from conspiracy theories concerning faked moon landings to MK Ultra mind control experiments; from symbolically reflecting the genocide of Native Americans or Jews during the Holocaust, to the retelling of ancient myths like Theseus and the Minotaur, Narcissus, Plato's "Allegory of the Cave," or Poseidon, Sisyphus, and, according to some interpretations, even Jesus Christ. Some have suggested it's all just a dream, others that it is about going insane, or being in hell, or even being the devil himself. Some argue it's also about the U.S. dollar being detached from the gold standard, or reincarnation, or sexual abuse, or a psychotic episode by Wendy or Danny or Jack, or even just the chaos of life in general. But what I saw staring back at me that night made it perfectly clear that, in a way, it was actually about all of these things, and a whole lot more.

Over the years, one perspective that appeared to have been overlooked about the movie was how various interpretations of *The Shining* were like six blind men each offering an interpretation of an elephant. If none of the blind men have any idea what an elephant looks like, and each is offering an interpretation based on touching only one of the different features of the animal, then the one who feels the ear might describe an elephant as being like a giant palm leaf, while another who feels the tusk may describe it as being like a giant spear; a third feels the trunk and says "it is like a giant snake;" a fourth feels its side says "it is like a great wall;" a fifth grasps only one leg and says "it is like a column of the Parthenon," and the last one feels the tail and concludes it is like a length of rope with a rabbits foot on the end of it. All the descriptions are correct, of course, but only in describing the sole area explored by the individual blind man. Each description is also incorrect whenever it is offered as the sole "infallible" definition of the entire elephant.

What those blind men cannot see (obviously) is how the various parts they have each correctly described all connect to a whole which is greater than, and certainly very different from, any single part. Naturally, the only people who know how these seemingly disparate parts are all interconnected with each other are those who have seen an elephant for themselves. That Halloween night, the pieces of Kubrick's puzzle suddenly unmasked themselves as being not just a story, but parts of an incredibly intricate game. Part of that game required figuring out how the different interpretations offered about the nature of Kubrick's elephant could be assembled into a single unified image. The problem is that each interpretation could be equally valid, even if they contradict each other. And this makes the different interpretations of an elephant by six blind men look a lot like the problem with string theory.

In the field of quantum physics, string theory is the idea that at the heart of every single atom in the universe is a string so small that, to see it, we would have to expand the diameter of an atom to the size of the orbit of Pluto. Only then would the theorized "string" inside that atom reach the size of a small tree. So small is this string, as such, that we are incapable of verifying it exists at all, even though the mathematics of string theory predicts that it does. Since everything is made up of these strings, according to the theory, differences in things are the result of each string in the atoms of any particular thing vibrating in a different way.

Like six blind men interpreting an elephant, there are currently five distinctly different string theories. And, despite their differences, each theory is independently mathematically consistent. Those five theories are also related by dualities to a sixth theory known as M-theory, which unifies all the other theories. Unlike the five mathematically consistent versions of string theory, however, M-theory often causes arguments among scientists because there is no way to test it to see if it is true. And each of these six theories can only operate in 10 dimensions or more. Those 10-plus dimensions don't just exist in theory. Like a reflection in a mirror, they also exist in the physical structure of the human brain.

Combining mathematics with neuroscience, a Swiss team of researchers known as the Blue Brain Project, discovered something about the human brain that may help explain why there are at least as many different valid ways of interpreting Kubrick's *Shining* as there are in interpreting string theory, let alone concepts of an elephant or a "God." Studying the brain's neural network using algebraic topology, a branch of mathematics that can describe systems with any number of dimensions,[3] they discovered that the brain is full of multi-dimensional geometrical structures operating in as many as 11 dimensions.[4] As mathematician Ran Levi pointed out, as the brain progresses through an activity in those 11 dimensions, it "resembles a multi-dimensional sandcastle that materializes out of the sand and then disintegrates." The question is whether or to what degree the six different string theories, which can only operate in 10 dimensions or more, are the result of the

---

[3] https://www.eurekalert.org/news-releases/834792
[4] https://www.sciencealert.com/science-discovers-human-brain-works-up-to-11-dimensions

complexity of the multi-dimensional "sandcastles" the brain can build in the 11 dimensions found operating within its own neural networks. How much are we only seeing things as we are, in other words, rather than as they are?

What does this have to do with six blind men and an elephant, let alone interpreting *The Shining* or even the meaning of the word "God?" Well, it illustrates how we forget how much "the observer is the observed," as Jiddu Krishnamurti, which means we are often wholly unaware of how much the latter reflects the former, especially when the latter has no idea how it may be doing so.

Think about it this way. The five string theories are all equally valid, mathematically speaking, even though each is at odds with the others in striving to understand the same thing: a string that, like "God," may or may not exist. Those six different string theories, as such, may be mere reflections of the structure of the human brain from which our mind emanates, like light emitted from a candle flame, and therefore be simply examples of the different perspectives we can generate in our attempts to understand something.

Now, apply all of this to the six blind men, to whom the elephant they've never seen is also an abstraction. Like the different versions of string theory, this means that each one of the six blind men investigating an elephant could potentially come up with their own personal yet equally valid mathematically consistent models of what they perceive an elephant to be, even if all their models contradict each other and none of them reflects the reality of the elephant itself, because an elephant is not an abstraction. Rather, each of their models of what they think an elephant looks like may look like six different paintings by Picasso, but nevertheless be equally mathematically valid. It only takes one of those six men to declare their own model infallible and the rest heretical, to give birth to a religion in which all must "believe" that only one of those men can be infallible, for fear that chaos will ensue without such authority. And with such a need, the spilling of blood will follow as sure as night follows day. And of course, God is infinitely more abstract to all of us than an elephant is to six blind men.

It may not look like it at first but, as we will see, Kubrick is throwing open the doors to such questions with the opening scene, of a three-dimensional ball in the form of Jack's yellow car which, over the course of the film, rolls its way to a two-dimensional ball of a black and white photograph Jack appears to end up trapped inside of. That transition invites us to play with ideas. It invites us to consider, for example, questions like, if we are three dimensional creatures with an 11-dimensional brain that can't even agree on an understanding of the nature of the three dimensional universe we inhabit, let alone fully understand our own consciousness or anything outside of the three dimensions we are confined to, then why do we pretend to understand a "divine intelligence" infinitely greater than our own that exists wholly outside of our three dimensional universe, which by its "infinite nature" would therefore operate within infinite dimensions, let alone believe we must strive our whole lives to honor and appease such an intelligence by practicing religions that command us to think in two dimensional ways of black and white, right and wrong?

Like those string theories potentially reflecting the model of the human brain, so Kubrick rolls the ball of these kinds of questions out to his audience. And while such a ball at first sight looks like Kubrick is inviting us into a maze devoid of answers and therefore no escape, he provides two equally consistent models for understanding exactly what is really happening in his film, one psychological and the other structural. And he invites us to follow both with the two overlooked elephants flanking the doorway to his maze.

Symbolically, elephants help demonstrate how to play Kubrick's game. Being matriarchal, elephant herds always follow the female, who is the leader of both the jungles and deserts. Even the lion and leopard follow the elephant because they know she possesses a vast memory – the very thing required to navigate a labyrinth – of watering holes and food sources.

Of the two, the first elephant we see stands between a ball sitting in a box on top of the filing cabinet and a painting entitled "The Great Mother" hanging on the wall just outside of Stuart Ullman's office; a symbolic nod toward Wendy of who the audience should follow. Note that the ball is red, and the elephant is green: two colors Jack is always wearing throughout the film. The second elephant we see is purple, a color we get by combining red and blue, and sits at the bottom of a poster board as dark as a shadow, that sits on the floor next to Wendy – who happens to be dressed in red and blue, the same colors that predominate in "The Great Mother" painting – as she "overlooks" "doc" and Danny after he awakens from his "episode" in Boulder. Add the only other color we see Jack wear in the film – his gold sports jacket – and we get sepia, like the old pictures Jack ends up in, and the dark color of the posterboard.

The timing, placement, and colors of those elephants are no accident, nor are they irrelevant to navigating Kubrick's visual maze.

Part of what makes those elephants so important, however, is how they also relate to the white porcelain bull seen over Wendy's head as she reads her copy of *The Catcher in the Rye*, and how the milk carton we see over her shoulder, under the twin bottles of Joy dishwashing detergent, is symbolic of a cow, and what both have to do with room 237 and Theseus and the Minotaur. But to even begin to understand the significance of these connections, and how they are part of the 'clew of thread' Kubrick begins unwinding for his audience with Jack's golden Volkswagen (which resembles a ball of golden thread), we should look into a history which is so often kept outside our own, in a book written in 1972, by a Lakota Sioux medicine man named John Fire Lame Deer.

Lame Deer was born on the Rosebud Indian Reservation in 1906. In his book, *Lame Deer, Seeker of Visions*, he elaborates on how much we have lost our ability to see what is right in front of our eyes, just like so many of the characters we see in the Overlook hotel. As he points out, "mass produced people" - which Nietzsche referred to as "herd animals" and the famed socio-economist Thorstein Veblen described as "fabricated consumers"- have been homogenized and alienated as much from the world around them as from each other and themselves, and even their own existence. In this, Lame Deer echoes concerns raised by countless others, including Leo Tolstoy, John Stuart Mill, Henry David Thoreau, Alexis Tocqueville, and Mahatma Gandhi, all of whom saw people who were increasingly conditioned to rely on such an ever-narrowing focus of themselves as corrosive to one's own sanity, the spirit of life in general, and especially morality overall. And religious bulwarks erected to prevent the moral erosion such unfettered consumption inevitably leads to amounts to trying to hold back a tidal wave with a tampon. In fact, some have theorized that this is why Abraham left the highly commercialized city of Ur, at the very time when the technologies of numbers, writing, and money were all invented, and also why Jesus angrily overturned the tables of the money changers in the temple in Jerusalem, because both knew just how toxic the whole process of reducing everything to a dollar value and a business transaction could truly be. And through the alchemy of commodification, a multidimensional reality is reduced to 1s and 0s, the many-colored coat of life is reduced to a black and white picture, and the meaning and spirit of life is reduced and imprisoned in the scripture of a balance sheet.

For the Lakota, any separation from nature ultimately resulted in turning a person's heart to stone, leaving them as bitter as salt, like the bags we see Jack sleeping on in the "story room," cut off from the rest of the world and the story as he is. As Lakota philosopher Luther Standing Bear explained, the Lakota "knew that lack of respect for growing, living things, soon led to lack of respect for humans too." Instead, *The Virtue of Selfishness* fueled by modernity – which was championed by Ayn Rand in her book of that name, mathematically validated by John Nash, and then applied as economic policy by Rand disciple and Chairman of the Federal Reserve, Alan Greenspan – becomes a religion of Narcissism masquerading as the benevolence of the business man and the butcher: the latter of which Jack aspires to become for the approval and acceptance masquerading as "love" of the former partying in the Gold Room; a veritable brood of vipers selling circus and bread.

With our modern dependence on technology and the almighty dollar, a person's ability to hear their own inner voice, and thus their ability to know their true "self," is muted, replaced with the clamor and din of those selling their own ideas of who we are and should be. In such a culture, Danny's intuition, which we hear in the voice of Tony, is seemingly demonized as a sin, or something to be weary of, while Jack's obedience to Delbert and the Overlookers is venerated as a virtue. If the former is the source of authenticity, the latter fosters a dependence upon a need for acceptance and approval through status signaling. As a result of striving for such approval and acceptance, "modern man is alienated from himself," as Erich Fromm pointed out, "from his fellow men and from nature." In such a cultural milieu, the main aim is "profitable exchange," the only satisfaction is to consume, and the morality of the game of life is reduced to an ethos that proclaims, "he who dies with the most toys wins," and those who are still alive lose the whole planet.

Rendered incapable of understanding anyone else by such self-alienation, such a man then prides himself more and more on his assumed understanding of "divine truths" as dictated by his preferred brand of religious orthodoxy, whether theistic or scientific in origin. Through such a process, man increasingly separates himself from the world around him, leading him to desire evermore for a life beyond the one he has been given, even as he separates himself from the "mother nature" that gave him that gift of life to begin with. And, thanks to an insatiable appetite for more, which is unnatural to his soul yet nurtured everywhere in him by his environment, he gains his schizophrenia by losing his ability to see how the "God" to which he prays for salvation is the very Earth which he crucifies as an expendable commodity. And of every species of life on the planet, "enlightened" Homo sapiens deny this truth, like Peter denying Jesus, and ritualizes that denial into an infallible religion.

So how does Kubrick's *Shining* help restore sight to the blind by shining a light on all of this? It does this with images. "Seeing comes before words," wrote media theorist John Berger in *Ways of Seeing* (1972), for "the child looks and recognizes before it speaks." And one way Kubrick invites us to become a child again and play comes in the form of the elephants that flank the doors to his Games Room. Although the easiest things in the film to overlook, they reflect the very kinds of symbolism Lame Deer was referring to. For Lame Deer, that symbolism showed us the true interconnectedness of everything in the world, a fundamental understanding that every child begins with, and which Native Americans had always understood and built their societies and cultures around. Among modern cultures, however, only the likes of Albert Einstein, Richard Feynman, and ecologists like Gregory Bateson and Margret Meade, have managed to discover the importance of such insight.

Likewise, Kubrick uses symbolism to reveal the deep interconnectedness he has created with every detail to be found in his film. To see this, and to illustrate the importance of memory for navigating our way around Kubrick's maze, we can start with the date July 16, and the years 1951 and 1969.

The number 16 is relevant in more ways than one. The sum of 8 + 8, or double infinites standing on end, we can compare it also to the date of July 4th. 4 squared equals 16. And as we will see, the square is even more of essence than time itself. On July 16, 1951, *The Catcher in the*

Rye was published; a book by J.D. Salinger which can only be fully understood by understanding Kubrick's *Shining*, because in many ways the latter is a unique interpretation of the former. The protagonist in Salinger's novel is Holden Caulfield, a name that reminds us that Danny was born with a "caul" over his face that gives him the gift of "second sight." Holden is the same age as Tony, who, in the novel, is Danny's older and wiser alter ego. About a boy who may have lost his mind, Holden wears a red hunting cap and says he "hunts people in this hat," while Jack hunts people in his red jacket. Wendy's copy of the novel has a red book jacket and golden letters, while Jack appears to lose his mind after Delbert spills three golden drinks on his red crushed velvet jacket. The book, as such, is "black and white and red all over," like Delbert and Jack. And in the end, Jack ends up in a black and white photo dated 1921: a date we get if we invert the 5 in 1951. And while Jack encounters an inverted twin in room 237, the date July 4, 1921, adds up to 24 (7+4+13); and, like light through a prism, so 2 x 3 x 7 = 42.

On the other hand, the Apollo 11 moon mission launched on that same day in 1969. At 9:32 in the morning, American astronauts Neil Armstrong, Edwin "Buzz" Aldrin, and Michael Collins, lifted off in the mammoth-sized Saturn V rocket from Cape Canaveral, Florida. The final critical landing phase of the Apollo 11 mission began at 20:05, GMT, an inverted twin in time, four days later, on 20 July, 1969. Just under 13 minutes later, **at 20:17 GMT**, the Eagle lunar module landed on the Moon. Armstrong and pilot Aldrin then landed the spacecraft, Eagle, on the moon's Sea of Tranquility. And if we flip the 9s in 1969 we get 1 followed by 666. And on Jack's first day on the job at the Overlook, we see a woman walk into the hotel wearing a hockey jersey with the number 13 on it.

Such 'coincidences' are fun to play with, of course, but they barely scratch the surface of a film that turns the cinema screen into a Pandora's Box chalked full of such twins, twists and turns, all of which hinge on the audience's willingness to engage its creativity, and to "come and play" with what they see, and hear, and think; and most of all, what they "believe."

Apollo, it must be remembered, is the Greek god of light, healing, disease, plagues, music, art, poetry, archery, reason, and knowledge, but also truth and prophecy. He is the son of Zeus and Leto, and twin brother of the goddess Artemis. Together, Apollo and Artemis are known as the Twin Archers. By comparison, Danny is wearing an Apollo 11 sweater outside of room 237, and he is throwing darts in the Games Room on Closing Day, while Jack drives to the Overlook hotel along the Going to the Sun Road and throws his tennis ball like lightings bolts at the mural of twins over the fireplace. And like the moon reflecting the light of its inverted twin, so Apollo was also the god of the sun, who rode his fiery chariot (yellow VW Bug?) across the sky.

Then there are the various bolts of lightning. On the ceiling in the bathroom to room 237 (which in the novel is room 217), we see a mirrored light fixture in the shape of a lightning bolt, while when Jack walks into the hotel we see at the top of the pillars "*Z Z Z*"; symbols that remind us as much of a sleeping cartoon as electricity and bolts of lightning being thrown down by the gods above. Notice too, the same shape is formed at the center of the massive maze by the mixture of shadows and light when we see Danny and Wendy reverse their direction, as God looks down from above like a "sky monarch," the twin to the "Ski Monarch" poster Danny sees while standing on a chair in the Games Room.

To see even more of how Kubrick layers his film with such symbolism, a perspective we must cultivate in order to assemble his puzzle, compare all the details just mentioned to the opening sequence of the film and Danny outside of room 237.

In the opening scene, we find ourselves flying over the 'tranquil sea' of St. Mary's Lake toward Wild Goose Island in Montana's Glacier National Park, as if to reflect Jack descending like Zeus in the form of an eagle or embarking on a wild goose chase through the frozen hedge maze. Like the Saturn V rocket, so too the Timberline Lodge, which is in Oregon, is V shaped, forming half of a hexagon, while the shape of the hexagon Danny is sitting inside of in the hallway outside of room 237, wearing his Apollo 11 sweater, is that of the launch pad at Cape Canaveral. In fact, at the North Pole of the planet Saturn, we also see a giant hexagon. And while Jack – a Stovington Eagle – lands in the Overlook parking lot (which just happens to look like he had landed on the moon) bathed in sunlight, Danny launches like a rocket "somewhere over the rainbow" of colors in the hallway carpet - which just happens to match the colors in the rainbow seen both on his bedroom door in Boulder and a picture frame on the wall in Stuart Ullman's office - after a tennis ball is rolled to him from no one. Hell, even the eye of the Hal 9000 computer depicted in the poster for Kubrick's *2001: A Space Odyssey*, is similar in color and shape to the hexagon from which Danny "lifts off" before crash landing in room 237. And while the emblem at the bottom of Danny's Apollo sweater is most often interpreted as the number eleven, it is also the Roman numeral II, and the astrological sign for the Gemini: the third astrological sign in the zodiac, a constellation representing a pair of twins. While the Torrance apartment is apartment 3, under the sidereal zodiac, the Gemini is a sign that the sun transits from about June 16 to July 16. And the translunar injection of the Apollo just happened to occur at exactly 11:16:16, eleven years before the launch of Kubrick's *Shining*.

Such symbolic parallels, which Kubrick has littered throughout the film, illustrate how the game Kubrick created operates like a multilayered puzzle. But that puzzle can only be assembled after first finding all the pieces, many of the important ones of which are disguised to look like mistakes, and others of which are only alluded to in the film. And while the film is indeed a puzzle, it is one which operates also like an assortment of games. One of those games is mahjong, where we must match various types of "twins," be they near identical or inverted, and another is what King described in his novel as "one of those pictures that said CAN YOU SEE THE INDIANS?" If you strained and squinted, King explained of such a picture:

> "You could see some of them . . . hiding in the rocks . . . their evil, merciless faces peering through the spokes of a covered wagon wheel. But you could never see all of them, and that was what made you uneasy."

Like that picture, what makes us uneasy about *The Shining* is that we never see all the "Indians"- that is, all the many meaningful details, changes, and inconsistencies - that Kubrick includes in literally every shot of the film. Nor do we ever see the many "merciless faces" that Kubrick includes at various points along the way, many of which are seen on Closing Day; some are even "hiding in the rocks." Indeed, most never even notice how much the emblem on the top of Jack's chair in the Colorado Lounge (CL) looks just like "the spokes of a covered wagon wheel," much like the bent rim on the dart board in the Games Room, which just happens to show the numbers 2, 3, and 7, across the bottom of it, like a blackface jack-o-lantern smiling with a mouth full of broken crooked teeth.

And while some have interpreted the parallels just mentioned as representing a veiled confession by Kubrick to faking the Apollo 11 moon landing – a theory he was possibly familiar with and thus may have intended to exploit – the film is littered with evidence that demonstrates that Kubrick included such details because he had a very different meaning in mind. If he had wished to simply draw our attention to the moon landing, for example, it would have made more sense to have the date affixed to the picture of Jack at the end as 1958, the year NASA was founded.

The simplicity of such a theory, which may appeal to those who enjoy a good conspiracy now and again, shows at least a willingness to accept Kubrick's invitation to "come and play" by trying to be as creative as possible in interpreting the symbolism that Kubrick clearly included intentionally in his film. As creative as such an interpretation is, however, there are plenty of other pieces Kubrick included in his cinematic jigsaw puzzle that reveals something even more unnerving. And make no mistake: *The Shining* is a cinematic puzzle unlike any other ever designed.

In an interview with the French daily newspaper, *Le Monde*, Kubrick stated that his "film is built like a jigsaw puzzle," one in which he had placed "the last piece in the final image."[5] Offering any ultimate "solution" or unified theory about "what it all means" therefore requires first finding all the pieces of the puzzle, rather than just some or most. The picture of an elephant, after all, is only complete when all the various interpretations are pieced together into their proper places, along with plenty of other pieces never noticed by the six blind men from earlier. However seemingly contradictory they may appear when considered one at a time, assembled, all those pieces must form a unified whole. Any attempt to offer an ultimate solution about what it all means, as such, requires explaining how each and every piece of the puzzle - including everything from why there is an "impossible window" in Stuart Ullman's office and why various items on Stuart's desk dance around without ever being touched or even noticed, to why we hear a faint "sha" sound numerous times throughout the film, as well as how and why Jack ends up in a black and white photograph dated July 4, 1921 - contributes to forming a single coherent picture.

In physics, offering a perspective that resolves the seemingly contradictory explanations found in the various branches of a tree of inquiry is called a "unified theory." And while there are countless numbers of theories about every element of *The Shining*, the investigation that follows is the only one that will map out the elements of a unified theory from a 360-degree perspective of even the smallest and most seemingly insignificant details of the film, including every anomaly and inconsistency Kubrick included.

---

[5] Patrizia Moraz, "Il faut courir le risque de subtilité," *Le Monde*, 23 October 1980

To see this, we must first understand why Kubrick worked so hard to include all the anomalies and inconsistencies to be found in the film. And to do that, we must be willing to be as meticulous in our consideration of such details as he was in working to include them, by looking at each one frame by frame, and even second by second. Our investigation here will provide not only a logically consistent explanation for every anomaly in the film, but will also demonstrate how Kubrick pulls every rabbit out of every hat without ever once having to rely on ghosts, ghouls, or other supernatural forces drooling under the bed, to explain everything that occurs in the film – including how Jack escapes the pantry *and* ends up in a photograph dated 1921.

Offering a unified solution for *The Shining* has been difficult for numerous reasons. Chief among those reasons is the fact that the film is more than just a puzzle: it is a puzzle wrapped inside of a riddle, wrapped inside a mixture of games, and hidden behind the smokescreen of a movie which is about something radically different from the novel the movie is based on. And it is only in the process of assembling this puzzle that the viewer can discover the true face of the Minotaur hiding at the heart of Kubrick's maze. *The Shining* is a puzzle, that is, which we must assemble to play, and a game, which must be played in order to be assembled. Properly assembled and played, however, the game reveals a face of horror that is far scarier than that of a family man quietly going insane for the holidays. Like *The Tell-Tale Heart* by Edgar Allen Poe, the sound of the heartbeat we hear in places like room 237 and on the plane with Dick Hallorann - "the sound a watch makes when enveloped in cotton" - is an audible clue that there is an "insidious heart" beating beneath the floorboards of Kubrick's film. And Kubrick is inviting us to play detectives and discover whose heart it really is, and how it got there in the first place.

Although the cryptic ending of *The Shining* can be used to spawn an ever growing number of alternate perspectives and interpretations, the details to be found under the floorboards in the bedroom of Kubrick's jigsaw puzzle can be assembled into a skeleton key that unlocks every door and answers every mystery, from whether the shadow of the helicopter in the opening scene is indeed just a mistake, to how Jack escaped the pantry and ends up imprisoned in a black and white photo dated 1921; and even what may be written on both the note he appears to be holding in his right hand in that photo, and the piece of paper being held in the hand of the woman behind him, and why the latter disappears from view. The trick, of course, is learning how to assemble that puzzle by heeding Lame Deer's advice to learn to see, in order to use that key. The problem is that many of the important pieces needed to do so, as already mentioned, are not included in the film directly, but are only alluded to. The audience is therefore left to fill in the gaps using the clues and the rules Kubrick illustrates for them in various ways by thinking outside the box of their movie screen.

Compounding the challenge of assembling this skeleton key is the fact that, in addition to the surface narrative of the film, there are also myriad layers of symbolism that, while intended to convey multiple meanings, can often operate as red herrings that produce sub-narratives that Kubrick either directly or more often subliminally invites his audiences to consider. While the point of including such layers is to encourage "out of the box" thinking among his audience (and the further outside that box the better), it also creates a visual maze littered with rabbit holes into which it is easy to fall, and from which - especially for the obsessively curious - there may be no escape. We see this with allusions to Native American genocide and symbols that trigger thoughts about the Holocaust and the moon landing, to name but a few of the more obvious examples. Such interpretations only hamper the process of assembling Kubrick's puzzle to the degree they prevent the player from continuing to play the game. What follows then is simply the story of how I discovered this key and found myself playing this game, and all entirely by accident.

Rather than the "accident" of which I am referring having occurred in a single instance, however, it began with another movie altogether, some years earlier, and then a chance observation in an art gallery in Brazil. The movie that started the ball rolling, coincidentally enough, was *The Exorcist*.

The Exorcist: A Shining Twin Challenge

A number of years ago, I re-watched *The Exorcist*, a movie that had terrified me as a child, to see if there was a way of interpreting or understanding the film from a purely scientific perspective. As my mind began to question the religious ideas I had been raised to depend on, I began to question my habit of always blaming "evil" on the devil, the supernatural, or the gremlins that came clamoring into my bed chamber in the middle of the night. Assigning such blame only ensured I would continue to "believe" in both the existence of devils and the God and Church I needed to save me from such spectacles. But if the "God" I was taught to fear and love was either a fable or at least unlike anything we call "God," what then was the true origins of "evil"?

Being raised a Roman Catholic meant there was nothing more natural to me than the supernatural. Yet the fear and anxiety that accompanied this belief compelled me to depend entirely upon the priests and nuns employed by a Roman Catholic Church rather than any actual "God," however one chooses to define such a word. As a result, I wore my Catholicism like a suit of armor. As I got older, however, that suit of armor felt ever more like a crown of thorns and as rigid as a crucifix. So, after graduating from law school and awaiting my results from the BAR exam, I felt compelled to apply the skills I had paid so dearly to acquire to quite literally become the devil's advocate.

To play the devil's advocate, I rewatched a film about the devil that had scared me the most into depending upon my brand of religion (by scaring the bejesus out of me, ironically enough). And by shifting from the prosecution to the defense, I began to argue against my own spiritual dependence upon a religion I had been raised to believe I had "freely" chosen, rather than raised to be emotionally dependent on. Discovering my own emotional bamboozlement only came from subjecting my own beliefs to the same acid-bath of criticism I had always enjoyed pouring over everyone else's beliefs. As uncomfortable a process as it was, however, it was only by doing so that I came to understand how my own spirituality had been crucified to a dependence on a particular Church in Rome, and "men in black" whose celibacy was even more unnatural and opposed to procreation than the homosexuality such men condemned.

Much to my surprise, that process allowed me to clearly see how all the events in *The Exorcist* film, unlike the book, are not the result of demonic supernatural forces. Instead, the film provides its audience with a much more disturbing interpretation of what was really going on with

Regan MacNeill; and who and what was really to blame for all of the "evil" in the film.

The author of *The Exorcist* novel was William Peter Blatty, a fellow Roman Catholic. The director of the film adaptation of that novel was William Friedkin, a staunch agnostic. These two perspectives reflected those of my own father and his older brother, respectively, between whom my young mind had often been batted back and forth like a tennis ball over the course of my life. As a result of these differences of perspective, differences which in some ways reflected the two warring sides of my own brain, I noticed how the film version of *The Exorcist* depicts a story that is subtly but significantly different from the novel. While the former based his story on competing supernatural forces, the latter does something very different. The problem is that most people missed the subtleties Friedkin included in his film because they were blinded as much by the storybook version written by Blatty as their own faith in the belief that evil has its origins in supernatural forces. Watch the film again while looking for those subtleties and you may discover, much as I did, that Friedkin includes details that suggest the evil he is referring to shares our own bed. Watch it again, that is, and you may see the ghost of Friedkin's agnosticism peering out through the wagon wheels of Blatty's supernatural tome.

When I sat down to again watch *The Shining* that Halloween night, I hadn't intended to subject the film to the same consideration as *The Exorcist*. But after watching a few minutes of Kubrick's film, like an involuntary reflex, part of me began to wonder if what appeared to be going on between Blatty and Friedkin was perhaps also going on between King, who was raised a Methodist, and Kubrick, whom King once referred to as a "visceral skeptic." If so, maybe Kubrick, like Friedkin, had also provided a means of interpreting his film without having to blame angels and demons, ghosts and ghouls, or things that go bump in the night. As it turned out, Kubrick not only did just that, but he did so more than any other director had ever done before in the history of film.

◊◊

As any fan of the movie already knows, *The Shining* by Stanley Kubrick is widely considered to be one of the greatest horror classics of all time. And it is, in part, because it is a movie that has largely left audiences struggling to stitch together a puzzle that appears to be infinitely malleable on the one hand, and missing a significant portion of the pieces needed to assemble it on the other. For 42 years, as a result, most of the pieces of that puzzle have either failed to be found or left unwittingly in the box, and the puzzle, even as the film has been studied and ruminated over by the most devoted of horror fans and cinephiles alike, has remained largely unassembled. While this has added to the allure of the movie itself, it has also kept hidden the true face of horror that Kubrick had surreptitiously assembled, and with it, perhaps the reason he felt the need to do so, which he appears to have taken with him to his grave (at least until that fateful Halloween night). Properly arranged and perceived, however, the fragmentary nature of the images in Kubrick's film reveals not only one of the most important films ever made, but in many respects, also one of the most frightening spectacles ever seen. And it is, because it preys upon the malleable and mercurial nature of human perception itself.

Only by unmasking the true face of horror that Kubrick hides from his audience in plain sight, is it possible to understand how Kubrick masterfully uses techniques to distort reality and disorient his audience. Seeing this makes it clear that, more than simply wanting to add to the creepy experience of his film, as he so often claimed, Kubrick also sought to illustrate just how much human consciousness can be both a blessing and a curse. It is a blessing, because it gives our species a unique ability to perceive reality with, as Hamlet said, all the seeming apprehension of a god. Yet it is also a curse, because the plasticity of human perception makes human consciousness not only infinity malleable, but also the easiest thing in the world to manipulate. Although the world we have built like a digital cocoon around ourselves has changed beyond anything that the first of our species could have ever imagined, the stories we have built for ourselves like an ark, which have taken many shapes, have always either venerated human sacrifice as divine, or eventually led human beings to a point where they no longer know why they exist. While human consciousness giveth us the unique ability to "intelligently design" for ourselves the meaning of life on the one hand, it also taketh away from life any semblance of meaning worth living for, on the other; even seducing some into suicide with dreams of martyrdom for a happily ever hereafter. It clings to the past because it is the devil it knows and shuns the change that survival has always required because it is the devil it knows not. It allows us to discern that fact is always stranger than fiction, but leads us to always prefer fantasy over reality, because stark reality has always seemed far too terrifying a spectacle to face without the pacifying effects of one grand illusion or another, to comfort and sustain us. And nowhere are all these paradoxical truths illustrated more clearly and more brilliantly than in *The Shining*.

At the heart of the two versions of the story offered by King and Kubrick, an intersection where fact and fiction so often become one, is a debate about human consciousness that is even older than Julius Caesar and Jesus Christ, or Plato (who was said by some to be the son of Apollo) and Aristotle. That debate revolves around questions concerning the nature of human perception and our ideas about good and evil. The difference between the two stories, however, is that one is a tale to be imagined, while the other is an experience to be engaged. While King's novel invites the reader to envision the events being described in black and white, Kubrick's film invites the audience to play a game in living color, by encouraging the audience to question everything, especially what they see and hear and "believe." The former relies on the audiences' willingness to believe in faith, while the latter hides the truth behind a curtain of confirmation biases designed and installed in our psyche by our religious beliefs. And to see the shining truth hiding at the heart of Kubrick's maze, we must be willing to find the phantom thread of truth that allows us to pull back the curtain of those beliefs.

To allow for the audience to ultimately find the phantom thread that runs throughout the film, like Theseus navigating his way through the labyrinth with an invisible string, Kubrick appears to have been far more meticulous in the making of this film than perhaps any other. As the details that follow will illustrate, it appears he did so in order to ensure that the only incongruities in *The Shining* where the ones that had to be there for one reason or another. If the pen moves on Stuart Ullman's desk, for example, we must ask ourselves if this is simply a continuity error, or if that movement was as intentional as the placement of the "impossible window" in Stuart's office?

Answering such questions can often create the paradoxical problem of both validating and invalidating all theories about *The Shining* simultaneously. It does this because *The Shining*, rather than being a dogmatized religion, is a living, breathing work of art. In fact, as we hear in room 237, it even has a pulse. And because it does, any interpretation of it can be determined, not by some minority of critics or experts or even the "Creator" of the art itself, but by each member of the audience, however they see fit. After all, there is no pope who can offer a single way of interpreting a piece of art any more than there is a single correct interpretation of a Rorschach inkblot; concepts of an infinite "God;" a line of poetry or sacred verse; what it means to be a human being; or even how to define the nature of reality itself. Indeed, art is purely subjective, because it is an invitation to come and play with interpretations, with each interpretation being as unique as the interpreter. And it does this because, in more ways than one, art operates like a mirror, one which invites the viewer to be an artist themselves and explore that art to the same depth they are willing to know themselves.

Unlike a religion, which often seeks to oppress our imaginative capacity by imposing a single "infallible" interpretation of a poetic verse of scripture (even though poetry is designed to produce a menagerie of interpretations), *The Shining* is pure art. And the point of all art is to hold up a mirror to the world. By doing so, it invites its audience into that mirror, to become artists as well, exactly as we are born to be. And an artist is someone who not only creates, but seeks a more artistic explanation for elements expressed in any art than that something was simply a mistake or an oversight, or a meaningless addition by the artist. While religion teaches us to see ourselves as the masterpiece of a perfect artist, even though we ultimately blame ourselves for expressing the sinful nature that artist designed us to have and prefer, art teaches us to look at what looks like merely a mistake and see how it is part of the magic that makes us who we really are.

Applied to *The Shining*, the continuity errors one sees (or thinks they see) in Kubrick's masterpiece, even if they are mere mistakes, invites us to imagine a better way of interpreting such mistakes, to be as creative as we possibly can in imaging what such mistakes could mean. What others call a "mistake," in other words, the artist sees as the medium of all creativity. Only by looking through the eyes of a child can we ever see how any mistake may simply be part of an illusion, one orchestrated by a cinematic magician who was perhaps without equal. In many respects, those continuity errors may in fact be the most truthful parts of the movie overall, which is why Kubrick worked so hard to include them and ensure he got them just right.

Because the movie is designed to allow the more curious viewer to exercise their creative intelligence to whatever degree they wish, the only interpretations of *The Shining* that could be considered "invalid" are perhaps only those that seek to prevent people from exercising their imagination and creativity. To do so is to discourage people from striving to look at something old in new and different ways. Every child is an artist, as John Lennon observed, until their willingness to exercise their creativity is disemboweled by "experts" that assure them they are not artists at all. Such naysaying led Picasso to remark that, while "all children are artists, the trouble is remaining one as an adult." Dogma crucifies imagination much as judgement acts like a crown of thorns on our curiosity, while art lives or dies through the curiosity and creativity of the audience. To unmask the secrets of *The Shining* we must resurrect our imaginations from the temples they have been walled up in, and breathe life back into our creativity. After all, as Albert Einstein said, creativity is simply intelligence having fun.

Ironically, those who have argued that to get lost in the tiniest of details in the film is to "fail to see the bigger picture" have ultimately failed to see the bigger picture because of their dismissal of Kubrick's insane attention to even the tiniest of details in his film. In 2013, for example, David Haglund published an article for Slate.com (on 03/28/2013, at exactly **12:07** PM) entitled "Yes, Super Fans of *The Shining* Are a Little Nutty."[6] In it, Haglund concluded that the documentary *Room 237*, which explores several deeper possible meanings in *The Shining* put forward by various fans, leaves you feeling pretty sure that finding such deeper meanings "is not the point." Yet the more anyone considers the level of secrecy and meticulousness, the record levels of retakes, and the incredible number of synchronicities that Kubrick took such pains to weave across his film, the more it appears that it not only *is* the point, but that it is actually Kubrick who is talking directly to those in his audience who make such dismissals when Danny says "there's hardly anyone to play with around here." We know Danny's comment is not true, after all, because just before we hear Danny say this, we hear children playing outside of the apartment

---

[6] https://slate.com/culture/2013/03/room-237-review-the-shining-documentary-is-misunderstood-by-the-new-york-times-video.html

complex, and even a dog barking (reminding us of the man in the dog suit "playing" with the man in the upper room). Yet even if Kubrick never intended for his audience to "come and play" with the details to be found stashed away like Easter eggs in every nook and cranny of *The Shining*, being nutty enough to play with his films as if he had hoped we would do so is one sure way of appreciating that advice of Robin Williams, when he said, "You're only given one little spark of madness. You mustn't lose it." Or as Jack Kerouac said of "the crazy ones:"

> "Here's to the crazy ones. The misfits. The rebels. The troublemakers. The round pegs in the square holes. *The ones who see things differently*. They're not fond of rules, and they have no respect for the status quo. You can quote them; disagree with them; glorify or vilify them. About the only thing you can't do is ignore them. Because they change things. They push the human race forward. And while some may see them as the crazy ones, we see genius. Because the people who are crazy enough to think they can change the world are the ones who do."

Besides, "some people never go crazy," as Charles Bukowski wrote, and because they don't, "what truly horrible lives they must lead." In this sense, perhaps Thoreau said "the mass of men live lives of quiet desperation" because they fail to be a "little nutty" every now and again. In fact, the only day of the year that some people do allow themselves to go a little nutty is Halloween: the very same day the Torrances start their winter holiday in the Overlook hotel. Indeed, for some, Halloween is the only day of the year when they allow themselves to unmask their true self.

In contrast to those interpretations that may have the effect of smothering in its crib the childlike creativity of those who like to play with ideas, perhaps the most valid way of interpreting the film, like interpreting any piece of art, might simply be one that not only encourages others to resuscitate their inner artists again, but alters the way a person watches every other film they see thereafter, and perhaps, even changes how they see themselves, and life itself. And who does that more than those who embrace their God given gift to "be a little nutty?" Hell, isn't that the whole point of art? Besides, even Jesus was accused of being "out of his mind" (Mark 3:20-21), and all because he dared to challenge people's beliefs. And that, on some level, is what every artist does.

"Unquestioned beliefs are the real authorities of a culture," Robert Combs wrote, and blind faith to such beliefs can lead to the same kind of madness Jack Torrance succumbs to, the same kind that burned witches and heretics and led the crowd to scream out "crucify him!" And this is far worse than what happens when people are willing to try being "a little nutty" enough to question such beliefs. And because they can, Kubrick created a movie that was really an elaborate game that challenged the audience to think about what they believe they are witnessing, and why. The question is whether we are curious enough to play Kubrick's game, so we can look at the reality of Kubrick's film unmasked from the biases and beliefs we too often project onto it, and even into it. In a world of illusions and deceptions, however, the only sin greater than seeking the truth is daring to speak one's own truth, "without reference or dependence on any other authority whatsoever," even if the whole world should hate us for daring to do so.

So, for anyone who is willing to do either one, what follows is a picture many people would prefer not to look at, and most work their whole lives to avoid seeing at all.   Or let me put it this way: when someone tells you "That some books should not be opened," you know that those books are the very books that need to be opened more than any other. This book is that kind of book. But you'll have to read it and make up your own mind about that.

And with that our little game begins.

(SCHISMO)GENESIS

All things are bound together. All things connect.
Chief Seattle, 1854

To think is to speculate with images
Giordano Bruno

KUBRICK HAD A PHRASE that he repeated like a personal mantra to deflect those who pressed him too much about the "meaning" of his work or his intentions:[7] "In all things that are mysterious, never explain." He borrowed the line from H. P. Lovecraft, a man who was as much a master of the macabre as Stephen King. This edict, which applies at least as much to Kubrick's work as to Kubrick himself, has left audiences to determine for themselves what, if any, deeper meanings may hide in the hearts of Kubrick's films. While some have dismissed investigations into such a question as mostly the idol worship of a director whose mythic status outshines his actual abilities, others cannot shake the gnawing sensation that there is something more sinister lurking just beneath the surface of some, if not all, of his films. And, for a growing number of fans, in no film is this feeling more palpable than in *The Shining*.

Of the many reasons that lead so many people to suspect *The Shining* is about so much more than meets the eye, four reasons standout. The first is the fact that, in an industry built upon public exposure, Kubrick

---

[7] *Stanley Kubrick, Director* by: Walker, Taylor and Ruchti, pg. 274

remained intensely private and secretive. This was also true of *The Shining*, with the film being made "with an excess of secrecy [with] no outsider ... allowed on the set, nor ... any interviews permitted."[8] Second, in addition to such secrecy, his insane attention to detail and penchant for repeated takes and sheer perfectionism while filming and editing have led many to wonder if Kubrick suffered from an obsessive-compulsive disorder. Third, despite Kubrick's potential OCD, under close examination, it turns out *The Shining* proves to be a film with more inconsistencies and continuity errors than any other film in history; so many in fact that they appear to be deliberate. This begs the obvious question: why would a man who was arguably the most meticulous director in history, put so much effort into, and maintain such secrecy around, the making of a movie that has more continuities errors than any other film ever made?

The last reason to suspect Kubrick's films are hiding something is because of one of Kubrick's favorite books. That book was not only used as a central plot point in his film *Dr. Strangelove*, it was also a book that, according to Kubrick's personal assistant for over twenty years, Anthony Frewin,[9] Kubrick felt was one of the greatest scholarly works of the 20th century.[10] By David Kahn, that book was *The Code Breakers: The Story of Secret Writing*, which laid out a detailed history of message encryption and decryption. And as it turns out, that book suggests that the music of

---

[8] https://www.sensesofcinema.com/2020/the-shining-at-40/king-vs-kubrick-the-origins-of-evil/

[9] Stanley Kubrick Archives, p. 518.

[10] http://www.collativelearning.com/RAtakeonRoom237controversy.html

Dies Irae playing during the opening scene of the film is a clue that, among other things, *The Shining* is also an encrypted message.

Although these four ideas make for a perfect plotline for the movie *Conspiracy Theory* – a 1997 film directed by Richard "Donner" about a NYC cabbie named Jerry (played by Mel Gibson), who is obsessed with reading *The Catcher in the Rye*, over and over again – a person need not be aware of any of them to be left, after watching *The Shining*, with a sense that what they had just witnessed begs for deeper consideration. Hell, a faded photo of Jack dated 1921 can alone do that. The question is whether to follow our curiosity or not, and if so, how, to what extent, and where to begin? As it turns out, the film itself provides the roadmap for answering these very questions. Like the opening ascent to the Overlook Hotel over a silver sea, the place to begin for all those who enjoy going a 'little nutty' now and then is with a bird's eye view of how the film itself ended up on the silver screen.

A Movie is Born in a Manger of a Mirror

A manger is an open oblong box, usually found inside of a barn, from which farm animals feed. Such a box is said to have served as the legendary crib for the most famous baby ever born, foreshadowing the food he would later be used as, at least by so many Western Europeans for whom domestication to authority was a prerequisite to striding the globe red in sword and cross. Coincidentally, if we are being creative, an oblong box also describes the shape of a movie screen, from which an audience feeds on food for thought. So how did *The Shining* manage to end up in the manger of a movie screen, and how should we best understand the relationship between the two versions of the story, and the world views held by the two men who created each one?

In 1977, Stephen King published a horror novel that he began while staying at, as if a foreshadow itself, the Stanley Hotel in Estes Park, Colorado. Stanley Kubrick then adapted that novel into a movie that was released "three goddamn years" later in 1980. Despite significant differences between the novel and the film, due in no small part to their different mediums, both became and have remained horror classics. But to best understand the relationship between these two men and the story they share, we should start by first understanding the relationship between two other men, and a postcard.

Consider these two other "faceless" men for a moment. One of them is a mythical character who, according to legend, is said to have walked the earth some four thousand years ago, while the other is one of the most notorious phantoms who ever lived. One is remembered as the greatest saint of all time and the founder of an ever-growing number of religions, and the other is one of the greatest sinners of modern history and has an almost cult like following. The former is most famous for attempting to murder his own son on a mountain top, much like Jack Torrance, while the latter was the first serial killer in history to enjoy worldwide notoriety, much like Jack Nicholson.

So, who are these two men, who seem like two sides of Jack? Well, the first was named Abraham, and is remembered today as the patriarch of three of the world's largest monotheistic religions. And the second was Jack the Ripper.

On the one hand, both figures can be seen in the image of Jack Torrance, a man who takes his son and wife into the mountains where he tries to murder them both out of obedience to the "Overlookers." On the other hand, the Rosetta stone required for simultaneously seeing how Jack Torrance is a composite of both Abraham and Jack the Ripper, as well as understanding the relationship between the men responsible for the two versions of the story written in 1977, is a postcard, sent from the past, about the true nature of what Shakespeare referred to as the greatest prison of all: human perception.

The earliest known form of the Rosetta stone needed for deciphering the relationship between the four men just mentioned comes from an image, the oldest version of which comes from an anonymous German postcard found in 1888: the same year Jack the Ripper was carving up working-class women in White Chapel. In 1890, a later version of that image was found on an advertisement for the Anchor Buggy Company. In 1915, yet another version of the image was published by William Ely Hill in a humor magazine with the title "My Wife and My Mother-in-Law."

The image, which has become famous among Psychology 101 students for illustrating the plasticity of human perception, is a black and white drawing of a woman's face. Depending on interpretation, the face you see is either one of a young and beautiful woman, with a delicate chin line and an elegant headpiece, or that of an old woman with a large bulbous nose and a protruding chin. Put another way, depending upon how our cultural formatting molds our perspective, we see either the Virgin Mary or the wicked witch of the West (Wing?). The image itself is seen in Figure 1.

E

Figure 1

This famous image, which serves as a much-needed compass for navigating Kubrick's *Shining* head maze, is designed to operate as an optical illusion. Of the different types of optical illusions, the image above is an example of an illusion based on perspective. Perspective illusions exploit the ways in which our brains can construct three dimensional images out of two-dimensional input. In 1980 (an anagram of 1890), Kubrick provided his audience with the most recent version of this image in the form of the woman in the bathtub of room 237. First, we see a young seductress, then, after casting her reflection in the mirror, an old rotting corpse; one is three dimensional, and the other two; one is "REDRUM," the other is "MURDER." This reversal – which was absent from King's novel – illustrates how the famous drawing causes the brain to switch between seeing the young girl and the old woman, a "wife" and a "mother-*in-law*," like reflections in a mirror. And as Jack is a writer, a similar thing happens when an oral tradition is written down: one as alive as a tree, the other as beset with the rigor mortis as a cross.

The point of presenting such a two-faced image, of course, is to invite the audience to question the nature of the images they see on the screen, as either one or the other; or even both, and neither. The difference is that with the images in the film, Kubrick is inviting the audience to construct two-dimensional images (the true nature of a photograph) from what we perceive to be three-dimensional information, which is how we interpret the images we see in a photograph or a film.

Throughout his film, Kubrick uses this perspective illusion to not only invite his audience to question their perceptions in numerous ways, but also to question what they think they know. One of the best examples of this can be seen in the famed controversy around the shadow of the helicopter. That shadow can be seen briefly in the bottom frame of the opening scene of the film but is only visible in its entirety in the release of the film formatted for old style TVs. Those who worked closest with Kubrick on filming and editing the opening scene have repeatedly insisted that the shadow is simply an oversight. Yet as we will see, there is amble reason to suspect that they may be mistaken.

For now, just consider some of the reasons why the shadow may only be intended to look like a mistake. In 1932, the Academy of Motion Picture Arts and Sciences dubbed the camera aperture setting 1.33:1 as the "Academy aperture," which remained the first standard ratio in film until the 1950s. The 1.33:1 aperture ratio just happens to be the same as the 4:3 ratio of a television screen in which the shadow of the helicopter is visible. In the book of Psalms, verse 133:1, we see the "Song of Ascents" (like Jack driving up the mountain, and Wendy running up the stairs), that tells King David, "How good and pleasant it is when brothers dwell in unity." Recall that Apollo has a twin named Artemis, and both are known as the "twin archers" – like Danny throwing his darts and Jack throwing a tennis ball which eventually lands in front of Danny. In

Matthew 12:25, in contrast, we see "a house divided against itself cannot stand" (just like a child's imagination when the digitally analytical hemisphere of his brain is conditioned to live in fear of the images generated out of the creatively analogue hemisphere of his brain), and Jack falls to the ground after Wendy and Danny leave the hotel. Also, if we combine the day the Torrances move into the Overlook and the number on the hockey jersey of the woman walking into the hotel, we likewise get 13 31. And at what time into the film do we see the shadow of the helicopter? At exactly 01:10 to 01:11: twins in time that look as much as the 11 on Danny's Apollo sweater as the zodiac symbol for the Gemini. As we shall see, there are a host of other details that Kubrick includes in the film, and even in the opening scene, that all invite us to take a much needed second sight of that shadow, and the movie overall.

If we look closely, we see plenty of other "errors" in the film. In addition to the shadow of the helicopter, for example, we can also see the chopper blades of that helicopter slashing across the top of the screen as we get our first 'overlook' of the Overlook Hotel. In fact, the more attention we pay to the details, the more obvious it becomes that the entire film is littered with such errors. A chair and a table go missing in the Colorado Lounge (CL); a cigarette disappears and reappears in the ashtray on Stuart's desk; lights switch on and off between shots, and several other various objects regularly move around on their own, including the black and white photos on the walls, or simply disappear altogether, like the lamps and the driftwood in the CL. And there are numerous other details that look like mistakes, but which appear to be clearly intentional nevertheless. Such details keep the viewer both disoriented and in a perpetual state of uncertainty (a bit like going to church and watching the nightly news), leaving the meticulous observer with the seemingly impossible task of discerning which anomalies may be simply accidents of poor editing and which may be intended to simply look like accidents. Like the two faces on the postcard, some mistakes appearing to be more intentional than others, how can we ever be certain which are which?

One of the most obvious incongruities of the film is the "impossible window" seen inside of Stuart Ullman's office. Since Stuart's office is interior to the hotel, those who notice this spatial anomaly are left to wonder why Kubrick would intentionally place a window that opens to outside of the hotel in a wall that separates Ullman's office from the hallway on the other side of it. Did he just like the lighting such a window provided for the scene, as some have argued, or is it intended to also help disorient the audience, or for some other reason as well? Whatever the reason or reasons, it nevertheless leaves the viewer to wonder: what kind of game is Kubrick *really* playing?

What Kind of Game Are We Playing?

In trying to figure out what kind of game we are being invited to "come and play," the perfect place to look is the final photograph of Jack, dated 1921. Properly understood, that photograph operates as the flipside of the postcard from 1888.

In 1921, the phrase "a picture is worth a thousand words" first appeared in print (i.e., in black and white). It is also the year that the ten images used in the Rorschach inkblot test were established. Developed by Swiss psychologist Hermann Rorschach, the test allows doctors to observe the unique way people construct a mental image from what is basically meaningless stimuli. Doing so helps to provide a better

I

understanding of how a person's experiences affect their perspective. Those perspectives determine why someone sees a young woman or an old lady; impish gremlins prowling about their bedroom in the dark of night; or even why some people can see Abraham is Jack Torrance's twin, while others see only Jack the Ripper.

So, why are the inkblots from 1921 and the postcard from 1888 needed to put Kubrick's puzzle together? Answer: because the opening shot of the film, as we fly over St. Mary's Lake, is as symmetrical as one of Rorschach's inkblots, while the final photograph of the film is an image that is both Jack Nicholson and Jack Torrance, standing in a posture that is reflective of both Jesus and the devil. And like the number of inkblots in Rorschach's test, Kubrick shows us ten black and white cue cards over the course of the film; cue cards that are obviously about more than simply wanting to provide the audience with a sense of timing. Combined, the ten cue cards and the two images that bookend the film are not merely intended to blur the line between categories of "good" and "evil," but to challenge the audience to notice how often followers of Abraham use the former to justify acting like Jack, whether Torrance or the Ripper, for their brand of righteousness. And the only difference between the two is not intrinsic to the violence being carried out, but, as even St. Augustine argued, who is using violence against whom.

In many ways, the optical illusion of the woman on the postcard reflects also the difference between how Kubrick and King interpret the nature of reality (at least for the purpose of their shared story): one seeing a witch and the other a seductress. In 1509 (an anagram of 1950, the year Wendy was born in Kubrick's version of the story - she was born in 1946 in the novel), this difference was captured in a famous fresco by the painter Raphael. Called *The School of Athens*, it was a hallmark of the Italian Renaissance, symbolizing the unification of art, philosophy, and science. At the center of the painting stand Plato and Aristotle, two men whose different interpretations of the nature of reality happen to mirror the different sources of "evil" at play in the two versions of *The Shining* offered by King and Kubrick. It also illustrates a perspective that Kubrick would become famous for: the one-point perspective. For Plato, like King, the "genus" to which a thing belongs possesses a greater reality than the thing itself, while for Aristotle, like Kubrick, the opposite was true.

A genus is a group of closely related species. For example, the genus Canis — which is Latin for "dog" — includes all domestic breeds of dog and their closest wild relatives, including wolves, coyotes, jackals and dingoes. Thus, every form of a dog is but a derivative of, and thereby points to the existence of, a greater reality: the "canis" collective. Whether that greater reality was comprised of a supernatural or divine ideal "dog," or an ideal comprised purely of the collective totality of all dogs in the mind of those capable of defining the word "dog," was never made perfectly clear. But later theologians would come to interpret it as the former, and torture or execute anyone who said otherwise, much as Socrates was forced to drink hemlock for doubting the theologians of his own day.

Applied to the events in *The Shining*, the difference between how Plato and Aristotle thought about what they both labeled as a dog is the same difference between what King and Kubrick defined as "God," and thus the source of "evil" operating in their two versions of the story. Like Plato, the evil operating in King's version of the story is more abstract. That evil precedes and is independent of Jack, who is but a puppet that must struggle to resist its influence. The evil operating in Kubrick's version of the story, however, has a symbiotic relationship with Jack, without whom it does not exist. For one, evil starts as something external to any given object, originating instead from a supernatural force like "Satan" or other demonic forces. For the other, evil is "unspectacular and always human," as W. H. Auden pointed out, which "shares our bed and eats at our own table." For Kubrick, in other words, evil has a purely psychological explanation, and depends on the kind of moral justifications offered by Jack in the novel, and St. Augustine for preferring torture to convert people to his Roman Catholicism.

The different interpretations of the nature of evil by King and Kubrick can also be seen in the difference between the two versions of *The Shining*. On the one hand, Stephen King was raised a Methodist but lost his belief in organized religion while in high school. While no longer institutionally religious, King's novels often rely on a belief in the existence of both supernatural forces and a binary moral universe governed by ideas of good and evil. On the other hand, Stanley Kubrick expressed his own "visceral skepticism"- as King referred to it, and which King insisted prevented Kubrick from being able to "appreciate the nuances of the supernatural forces at work in his novel" - in a 1969 interview with *American Cinematographer*. Replying to whether there was an unseen cosmic intelligence or "God" operating behind the events in his film, *2001: A Space Odyssey*, Kubrick exclaimed:

> The whole idea of god is absurd. If anything, *2001* shows that what some people call "god" is simply an acceptable term for their ignorance. What they don't understand, they call "god"... Everything we know about the universe reveals that there is no god. I chose to do Dr. [Arthur C.] Clarke's story as a film because it highlights a critical factor necessary for human evolution; that is, beyond our present condition. This film is a rejection of the notion that there is a god; isn't that obvious?

While Kubrick rejects the notion of God during this interview, at least as it relates specifically to *2001*, during an interview with Michael Ciment in July of 1981, he appeared to modify his position on such a question. Ciment asked:

> You are a person who uses his rationality, who enjoys understanding things, but in "2001: A Space Odyssey" and "The Shining" you demonstrate the limits of intellectual knowledge. Is this an acknowledgement of what William James called the unexplained residues of human experience?

To this, Kubrick replied:

> Obviously, science-fiction and the supernatural bring you very quickly to the limits of knowledge and rational explanation. But from a dramatic point of view, you must ask yourself: 'If all of this were unquestionably true, how would it really happen?' You can't go much further than that. I like the regions of fantasy where reason is used primarily to undermine incredulity. Reason can take you to the border of these areas, but from there on you can be guided only by your imagination. I think we strain at the limits of reason and enjoy the temporary sense of freedom which we gain by such exercises of our imagination.[11]

A second look at Kubrick's reply leaves us to wonder if even this answer is but a veiled invitation to "come and play." Notice, for example, that Kubrick poses the question "if all of (what is happening in *The Shining*) were unquestionably true, how would it really happen?" This, in fact, is the very question that unlocks the door to Kubrick's *Shining* game. But are we up to the challenge of explaining the evil unfolding in the hotel without blaming it all on supernatural forces? He then mentions that, while reason can take us to the border of fantasy, it is not mere faith in one supernatural force to save us from another that can guide us beyond that border, but *imagination*.

Like the Romantics who pushed back against the overly mechanical rigidity of logic that had grown to feel like a straitjacket during the Age

---

of Reason, and the transcendentalists of the 1830s like Ralph Waldo Emerson and Henry David Thoreau, "freedom" for Kubrick came from escaping from "the limits of reason" through the "exercises of our imagination." For as Einstein observed, imagination is merely the act of having fun with one's own intelligence. And when we think about it, is Kubrick not inviting his audience to do just this, to engage in the "exercise of our imagination," by making a film as uniquely intricate and meticulously designed as *The Shining*? Might this be why the Grady twins issue their spooky invitation to Danny, to "come and play with us," while looking directly at the audience?

King's *Shining* Duality

Contrary to popular opinion, King's reliance on a belief in supernatural forces in his *Shining* novel is anything but black and white. Ideas of "good" and "evil" tend to exist in binary opposition in most major religions. King, however, shows a sophisticated talent for illustrating the tension between these binary opposites, and mixing them together to create subtle forms of grey in his novel.

Consider how King uses various methods to blur the line between ideas of good and evil. One example comes from having Jack Torrance use language to justify his attempts to kill Danny that remind us of God commanding Abraham to murder his son Isaac in Genesis 22. As a result, King depicts Jack with the duality seen in both the image of the woman on the postcard from 1888 and in the final photograph of Kubrick's film: the embodiment of opposites, the yin and the yang.

That duality challenges readers with the paradox posed by religion, which so often teaches us to see good and evil as having two distinctly separate faces while hiding the fact that those two faces are the same, just like the postcard from 1888. King even captures this paradox in a conversation between Delbert Grady and Jack that could just as easily have been a conversation between Yahweh and Abraham. In the following exchange, Delbert is asking Jack to offer up Danny as a sacrificial lamb to the Overlook:

> Delbert: You would bring us your son?
> Jack: Yes, Yes, I swear it! My word, my promise, my sacred vow!
> Narrator: Then a voice much deeper and much more powerful than Grady's, spoke from somewhere, everywhere ... from inside him. ("Keep your promise, Mr. Torrance.")

For the reader, the "much deeper and much more powerful" voice that summons Jack to sacrifice his son Danny is assumed to be evil incarnate, like the devil. Yet the "sacred vow" Jack gives in response to that voice echoes the idea of the "covenant" established through Abraham's willingness to Ginsu his own son out of obedience to the "much more powerful" voice he labeled "Yahweh" (which sounds like he's saying "yeah, your way, not mine," which is what Jesus ultimately says before he's skewered like a shish kebab for sinners everywhere). Like Jack waking up in the "story room" to the voice of Delbert Grady, however, this is like the relationship between Ed Norton's character and Tyler Durden (played by Brad Pitt) in *Fight Club*, or John Nash following the advice from his imaginary roommate in college. King even presents the idea of obedience to his own "belief" as being at least part of the problem, by describing Jack as thinking:

O

> "He knew that many times they didn't like his understandings and many other times refused to believe them. But someday, they would have to believe."

Jack's belief that "someday, they would have to believe" what Jack believes about the "higher voice" he seeks to obey is the same belief that led St. Augustine to advocate for the torture of those who failed to accept his Roman Catholic "beliefs" to be infallibly "true." Such justifications would later snowball into Crusaders, Inquisitions, slavery, Witch Trials, and even 9/11.

On its face, King presents his readers with a simple paradigm of good versus evil. Below the surface, however, he gives his audience another face. Although he is assumed to be beset by demons, Jack often speaks in the language of religious righteousness to justify the murders he seeks to commit; and all to please a voice much "more powerful" than his own, even if that "voice" is only a schizophrenic symptom of alcohol withdrawal mixed with cabin fever. Jack is the only one in King's novel who repeatedly claims, "By God!" and "By Jesus," as if by labeling the voice he wishes to please as "God" he is effectively transferring any guilt he may incur for his sins to a "savior" who has already paid for those sins in full already. Perhaps this is one reason why Jack's drink of "redrum," which calls to mind the sacrament of turning wine into blood, is "on the house." If Jack truly "believes" he is serving God and Jesus, then killing his wife and son is already paid for in advance, much like those who burned witches and crucified heretics out of a desire to remain in good standing with their own "God" (i.e., faith community).

King also has Jack justify his murderous desires is by labeling those Jack seeks to murder as "disobedient." Like the Sanhedrin accusing Jesus of being disobedient for healing people on the Sabbath, so Jack uses ideas of disobedience to transfer the responsibility for his actions to his victims and his God. After all, by being disobedient to Jack himself, Jack believes his family is being disobedient to a God who requires them to be obedient to him. In the novel, Jack even whispers to himself such a justification: "Now, by Christ, where was Danny? He had business with his trespassing son." But who is Danny allegedly "trespassing" against? In similar fashion, God sought Adam & Eve in the Garden of Eden for trespassing upon a tree of knowledge, as if God had commanded them to remain as animalistic as apes, even as Christianity saw non-Christians as "savages" and wants us to believe we are born sinners, and thus even worse by nature than apes. As if to confirm this, we even see a voice reply to Jack say, "no one here knows Danny from Adam," as if Danny and Adam were the same as Danny and Tony.

At first sight, King's depiction of evil looks straight forward. On second sight, however, he blurs the line between good and evil, leaving it hard to tell if the ultimate evil in his novel is because of Jack's obedience to God or to a devil masquerading as God, or even a God masquerading as the devil. Or are God and the devil just like Danny and Tony, Jack and Delbert, Verbal Kint and Keyser Söze ? Either way, King leaves his readers to wonder about the difficulty that fallible sapiens have of ever being able to truly know, let alone always clearly discern, the difference between the two; or if there is any.

As W. K. Clifford warned, this same difficulty can lead us back to savagery that plagued eighteenth century America. At that time, different brands of Christianity all sought to improve upon the human nature they were nurtured to distrust and fear. Relying on their different rules as both

Q

their swords and their shields to safeguard against such differences, different Christian sects sometimes attacked each other like the cowboys and Indians from old western movies, or the gangs in Martin Scorsese's *Gangs of New York*. They did so out of fear that those following a different brand of "God" and beliefs were unwittingly following the devil. And when disobedience to a "more powerful voice" is believed by all such followers to be a greater sin than murdering fellow human beings who threatened to infect them with their disobedience, since all of humanity is born with the spiritual gene for such disobedience via the stain of original sin, "morality" becomes a byword for murder for our preferred brand of "God." And, thanks to the moral relativism championed so often by saints like Augustine, who merely followed in the example of a divine double standard practiced by God from Noah to Jesus, the willingness to commit murder and impose suffering for one's brand of "beliefs" has become the surest way of avoiding an eternity of such suffering in the afterlife for failing to have "the belly" to kill each other to prove one's obedience and devotion to their brand of "God."

In response to Jack seeking to prove himself worthy of an eternal reward from an unseen "overlooker," Danny, like a transcendentalist, naturally consults his inner voice or intuition: Tony. Among other things, Tony appears to be Danny's own conscience. Like Isaac armed with a "sixth sense," in the novel, Danny even asks Tony, "is it my daddy that's coming to get me?" And when Jack finally screams at Danny to come out from his hiding place, we see Danny's disobedience in the form of resisting the temptation to be as obedient to his father's "voice" as his father has become obedient to the sound of that "more powerful voice." As King puts it, "obedience was so strongly ingrained" in Danny that he "took two automatic steps toward the sound of that voice before stopping." After all, is it not the child's duty to obey his parents, much as Isaac was obedient to Abraham and Jesus said to his Father in Heaven, "not mine, but thy will be done"? Danny, as such, is disobeying his "father," just like Adam did, and Isaac surely would have done had he known that Abraham had intended to treat him like a turkey on Thanksgiving Day.

At one point, King even captures one of the most important underlying assumptions necessary for all religious belief. The believer must assume that, if their own brand of beliefs is necessarily "the one true faith," and that "free will" is a prerequisite for both damnation and salvation, then all those who accept those beliefs can only deserve heaven for claiming they "understand" those beliefs, and all those who reject the validity of those beliefs can only be damned for "willfully not understanding" those beliefs. This is an important part of religious claims to righteousness, because without the "willful" part, there could be no justification for eternal rewards or the punishing of infidels or burning of witches, let alone the existence of purgatory and eternal hell. This, in fact, is exactly the conclusion that Jack is eventually forced to reach, for how else could he justify to himself the morality of murdering his own family, regardless of how possessed or insane he had become? As Jack reasons in the novel, they deserved to be punished because:

> They were willfully not understanding . . . And if his son and his wife had willfully set themselves against his wishes, against the things he knew were best for them, then didn't he have a certain duty – ?

While such reasoning comes from a mind we assume to be suffering from madness, Jack's comments are nearly identical to those offered by the great St. Augustine. Like Jack, the saintly Augustine argued that it was right and proper, and in his own opinion even preferable, to use torture to convert "non-believers," especially Jews, to his own brand of Roman Catholic beliefs. In his Discourse on Psalm 37, for example, Augustine's justification for such torture is nearly indistinguishable from Jack's rationalizations:

> "My son, reject not the correction of the Lord, and do not faint when thou art chastised by Him: for whom the Lord loveth He chastiseth, and He scourgeth every son whom He receiveth."[12]

Jack's aping of Abraham while espousing Augustinian justifications leaves us to wonder whether Jack's attempts to murder his family are because of a deficit of religious beliefs or, like those who burned heretics and "witches," a surplus. Jack, after all, sounds more like a member of the Taliban engaging in an honor killing than an atheist or an infidel. The reasoning Jack is offering to justify punishing his own child is a bit like the script religion installs in its followers to play as their inner dialogue to keep them fearful of damnation, and to convince them of their need to "obey" their brand of God or there'll be hell to pay. Indeed, are not those who engage in "slut shaming" and the denunciation of homosexuals as "sinners" simply externalizing the inner dialogue they have been conditioned to rely on to keep themselves from being seen by those they surrounded themselves with as either a "faggot" or a "slut"? Are not the stones of judgement we cast at others the same ones we fear

---

[12] Discourse on Psalm 37, p. 353.

will be cast at us by those who believe as we do, and by engaging in the former are we only expressing our underlying resentment or fear over the latter? Put more simply: we cast only those stones which we fear will be cast at us, by people who believe the same things we've been taught to believe, even if our beliefs are untrue. And, since he is a writer, might the cause of such madness have anything to do with the stories Jack is telling himself, much as I was about those gremlins? Might his own madness be simply the result of Jack defending his "belief" in the inerrancy of his own "holy" words?

Kubrick's *Shining* Twin

Kubrick's film can be thought of as the inverted twin of King's novel on virtually every level, except for the moral ambiguity of whether Jack is more like Abraham or Jack the Ripper. From the red VW Beetle Jack drives in the novel to the yellow one he drives in the film, to Wendy being a brunette rather than a blonde, to Jack freezing in the maze rather than burning alive in the hotel, Kubrick reverses nearly every detail in King's story in order to fit his own design. In the novel, malevolent powers in the Overlook work to unlock the evil that resides within Jack to begin with. Fearing the director was "a man who thinks too much and feels too little," however, King therefore concluded that Kubrick "could not grasp the supernatural elements of the story." Such overthinking, King argued, made Jack a lunatic to begin with, and Kubrick's film "a Cadillac with no engine; all style and no substance."

Despite these differences and criticisms, Kubrick may share a similar thread of moral ambiguity to one we can imagine running through King's novel in changing the color of Jack's VW. In 1895, Robert W.

Chambers wrote a book of short stories entitled "The King in Yellow." It includes a story of a book that, when read, drives people mad. Simply reading such a book convinces people they have ingested knowledge from a divine intelligence that allows them to know, infallibly, the sum of all that is good and evil in the universe, and who deserves to be punished and who rewarded for doing the punishing, and claiming they were only doing "God's will." Is this why Jack, who aspires to become Overlook royalty, is seen driving a yellow VW along the Going to the Sun Road in the opening scene? And is the scrapbook of the hotel not a story book that is hypnotizing Jack to imitate the horrors pouring out from its pages, much as the Bible appears to inform "believers" what God expects of them to defend His words, and save themselves from hell?

King's opinion of Kubrick as a director for making so many changes is not all bad, however. He appreciates Kubrick's masterful use of subtle details, for example. Writing in his non-fiction book, *Danse Macabre*, King compliments Kubrick for having "an almost exquisite sensitivity to the nuances of light and shadow." What King never fully understood about Kubrick's version of *The Shining* is that, in the same way Kubrick changed nearly every other thing in the story, so too the "evil" operating at the center of Kubrick's version of the story depended, in more ways than one, on the nuances of light and shadow.

Like the image on the postcard from 1888, when King watches Kubrick's *Shining*, the Cadillac of light and shadow he sees staring back at him is mostly the face of his own novel, not Kubrick's film. The Cadillac King sees, in other words, is simply a false-face. Behind that face, Kubrick's film is more like a ticking time bomb, slipped under a table, at which sit two people trying to defuse it by playing chess. The catch is that there is only one person playing chess while sitting in front of a mirror. And the bomb can only be defused when that person figures out which of them is real and which is merely a projection of how they wish to be perceived by others.

In the novel, King depicts Jack Torrance as a complex character trapped between end-zones of good and evil, a character who struggles to free himself from the clutches of the latter in his quest to reach the former. Yet Jack also appears to be chasing a reflection, since nothing produces greater evil than those who think they are defending the greatest of goods. Kubrick, on the other hand, creates a much simpler version of Jack - one that happens to look more like a composite of Jack Nicholson than anything else - and drops him into the middle of an ever-morphing visual maze. What we are left to wonder about this alteration is to what extent Kubrick's changes to Jack's character are directly related to the change Kubrick made to the ending of King's story. Kubrick fashions Jack Torrance from the clay of Jack Nicholson, in other words, in part because Kubrick appears to have wanted to blur the line between fiction and reality. And he does this so it would be unclear exactly which Jack is smiling back at the audience from the final photograph: Torrance or Nicholson, or both. And could it be neither one?

More important than the changes to Jack's character are the changes to the story itself. Despite appearances, those changes lay out a discernable thread that stretches from the very opening shot to the final photograph, and even the final credits. The trick, again, is figuring out how to weave together the thread needed to find one's way in and out of the maze Kubrick created, especially when that maze constitutes a

w

physical space that appears to defy both geometry and logic. And it does so because the true danger in the Overlook does not come from Jack as the Minotaur, but from the maze itself. In some ways, that is, the maze itself *is* the Minotaur. And for all the criticism heaped upon Duvall's portrayal of Wendy as little more than a Kubrickian "scream machine"- which was even less mania than Duvall thought a woman like Wendy would exhibit in such a terrifying situation - Wendy is the only character in Kubrick's version of the story who ever actually manages to figure this out. The audience just never quite understood how she does so, or why. But I'll give you a hint: it has to do with a man named Seymour Glass, the "twin" story of the book she is reading when we first meet her in the kitchen with Danny in their Boulder apartment. But I'm getting ahead of myself.

Simply put, the different world views of King and Kubrick invite the audience to consider whether the film they are watching is one haunted by supernatural forces or something else they have overlooked. Most people naturally conclude the former to be the case, but they do so only because that is what King leads his audience to believe is at work in his novel. And at first glance, this seems to be the case in the film as well. In truth, King's story is simply the "false face" of Kubrick's Trojan horse, within which hides the silver key to unlocking the "story room" door to Kubrick's cinematic games room.

Second Sight of Kubrick's *Shining*

If you're a true fan of Kubrick's version of *The Shining*, you probably know at least some of the theories and speculation that have surrounded the film since its release. To name just a few examples, it is notorious for its disappearing and reappearing props, impossible windows, and functionally disjointed set design. Such "errors" should prompt the viewer to ask themselves a question. What's more probable: that the most meticulous director in history created a film with more continuity errors than any other film in history, and solely for the purpose of disorienting his audience (as Kubrick always maintained), or that, in addition to this reason, he had also done so for another reason as well, and that his claims to the contrary were all part of the mirage?

Kubrick's "visceral skepticism" prompts us to ponder a few other questions as well. Should we simply accept that there must be supernatural forces at work in Kubrick's version of King's novel, for example, or is Kubrick simply using smoke and mirrors to manipulate the fears and superstitions of his audience into thinking so? Why work so hard and strive for such precision, and indeed require such secrecy, if the same "disorienting" effect could have been obtained by simply choosing not to care about any continuity at all? Why be as meticulous to detail as Raphael, in other words, when the same effect could've been more easily and perhaps even more effectively achieved by being as random as Jackson Pollock? In the end, is Jack smiling because it is Kubrick who gets "The Last Laugh"? In fact, like the helicopter, we even see the shadow of such a 'last laugh' in the *Shining*.

To see the shadow of Kubrick's last laugh, pay attention to the scene of Wendy walking up the stairs to discover two men in an upper bedroom appearing to be engaged in a sexual act. As she does, Kubrick uses Wendy's shadow to pay homage to the famed German director F. W. Murnau's *Nosferatu: A Symphony of Horror*, from 1922. In 1924 (42?), Murnau released the silent film, *The Last Laugh*, about a nameless and aging hotel doorman who is demoted to a washroom attendant, a bit like Delbert Grady. In it, Murnau tried to avoid "the intertitles (title cards) of spoken dialogue or description that characterize most silent films, in the belief that the visuals themselves should carry most of the meaning." To do this, he created new perspectives and impressions for viewers by being the first director to begin moving the location of the camera and taking particular care of how shots were decorated and presented.

In Kubrick we can see the shadow of Murnau. Like Murnau, Kubrick is the first director to use the Steadicam that follows Danny around on his trike. And, when we know what we are looking for, it becomes clear that even the smallest details in every frame of *The Shining* carry most of the meaning in the film. And while Jack is first seen walking through the front doors of the Overlook, "nameless" until he introduces himself to the receptionist, his is also the last "laughing" face we see before cutting to the final credits. Lastly, the person responsible for the sole cue card seen in *The Last Laugh* was none other than Alfred Hitchcock. And while all of this is merely speculation, it is just such subtle but ever so curious details that serve as the very things Kubrick relies on to lure the inquisitive viewer into his labyrinth.

And what kind of labyrinth is it, and what do we know of the Daedalus who created it? Widely regarded as one of the greatest and most influential psychological horror films of all time, *The Shining* was produced and directed by an American film director, screenwriter, and producer, who is considered to be one of the most influential filmmakers in cinematic history. Comprised mostly of adaptations of novels or short stories, his films cover a wide range of genres. Along with his unique cinematography, extensive set designs, and evocative use of music,

Kubrick used realism and dark humor in his films to communicate to his audience in a way that often suggested there was an underlying point to his message. That point always remained elusive, implicit, or inferred, however. And in many ways, *The Shining*, which is Kubrick's only foray into the horror genre, may truly be his magnum opus in this respect. Watch *The Shining* a hundred times and you will likely notice things each time that you had failed to notice in the previous viewing, with each new detail unfolding an ever-deepening mystery like a Venus fly trap in the middle of a little shop of horrors.

On the other side of the screen is the original author of the story, Stephen King, who both detested Kubrick's adaptation of his novel and disliked Kubrick. In fact, King, who typically only shared his thoughts about those adaptations he enthusiastically supported while refraining from criticism of those he did not, reversed this habit with Kubrick. He not only went on record many times to speak about his displeasure with Kubrick's adaptation, he's also repeatedly explained why the film fails to capture the various nuances that King felt were so important to understanding his story.

For a time, King briefly curtailed his criticisms of Kubrick's film. After repurchasing the rights to his story back from Kubrick, however, King resumed his attacks, escalating them after Kubrick's death in 1999. Why? Well, unlike his other stories, *The Shining* was personal for King. As King explained it:

> Not that religion has to be involved in horror, but a visceral skeptic such as Kubrick just couldn't grasp the sheer inhuman evil of The Overlook Hotel. That was the basic flaw: because he couldn't believe, he couldn't make the film believable to others. Kubrick's

version of *The Shining* is that it's a film by a man who thinks too much and feels too little; and that's why, for all its virtuoso effects, it never gets you by the throat and hangs on the way real horror should.

Ironically, King may have felt like Kubrick's adaptation never grabbed him "by the throat" because he may never have quite understood exactly how to open the door to Kubrick's games room, nor what it was that grabbed Danny by the throat in room 237; because it sure as hell wasn't the ghost of Mrs. Massey.

King also felt that the difference in the respective finales of each version of the story "tell you all you need to know" about the differing approaches to the material. What King may not have known at the time he made these comments was just how right he was. In an interview with The Paris Review, King explains: "Near the end of the novel, Jack Torrance tells his son that he loves him, and then he blows up with the hotel. It's a very passionate climax. In Kubrick's movie, he freezes to death." Yet the different endings may not be as different as King thinks, since Jack only freezes to death in the film because he never uses his axe to chop his way out of the hedge maze, the way he chopped his way into their apartment, and quite easily at that. Failing to do so implies that Jack may well have made a choice to die in the maze, rather than trying to escape from it.

In addition to his displeasure with Kubrick's ending, King also disliked Kubrick's portrayal of Wendy Torrance by Shelley Duvall. In that same interview in the Paris Review, King described the movie's characterization of Wendy as "insulting to women," because Kubrick had turned her into "basically a scream machine." And King was not alone in this assessment.

Duvall's portrayal of Wendy was, by Kubrickian design, one of the most heavily critiqued elements of *The Shining* when it was released. Not only was she nominated for a Razzie Award for Worst Actress, but since then, reports of what she endured on the set have become part of the movie's lore. Among other things, Kubrick's notoriously meticulous style of directing forced Duvall into dozens of takes of anguish-stricken scenes that, as the actor detailed in her book *The Complete Kubrick*, resulted in her being pushed to such extremes that it left her "in and out of ill health." Adding to this strain, Kubrick was often intentionally cruel to her, even instructing members of the crew to ignore her between takes. And one of the reasons he did all of this was not only to create an almost cartoonish caricature of Wendy Torrance, but because the more frazzled Duvall was, the more unlike the novel version of Wendy she would become. Even more than that, however, Kubrick's treatment of Duvall on the set was a clue about what Kubrick was really doing, and why.

Even more than his criticism of Duvall's portrayal of Wendy, King's biggest complaint about Kubrick's film was with the casting of Jack Nicholson as Jack Torrance. By casting Nicholson right after his starring role in *One Flew Over the Cuckoo's Nest* in 1975, King complained that the audience would see Jack as mad from the beginning: "he's a villain from the moment we meet him." In the novel, on the other hand, King presents Jack in the "sympathetic portrait of a man cursed with the burden of alcoholism and trying to balance his work life and personal life." Such a portrait was intended to show how King was more "interested in what's under the surface of a man's exterior, and the dark, private thoughts he keeps bottled to himself, until the supernatural forces them out." Kubrick's reversal of so many other details between his film

cc

and the novel, however, reflect the idea that Kubrick is using such "dark thoughts," which manifest themselves in the guise of Delbert Grady in a tuxedo, as something coming both from within Jack, and also trying to force their way into Jack's mind, at the same time.

In contrast to King's desire to explore 'man's dark private thoughts,' Kubrick once told a friend in 1966 that he had long desired to "make the world's scariest movie, involving a series of episodes that would play upon the nightmare fears of the audience."[13] To do this, Kubrick sought to toy with people's imaginations, much like that postcard from 1888, leaving his audience to wonder whether the events in the hotel were the result of supernatural forces or a form of shared psychosis, or even something else entirely. To the "visceral skeptic," after all, fact is always stranger than fiction, and therefore potentially a great deal scarier. And it is, because what is far scarier than supernatural evil is evil that is "unspectacular and always human," to quote W. H. Auden again, which "shares our bed and eats at our own table."

In 1963, the Bronx Zoo in New York captured this very idea in an exhibit. Above that exhibit was the inscription, "The Most Dangerous Animal in the World." Below the exhibit was written: "You are looking at the most dangerous animal in the world. It alone of all the animals that ever lived can exterminate (and has) entire species of animals." Between these two inscriptions was a mirror.

Kubrick once expressed his thoughts on the nature of what we call "evil" during that interview with French film scholar Michel Ciment.

---

[13] Baxter, John (1997). *Stanley Kubrick: A Biography*, Harper Collins, p.302.

Ciment asked Kubrick what he thought about King's book, and Kubrick replied:

> I thought it was one of the most ingenious and exciting stories of the genre I had read. It seemed to strike an extraordinary balance between the psychological and the supernatural in such a way as to lead you to think that the supernatural would eventually be explained by the psychological: 'Jack must be imagining these things because he's crazy.' This allowed you to suspend your doubt of the supernatural until you were so thoroughly into the story that you could accept it almost without noticing ... It's not until Grady, the ghost of the former caretaker who axed to death his family, slides open the bolt of the larder door, allowing Jack to escape, that you are left with no other explanation but the supernatural.

Here, Kubrick's claim that the supernatural might "eventually be explained by the psychological" was exactly what I was trying to do with the gremlins that stalked my bedroom when I was a child and began to wonder about both *The Exorcist* and even *The Shining*. Yet he also mentions that, with Grady opening the larder door, we "are left *with no other explanation but* the supernatural." No other? Really?

So, is that it? Is Kubrick telling us, once and for all, that his entire movie is about nothing more than ghosts and "the supernatural"? Being the visceral skeptic that he is, his claims above should elicit second thoughts. To accept the idea that Kubrick really believed such a claim is to conclude that, however many other details Kubrick changes and reverses from the novel to the film, he nevertheless wanted the audience to accept that the overall animus for the "evil" in his film is exactly the same as the one operating in King's novel.

But again, if it really is as simple as that, then why did Kubrick feel the need for such secrecy, such an insane number of retakes, and litter his film with so many continuity errors? If he is telling the truth, then his

Shining doesn't even come close to being "the world's scariest movie," not only because it fails to explain the supernatural by the psychological, but also because it would be nothing more than a ghost story about a haunted hotel. Hell, Alfred Hitchcock had surpassed that two decades earlier with *Psycho*: which was perhaps the first film that both replaced and explained supernatural evil with the psychological. If Kubrick is to be taken at his word, then all he would have created was a film where what looks like the supernatural *could be* explained by the psychological is simply a ruse, one Kubrick uses to lure his audience into a maze of questions they never need to enter in the first place, because the answer to all those questions is obvious: the devil made him do it.

Like the film itself, the contrast between what Kubrick said he wanted to create and what he suggests he created only leads us wonder even more if Kubrick's explanation is designed to hide some bigger picture. Is it foolish or wise to wonder if Kubrick's comments confirming the presence of "supernatural forces" in his film are perhaps part of a smokescreen that helps to conceal the true face of Kubrick's grand illusion? Like the 2006 thriller, *The Prestige*, what if the real magic in *The Shining* is not just what we see on the screen but everything Kubrick did and said off the screen, throughout his life, even to his grave?

One reason why Kubrick might have wanted to pull off such a magic trick is, in part, because of his visceral skepticism. For the skeptic, explaining the supernatural "by the purely psychological" can be far more terrifying than explaining otherwise inexplicable events in terms of supernatural causes. What could be scarier, after all, than the idea that everything happening in *The Shining* is in fact the result of something *other* than the stuff of spooky bedtime stories? Or think of it this way:

what if behind the mask of a film that looks like *The Exorcist*, beats the heart of a film that operates more like *Soylent Green*? Even scarier still, what if the Bible works the very same way?

Yet Kubrick's film leads us to wonder about an even more troubling problem, one that may help to explain why Jack Torrance can justify his attempts to murder his family with the same reasoning used equally by both St. Augustine and real-life serial killers. What if what leads Jack to want to murder his own family is because he is asleep? Worse, what if he is only partially asleep? What if, in other words, only part of his brain is asleep, but it just happens to be that part that allows him to feel any sympathy or empathy for anyone else? And what if the thing that anesthetizes that part of his brain that allows him to feel empathy for others, especially those most different from himself, just happens to be the stories he tells himself, that lead him to fall in love with his ideals of perfection; ideals that become more important to him than even life itself, including his own or anyone else's? Put another way, what if Jack is aspiring to becoming one of the faces he sees in the black and white photos on the walls of the Overlook, because to his mind, they constitute the "saints" of a sacred tradition, and all he must do to win such a reward is follow in the footsteps of the saint who started it all: Abraham?

One thing that seemed to hint at an answer to such questions came in the form of a painting of a horse charging toward a train in the Torrance apartment in Boulder. For me, that painting suggested that one way to understand Jack's transformation was from the inside out, starting with Jack's mind. And to do that, I considered Jack's behavior in light of the trolley problem.

Jack's Mind as the Train Tracks to Kubrick's Trolley Problem

To consider the trolley problem in real terms, and how Kubrick's film serves as an invitation to consider it, we need to first consider how or why Jack converts from being a father and husband to being an aspiring serial killer for his faith in the Overlook. Then, we need to take a train ride back to the fourth century, to look at a real-life example of how a person's thinking can jump from one set of synaptic train tracks in their mind to another. But before we get to that saint, let's start with Jack.

One way to see Jack Torrance is as a man who has a conversion. This conversion starts much like that of St. Paul on the road to Damascus. As the story goes, Paul was struck by a brilliant light and fell to the ground. He also heard a voice saying, "why are you using violence against me?" Like Paul, so Jack's conversion from a father to a psychopath starts with his fall to the floor. Also, like Paul, whose name was originally Saul before his fall and adoption of a split personality as his "true self," so Jack changes too, in color: from green shirts or sweaters to a red jacket. And while Jack begins the film as a loving husband and father, he ends as a monster. So, was Jack always a monster who had simply mastered the art of hiding it, or did something happen that shifted gears in his brain and drove him from caring about his family to caring more about his faith in the Overlook? More than St. Paul, the saint who may shed some light on this question is St. Augustine.

Before his conversion in 386, which he delayed for as long as possible with the prayer "Lord, make me chaste (sexually pure) – but not yet," St. Augustine spent much of his youth frequenting the brothels of Rome. After his conversion, at the ripe old age of 31 and only shortly after his brain had finally fully formed, that which he had previously enjoyed in his youth became the object of his hatred and scorn. In the process, as necessity would have it, he separated love from sexuality and assigned the former to God alone (even though "love" is the opposite of judgement), and the latter he concluded was but the fruit of evil, proof of his sinful nature, and the doorway to eternal death. In his youth, to put is more simply, Augustine saw sex in the form of the woman in the bathtub in room 237, while after his conversion, he saw sex in the form of the old dead hag, as if he'd stepped through a mirror.

Loathsome and ashamed of his own sexual desires, Augustine eventually came to the "infallible" conclusion that the "original sin" of Adam and Eve was necessarily sexual in nature. His evidence for this conclusion came not from scripture or any tradition, but from his own lustful desires and, according to his *Confessions*, his memories of preexistence (always a solid source of evidence). These alone were enough evidence for Augustine to conclude that Adam & Eve "were ashamed and covered their sexual parts with fig leaves," as it said in the Bible, because the "original sin" they had committed came from daring to take pleasure in using their "sexual parts" as God had designed them to be used, so that they could fulfil God's command to "be fruitful and multiply." Naturally, as only a saint can see, this reasoning makes perfect sense.

It was not the act of love making itself that so disgusted Augustine, however, but the pleasure they enjoyed in the process, which was simply a reflection of Augustine's disgust for what he described as his own "insatiable lust." "Thus, according to Augustine, sexual intercourse, or more precisely, sexual pleasure (even within marriage), is what carries original sin on and on, from generation to generation."[14] To avoid the stain of sin that was inseparable from what he called the "defilement" of sexual pleasure (Enchiridion 13, 41),[15] Jesus had to be conceived without any sexual pleasure whatsoever, which is why the whole procreative act was simply bypassed altogether. Jesus's mother, Mary, on the other hand, while born via natural sexual relations between her own mother and father, was thought to have been conceived "immaculately" because, according to Augustine, they had managed to have sexual intercourse with neither one managing to take any pleasure in the act itself. Talk about a "miracle" of faith!

In effect, Augustine's conversion to Christianity, which led him to his conclusions about Jesus and his mother Mary, was also a conversion from the pleasure of sex to the pleasure of castigating the pleasures of sex. It seems that for Augustine, many of whose ideas still underwrite the Roman Catholic Church's teachings about sex and sexuality, the holiest form of procreation can only be achieved using test tubes and artificial insemination. Short of that, the only way the act of "making love" was not a sin of the flesh, according to Augustine's perspective, is if the people engaging in such love making ensured they hated every minute of it.

What Augustine's conversion leaves us to wonder about today is how his views on sex led him to see women in the same light that Jack sees the woman in room 237: first as the object of his desires, and then, after he kisses her (a bit like Judas kissing Christ), as little more than "the

---

[14] Ranke-Heinemann, Uta, *Eunuchs for the Kingdom of Heaven*, Germany, Doubleday, 1988, p. 77.
[15] Id.

gate to Hell," as the first century church father Tertullian described all women. So, what the hell happened? Why such a dramatic reversal? Had the testosterone that had fueled Augustine's appreciation for the prostitutes of Rome in his youth suddenly, as a man, shut off that part of his brain that allowed him to feel anything for women but disgust and contempt?

It is curious to note that Augustine reversed his position on sex at age 31, because not only is this more than a decade after a man's peak testosterone production, but it is also shortly after his brain has fully formed, including that part of the brain – the frontal cortex – that helps regulate sexual desires and exercise feats of orgasmic philosophical speculation, especially about what 'dark supernatural forces of evil' may be animating the desires of his own genitalia. With his conversion, Augustine's mind was weaponized with sacred "beliefs" to blame women for the fact that Augustine's own struggle was really between his brain and his testicles, one being underdeveloped to the same degree the other was overly productive. And when finally, a harmonious balance had been achieved between the two, his love for the former was transubstantiated into a hatred for those who enflamed the latter. It had never occurred to Augustine to blame God for this imbalance, of course, for it was in His image and likeness that he had been made which dictated that one would develop faster than the other. Otherwise, a species possessed by its high ideals might conclude it is far better to live like priestly eunuchs and ponder the secrets of eternity, as its religion requires, than engage in the sinful pleasures of propagating its own species, as that mysterious God had commanded.

KK

Augustine's conversion from a love of women to a loathing for sex as the root of all sin illustrates how we can switch from seeing something we previously perceived as "good" to suddenly being "bad." In truth, however, Augustine's conversion to Christianity seemed to transform his previous love of sex, in which he treated women as objects, into a hatred of women, in which women became the object of his hatred of his own uncontrollable lust. Is this because he held women responsible – and not his own God given hormones or underdeveloped brain – for triggering his "insatiable lust"? This same reversal can even be seen in the change we see in the woman in room 237, from a seductress into death itself.

Jack's Religious Conversion

Like Augustine, Jack also undergoes a conversion, from caring about his son upon returning from room 237, to wanting so badly to stay in the Overlook that he is willing to ax his family into pieces to do so. The questions both conversions invite us to ask are how does this happen, and why? Is it simply the result of a physiological change in the brain – with Augustine's brain fully forming and Jack suffering from alcohol withdrawal and cabin fever – or has some idea or ideal sunk its teeth so deeply into Jack's mind that it has not only superseded the love he must have had at some point for both his wife and child, but also caused that love to mutate into a murderous hatred of them instead, as obstacles barring him from a wishful paradise?

Is shame, that vehicle that religion uses to cattle prod congregants away from sin and into religious conformity, driving Jack to morph from a father into a full-blown serial killer? Like Augustine's hope for the pleasures of heaven (or just his fear of the tortures of hell) growing in tandem with his hatred for the pleasures of the flesh (and his spiritual lust for eternal life), is there a belief in some "heavenly" reward (or a fear of some version of hell, like personal shame, of "shoveling out driveways" or "working in a carwash") driving Jack to murder his wife and son? In attacking Wendy, we see his fear of shame when he mentions how "failing to live up to (his) responsibility" to the contract he signed would damage his "reputation." In the novel, that "contract" or covenant was signed with the "deeper voice" that warned Jack to keep his "promise."

I have seen this before. Religious conversion, which most people assume makes someone a "better" person, can often lead people to make dramatic changes in their perspectives. That change can turn someone from being accepting or at least tolerant of other people's different religious or sexual habits before conversion, to being adamantly and sometimes aggressively opposed and intolerant of those same differences after conversion. For the "believer," and the group they wish to assimilate into, such a change is seen as a blessing or even a "moral improvement," even though, to the cohesion of society overall, such a change is necessarily a curse until everyone agrees to adopt it (even though no one can agree about what "it" really is or isn't). Not only can this be achieved by first overriding any sense of individual "free will," it also requires seeing the spectrum of human diversity that reflects the true complexity of homo sapiens as a sin, as if we are only saved from an eternal incinerator by thinking and acting like robots. In fact, the great historian Edward Gibbons felt this perspective explained how Christianity, in part, contributed to the fall of the Roman Empire.

Major shifts in one's moral goal posts, like we see with Jack and St. Augustine, are often part of a conversion experience. Nor is such an experience limited to less educated demographics. People join cults like the Branch Davidians and Jones Town from across the spectrum of educational backgrounds, including doctors, both medical and academic, and lawyers, whose job it is to question everything, including the facts. Even those who agreed to implement the "final solution" in Germany, who prided themselves on their high ideals and were convinced of the moral and physical supremacy of their Arian heritage, were Christians and doctors and lawyers. No religion or level of education, it seems, can ensure we will not fall victim to the snares of one devilish "belief" system or another. Such systems find their way into our hearts and souls by preying upon all our hopes and our fears. Jack hopes to graduate to Gold Room status but fears he will end up shoveling out driveways or working in a carwash. Yet Delbert provides Jack with the means to achieve the one and avoid the other: obey, sacrifice your son, and you will have eternal life in paradise.

How does this happen? How do we decide to surrender control of our own mind to that of a belief that we then decide we will serve and obey?

Jack's sudden change, like that of St. Augustine, was like the throwing of a switch in his head. Then I noticed a painting hanging in the Torrance apartment in Boulder. That painting reminded me of the throwing of a switch in something called "the trolley problem."

Religious Conversion & the Trolley Problem

Framed in the Torrance's Boulder apartment is a painting of a dark horse charging down a set of railroad tracks toward an oncoming locomotive. Entitled "Horse and Train," it was painted in 1954 by Alex Colville, a date that, if we flip the five and reverse the last two numbers, gives us 42. It was that painting that reminded me of a famous psychological experiment called "the trolley problem."

The trolley problem works like this: imagine you are standing on a platform watching a runaway train headed for five people who are trapped on the train tracks ahead of it. The only way to save them is to pull a lever and redirect the train onto another track, where only one person is trapped. What would you do? More importantly, however, is whether such a question may help offer a psychological explanation for Jack's conversion from a family man to a psychopathic killer.

To this problem, the philosopher Judith Jarvis Thomson proposed a slightly different scenario. Instead of having to pull a lever, Thompson proposed you could stop the train and save the five people stranded on the track by pushing a fat man into the path of the oncoming train, killing the fat man but halting the train.

Cambridge psychologist Dr. Kevin Dutton addressed this very question in a book on psychopaths called *The Wisdom of Psychopaths: What Saints, Spies, and Serial Killers Can Teach Us About Success.* (That a psychopath can only teach us how to be "successful" in a system that rewards us for behaving like a psychopath, much like Jack, is a telling statement about the society in which we live.) In it, Dutton references Harvard psychologist Joshua Greene, who studied the differences between normal and "abby normal" or psychopathic brains. According to Greene, one of those differences is that the psychopath suffers from a profound emotional deficit, so that a serial killer is as indifferent to the pain of his victim as that rich man was to the starvation of the crumb-eating Lazarus. Elaborating on this deficit in an article entitled, "The Cognitive Neuroscience of Moral Judgment," Greene explained that the brain of the psychopath "exhibits normal electrodermal responses to threat cues (e.g., a picture of a shark's open mouth), but reduced responses to distress cues (e.g., a picture of a crying child)."

Expanding on Greene's work, Dutton points out that the variation of the trolley problem results in a "personal moral dilemma" for most people, one that "hammers on the door of the brain's emotion center, known as the amygdala." For "normal" people, their amygdala revs up their emotions, and thus their empathy, which then makes pushing someone to their death impossible. But for a psychopath, their amygdala does not factor into the cold calculous needed to "succeed," which in this case means saving five people by turning one into a sacrificial lamb, even if that one never agreed to it. Having the ability to push the fat man to his death, as such, is one of the "virtues of selfishness" Ayn Rand championed in her book. Such apathy is "right" because its' cold unemotionally involved calculus makes it the more perfectly logical thing to do. Such a conclusion is as devoid of emotional influence as a computer, an accountant, a Wall Street trader, Mr. Potter to George Bailey, Ted Bundy, members of the German SS, or St. Augustine saving souls through torture.

Is there a way to see the differences between the brains of normal people and psychopaths? Yes, there is. Hook a "normal" brain to an fMRI machine, Dutton explains, and the amygdala would "light up like a pinball machine" when presented with the "personal" version of the trolley dilemma that involves pushing a fat man into the path of an oncoming train. Perform the same test on a psychopath, however, and in the area of the amygdala, "I would see only darkness." Show psychopaths images of famine victims and we get the same results: their brains "merely pull down the emotional window blinds and implement a neural curfew." This idea of pulling down the "window blinds" is like the curtains being drawn both in room 237 and in the lobby when Jack kills Dick.

Frighteningly, Dan Ariely, a professor of psychology and behavioral economics at Duke University, pointed out that similar behavior is found when the "lever" being pulled that sends the fat man into the path of the oncoming train is a financial instrument like a stock or a credit default swap. As a result, real people are thrown into the path of a financial tsunami in order to save artificial people known as "corporations."

Is this what happens with Jack? Does he try to kill Danny and Wendy because his amygdala simply shuts down, or has it been redirected to light up for something else, rather than someone? Or did it perhaps never really work in the first place?

What Augustine's conversion helps to illustrate about Jack is how the problem may not be that the emotional centers in Jack's brain just stopped working. Instead, like Augustine, those emotional centers may have been rerouted onto another set of synaptic railroad tracks, inside of the head of both Jack and Augustine, displacing the love and empathy previously held for some*one* with a love for some*thing* far greater, and for more selfish reasons: the eternal reward of avoiding eternal punishment. And, to the extent the love of the former is believed to pose a threat to the latter, the insecurity one feels toward the latter can produce a proportional degree of hatred for the former. The conversion of Augustine, as such, switched his love of sex to a lust for salvation, with his passion for the latter rising in tandem with a proportional amount of hatred for the former. This turnaround is even reflected in how the woman in room 237 flips from a steamy seductress dripping with temptation into an old witch luring Jack to join her in eternal death, in the "mirror, mirror, on the wall."

Real world examples of this abound. Langdon Gilkey, for example, saw something similar to Jack caving into the pressure to honor his contract (or what the Bible calls a "covenant") with the Overlook. In *Shantung Compound: The Story of Men and Women Under Pressure* (Harper and Row, 1966), Gilkey tells the story of the moral problems that come with life in a Japanese concentration camp in China. While none of them were tortured physically, inmates there suffered from hunger, lack of sanitation, crowding, even boredom. Such conditions led him to "marvel at the way we can fool ourselves," Gilkey recalls, as "we don some moral costume so as to hide from ourselves our real desires and wants. Then we present to the world a façade of objectivity and rectitude instead of the self-concern we really feel." And while Jack's self-concern is to avoid leaving the Overlook, the great St. Augustine wanted to avoid both hell in the next life, and the loss of the power his claims to divine knowledge allowed him to enjoy in this one, the butterfly of which resulted in the hurricane of witch hunts that ravaged Europe and America from 1300 to 1782, and then again in Germany after 1945, as detailed in the utterly fascinating book, *A Demon-Haunted*

Land: Witches, Wonder Doctors, and the Ghosts of the Past in Post-WWII Germany, in which historian Monica Black explores how Germans sought to destroy their sense of fear and guilt about the war by projecting it all onto a class of scapegoats they labeled as "witches." Yet it is only after we stop blaming such scapegoats, from Jesus to witches, that we find the true origins of droughts, famines, and disease.

From this perspective, Jack's quest to sacrifice Danny to the Overlookers can be seen as a recurring religious ritual intended to produce transformation. In *Violence and the Sacred* (1972), French polymath René Girard offers a universal theory of religion and culture through the lens of such violence. For Girard, ritual sacrifice is functional, for it appeases and channels humanity's innate desire for violence. This "mimetic" desire develops from jealousy for what others have, like Jack in the Gold Room. Left unchecked, this violence seeps into an amorphous being and will eventually find a victim. That victim will then seek more violence, leading to a destructive circle of vengeance that, like the Hatfields and McCoys and Christians and Pagans in Rome, can lead to a society's destruction. Sacrifice offers a solution to this problem through channeling violence into a sacred moment. A surrogate victim is chosen; a third party to the conflict who is usually the most innocent of all. In an act of deep catharsis, the communal need for violence is then pinned on this sacrificial lamb, who functions as a scapegoat. Indeed, this may have been one reason Constantine decided to make Christianity a favored religion in Rome.

Jack's conversion in the Overlook looks like that of St. Augustine, along the rails of reasoning laid out by Langdon Gilkey. From loving his wife and child to having that love superseded by his love for the

Overlook itself, and the Overlookers he sought to please, the latter appears to create a hatred in Jack for the former so intense he is willing to murder them to obtain his little piece of Shangri la. After all, who would not be willing to murder the whole world if they thought they had to do so in order to win paradise and avoid being tortured for all eternity?

◊◊

And this is exactly what makes Kubrick's game so much fun to "come and play." It invites viewers to ponder questions about everything from morality to the human mind to why believers who want to usher in the apocalypse are admitting God is genocidal maniac who threatens to torch them for all eternity if ever they object to the His "divine plan" in this game of eternal life and eternal death. But if Kubrick is inviting his audience to grapple with such questions, then the last place we would expect such a visceral skeptic to hide his answers is in the supernatural, while the first place we would expect for him to do so would be in the purely psychological.

Three Final Points

Trying to find a psychological explanation for what appears to be the supernatural events unfolding in *The Shining* is merely the first step to assembling Kubrick's puzzle. But while such considerations certainly start the ball rolling, to truly appreciate the complexity of the game, and the film, it is critical to understand three important points.

The first point to understand is that the special effects in the film were accomplished before the age of CGI, and, for the most part, there are therefore no in-camera special effects throughout the entire movie.

As a result, almost all the anomalies and special effects to be found in the film had to be performed manually, through an almost insane attention to detail. Such precision indicates that each anomaly, however seemingly irrelevant, must be there for a reason. Nor does it make sense to accept that such effort was exercised for no other reason than to disorient the audience, for such an effect could have been achieved with much less effort and expense. And the fact that Kubrick exercised such efforts suggests that every single detail in the film is just as important as any other, including the continuity errors. Kubrick, in short, wants to see who is paying attention.

Part of what Kubrick is doing is testing our powers of observation, to see if we are as oblivious to what he is doing as the characters are to what is going on around them. Is it a coincidence, for example, that Wendy is as unconcerned about the disappearance of Susan Robertson as the newscasters are indifferent to the fact that she was most likely murdered by her husband, with whom they report "she was on a hunting trip"? Like the swiveling pen and vanishing cigarette during the interview, Bill Watson and Stuart Ullman are also oblivious to Jack, on his first day on the job, sitting in the lobby of a grand hotel reading a Playgirl magazine. We assume that such details, like the continuity errors between shots, are ignored because they either do not register with them or they are in fact invisible to them. But the Playgirl magazine, and other things, all suggest that even this assumption may be wrong.

To see how Kubrick challenges his audience to consider what they are seeing, take the man stacking dishes in the utility hallway behind the lobby. Dressed in greenish overalls and wearing golden boots, Stuart watches him slip through the backdoor to his office on Closing Day, and never objects. Is this because Stuart is "in on the game," which means he knows why that man must enter through the back door of his office, and Stuart was looking to make sure that he does, right on cue? When we first see that man, he is stacking dishes on top of a cabinet at the same time his face is just a few inches from a large sign that says, "KEEP THIS AREA CLEAR." The point of how oblivious these people are appears to be just one way in which Kubrick tries to tell his audience that the bigger picture can only be seen by paying attention to small details. The copious number of signs posted all over the Overlook hotel, which are as regularly ignored by the people in the film as the signs Kubrick shows his audience are overlooked by the audience, is just one way Kubrick is asking his audience "Can't you see the signs," as the song goes, for "everywhere are signs."

The second point to understand is that, from what we can tell, it appears Kubrick never let anyone in on the secret of why he orchestrated the countless details and continuity errors he sought to ensure in each shot of the film with such meticulousness. For perhaps most people, such an obsession to detail is meaningless, at least until you start asking questions.

So determined to produce perfection while at the same time hiding from everyone the true nature of what it was he was doing, Kubrick would often require as many as 70 or 80 retakes of the same scene. After being forced to perform the iconic and exhausting baseball bat scene 127 times, for example, Duvall, who Kubrick intentionally and repeatedly isolated and argued with, then presented Kubrick with clumps of her hair that had fallen out due to the extreme stress. So too, the bar scene with Lloyd the bartender was shot 36 times, while the kitchen scene between the characters of Danny (Danny Lloyd) and Dick Hallorann (Scatman Crothers) ran as high as 148 takes.

In, *Stanley Kubrick: A Biography*, John Baxter even describes how Scatman Crothers eventually broke down, crying out in frustration, "What do you want, Mr. Kubrick? What do you want?!'" The answer Crothers was looking for was the perfection needed to arrange the pieces on the game board just right, without which the true game Kubrick was creating could never begin, and the puzzle never pieced together.

As a result of such secrecy, there is only one way to determine whether the claims of this author, that Stanley Kubrick died with a secret he never told a single soul, but which he left in plain sight, are valid. The only way to do that is weigh the evidence and decide for yourself.

The third critical point to understand is that the golden cord needed to navigate Kubrick's cinematic maze must be woven together by the player from three threads. The first thread needed to fully piece together Kubrick's puzzle comes from first watching the full-length version of the film. The second thread comes from then reading the original novel by Stephen King, paying attention to even the smallest differences between the two. And lastly, but most importantly, the third thread comes from understanding which pieces of the puzzle are provided directly, in the form of the rules needed to play his game, which he illustrates through pantomimes, and which are only alluded to by Kubrick, and always in accord with the internal logic by which everything in the film is forced to operate: a rule of twins.

With this third "shadow thread," the two former threads – the book and the film – can be laced together. And while the first two threads are parts that anyone can easily perform, the third, which in some ways is the most crucial of all, requires all the creativity, curiosity, and perhaps even the clairvoyance, of Danny Torrance talking to Tony or Jack talking to Delbert Grady.

Woven together into a single cord, the three threads just mentioned form a kind of "phantom thread" that stitches together the great puzzle Kubrick created, and along with it, the secret he appears to have taken with him to his grave as to why he did so. That secret was that, while King relied upon supernatural forces to terrify his audience, Kubrick sought to use people's beliefs in the legitimacy of those forces to show his audience a nightmare that has been playing out since the dawn of time, but not the "time" you may think. The point, however, may have been less about showing his audience how one could be scarier than the other, and more about showing them instead how the latter has always been used to fan fears of the former, fueling a cycle that Fredric Nietzsche called "the doctrine of eternal recurrence."

Why bother playing such a game at all, you ask? Because the maze in Kubrick's movie is merely a reflection of the one we are born into. Yes, a bit like Neo in *The Matrix*. And the only way to show you what that maze is, is by showing you how to piece together Kubrick's puzzle, so we can escape being trapped in either one "forever and ever and ever."

So, with all that being said, let us play.

ONE

Seeing the Game Board: Inside & Out

Let's sit down here, all of us, on the open prairie, where we can't see a highway or a fence. Let's have no blankets to sit on, but feel the ground with our bodies, the earth, the yielding shrubs. Let's have the grass for a mattress, experiencing its sharpness and its softness. Let us become like stones, plants, and trees. Let us be animals, think and feel like animals.

John Fire Lame Deer

When the human race leans to read the langue of symbolism, a great veil will fall from the eyes of men.

Manly P. Hall

TO BEGIN ASSEMBLING KUBRICK'S PUZZLE pieces into a unified whole, we must first become more acquainted with his game board. That game board exists on two sides of a mirror that is the silver screen. And while one half is reflected back to us from the screen itself, the other half is the ghost that lives behind our eyes, inside our own head. To see the one, as Lame Deer explains, we must free the other, and learn how to see with the wildly curious eyes of child. We have to be reborn, in short, with "second sight."

Let's start first with that half of the game board that is the movie screen, and what we know about the artist who paints that canvas with moving pictures. There, our three-dimensional reality is cramped into a two dimensional space. In that space are at least five defining features. The first is its mirrors, the first of which we see with the lake in the opening shot, and the second we see just beside Jack as he first walks through the foyer of the hotel into the lobby for his interview. The opening shot of the lake is telling us that virtually everything is either a mirror or operates like one. The Grady twins, for example, mirror each other, while the woman in room 237 is an inverted reflection in one body; a seductress that looks like "red rum" and an old hag that embodies "murder." The second feature is lighting, with the shadows operating as clues about how the pieces move on the board. The third important feature is the colors, which Kubrick uses like semaphores to telegraph underlying symmetries. Fourth, are the details themselves, where the movement and disappearance of items are as relevant as every other item and detail to be found in the film. And lastly, there is the time-space dimension of the hotel. In this film, "time is out of joint," as Hamlet laments, "oh cursed spite, if ever (we) were born to set it right." Like time, so too the characters often appear to move in directions that seem contradictory, almost as if they are pieces in a game Kubrick used to play for money on the streets of New York as a young man: chess.

Kubrick loved to play chess. Such a fan of the game was he, in fact, that, on occasion, he would even delay filming in order to "push" a game or two. One person he enjoyed playing with perhaps the most during filming, who he considered to be the best player among the members of the cast and crew, just happened to be "Tony" Burton.

Knowing about Kubrick's love of chess may tell us something about why pieces of driftwood and wooden chairs often move around in various scenes throughout the film. In the same way the ball rolling to Danny in the 237 hallway is the visual equivalent of "come and play with us," the movement of such items is also a visual example of a slang term used for playing chess or describing an untalented player: "pushing wood." As we will see, even the mysterious jump between the C4 and C3 freezer doors in the kitchen on Closing Day reflects an opening move in chess known as a Queens Knight Defense. Noticing how Kubrick moves his pieces around on the board helps us to begin to understand why those pieces move as they do, when they do, and where they do.

More than just a game of chess, however, *The Shining* is also both a puzzle, as Kubrick claimed, and a labyrinth. As a puzzle, we are tasked with sorting out different pieces according to shapes and, most importantly of all, colors. By doing so, we begin to discover pieces of the thread Kubrick provides to his audience with which they can navigate their way through his maze. Following that thread reveals a repeating set of patterns. Those patterns reveal how Kubrick, in the most subtle of ways, begins laying out the rules of his game in virtually every shot of the film. In this respect, Kubrick is like Daedalus, who was not only the architect of the maze that housed the Minotaur, which Theses was tasked with navigating, but also provided Ariadne with the solution for entering and exiting the maze successfully.

Kubrick begins unwinding the thread needed to navigate through his maze even with the silent black screen that precedes the opening shot. As if being birthed from the blackness, suddenly we find ourselves in midflight. Mountain ranges flank either side of the screen like Mother Earth opening her legs and birthing us forth, and as much from her womb as into it. Like Peter Pan soaring on gossamer-wings, we open our eyes like a newborn child and an angel falling from the sky. Our wings catching the wind, we glide over a tranquil sea that acts like a mirror; propelled straight toward a small island in a shining desert of water. With our fall, somber tones of a funeral hymn pulsate in our ears like a heartbeat or a war drum. The contrast of life and death clothed in the guise of sight and sound reminds us that every birth carries with it a death sentence.

More than anything else, what we hear provides us with the most important clue of the entire film. Those sounds are an audio reference to one of Kubrick's favorite books. That book suggests the movie we are about to watch is, in fact, encrypted. And part of the key needed to decrypt it is offered in what the camera zeros in on: Jack's yellow VW Bug. What's Jack's car trying to tell us? Follow the ball of thread Kubrick is unspooling right before our eyes.

The lake acts like a black mirror, casting a shimmering reflection of the sky in the water, with the waterline cutting across the middle of the frame reminding us of falling through the star-gate in *2001: A Space Odyssey*. As a result, we are falling through a pair of double mirrored doors, with the reflection of the island in the water giving it the shape of a diamond in the center of the monolithic manger that is our screen. Combined, the two shapes reflect the idea of a hexagon, with the diamond shape of the island reflecting the window in the Overlook elevator in King's novel.

In contrast to the symmetrical reflection of above and below, the left and the right sides of the frame stand in opposition to each other. The left side looks like three jagged fangs clothed in shadows, or the teeth of a jagged saw blade. The right side rises in a smooth slope bathed in golden light, and resembles an outline of the profile of a predator hunting its' prey. Both ranges intersect at a vanishing point of a small and distant mountain peak that lay beyond. That peak sits at the back of a shot that

4

exemplifies a technique known as the "one point perspective" (which we will discuss in more detail later), and toward which we are helplessly thrown and drawn. We have been reborn as Alice falling through the looking glass.

Passing over the island, which reflects both the red and black diamond pattern emblem which we see Jack first walk over just inside of the Overlook hotel and the diamond-shaped window in the center of the elevator door mentioned in the novel, the camera veers off course to the right, like Jack veering to the right as he angles toward the reception desk to introduce himself. As it does, it skews the symmetry that previously divided the screen, tilting the tabletop of the waterline like a pinball machine, the audience now flying straight into the side of the mountain, like Dick Hallorann flying to meet his grizzly demise at the hands of a man who, by that point, had become as savage as Caliban, as we head into a tempest. As the sloping mountain ridge slashes diagonally across the screen, its giant edifice is reflected in the water, taking on the profile of two giant golden wolves sniffing at the same shining mountain morsel in the distance.

The brief image of two wolves serves as a visual reference to the old Cherokee story about the two wolves that inhabit each of us: one good and the other evil, with the victor being the one we feed the most. In religious terms, those same wolves are called love and judgement: two ideas that are often conflated even though they are mutually exclusive opposites. And, like the two faces in the same image on that famous postcard, the mask of one is used to hide the true face of the other. And here we sit, about to watch the prize fight between those wolves as much over the soul and sanity of a man and his family as the minds of the audience. We are, in short, looking into the mirror of human history.

The tracking shot we encounter at the opening of the film reflects the tracking shot at the end, but contrasts with it as well. The former is an expansive landscape filled with life and color which seems like a never-ending dream, a visual splash of color that reflects the language with which Mother Nature speaks in pantomime. The latter, ending in the lobby of the Overlook, cramps us into a black and white coffin of a picture frame, like the pages of a book, with Jack standing at the foot of the frame like a coffin nail, the same nail on which the picture hangs, only upside down.

Like playing mahjong, the symmetry and dissymmetry of the opening shot are likewise reflected in the posture Jack holds in the final photograph. His left hand extended down to the floor with his right hand held up, as if waving at the audience both hello and goodbye, reflects both Jesus Christ and the posture of Baphomet.

Baphomet is a deity of occult and mystical traditions that has been associated with the Sabbatic Goat, an image drawn by Eliphas Levi. For Levi, that Sabbatic Goat symbolized the equilibrium of opposites, and the use of astral lights to manufacture perfect social order. The goat also reminds us of the ancient Hebrew tradition of scapegoating, which involved two goats: one to be slaughtered, the other to be banished. That tradition is reflected in the ram that Abraham eventually sacrifices in place of his son, Isaac. Even though God was willing to forego human sacrifice at that particular moment, preferring to have us murder his own son a couple of thousand years later, He still craved red rum to slake His desire for death; and perhaps because it was the very thing that, like a vampire, He could never find for Himself. Killing Jesus, from this perspective, was simply a way for God to experience one thing a God who was said could do anything, could never do: die.

The telescoping effect seen in these two tracking shots, which are seen numerous times over the course of the film, mirrors a 1967 film entitled *Wavelength*, by experimental filmmaker Michael Snow. *Wavelength* is a forty-five (42?) minute film where the camera, indifferent to everything in a large mostly empty room in which the entire film takes place, simply and slowly narrows its focus into a photograph that hangs on a rear wall of the apartment; a black and white photograph of "waves" crashing in the sea. In one we start in a strange room and end in a picture of waves in the sea. In the other we start by flying over the sea and end seeing a black and white photo of people cramped inside of a strange room we have not seen before in the film, as Jack smiles and waves. The similarities between the two serve as a cryptic suggestion that to decipher *The Shining*, we must first strive to get on the same wavelength as Kubrick himself.

The wild goose chase Kubrick has designed for us begins with the audience gliding toward Wild Goose Island as *The Shining* opens, like Jack chasing Danny in the hedge maze. That island sits in the middle of St. Mary's Lake in Glacier National Park, Montana. The camera veering off to the right, toward a profile of a big bad wolf bathed in gold, visually echoes Jack's comment: "little pigs, little pigs, let me come in," a line Nicholson adlibs that Kubrick could surely appreciate. That our vantage point is from the Going to the Sun Road reflects the fact that in the pantry - which Dick refers to as "the story room"- the camera walks toward Danny, behind whom we see numerous boxes with the words "Golden

Ray" written on them, as if Kubrick is putting us in Danny's shoes. In fact, this is likewise hinted at when the camera gives us a vantage point from Danny's eyes as he walks into the foyer of room 237, the two mirrored doors operating like the mirrored reflection in the opening scene but turned 90 degrees.

The opening scene then crossfades to an eagle's eye view overlooking a yellow VW Beetle skimming along a serpentine road that carves its way through a veritable Eden of evergreens. Visually, it looks like a pinball rolling along a track or a mouse snaking its way through a model hedge maze on a tabletop. Flanking either side of the road, evergreen trees stick up like the spikes in an iron maiden or a bed of nails. The scenes that follow become increasingly angular; the path of the bug aimed always toward the mountain tops in the distance. And with the ominous sound of the ritual Latin hymn sung in a mass for the dead, Dies Irae, which portends of Judgement Day or the "Day of Atonement," and Jack's undying love of the Overlook, Jack drives to his interview like a little lamb being led to slaughter. And all the while, Jack is being lured with the promise of eternal life, if he will but obey his Overlookers.

Despite starting with a vantage point from the Going to the Sun Road, the opening scene ends when we arrive at a gothic hotel called The Overlook, which looks like a castle or a monastery that we might find erected on a mountainside in Transylvania. Set in a landscape of mostly white and gray hues that looks like we just landed on the moon, or an alien world in which the inhabitants think in binary forms of black and white, the grey stone of the hotel and the mountain, as well as Jack's sports jacket, allude to the idea of blurring the distinction between right

8

and wrong. The result: we are left to wonder which wolf we are watching walk into the hotel, and which are we feeding by doing so.

What is clear from the opening scene, and especially the music, is that we are no longer in the Kansas of a Stephen King novel anymore. Rather, the first shots of the Overlook resemble a concrete bunker, as if the audience has just been ferried across the river Styx to the spiritual equivalent of Shawshank prison. In fact, Jack waking up in his Stovington Eagles shirt "a month later" even suggests the Overlook is like a Nazi basecamp on the moon. The Overlook, in other words, is an eagle's nest.

The Eagle's Nest was a famed resort built by the Third Reich atop the summit of a rocky range of mountain in Bavaria, near the town of Berchtesgaden. Even the word "Adler," which is the brand of Jack's typewriter, means "eagle" in German. Like the Overlook hotel itself, the Eagle's Nest was used exclusively by Germany's social elites, which naturally included the "royalty" of the Nazi Party – those who were considered to be "all the best people." There, they drank fine wines and enjoyed the most cultured music and cuisines, and gushed over their dream to conquer the world, spread (i.e., "impose") their "cultural superiority," and kill everyone who failed to live up to their enlightened ideals, especially their ideals about Aryan blood. Those ideals were grounded in the science of the day, which was built on a pseudoscientific religion in which there exists only one infallible law: "survival of the fittest." But who gets to define what "fittest" even means? Those who, like Jack, God gave the authority to use violence as He, and they, see fit.

Like Jack for his interview and in the final photograph, Germany's social elites dressed in grey or tuxedo-black military uniforms and saw the world in black and white: they were right because they were white, and everyone else was wrong – period. And, as they saw it, the reason they had the military might to prove this was so because, as they proclaimed by embroidering it on the belt buckles of their uniforms, "God is with us:" a belief that everyone equally shares, especially in times of war, even as each one is equally convinced that they alone are correct in thinking so.[16]

Speaking in Living Color

Among many other things, the opening scene invites us to follow Lame Deer's advice, not only by taking a birds eye view of what follows, but by also considering how color operates like a language all its own. The problem is that color is a language we have increasingly lost our ability to appreciate or listen to, let alone speak and understand. Like Murnau's *Last Laugh*, part of what Kubrick invites us to do with the opening scene is to stop relying so exclusively on words - to stop listening to the voices in our head, as it were - and to tune-in instead to what all our other senses are trying to tell us.

To do that, we have to back-track like Danny in the maze, to a time before the supremacy of words alone reigned over the whole of the

---

[16] One "miracle of religious faith" is that, even though everyone knows this is true, everyone equally strives to both deny such a truth, and to prevent the (evil of) "doubt" such an infallible truth tries to introduce into their brain, even when that doubt is in fact trying to save their own life in a foxhole somewhere, and free their soul from a belief that it is nobler 'to die for a belief than to live humbly for one.' Avoiding any entertainment of such doubts is necessary, of course, because it may lead all those who do entertain it, even in the least, to realize that the very religion they have relied on as necessary for peace, morality, and love for their fellow man (out of a fear of God), is now compelling them to fear, hate, and kill their fellow man, out of a love for, and fear of, that very same God.

human mind, through the sacred scepter (and deception) of a symbolic language. We must return to a time when being alive meant more than simply being frozen in thought about a sacred sentence scrolled on the flesh of a dead tree, like a dead body in a tomb. We must return to when the language of life came, not from words alone, which are merely the vacuous symbols of reality posing as manna from heaven, but from all of our other senses combined. We must return, that is, to when being alive was to *experience* life, not dream about ways of converting and controlling life by locking it inside a prison house of language and crucifying it to a cross of a balance sheet.

Simply put, to find the invisible thread that runs through Kubrick's *Shining*, one which will suture everything together into a single unified whole, we first must find our way into the game. The difficulty of finding that thread can be seen from the fact that not only did Kubrick create it, but he also then spent the rest of his life either denying it was a game at all, or downplaying such an idea by claiming the movie wasn't supposed to make sense. But it is a game, and if we learn how to play it, it makes perfect sense. And while noticing colors is not necessarily where a person must begin to solve Kubrick's little Rubik's Cube of horrors, it is probably the best place to start by far. In fact, that's the thing that first caught my eye. What's creepy is how and why.

The How and Why

Right after Wendy, Jack, Bill Watson, and Stuart, all mysteriously jump out of the way of a car that was just about to flatten them like a pancake, Stuart mentions that the hotel is built on an Indian burial ground, a reference which reminds us of the trilling voices of Indian

11

chants heard mixed in with the funeral march during the opening scene. Those voices began just before Jack drives through a tunnel and out the other side. Is this really just a coincidence? And is that mysterious jump really something Kubrick just wants us to, say, 'overlook' as altogether meaningless to piecing his puzzle together?

The reference to Indian burial grounds reminded me of the quote from Lame Deer at the top of this chapter, from the book *Lame Deer, Seeker of Visions: The Life of a Sioux Medicine Man*. It is the opening paragraph of Chapter Seven, entitled "Talking to the Owls and the Butterflies." The visual invitation being issued by Kubrick to his audience with the opening scene, an invitation to pay attention to the scenery, is articulated by Lame Deer entreating us to "think and feel like animals." To do that requires listening and seeing what the "Great Mother" Nature has to say through a language that she speaks in everything but words. And to do that, we first have to understand how, for the Sioux, everything in the world is not only alive but, when compared to those of us tethered to the umbilical cord of one electronic device or another, is even more alive than we are.

In contrast to those who sought to worship the spirit of life by always condemning the flesh in which it dwelled as necessarily "fallen" and sinful - and presumably from the lofty heights from whence they claimed their own "sacred ideals" about our putrid flesh reigned supreme - the more pantheistic and panpsychic beliefs of the Sioux interpreted everything in the universe as being both inseparably connected and equally divine. European monotheists, who were limited to viewing such "beliefs" through the lens of the pagan and polytheistic religions which had given birth to their own religious traditions, mistakenly interpreted this perspective as one in which the Sioux believed a kind of small human or humanoid creature, which the Greeks called a "homunculus," existed in everything. Europeans did this, of course, because they saw all "gods" much as they saw their own: as made in the image and likeness of themselves. But the Sioux saw something else entirely.

For the Sioux, the idea of "God the Father" represented the immaterial masculine consciousness that served as the author of all, while Mother Nature was the feminine made flesh in the form of physical reality, which was alive. And if one was the seed of a thought, which the Greek philosophers sometimes called "Logos," the other was the deed that had given life to those ideas in an ideal form. The Virgin Mary, from this perspective, was simply the personification of physical reality itself, with Earth being as much her womb as the Garden of Eden, from which all life sprang eternal. The "immaterial" Father, by extension, was the crown of stars and the shining sunlight in the sky above. To separate the two, as St. Augustine would later do with love and sex, was to worship a perfect "Creator" by only ever condemning His creation as His greatest sin.

This same contradiction is even reflected in the opening shot of *The Shining*, with the expansive views of nature being accompanied by the vituperative judgements of a funeral march. God is thought of as a divine ideal, even while His creation is treated as the seed of His greatest shame. Homo sapiens were only unique, from this perspective, not because they were separate from or above nature, but because they alone were gifted with a level of conscious awareness that allowed them to understand the intimate interconnectedness of all things; and that they, like all life, were but the offspring of a divine marriage of earth and light. Yet we divorced the two and ravaged the womb of the one while claiming to love only the other.

Our conscious awareness, which has so often led medieval man to love his own "beliefs" and his ideals more than his divine mother or his fellow man, for the Sioux, came with a responsibility. That responsibility consisted of the need to honor the father by protecting the physical body of the divine heavenly host who bore us from her womb and carried us on her back. While our earth could easily provide all of her inhabitants with a greater abundance than they could ever need, forced to be a slave of profit motives crucifies her on a cross of greed.

For the Sioux and other native tribes, in stark contrast to the empires of Europe that preached love and forgiveness while practicing conquest and genocide, more value was given not to what a person amassed for themselves, but what they gave away. Described as the basis of a "gift economy" by anthropologists like David Graeber, such value systems were part of a larger ethos that thought not in terms of rights but obligations, for we are only granted the former from those that would rule us, while we are born with the latter. And the highest obligation of all was a duty to honor all the generations who had come before by doing one's share to protect the earth for at least the next seven generations to follow. And to do that required a devotion to defending our "great mother" as the heavens commanded, so she could continue to provide for all her children through the nourishments, as much physical as spiritual, of her own body and blood, spirit and soul.

The idea that we are all connected to everything in the universe, not to just those who think and look and act as we do, which was as familiar to every Native American child as the stars above, has only bubbled up from those minds that have found the truths buried among the bones of our ancient ancestors. Among others, and along with other insights about the true nature of reality, souls like Albert Einstein discovered and preached about the deep interconnectedness to all things as an infallible truth. As Einstein put it:

> We are part of the whole which we call the universe, but it is an optical illusion of our mind that we are separate. This separate is like a prison for us. Our job is to widen the circle of our compassion, so we feel connected with all people and situations.

Here, Einstein touches upon how our various cultural belief systems are used to format our minds into partitions that then perceive the stratifications upon which our societies are built and depend as a "natural law." We accept this idea as easily as breathing, even though we are the sole authors of such a law, and the law itself is at variance to both our abilities and the truth being preached by nature itself. Nor can walking in a sacred circle free us from such illusions, but only by "expanding our circles," like the spiral of a universe, can we hope to escape the cultural conditioning that celebrates the insanity of doing the same thing and expecting a different outcome as a sacred tradition.

The importance of cultivating our connection to the earth and Mother Nature was not fully alien to Christianity and Western culture. Thomas Aquinas, for example, acknowledged that plants have souls. In fact, for Aquinas, humans shared the soul world with plants and animals, as well as spirits and angels, and functioned as mediators between these two realms. Among others, D. H. Lawrence saw things the same way. As he put it,

> The whole life-effort of man is to get his life into direct contact with the elemental life of the cosmos, mountain life, cloud life, thunder life, air life, earth life, sun life. To come into immediate felt contact, and so derive energy, power and a dark sort of joy. This effort into sheer naked contact, without an intermediary or mediator, is the root meaning of religion.

Like Lawrence, Herman Hesse pointed out that "trees are sanctuaries," and that whoever learns to converse with them "can learn the truth." Cut that tree down and turn it into a cross, however, and violence will always be needed to defend the "belief" that faith in the latter is more important to life than the oxygen - the "breath of life" - provided by the former.

Hesse and Lawrence were merely expressing what the visionary German naturalist Alexander von Humboldt (1769-1859) had illuminated for the Western world. As Andrea Wulf pointed out in *The Invention of Nature*, Humboldt created the way we understand nature today. He did this by discovering what every Native American knew from childhood: that all of nature is intimately and inseparably connected. And hell is a religion that teaches us we are separate from that God in order to lure us into striving our whole life to reconnect to a brand of "God," even though this is like convincing a fish it is disconnected from the water it lives in, and the atoms it is made of.

Humboldt's insight can even be interpreted as explaining the meaning behind the process by which Jesus restores the sight to a man born blind. As it says in the Gospel of John 9:6 (inverted twins?), Jesus does this through a seemingly meaningless series of steps. First, he creates mud with his own spit. Then, he rubs that mud in the man's eyes. (Gross!) Next, he tells that man to go washout his eyes in the river.

Why would Jesus need to engage in such theater when one woman healed herself just by touching Jesus's robe? Is he communicating something to those who have eyes to see and ears to hear? The mud Jesus makes is clay, the stuff of Adam, and the day he performs this "miracle" restoring such sight is the Sabbath. Maybe Jesus just wanted the man to see that, as it says in Genesis 2:7, the "image and likeness" of the God in which man was created was not an image of his own reflection, of which the story of Narcissus was a familiar warning in a Roman Empire that prided itself as inheriting all of its wisdom from ancient Greece, but of their own Mother, from the clay of water and dust. We are, after all, more than 60% the former, and to the latter we shall return. In our Mother's image of Earth and water, we are made of flesh and blood. Maybe that's why blood and water pour from the side of Jesus after he was pierced with a spear, like a pen piercing a page, until the letter of the law becomes a cross of obedience to those who wield the scepter of royal decree.

Kubrick mixes the significance of returning to the earth after we die by showing us an opening scene of nature while listening to a funeral march, a contrast as stark as the woman in room 237. This same contrast is seen in our own societies today.

Reacting to the constricting effects that were being imposed upon the human mind by a love for the rigors of logic during the Enlightenment, as Florence Williams points out in *The Nature Fix: Why Nature Makes Us Happier, Healthier, and More Creative*, the Romantic movement sought to return to the idea of "nature as the salvation of the mortal soul and the mortal imagination, with poets penning odes to high peaks just as industrialization was beginning to choke its way through Europe." Aquinas's appreciation for the spirit of nature could be seen from Wordsworth who wrote of a fusing of "the round ocean and the living air, / And the blue sky and in the mind of Man," to Beethoven dedicating symphonies to landscapes and exclaiming "The woods, the trees and the rocks give man the resonance he needs." Both men were speaking of "a melding of inner and outer systems."

As Williams further points out, science is now demonstrating the healing and beneficial effects that nature has on our brains, improving our mood and well-being along with our ability to think, remember, plan, create, focus, and daydream. It even improves our social skills. She even points out that, while "scientists used to attribute myopia to book-reading," today, "it instead appears to be closely linked to time spent living like mole rats, away from the 'golden rays' of sunlight, because "the sun primes the retina's dopamine receptors, and those in turn control the shape of the developing eye." Sunlight and nature in general, in other words, are what enabled Jesus to restore the sight to the blind man, who had been living like a mole in a temple: a manmade cave in which he worships an idea of "God" rather than an actual God which can, by simply beholding the cathedral of the world with its ceiling of our universe, restore sight to the blind with the power of the heavens themselves.

By mixing the funeral hymn played in the opening scene with Native American chanting, Kubrick echoes Lame Deer's invitation to his readers to think and feel like the animals. By doing so, Kubrick also invites the audience to look past the surface narrative and the characters on the screen that look like ourselves,' and to see more. In effect, both are inviting us to imagine what it must have been like to experience reality before our interpretation of that experience began coagulating into the symbols we now venerate as our god: words.

Such veneration is even expressed in the opening lines of the Gospel of John, where the author christens words as our one true "god" by writing, "In the beginning was the Word, and the Word was with God, and the Word *was* God," and "the word was made flesh." Jack's name in the novel, by the way, is John, while the verse above is John 1:1 or 11 (and Jack Nicholson's real name is John also).

Nor is it a mere coincidence that 4 in 10 Christians believe the world began between six to ten thousand years ago, because that is when man first invented the technology of the written word. And we first did so, as Yuval Noah Harari pointed out in his book, *Sapiens: A Brief History of Humankind*, in a business contract written on a tablet made of the same stuff as Adam: clay. And sitting on the top of his wooden chair in the CL is a wagon wheel that looks like an unfinished spider web – a spider web of the words Jack hacks into his paper with his machine, much as he plunges his ax into the heart of Dick Hallorann, as if he were saying a pledge of allegiance to his own sacred words, and the machine with which he set them down.

Today, we become ensnared in that web when we wallpaper reality itself with words, labeling everything our eyes survey with the stick-em note of a name and, by extension, a meaning. As Jiddu Krishnamurti pointed out, "to tell a child the name of a bird ensures the child will no longer see the bird." Tell a person that *The Shining* is a horror movie, and they stop *seeing* the movie for what it really is. They'll remember lines of dialogue, but overlook and forget the details that matter most –

the ones that allow us to navigate the maze and slay the Minotaur living as much within it as ourselves.

As a result of our dependence upon words, as Anthony de Mello points out in his book *Awareness*, "Human beings react to words, feed on words, rather than on reality." Part of the effect of the opening scene in *The Shining* is to raise our awareness of De Mello's point, to stop listening to just the lines being spoken, along with the voices in our head, so we can start using all our other senses to notice the real story Kubrick, like the world overall, is trying to tell us through everything else.

Our Divided Brain

As mentioned already, part of the problem we have with experiencing what it means to be alive is that we live in a divided house. That house is comprised of a bicameral brain with two hemispheres. Along with our analytical faculties like logic and math, language is largely a function of the left hemisphere of our brain. Like that miser Ebenezer Scrooge, it spends its days tabulating experience. And like a computer, it processes information gathered through our senses from a fluidly analog environment and converts it into a simpler more binary perspective, one which language allows us to access in a linear fashion. And since words are mere audible symbols of reality, to see God as "the Word," as it says in the beginning of the Gospel of John, is to reduce the universe to a Polaroid, and then treat the Polaroid as more important than real thing.

The right hemisphere of our brain, on the other hand, houses our more creative, intuitive, adventurous, and holistic ways of thinking. It is more like Tiny Tim and thinks in terms of everyone, not just those who make you a profit or pick your pocket every twenty-fifth of December. It processes experiences into a more analogue and nonverbal format, converting information in a serial fashion into images and intuitions.

And as the faculties housed in our left brain have been venerated by philosophers and warriors and associated with masculinity, with the "word" being elevated to a "God," the faculties exercised by our right brain - which tends to be more reflective of empathy, creativity, and experiences of awe and wonder - have more often been denigrated as soft and weak, and associated with femininity. One side thinks in blocks of ice cubes, while the other side swims in the ocean. Or, put another way, one relies on the letter of the law to sting those who draw outside the lines laid down by a priestly class of vipers, while the other is as gentle as a butterfly on the breeze.   And while one is consider more "conscious," because of our heavy reliance on words, the other is more unconscious.

Qualifying the two hemispheres of our brain as if they were different genders demonstrates how even our ideas are the product of the union of such differences. Today, however, the dominance of one too often results in it domestically abusing the other. Long before the rise of monotheistic religions dominated by male gods that have most often been worshiped through warfare, gods which all arose with the invention of words and numbers and money and even chattel slavery, most of the ancient gods were female. The former warred over scarcity like apes around a watering hole, while the latter shared the abundance of her fertility like a mother with her children. And sex, far from being vilified as being the greatest carnal sin, was celebrated as much by sapiens as their gods, as an inseparable part of the gift of love and life itself. And as male gods ruled by judgement and war, female deities brought forth life through the procreative means of communing with the divinity of nature itself.

Perhaps unwittingly, our information culture has helped to cultivate a never-ending conflict between these two hemispheres of our brain, between a more analytical, linear, and binary way of thinking on the one hand, and a more analogue and holistic way of perceiving on the other. This conflict is reflected in much of what we see happening in *The Shining*. Jack is a writer, after all, and other than sleeping, drinking with imaginary friends, or ambling aimlessly around the hotel, he spends all his time pounding away on his typewriter like a literary phantom of the opera. Words, from this perspective, are Jack's God, that he "makes flesh," in the form of Lloyd, Delbert Grady, and the woman in room 237. On the other hand, Wendy, Jack's other half, cultivates her inner child by regularly playing and spending time with Danny. As seen from the plethora of books found all over the Boulder apartment and the books we later see in the bookshelf in their Overlook apartment, she also cultivates her curiosity by reading virtually anything and everything. And while Jack dies after being divided as much from his wits as from his typewriter, his sense of play, and his own family, Danny becomes unified with Tony, and then Wendy, escaping the labyrinth of language he had fallen into without ever saying a word. And he does this by using his intuition to escape the box of a book written in black and white and veiled in the sacred robes of a red velvet jacket.

In the opening scene of *The Shining*, Kubrick even appears to allude to not only how we are falling into a labyrinth, but that to escape it, we must learn to bypass the left hemisphere of our brain, with its dependence upon words alone. This stretch of the imagination comes from the camera passing Wild Goose Island and veering to the right. In doing so, it's as if the camera is steering us toward the synthesizing, non-verbal right hemisphere of our brain, escorting us like an unseen Virgil into the steerage sections of our mind which are more holistic and intuitive. Add to this the fact that we are clearly looking through the eyes of a bird during the opening scene, and it becomes clear that we are being escorted into the film in a way that alludes to the kind of perspective Lame Deer invites us to consider: to think and perceive like the Owl and the Butterfly.

In contrast to how the left hemisphere of our brain makes sense of the world, the right hemisphere of our brain thinks less in words and more in images, shapes, and colors; that is, more like other animals. To learn its language, as such, is to become a little like Dr. Doolittle. And this is because animals know only too well how to speak the language of color.

Seeing in Living Color

Of all the species of animals known to man, it turns out that birds and insects just happen to have the most advanced color vision and the highest form of color discrimination of all. While mammals generally tend to have a relatively weak color vision compared to other species, with humans possessing the most advanced color perception among all mammals, even the human ability to perceive color pales in comparison to that of certain birds and insects, especially the owl and the butterfly.

Animals tend to understand colors better than humans because, ironically enough, they are more acquainted with light. Humans tend to

23

have trichromatic vision, which means our eyes have three types of the photoreceptors known as cone cells, which are sensitive to the colors red, green, and blue - the very same colors Kubrick relies on the most for the costumes throughout the film. Animals tend to process light differently, with some creatures having only two types of photoreceptors, which render them partially colorblind; others having four, which enables them to see ultraviolet light; and still others having the ability to detect polarized light, meaning light waves that oscillate in the same plane. What's relevant here is that it was the oscillation of the colors in Kubrick's film that first caught my eye.

Noticing different colors is easier for some people than others. This is because, like some species of animals, some sapiens possess four types of photoreceptors. Known as quadchromatic vision, this trait is rare among men, who are more likely to be color blind or unable to perceive as many colors as women due to inherited abnormalities in their cones. According to a 2010 study, nearly 12% of women possess this fourth color perception channel.

If Wendy is the "queen of the maze" - as hinted at in the dissolve from their apartment bathroom in the Overlook to them walking by the opening of the hedge maze on Closing Day - this trait becomes more than simply an interesting parallel to the story. This same idea is even reflected in the "Great Mother" painting hanging on the wall just outside of Stuart's office. That painting not only depicts a figure that strongly resembles Wendy, but it also appears to have four eyes, including one on the back of her head. Is it that fourth eye that gives her the "second sight" to see what she sees later?

With the colors in the opening scene and the bird's-eye-view of the ascent, Kubrick invites his audience into his masquerade ball in which he wants us to consider colors, not as simply a backdrop, but as clues. What's more, we should consider colors as a language unto themselves, a language which communicates to that part of our brain that is not pilloried by a use of words to derive all its meaning and understanding.

Seeking to experience life less through words and more through color led me to notice wormholes in an art gallery that would become the first clue of piecing Kubrick's puzzle together.

The Woman in the Wormhole Gallery

Picture, if you will, an art gallery, in which the paintings on the walls begin crawling off of their canvases and out of their frames to walk among the living, like that little girl in the horror movie *The Ring*, while the souls of the living are slowly sucked into those empty frames and absorbed onto those canvases, like that other little girl in *Poltergeist*. In 2015, I found myself wandering around just such an art museum in Rio de Janeiro. Unbeknownst to me at the time, what I was really seeing were the first sparks of Kubrick's masterpiece speaking to me through the medium of colors.

With three floors and too many rooms to count, the fateful museum I happened into one sunny day was a bit of a maze unto itself, with each room containing various kinds of art. After touring most of its galleries I ended up in a room filled with the most abstract paintings in the museum. It was there that my awareness underwent a metamorphosis, dropping me out of the pages of a Franz Kafka story to become a fly on the wall. In that room, art came to life, literally.

Shaped like a giant shoebox, or a manger, or even a movie screen, the room was maybe eighty by thirty feet in dimensions. A wall ran lengthwise through the center of the room. Being shorter than the length of the room overall, that wall left openings on either end. People mulled about in both directions around that wall like monkeys ambling around a monolith, looking at the paintings hanging on both the outside walls and either side of the central wall.

Into the sea of onlookers that were circumambulating around the center wall like Muslims walking around the Kaaba in Mecca I went. A painting halted my feet before long, and there I stood, gazing, peering into it, wondering who, and why, and when. After a few minutes, my head swiveled toward a young woman who had likewise been stopped in her tracks by a similar painting hanging on the wall across from mine. Moments later she walked on. And when she did, I was awestruck by what I saw looking back at me: the painting into which she had been gazing was her doppelganger in abstraction.

Like a mirror that cast her reflection through a prism, the painting she'd been gazing into was colored in red and black and resembled the iris of an eye or a flower. The paint itself looked like it was splashing out of the frame, with the composition resembling a bird's eye view looking down into the mouth of an erupting volcano. And like the gremlins in my room pouring out of my picture Bible, the contents of the canvas looked as if they had poured through the open window of an abstract painting hanging on a wall, and into the physical form of the woman looking into it. The paint itself, which was thick and clumpy and seemed almost as if it were grasping with mangled fists at the canvas, reaching desperately for the edge of the frame like a man buried alive crawling from his would-be grave, looked also like a child clutching and clawing in terror at their bed covers in the middle of a moonlit night. As my mind was drawn into its vomiting mouth, I was reminded of that line from T. S. Eliot's "Hollow Men,' which seemed to capture with words the image I saw staring back at me from that portrait, an image of "paralyzed force, gesture without motion."

Struck by how much the young woman looked like the physical manifestation of the painting she had just been gazing into, I wondered if I had been the only one in the gallery to notice that she had been looking into a mirror of what she would look like if she were but light diffused through a prism. Indeed, the prism through which she had been diffused was another person's eye, which had passed into their mind and out through their paintbrush. It was as if the right hemisphere of that artist's brain had perceived her image standing before his canvas, and the left hemisphere had endeavored to record that vision for posterity, which included her. Or more simply, she had been looking at herself in the mirror the artist's eye, forming a kind of entanglement between the artist and the onlooker, between the actions of the past and the unfolding of the present.

At the time, I could never have imagined just how much such an experience would portend my chess match with Kubrick's ghost, years later. And that's because it was this very experience, and indeed this same thought, that led me to notice how often the very same thing seemed to be happening with the paintings and other forms of wall art in *The Shining*, again and again and again.

Blessed with skin as dark and smooth as volcanic glass, the young woman wore a red single piece outfit comprised of shorts and a halter top: two colors that perfectly matched the only two colors used in the painting into which she gazed. To see her standing in front of it looked as if the painter had hurled his paint with such force at the canvas that it had passed through a wormhole in the fabric of time, like starlight hurtling through space from a distant star that had long since ceased to exist. And by doing so, that paint now poured out of the other side of that window and into physical reality the very person who now gazed upon it. Indeed, she was comprised of the very same colors as the elevators and the doors in the Overlook hotel! And like Wendy, it was as if that woman had walked in through a door and out through a mirror.

Only then was I likewise struck with a sudden realization that she was not alone in having been poured through a picture frame, by that same painter, into the same room in which we both stood. As my head suddenly swiveled back like the dialer on a rotary phone, I looked again at the painting that hung before me, remembering vaguely that its colors also seemed strangely familiar. It was then that I discovered that I too had been looking into the very same mirror as the woman across from me, for the painting that hung before me was also a mirrored abstraction of myself.

Much like the red and black painting on the opposite wall, the painting I had been looking into – which sat across from the red and black painting at the same angle of difference with which the C3 walk-in freezer door sits in relation to the C4 walk-in freezer door – was of a similar composition, but looked like the iris of an eye that was mostly colored in shades of dark blue, with slight hints of lighter blues and a small amount of yellows and whites erupting from its center. Shifting my eyes suddenly to review the colors of my own attire, I was awestruck to discover that the colors of my own painting were as much of a reflection of me in abstraction as the painting on the opposite wall had reflected the woman in red. And if her painting reflected herself in one of the eyes of the artist watching who would eventually come to eye his work, the painting before me reflected myself in his other eye, doing the same thing, at the same moment in time!

What were the chances, that a painter of two abstract pieces of art would not only have those painting hanging on walls across from each other, but would then have two people from different sides of the equator standing there looking at them, at the exact same moment in time, and be exact human manifestations of the paintings themselves?

This experience - which I came to refer to as "the woman in the wormhole gallery" - led me to pay attention to the paintings in *The Shining*. And this led me to wonder if Kubrick was doing with the opening shots of his film what Lame Deer had admonished us to do when he invited us all to "think and feel like animals." As it turned out, it was colors, which have so often been used to divide and conquer the seamless garment of homo sapiens through the scepter of the pseudoscientific religion of "race," that Kubrick was using to show just how interconnected everything in the movie really is, despite appearances to the contrary. But to see this we must relearn the language of colors Kubrick is speaking throughout the film.

Bird Watching & the Language of Color

If we pay close attention to the colors in *The Shining*, it becomes clear that they play a larger role in the film than simply window dressing, or even Jack Nicholson and Shelly Duval. Of the different colors of green paint on the walls of the utility hallway behind the lobby, for example, first seen as Stuart, Bill, Wendy, and Jack head to check out the boilers on Closing Day, the bottom and top halves of the wall are comprised of two shades of green. The top half is a lighter shade of green than the bottom, and both just happen to match the dark green sweater and light green shirt Jack is wearing in that same scene. In the utility hallway that runs behind the fireplace in the CL, on the other hand, the colors on the wall are like, but not exactly, a dark greenish grey below and a golden yellow above: colors matching Jack's sports jacket and green sweater. The pipes "running" overhead in both hallways are blue and red, the same colors Danny wears when riding his tricycle down those hallways later. Even the colors Wendy wears when she chases Danny playfully into the maze are identical to the colors worn by Jack when he chases Danny into the maze like Wile E. Coyote chasing the Road Runner. And Danny is dressed almost the same in both scenes in the maze. Is all this really just pure coincidence, especially in a Kubrick film?

The experience in the art gallery in Rio de Janeiro led me to begin noticing the colors in the Overlook. Noticing colors led me to notice how the paintings in the hotel appeared to be more than just wall art. Although plenty of the paintings seen in the film clearly have deeper meanings, the first two paintings that caught my attention as particularly intentional looked harmless enough. At second sight, however, they looked as if they were just begging for someone to notice them. Those paintings sat at the far end of the utility hallway in the Colorado lounge (CL).

At the end of his ride around the CL "a month later," Danny rides his trike behind the grand staircase and then turns left to reenter the utility hallway to finish his ride where he began. Doing so closes the circle in which he rides, in a room that is shaped like a giant square. Danny's ride around the CL, in other words, is a squared circle: a contradiction in terms, like a boxing "ring." As he turns left to reenter that utility hallway, he passes two paintings of birds on the wall in front of him. Those paintings hang above a large wooden table similar to the ones we see under the mirrors in the Gold Room hallway, which are all smaller versions of Jack's writing table. One painting is of a bird in flight and the other is of a bird perched upon a branch or a railing. Although easy to overlook, they appear to confirm what Dick told Danny about the hotel on Closing Day: "Sometimes we see things that haven't happened yet." They are also "just like pictures in a book." But they are more than that. They are also foreshadows on the wall of Jack's writing cave.

What made those two paintings appear to jump off the wall at me, like the paintings in the art gallery in Brazil, were Danny's blue jacket and Jack's green t-shirt. "A Month Later," Jack wakes up in the vanity mirror, lying-in-wait for breakfast in bed. When he does, he is wearing his Stovington Eagles shirt. In the novel, Stovington was the school where Jack was previously employed. While not covered in the film, Jack had lost that job when he violently assaulted one of his students; an idea that reminds us of the violent assault Jack recounts with Danny and that Danny will encounter in room 237.

Much like the red eagle on Ullman's windowsill, the eagle seen on Jack's t-shirt is depicted in attack mode, with talons drawn as if swooping down to snatch a small child or Jack's car from the road. The colors of the shirt itself just happen to match the colors of the green paint on the wall in the "twin" utility hallway behind the lobby – the same hallway Jack will later chase Danny down after killing Dick. Like the two shades of green in the lobby hallway, the eagle on Jack's shirt is dark green while the shirt itself is light green. Sure, I thought, this could all be mere coincidence, or even an intentional parallel Kubrick included for no special reason. But then I recalled that, on Closing Day, we first see the word "LYERS" emblazoned in red letters across the back of Danny's blue jacket, just before he turns to see the Grady twins in the Games Room – a jacket with the same colors as the pipes "running" overhead in both utility hallways. Later, we see that the full spelling of the word on the back of Danny's jacket is "FLYERS." And Danny is wearing that jacket both when he first sees the Grady twins in the "Games Room" and when he goes to get "eye scream" with Dick, right after they "shined" in the "story room" – hinting at a connection between the two rooms. And in the Games Room, we see the numbers across the bottom of the dart board 237, both forward and backward.

Again, my Spidey sense was tingling, leaving me to wonder: was all this really just coincidence? Maybe.

However coincidental those paintings appeared to be with Kubrick associating both Jack and Danny with birds, the details and the colors in those paintings suggested they were as intentional as Dick saying "what's up Doc" after we saw Danny wearing a shirt with Bugs Bunny on it, and the Dopey sticker disappearing from his bedroom door (because Dopey of the Seven Dwarfs was a friend of Doc's). Of those two paintings, the one seen on the left as Danny turns left to reenter the utility hallway is of a bird flying, as if down the same hallway and in the same direction that Danny is riding his tricycle. At the bottom of that painting is a splash of red, of a red banister, while the floor in the utility hallway Danny is ridding into happens to also be red. It's like Danny is being ferried along down that hallway by the blood pouring out of the elevators. In the painting to the right, by comparison, a bird sits on a branch, an image which seems to portend the image of Jack holding an axe and standing at the end of the hallway in the lobby in his red jacket, right after cutting down Dick Hallorann for sport, and yelling "Danny boy?"

Again, is it really just a coincidence that Danny happens to run from Jack down the hallway in the lobby, or that he rides in the opposite direction down that same hallway just before he jumps a floor and encounters the twins outside of their apartment, chopped up into little pieces? And when he does, he's wearing a red jacket: like father, like sonny-side up.

Even Jack saying "Danny Boy" appears to be a cryptic message intended to call our attention to the pipes running overhead in those hallways. The phrase comes from a ballad written by Fredric Weatherly in 1913 and set to the traditional Irish melody of "Londonderry Air." The latter melody reminds us of the phrase, "dairy air," which is a common misspelling of the French word "derrière," which refers to the buttocks. (Recall the man in the upstairs room wearing the bear suit with his bare "derriere" hanging out.) As if to echo the music of Dies Irae in the opening scene, "Danny Boy" became popular for funerals and memorial services after it began to be considered an unofficial anthem by Irish Americans and Irish Canadians. The lyrics of the song bade us to notice not only the colors of the pipes running overhead in the utility hallways, but also Danny sliding down a mountain of snow outside the bathroom window:

Oh, Danny boy, *the pipes, the pipes* are calling
From glen to glen, and *down the mountain side*.
The summer's gone, and all the roses falling,
It's you, it's you must go and I must bide.

But come ye back when summer's in the meadow,
Or when the valley's hushed and white with snow,
I'll be here in sunshine *or in shadow*,
Oh, Danny boy, oh Danny boy, I love you so!

Note that the phrase "summer's in the meadow" reminds us of *Summer of 42*, the film Danny and Wendy are watching in the lobby, while "the valley's hushed and white with snow" reflects the blizzard outside as they do. Even this reference to "sunshine" and "shadow" reminds us of the shadow of the helicopter during Jack's drive along the Going to the Sun road on a sunshiny day, but more on that later. And Jack Nicholson just happens to be an Irish American.

What portents was this? Like the paintings I had seen in the art gallery in Brazil, the bird paintings in the CL, which flanked either side of a mirror toward which Danny rides and the Torrances walk as they end their tour of the CL on Closing Day, seemed to preview what would happen between Jack and Danny on the 'closing day' the Torrances are in the Overlook. Like the woman in the wormhole gallery, later events in the film suggested the ominous images in those paintings had somehow crawled off their own canvases and come to life in the hotel. Or worse, it was as if Jack and Wendy had walked through the "mirror, mirror, on the wall" between those paintings, and out the other side came Jack in his red jacket chasing Danny down the green hallway behind the lobby, just like the Coyote chasing the Road Runner on Danny's TV. And just as the scene of the CL tour ends with Wendy and Jack turning left and walking toward the mirror between those two bird paintings on Closing Day, Danny turns left in the hallway before seeing the twins cut to pieces, like ghosts of Christmas yet-to-come.

So, was the hotel operating like Plato's Allegory of the Cave, with the images telegraphing what was to come? Was it feeding its audience – Jack, Wendy, and Danny – subliminal messages, and thereby conditioning them in the ways it wanted them to behave? Was it fueling Jack's aggression, normalizing extreme competition and the virility of a "lone wolf" machismo? Or was Jack somehow writing those pictures into life, conjuring the "words" to become "flesh"? Or was it all just a coincidence and my experience in Brazil had simply left the smell of burnt toast in my eyes, one that led me to read more into those paintings than was actually there?

What suggested the paintings were indeed intended to be as much a reflection as a preview of what was in store for Danny and Jack? In the next scene, we see Jack eating his bacon and egg yolk in bed. Recall that Danny had been watching Road Runner cartoons earlier. Well, Nicholson had starred as a cuckoo bird in his previous film. Like rabbits and even chickens, cuckoos have been known to eat their young and their own eggs. And Danny is obviously Jack's "yoke," while Jack is eating an egg "sonny" side up: just the way he likes them. But again, despite talking about cannibalism and Jack drinking Jack Daniels, my first instinct was to doubt myself, and dismiss all this as just more curious but ultimately meaningless coincidences. Having grown up in a society that prospers by selling insecurity, the one virtue I'd practiced more faithfully than any other over the course of my life was self-doubt. So, doubt myself I did, faithfully and devoutly.

But then we see Danny running into the maze with Wendy. Not only has Danny mysteriously changed his clothes, leaving us to wonder why, but Wendy just happens to be dressed just like Jack will be when he chases Danny into the maze at the end of the film. This also was curious for a couple of other reasons. First, because Danny is dressed like Wendy in Boulder, with blue overalls and a red sweater, with the back seat of his trike and the straps of his overalls resembling the shape of the dresses worn by the twins. Also, on the last day we see Jack, he is typing away in his green shirt before he likewise changes his outfit back into his red jacket and blue jeans when Wendy comes to knock some sense into his head with her trusty baseball bat – as if she were "Bat Woman."

It was then that I remembered something else. Long before I ever noticed how the paintings in the CL served as a prologue to a play, what first struck me as curious about the film were the colors of the attire worn by Jack, Wendy, and Danny. What caught my eye about those colors was how they tended to mirror each other in one way or another, and flip like a light switch over the course of the film. The simplest example is how Jack and Lloyd wear red jackets, while both Delbert and Jack in the final photograph wear black tuxedos, and Jack talks to both while looking into a mirror. We also see this with the color of the outfits worn by Jack and Wendy over the course of the film, with the former wearing greens, gold, then red, and the latter wearing red then yellow then green.

Then there is the fact that some of their wardrobe sometimes appears to mirror each other. Jack gazes out of the "impossible window" in the Overlook apartment, for example, while wearing a bathrobe that is similar in color to the one Wendy will be wearing when she wakes up on Jack's side of the bed after locking him in the "story room:" blue. And, when Danny watches Road Runner cartoons again while in the Overlook apartment, he not only sits where Wendy sat as Jack ate his egg yolk, but also in the exact same spot on the bed where Jack sat in the earlier scene as Jack stared out the window behind the TV (or was he staring at the TV, like Danny does?). And when all three of them sit in the same spot, they are each wearing a bathrobe – a *bath*-robe which is conspicuously absent from the woman in the bathtub in room 237.

Notice also the directions they face and how the colors of their robes appear to reverse. Wendy facing Jack is 180-degree difference from when Jack turns to look at Danny in his Mickey Mouse sweater, for example, while both Jack and Danny face the TV and the window. When Jack sits on the bed, he wears a blue greenish robe over dark blue long-johns, similar in color to Danny's Mickey Mouse sweater, while when Danny sits on the bed, he wears a brown bathrobe that reminds us of his bear pillow in Boulder, over a bright red one-piece pajama. That bear pillow was also a sleeping bag you could crawl into, while the one-piece red pajama reminded me of the union suit worn by Wendy when Danny watched Road Runner cartoons for the first time in Boulder. And as Juli Kearns pointed out, Wendy is not wearing just one union suit, but two!

Were such details meaningless or did they hold some significance? Again, my talent for self-doubt and dismissing my curious nature, honed through decades of Catholicism that encouraged me to trust my religion more than my instincts and to steer clear of asking too many questions, led me to dismiss it all as simply random patterns that were ultimately meaningless. "Bah, humbug!," I told myself, "tis simply my pareidolia entreating my feeble brain to the cliffs of insanity, and nothing more."

Alone, the bird paintings in the CL amounted to just slightly more than nothing at all. But when I remembered how my curiosity had been aroused by the alternating color patterns I had previously noticed in the respective bathrobes of Danny, Jack, and Wendy, the latter seemed to reinforce my earlier suspicion that some deeper design was afoot with the former. Both became breadcrumbs that invited me to follow my tingling Spidey-sense, because these "coincidences" looked like two pieces of a puzzle that were suddenly fitting together as part of a deeper repeating pattern. Of course, I still had no idea as to why or how these two pieces seemed to fit so nicely together, let alone if they even mattered. All I knew was that it was just possible they were trying to tell me something about the nature of Kubrick's legendary secrecy and meticulousness, but only if I was patient enough to learn their language.

Aware of the rumors about Kubrick's insane attention to details, I was still left to wonder just how insane he had been. Had every piece of wall art, and the color of every item in every shot of the film, been deliberately chosen to conform to some larger scheme or design? And if so, why?

Enter Through the Games Room

The more attention I paid to the colors and patterns throughout the film, the more it appeared that the Road Runner, Bugs Bunny, and the paintings in the CL, were not the only coincidences to be found. Nor were the patterns of alternating color symmetries limited to their wardrobes; they extended to the environment as well. And the first place this jumped out at me was in the Games Room.

Kubrick's careful orchestration of colors in the Games Room is all too easy to overlook. That's because, to notice it, we must remember not only the colors of the dresses worn by the twins, but also the colors found in the rest of the Games Room. Compare those colors to what we see in the scene that immediately follows: the all-blue wallpaper in the hallway outside of the Torrance's apartment in the Overlook hotel. The colors of the wallpaper and that of the dresses worn by the Grady twins are practically the same. Even the ceiling was white, reflecting the white ribbons worn like waist belts by the twins. Again, is this simply a coincidence? Alone, the similarity between the colors of the Grady twin dresses and the wallpaper outside the Torrance apartment raised no red flag, so to speak. What did was what came next.

As Stuart walks Jack and Wendy to the front door of their apartment, we see two women trotting down the stairs and making a U-turn. As they do, they say "Goodbye Mr. Ullman." Notice both the path walked and the attire worn by those two women. Like the Grady twins in the Games Room, the two women coming down the stairs, who could also be twins, exit the scene as they make a U-turn, turning to their left, while the Grady twins turned to their right. The thought of whether this was evidence of mirroring prompted a reflexive "Bah, humbug!" until their attire caught my eye.

Like the Grady twin dresses and the wallpaper in the hallway outside the Torrance apartment, the women walking down the stairs are wearing colors, and indeed even patterns, that look too coincidental to be a coincidence. This is because their wardrobe reflected the colors and patterns of the couches, chairs, and even the walls found in the Games Room. And while Danny climbs to stand on a wooden chair, the two women had just come down the stairs; stairs that, along with the banister, happened to be the same beige color as the chair Danny climbs on to retrieve his darts. Like Danny spinning around to see the Grady twins, so Jack also spins around to stare at the women trotting down the hallway, even pausing at the door to get a "second sight" at them. And as Danny's vision is attributed to his "second sight," Jack turns first to his right, then to his left to get his own second sight.

Sure, such mirroring seemed to be pure coincidence. Combined with other details, however, it began to look also like a repeating pattern, both in color and motion. Yet it still seemed rather presumptuous of me to interpret such coincidences as anything other than coincidences. Was I *really* seeing emergent patterns that were inviting me to "come and play with us," or was all this just an example of the tendency we have for seeing familiar shapes and images in clouds or things, like the face of Jesus or the virgin Mary in a water stain or a piece of burnt toast? And if it were the latter, was this something Kubrick was intentionally trying to trigger, and for no reason other than to mess with the minds of his audience? Or, if in addition to this, was it possible he was doing it for other reasons as well?

By chance, a few years earlier, I had read a book by Cambridge Neuroscientist, Daniel Bor, entitled *The Ravenous Brain: How the New Science of Consciousness Explains Our Insatiable Search for Meaning* (2012). From that, I knew about my pareidolia: our mind's highly developed sense of pattern recognition. This ability gave our mind an incredible knack for finding patterns in altogether random information. For Bor, pattern recognition was largely a talent that we had developed to survive in the jungles of pre-civilization, one which had outlived its usefulness in the modern world. In truth, pattern recognition is how we synthesize information, and learn.

Initially, like my own Catholicism, Bor's insights and conclusions led me to put my faith more in my own self-bout than in my own curiosity. As a result, I suspected that I was simply seeing something that wasn't really there; much like the gremlins I'd spied creeping into my room, and like Jack who appeared to be seeing "ghosts" in the Overlook hotel. All I was seeing, in other words, was my own mind's "search for meaning" in random coincidences. Plus, if Kubrick really was orchestrating such details to form repeating patterns, how could I know he wasn't doing so to simply lead me into a maze, like Jack?

Maybe the patterns I was noticing were simply designed to titillate my pareidolia in order to lure me into an endless search for meaning in a maze of mirrors, where no ultimate rhyme or reason existed. Were they simply patterns reflected into infinity? Maybe Kubrick was using a person's pareidolia to lure them into an obsession that they couldn't break free from, until they were frozen in thought about a problem that was intentionally designed to only look like there might be a solution, even though there wasn't. And how could anyone determine if such questions had any answers either way? In fact, this same question was reflected in "the halting problem" theorized by the great code breaker and mathematician Alan Turning, in which it could be impossible to determine whether a computer would halt after finding a solution or run forever and ever. It was just such a problem that now suggested that anyone who decided to enter Kubrick's maze should "Abandon All Hope Ye Who Enter Here."

Bor's perspective colored my own, leaving me unsure either way of what I was seeing or why I was seeing it. Despite this, the more I looked, the more definite patterns seemed to emerge. And while the colors were not always exact matches, neither were the Grady twins. And like the Grady twins, even when the colors were slightly different, the similarities always seemed pretty close, while the frequency of those similarities seemed too frequent to be the result of chance alone, especially with a man famed to be as meticulous as Kubrick at the helm.

To give but a few examples, consider the costumes worn by Wendy and Jack I mentioned earlier. Note that Jack is dressed in the same colors toward the second half of the film that Wendy wears in the beginning of the film, only inside out. Also, Jack's red jacket outfit is the same as Danny's when Danny first arrives at the Overlook, only the colors are reversed, with Danny wearing a blue jacket with red letters on it. Note too that when Danny encounters the bloody twins in the hallway, he is also wearing a red jacket with a hood on it. During his two rides around the CL and 237 hallways, with the camera chasing him, the back of the seat of his trike blends with the shoulder straps of his overalls to not only resemble the dresses worn by the twins, but also Wendy's outfit in Boulder. And, during both of his scenes in the maze, despite several costume changes between the two scenes, Danny is wearing the same outfit, only in the second scene he is without the protection of a jacket and his toy Star Trek phaser. While we first see Danny eating lunch with his trusty phaser beside him, Jack is armed with his trusty axe as he and Danny play hide-and-seek like the Coyote and the Road Runner. Yet despite Danny lacking a jacket to protect him from the cold, it is Jack who freezes to death in the maze, despite his jacket, and his axe, while Danny never appears to get cold at all.

Of course, all of this looked like little more than my own pareidolia run amok. And I had to wonder if Bor was right, and maybe that's all it really was. But then I recalled some of Carl Jung's concepts that got my head spinning again. Jung talked about synchronicity, which he said, "described circumstances that appear meaningfully related yet lack a causal connection." The contrast between the various patterns that appeared to be orchestrated with precision on the one hand, and the countless continuity errors that seemed to plague the film on the other, looked like just that: something that appears related but appears to lack a causal connection. But why?

Why would Kubrick juxtapose such precision with so many mistakes; so many in fact it looks as if all of them are equally intentional? Was the entire film reflective of the same "harmony of opposites" we see in both the opening shot and the final photograph of Jack, where he stands like both Jesus Christ and Baphomet? Or was there more to it than that? And most importantly of all, would asking such questions help me piece together Kubrick's puzzle, or was there no puzzle, just the scent of one that was designed to lead us around by the nose until we were trapped in the gravity of chasing our own tail?

Hell, for all I knew, plenty of people had already seen these very same patterns. But that didn't mean such patterns proved an underlying synchronicity was operating in *The Shining* that actually led anywhere or could be used to understand anything. None of it proved there was any kind of final solution to Kubrick's mind-maze. But that didn't change the fact that I wanted to know, maybe even needed to know, if there was.

And since my initial intention was to consider whether everything that was going on in *The Shining* could be explained without having to blame the devil or forces of "supernatural evil," my first instinct was to consider whether Kubrick was using the "magical medium" of the silver screen in a whole new way, as either a theater or an impossible window into the mind of Jack.? The former invited me to consider what I knew about the theater, and how mistakes could often be used intentionally to call the attention of the audience to think outside of the box of the stage, or in this case the screen. And the latter invited me to consider if what was contributing to Jack losing his mind were not ghosts or demons, but the "shining" itself, which both he and Danny seemed to have, or be suffering from. After all, Dick mentions to Danny that even the Overlook Hotel has something like the shining to it. This may be why it is only later in the film that Wendy begins to exhibit such "shining" abilities when she sees the things she sees. So, since the most automatic and natural thing our brains do is spot patterns, I wondered if the patterns I was seeing where an invitation to be an artist myself, and dare to see *The Shining* in a whole new light. If *The Shining* was really an inkblot test, then it was inviting me to explore the possibilities of what it could teach me about myself. And to do that, I had to explore the theater of the mind that Jack built.

TWO

THE THEATER OF THE MIND OF JACK

All the world's a stage

William Shakespeare

The mind is its own place, and in itself,
can make a heaven of Hell, a hell of Heaven

John Milton

IS KUBRICK REDUCING ALL THE WORLD'S STAGE down to the level of Jack's mind? One clue that he may have been doing just that is the disjointed nature of the hotel itself. Another is how Kubrick juxtaposes various scenes. On a stage, characters are free to enter and exit through any of the three or four walls available to them, and do so with a fluidity and naturalness that only seems strange when looked at from the perspective of the real world. This is the same perspective an audience unconsciously relies on when watching a film. We see examples of this when Jack and Wendy enter the lobby from opposite ends via the kitchen; when Stuart tells Wendy and Jack about the hedge maze only as they and Bill Watson all *return* to the hotel, as if they'd missed it (like the audience did in the opening scene) when they supposedly walked past it to wherever we then see them returning from; and even Danny riding his trike from the utility hallway in the lobby to the hallway outside of their apartment one floor above.

Like casting Danny Lloyd and Jack Nicholson to play Danny and Jack Torrance, the shifting nature of the hotel seems intended to, at least in part, suggest the silver screen that forms the boundary between fact and fiction is less a wall of separation and more like a permeable membrane. In fact, the belief in such a wall operates as the real illusion. We think we are watching a film even as the disjointed set design of the Overlook suggests we may in fact be watching a "play;" a "play" in which Nicholson gets to act like an "adult boy." In the novel, it was a play that Jack had begun to write, before he discovered the scrapbook and decided instead to write a tell-all book about the Overlook.

In addition to the idea that "all work and no *play*" suggests Jack is working on a play, evidence that Kubrick is using the silver screen like a theater stage can also be found in the various items that move around or simply disappear, both in the hotel and in the film overall. From the cigarette that appears to come and go from the ashtray on Stuart's desk during the interview, to the chair and table that disappear behind Jack in the CL when Wendy offers to bring Jack a couple sandwiches, to paintings and even the black and white photographs seen in the Gold Room hallway, the displacement of such items suggest there were invisible "stage hands" – people who work behind the scenes moving around props and building the scenes during a performance, like the bloody hand print we see on the seat of the woman's dress who causes Delbert to crash into Jack – who were working behind the scenes, as it were, on the stage of Kubrick's silver screen.

The idea that the world is really a stage and life is a play is not exactly new. It was first used as part of a short story in 1941 by Theodore Sturgeon entitled, "Yesterday Was Monday." And, if we do the math, it turns out the first day we see the Torrances alone in the hotel, "A Month Later," was December 1, 1980 – a *Monday* – while the first cue card we see announcing an actual day of the week is Tuesday. This same idea later turned up in a 1986 episode for "The Twilight Zone." Entitled "Matter of Minutes," that episode was about people who inhabited a world where the fabric of material reality, rather than being a fixed thing, was instead built second by second, and minute by minute, by an invisible corps of builders. In 20*11*, a similar idea was used to underpin the material reality of characters in *The Adjustment Bureau*, with Matt Damon and Emily Blunt.

Curiously, this idea traces its origins back to a heretical scientific sect of Islam known as the Mutakallimūn. For them, this was in fact how material reality actually worked. And when did the Mutakallimūn argue that reality was like a theater stage upon which the props of the present had to be built second by second and minute by minute? The *eleventh* century.

From this perspective, all of the inconsistencies found in Kubrick's *Shining* may be the result of the inability of those stagehands – that worked everywhere around the hotel like my own shadowy gremlins – to always keep up with the task of building the present moment. And again, such a perspective offered at least one way to explain the disjointed nature of the Overlook hotel and the inconsistent directions characters often come and go from scene to scene.

Kubrick also saw the silver screen as "a magic medium," through which someone could communicate to an audience in multiple and often indirect ways. And because he did, he further felt that the best way to use that medium was to communicate in ways that invited the audience to participate in deciphering his meaning or his message. In fact, this idea serves as the basis of one of Kubrick's favorite books: *The Code Breakers: The Story of Secret Writing*, by David Kahn. As Kubrick explained:

> If you really want to communicate something, even if it's just an emotion or an attitude, let alone an idea, the least effective and least enjoyable way is directly. It only goes in about an inch. But if you can get people to the point where they have to *think a moment what it is you're getting at, and then discover it, the thrill of discovery goes right through the heart.* (Emphasis added)

Perhaps more than any of his other films, every error, and in fact even every anomaly, in *The Shining* – whether included intentionally or otherwise – invites each member of the audience to play with the idea of "whether there are other better ideas" that may explain why a man as meticulous as Kubrick decided to include them. Each error, as such, operates as an invitation to the audience to become artists themselves, and to potentially experience the "thrill of discovery" that "goes right through the heart" that can come only from discovering a new meaning to the events in the film which was just waiting to be drawn out of the screen like King Arthur drawing Excalibur from a stone. However easily overlooked, perhaps such errors, which constitute something "only those who shine can see," are part of Kubrick's true art. And this is because Kubrick's inclusion of various errors in the film, while they may look like mere oversights to the novice, to an artist look like a reliance by an auteur on a technique known as "the distancing effect."

The Distancing Effect

After Jack sits at the bar wishing he could sell his soul for a "goddamn glass of beer," he covers his eyes with his hands the way Danny did when he saw the bloody bodies of the Grady twins in the hallway. After pulling his fingers down over his eyes, giving his eyes the shape of the eyes on the bear costume and mirroring Danny looking through his fingers after he sees the twins in the hallway outside of their apartment, Jack then looks directly at the camera, and the audience, and says "Hi Lloyd!" In doing so, Jack breaks "the fourth wall," which is the movie screen itself, in order to address the audience directly. And by doing so, Jack has the same effect on the audience as both the various black and white cue cards and the shadow of the helicopter seen scurrying along the base of the mountain in the opening scene. What all three of these events have in common, even though two are clearly intentional and one looks like it is clearly a mistake, is that each is an example of a theatrical technique known as the distancing effect.

Also known as the alienation effect, or a-effect, the distancing effect is an idea central to the dramatic theory of the German dramatist-director Bertolt Brecht. Brecht conceived of this effect and used it as part of a political mission in the theater. Inspired by the philosophies of G.W.F. Hegel and Karl Marx, and by Viktor Shklovsky's theory of *ostranenie* ("making it strange," or defamiliarization), it involves the use of techniques designed to distance the audience from mere emotional involvement in the play through jolting reminders of the artificiality of the theatrical performance.[17]

---

[17] https://www.britannica.com/art/alienation-effect

For Brecht, these jolting reminders were designed to help spectators understand the complex nexuses that historical development have in creating societal relationships. By creating stage effects that were strange or unusual, Brecht intended to assign the audience an active role in the production by forcing them to ask questions about the artificial environment of a theater stage, and how each individual element related to real-life events.[18] The point in doing this was so "the audience could no longer have the illusion of being the unseen spectator (like those sitting in the helicopter) at an event which is really taking place,"[19] an idea Kubrick alludes to every time Jack, the Grady twins, Danny, or whoever, looks directly into the camera. Brecht used such a technique to draw the audience into the story, in the hope that by doing so they would distance themselves emotionally from problems that required intellectual solutions and new ways of perceiving and thinking.

Two reasons make sense for why such mistakes are intentional. The first is how Kubrick's use of the one-point perspective, which he used so often in his films that it is seen as his signature style, likewise draws an audience into the shot. The second is that what we call mythology today, and *The Shining* is clearly the retelling of various mythologies mixed together, was also designed to invite the audience to come and play a role in the story. By doing so, mythologies were intended to invite the audience into helping find solutions to the social problems the story illuminated. And the oral tradition that conveyed those stories, unlike the written word, assured those myths reflected current events and problems.

---

[18] https://en.wikipedia.org/wiki/Distancing_effect#cite_ref-8

[19] John Willett, ed. and trans., *Brecht on Theatre* (New York: Hill and Wang, 1964), 91

In addition to the cue cards and Jack looking directly into the camera and saying, "Hi Lloyd," we also see an example of the distancing effect when Jack says "a little slow tonight, isn't it?" Not only does Jack make this comment while staring at the audience, but it is also as much a comment being made by Jack Torrance regarding the Gold Room as it is a comment by Nicholson addressing the audience about the movie. Up to that point, the movie has been pretty slow on action or drama, especially for a movie Kubrick called "a masterpiece of modern horror." Just as we thought we were about to see something scary as Danny wanders into the dreaded room 237, which served as one of the more chilling scenes in the novel, much to our disappointment, our voyeuristic ambitions evaporate as the camera crossfades to Wendy in the boiler room.

Other examples that operate like the distancing effect include the spatial impossibility of the rooms in the Overlook hotel itself, which makes the hotel appear more like a theater stage than any physical space that could exist in reality. As mentioned already, in addition to the inconsistent angles from which characters enter and exist scenes, which are clearly intended to demonstrate something strange about the space within the Overlook, even the furniture and other various items that move about or simply disappear reflect the idea of stagehands moving stage-props around between scenes during a play. In fact, even the woman in the gold dress who causes Delbert to crash into Jack has a bloody red handprint on her derriere ire. Perhaps even more interesting than this, however, is how the mind itself is a place, as John Milton pointed out, which can operate just like a theater stage, that "can make a heaven of hell or a hell of heaven." And in Kubrick's *Shining*, the

Overlook appears to look like one to Jack, and the other to Danny and Wendy.

Into the Theater of the Mind of Jack

Since it seemed clear that Jack was going insane from "cabin fever," regardless of anything else, the first place to look for answers to Kubrick's puzzle was in the mind of Jack. More than just reflecting the nature of a theater stage and how fact and fiction are often distinctions without a difference, the disjointed nature of the hotel layout, like the moving and vanishing of items throughout the film, also reflected the fractured nature of the human mind itself, especially in our dreams. Indeed, the nexus between all fact and fiction is the human mind that labels everything as one or the other, especially as we age. From Alzheimer's to schizophrenia to forgetfulness to the forging of false memories, our mind often works just like a theater stage or a movie screen. Even our ideas become moving pictures in our head that we reshuffle from time to time, filling in gaps where they occur or conflating details that we are convinced are accurate, even when they're not. Oblivious to the unconscious editing we do to our memories, we enjoy the bliss that comes from a mind that unconsciously stitches such gaps together into a seamless role of film, one we interpret as gospel fact, even if it is mostly or purely fiction. The question, of course, was whether this was what Kubrick was intimating with his choreography of dancing details that all foreshadowed what fate had in store for the Torrances.

While not a new idea, the "theatre of the mind" is useful for understanding events in both *The Shining* and our own head. Since the days of Aristotle, such a perspective has been used to try and understand consciousness. And in trying to understand Danny's "shining" episode, perhaps it suggests a connection between the bear pillow we see Danny wake up on in Boulder; the bears we see in the picture over Danny's bed in the Overlook apartment; the bearskin rug seen in front of the fireplace in the CL where Jack types his play; and the bear suited man in the upper room "playing" with the man dressed in a tuxedo, like the one worn by Delbert Grady and Jack in the final photograph. Like the paintings in the art gallery in Brazil, what's odd is how the thing that led me to connect those bears was how they broke the fourth wall by reaching out of the screen to remind me of a fellow who wrote a book in 1997 entitled, *In the Theater of Consciousness: The Workspace of the Mind*.

The author of the book that the bears brought to mind is a theoretical neurobiologist, Bernard J. Baars. In his book, Baars presents consciousness as a "stage" on which our sensations, perceptions, thoughts, and feelings, play to a vast yet silent audience. That silent audience is the immensely complicated inner workings of the brain's unconscious processes. Like the map of the world on the wall in Stuart's office, the more official name for Baars' theory is the Global Workspace Theory, or GWT.

According to GWT, consciousness operates like a stage light in a theater of one's own mind. "Conscious contents resemble a bright spot on the stage of immediate memory," Baars explains, "selected by a spotlight of attention under executive guidance. Only the bright spot is conscious; the rest of the theater is dark and unconscious;" much like where the "shadow side" that Carl Jung said inhabits our subconscious tends to grow; like the devil's ivy seen in Stuart's "head" office.

In the novel, Stephen King even uses language that reflects Baars' observation. He does this when he describes Dick and Danny as having a "tight" relationship because they both share "the shining," which operates like "a kind of searchlight in their heads." Coincidentally, in one version of the myth of Theseus and the Minotaur, Ariadne gives Theseus a shining crown that acts like a headlamp that allows him to see his way through the maze.

Nor is this relationship limited to just Danny and Dick. King even suggests the idea that Jack, Wendy, and Danny, may all be trapped inside the maze of one shared theater of mind – a single mind-space, as it were – when he writes of Wendy, "in sleep . . . she felt that the three of them had been permanently welded together," fused together in "their three/oneness."

Baars' ideas about "the theatre of mind," King's "three oneness," and Kubrick erasing the line between fact and fiction at the nexus of human perception, led me to wonder if the "shining" – which Jack, Wendy and Danny all appeared to share on some level, or which the Overlook Hotel somehow constituted or provided them – was the result of all three of them mulling around in the same dark theater of a single yet collectively shared mind-space.

Maybe that was what Kubrick's "shining" really was. Maybe it was a way in which each person could "shine" their conscious awareness, like a flashlight or spotlight, onto the subconscious thoughts that one or more of the others were having, even if those others were wholly unaware that they were having them, let alone that anyone else was privy to them. Were their most private thoughts as open to each other as they supposedly are to, say, an "all seeing God"? Today, various institutions

54

collect and mine the endless amount of information we generate online to find patterns and learn our most intimate secrets. Hell, according to Edward Snowden, the NSA has been doing this for years!

So, was that it? Was each of them, as a result, therefore operating like the East German "stasi" or Thought Police – otherwise described as "thinkpol" in George Orwell's dystopian novel, *1984* – of the other person's mind? But instead of living behind the wall in East Berlin or America, each of them was unaware that the hotel was empowering them to "overlook" the contents of each other's minds, so that 'nothing was their own,' as Orwell wrote in *1984*, "not even the few cubic centimeters inside your skull." Like that wall separating East and West Berlin, the walls of the hedge maze are also "thirteen feet high." And like the final photograph, this idea was central to the dystopian novel by Russian writer Yevgeny Zamyatin, entitled *We*, which was published in... drum roll please... 1921.

Mind-Space Twins

Fact being almost always stranger than fiction, there are at least two real world examples that reflect the reality (or at least the idea) of twins sharing the same "theater of the mind" or mind-space, much like Jack and Danny, Danny and Dick, and even the Grady twins, all appear to do. One of those examples is both physical and mental, while the other is purely psychological. An example of the first can be found 600 miles north of Timberline Lodge, in Vernon, British Columbia, in a pair of identical twins named Krista and Tatiana Hogan.

Like Alexie and Alexa Grady, the Hogan sisters are identical twins, but they are also conjoined at the head and brain, with each facing in opposite directions. Defined as "conjoined craniopagus twins," the two sisters are connected at the back of their heads and, as a result, happen to share the same physical brain. Because they do, they are an example of two minds dwelling in the same "theater" of a shared brain. What makes their unique situation so intriguing is that they undermine any belief in a perfect prism of subjective experience. And they do because, to some degree, each is privy to the "subjective" experiences of the other.

Like Tatiana and Krista, it appears that Jack and Danny also constitute a kind of mind-twins, or two degrees of consciousness – one of a man and that of a child – living under one roof. In fact, this very same idea is how trauma is sometimes understood to fracture a person's mind, between an adult on the outside and a wounded child on the inside. And while described to have been physically abused by his own father in the novel, Jack also admits to abusing Danny in the film, right around the same time Danny splits into both Danny and Tony. Through their mutual ability to "shine" (although it is not entirely clear whether Jack can "shine" or not), each therefore seems to be capable of experiencing the other's reality, and therefore the other's trauma. Maybe this is the result of the fact that both Jack and Danny appear to be not only telepathic and clairvoyant – with Jack even apparently becoming telekinetic enough to free himself from the storage room – but because they are, they are both also suffering from the problem of having someone else's voice, and even someone else's trauma, inside their own head: two conditions typically associated with schizophrenia.

One of the hallmarks of schizophrenia is a genuine belief that the voices within your own mind are not your own. We see this when Jack talks to Lloyd and Delbert, and when Danny talks to Tony, with the former feeding on Jack's baser instincts and narcissism, and the latter giving Danny warnings about the future, warnings which Danny tries to avoid by either blacking-out or covering his eyes. Many schizophrenics are convinced that some part of their own experience is at least partially someone, or some*thing,* else's, and often that "something else" is a god or a ghost, an angel or a demon. For serial killer David Berkowitz, otherwise known as the Son of Sam, who began his killing spree in July of 1976, this "other voice" came from his neighbor's dog, Sam. For Danny, this other voice is Tony, a guardian angel of sorts, whom Danny describes as "the little boy who lives in my mouth." Likewise, Danny talks to, and Tony talks through, his own index finger, while Jack is a writer, who basically does the same thing through all his fingers. In fact, when we see him talking to Delbert Grady in the Gold Room bathroom, Jack is also wiggling and, on occasion, looking at his fingers, the same way Danny does when he first talks to Tony in the Boulder bathroom. By talking to their own fingers, are both Danny and Jack just talking to themselves? Or might they even possibly be talking to each other, without realizing it?

How does the ability to "shine" affect both Jack and Danny? Because their ability to shine may allow them to hear the voice of the other person's mind in their own head, is it the cause of a shared schizophrenia between them? Kubrick even suggests as much by showing us Danny while we hear the echo of first Wendy's voice, after Jack returns from room 237, and then hearing Jack's voice, as Wendy backpedals from Jack in the CL. Lloyd and Delbert may simply be Jack's hallucinations, the equivalent of the tricycle and toy cars Danny tends to play with. Danny's ominous visions, on the other hand, may be mere snapshots of thoughts floating through the internal wiring of Jack's mind, or Wendy's, either because Jack is writing his story or because Jack is going insane, or both. While Danny sees the elevators of blood in a vision, Wendy sees them firsthand. Jack and Danny, as such, may simply be experiencing another person's subjective experience of reality, just like the Hogan twins.

However wired together the Hogan twins are physically to each other, Jack and Danny appear to have (at least potentially) a purely psychological (i.e., wireless) connection. Jack and Danny may be less like the Hogan twins, as a result, and more like another pair of mind twins: June and Jennifer Gibbons. If the former constitutes a conjoined brain that houses two minds, the latter are an example of two separate brains living in a conjoined mind. If the brain of the Hogan sisters is like a house with two ghosts living in it, in other words, the Gibbons have two houses between which they play a constant game of tug of war, their brains operating like hands, their single mind functioning as the rope.

Born in Aden in 1963, June and Jennifer Gibbons were identical twins that grew up in Wales. In 1987, they became known as "The Silent Twins" after Marjorie Wallace published their biography in which she details the strange and silent relationship that existed between them. As children, they only communicated with each other, and then only on rare occasions. When they did communicate with each other, they often used a secret language they had created for themselves, one which included the mirroring of each other's actions; like Hallorann and Danny do in the kitchen and Jack and Delbert do in the Gold Room bathroom. A bit like Jack, the Gibbons sisters used their secret language to build an elaborate fantasy life. But then, when the hormonal havoc of puberty set in, the two eventually plunged into a wild spree that led to their incarceration in a hospital for the criminally insane, much like Randle McMurphy.

During their stay in the psychiatric hospital, June and Jennifer began to believe it was necessary for one of them to die. Eventually, Jennifer told Wallace that she and June had agreed that the death of one of them was required for the other to survive. After much discussion, Jennifer agreed to become the sacrificial lamb, a martyr for the normalcy and peace of mind of the other. A few days later, much to Wallace's surprise, Jennifer passed away. With no evidence of drugs or poison ever found in her system, Jennifer's death remains a mystery.

Visiting the hospital a few days later, Wallace recounted that June "was in a strange mood," exclaiming, "I'm free at last, liberated," and "at last Jennifer has given up her life for me." According to Wallace, the girls had a longstanding agreement that if one died, the other must begin to speak and live a normal life.

Such an agreement leaves us to wonder if the pain they shared was a result of living in a world filled with people who were simply incapable of understanding what it must feel like when one person can "shine" in such a way with another. It also leads us to wonder if the relationship between Jennifer and June Gibbons is the same one we see developing between Jack and Danny, much like between Dick and Danny, and whether they know it or not. And while the latter relationship is more compatible, the former is more antagonistic.

If there was anything to the idea that Jack and Danny, and perhaps even Wendy and Dick to some extent, were indeed sharing the same mind space, then I was left to wonder if some or all of the mistakes and continuity errors to be found in the film were designed to reflect the idea that two perspectives were being layered over each other, with each person perceiving two realities at once: their own, and part of someone else's, just like the Hogan and Gibbons twins. As Danny watches a TV, for example, Jack faces an impossible window, as if that window is less a part of the actual hotel, and more just a projection of what Jack sees because, without realizing it, he is seeing with both his own mind and through that of Danny's as well. Perhaps this is also why the cigarette in the ashtray on Stuart's desk, directly in front of Jack, tends to come and go, because Jack's perspective – and we only ever see the cigarette from Jack's perspective in Stuart's office – is shifting between his own channel of perception and one partially colored by Danny's perspective, across from whom sits Wendy smoking her cigarette.

Kubrick even shows us that Danny and Jack have access to each other's minds. We see this when Tony tells Danny that Jack already got the job and is about to call Wendy, while in the Gold Room bathroom, Jack knows that Danny is calling Dick to the Overlook from Miami to help with the "situation." So why is the cigarette sometimes in the ashtray in front of Jack and sometimes not? Well, from Danny's perspective, because Wendy is sometimes holding her cigarette and sometimes she puts it down in the ashtray in front of her.

This theory, if you could call it that, led me to start tracking down continuity errors to see if they reflected synchronicity. And what I found surprised me, not because it validated my theory, but because it revealed something even bigger than that was really going on. But I only saw such a pattern by hunting down every error I could find. And as I did, a clear pattern began to emerge that revealed that Kubrick's continuity errors were not nearly as random or meaningless as they looked at first sight.

Give them a second sight, and you'll begin to see a whole new face peering out from behind the images being splashed across the screen. When I did just that, the game really kicked into high gear. And I couldn't stop playing until I found what I was looking for: the answer to why.

THREE

HUNTING ERRORS

What we call chaos is just patterns we haven't recognized.
What we call random is just patterns we can't decipher.

Chuck Palahniuk

Mistakes are the portals of discovery
James Joyce

WHY WOULD THE MOST METICULOUS director in history make a movie with more continuity errors than any other movie in history? The only way to find out was to be as meticulous in finding and examining all the errors in *The Shining* as Kubrick had been in committing such errors in the first place. Only then could I determine if all the continuity errors in the film were also operating according to a rule, a rule in which each error was relatable to another character's experience in the film, a rule of twins. If they were, would focusing on even the smallest of errors to be found in the film be a complete waste of time, or reveal a pattern of error-twins just like paying attention to colors appeared to reveal a pattern of color twins? If so, then the various items that moved about on Ullman's desk, which looked so random, might instead be the result of an entanglement to other objects in the film. If they were, then they must therefore be operating in some decipherable pattern, just like the various colors in the film. That meant that the pen and the cigarette on Stuart's desk were all moving because of something else happening somewhere else in the film. And if this were true, then potentially every detail in the film was entangled with every other detail in the film. Seeing Kubrick's bigger picture meant trying to connect the errors we see to the events that are entangled with those errors, like connecting dots in a children's coloring book. The question was whether trying to do so might reveal a set of patterns that constituted the fabled "Kubrick Code" that was rumored to exist but had yet to be discovered, let alone cracked and deciphered.

Presented with these and other questions, I was unsure how, or whether it was even wise, to proceed. It was as if Kubrick was luring me into being both Elmer Fud chasing Bugs Bunny, and Wile E. Coyote chasing the Road Runner. Kubrick opens his film with both, even though both Fud and the Coyote are simply modern versions of Sisyphus, which is why they never succeed at catching their prey (much as God chooses to never defeat the devil, even though one is like the sun and the other an ant). And perhaps that was the real point of Kubrick's maze: to turn anyone star-gazed enough to enter into his maze into a Sisyphus who is unable to stop pushing the stone of their own curiosity around inside of it, forever and ever and ever. Wondering about such concerns were futile at this point, however, because my curiosity was already hooked on the patterns I'd found, and there was no way to unhook myself from my addiction to wanting to find more, even if those patterns were only leading me around in a circle, "forever and ....," yeah, you know the rest.

Kubrick's mind-maze, in short, had become my new religion. Like Indiana Jones, the only way to determine if the secrecy that surrounded the filming of *The Shining* was in fact proof that Kubrick had a big shining secret was to dive into it. So, surrendering to the addiction of my own curiosity as any child would, like Nancy Drew or the Hardy Boys, I decided that the best place to start hunting for rabbit tracks that might operate as wormholes between scenes was to begin by cataloging some of Kubrick's mistakes. Only then could I determine if they were indeed, as James Joyce said, a portal to discovering what might prove to be Kubrick's best kept secret. And as it turned out, they were.

Hunting Error Twins in Ullman's Office

Looking for an underlying relationship between Kubrick's continuity errors and other details alerted me to the mistakes we see in Stuart's office. This in turn made me aware of what we hear as Jack enters the manager's office, which also seems like a mistake, even though we never notice it as such. That continuity error is the typing we hear, and the faint sound of a ringing telephone may even be a clue that the typing we hear is Kubrick trying to tell us something through his attention to details.

As a director, Kubrick's attention to detail was nothing short of legendary. Stories about how even the slightest variation between shots, in everything from the lighting to the smallest prop, might send him into a tirade. And it is that same meticulousness that keeps audiences coming back to study his films, again and again, looking for details that may reveal a meaning behind such madness, some deeper or even coded message lying just beneath the surface of his films.

In contrast to stories of such obsessive attention to detail are other stories, stories of how Kubrick would sometimes make changes to a scene intentionally. Asked why, he would simply reply, "no one will notice it anyway." But why would Kubrick be so OCD about details on the one hand, only to then alter such details on the other? Nor were the changes he would sometimes make between shots few in number. In fact, in *The Shining*, Kubrick would sometimes make an incredible number of changes in a scene, but mostly to details that were so minor they would only ever be noticed by the likes of Rain Man. Indeed, sometimes he makes so many changes from shot-to-shot that it makes no sense at all. When catalogued, the intentional injection of so many micro-errors into a scene don't just look like overkill, it looks like those changes are part of some larger design. And if some people believe there are no coincidences in life at all, it was at least as possible that there were none in Kubrick's film as well.

To illustrate the surprising number of seemingly meaningless changes Kubrick would make to a given scene, just consider the many changes made to Stuart Ullman's office during Jack's interview. In addition to the impossible window behind Ullman's desk - which is clearly an intentional continuity error even though, given the disjointed set design of the film, the awareness of it being spatially "impossible" is anything but obvious to the audience - the black fountain pen sitting near the ashtray on the left of Stuart's desk is probably the next most noticeable item in the room to change position between shots, pivoting between pointing toward Stuart's head and pointing toward the impossible window behind him. Other changes include the chairs having been moved closer together; the brown binder and red book on Ullman's desk turn from parallel to slightly askew; the bottom folders in the rack under the window, which are perfectly flat as Jack first enters Ullman's office, tilt like the waterline of St. Mary's Lake; a blue and white notepad moves from the credenza to inside of a brown binder on Ullman's desk, a large manila envelope taking its place next to the radio; the calendar book on Ullman's desk shifts left, and the corner of the page in it becomes dog-eared like the page seen in Wendy's book; Ullman's name plate moves to the left, as does the American flag; the ceramic red eagle on the windowsill behind Stuart slaloms left to right, with the tips of the eagles wings occasionally pointing up behind Stuart's head like devil horns; the eye glasses which Stuart places on his open notebook in the middle of his desk when Jack first enters the office, ends up between the clear pencil sharpener and the steel cup; items change and are added to the open briefcase behind Ullman; more pens are added to the steel cup on the desk; a white pen suddenly appears between the clear pencil sharpener and the date book under Ullman's arms; along with the black fountain pen, that white pen repeatedly pivots or spins around in various directions almost in tandem; the ashtray on the left of Ullman's desk slides toward the paper tray; the cigarette in the ashtray on the right side of Ullman's desk, sitting in front of Jack, the yellow filter of which suggests it is Jack's brand of cigarette rather than Wendy's (which is solid white), comes and goes; Ullman's hand gestures are often reversed from frame to frame and appear to move in tandem with the pivoting of the pens; and a large dark book that looks like a photo album or the scrap book we later see Jack thumbing through appears out of nowhere directly in front of Ullman in the wide shot of the room, that is not there when either Jack or Watson enter the office, and appears to be absent for the rest of the scene.

So many changes to a Kubrick scene could never be purely by accident, let alone go without Kubrick's notice or concern. Nor is this list exhaustive. And of all of them, the most noteworthy is the notepad with the blue and white spine on it, and how it connects to what we see in the Boulder parking lot, and the Overlook parking lot on Closing Day.

All these changes beg us to consider more closely what else Kubrick may be telegraphing to his audience via these changes. Is there some devil to be found by examining Kubrick's details? As Jack first enters the secretary's office, for example, we hear typing, even though Suzy, Stuart's secretary, is standing in Stuart's office. So, who, or what, is doing the typing? Before we hear the typing, we hear a telephone ringing immediately after Jack leaves the front desk, at 3:21 into the film, along with a garbled voice over a PA system somewhere, like the PA we hear behind Dick Hallorann in Stapleton Airport. Yet the only place we happen to see a PA speaker is in the upper corner of the Games Room when Danny goes to retrieve his darts. So, is Kubrick suggesting with that voice, one which echoes our own questions (like where was the hedge maze in the opening shot of the Overlook?), that we, along with Jack, have just walked into his cinematic Games Room?

Like the fact we hear typing even though Susy is in Stuart's office, so the telephone ring we hear is too distant to be coming from either the reception desk or the manager's office. So, it must be coming from either behind the cashier window, which Jack walks by as he then walks in front of the "Camera Walk" sign, or the black payphone we later see in the utility hallway (seen behind Jack as he flings the silver "rings" on the floor). Clearly, the ringing phone is deliberate, as is the fact that it is coming from somewhere other than the reception desk or the manager's office. And, when we look at it more closely, its timing seems too precise to be completely meaningless.

So, is there a meaningful relationship between the typing and the ringing? Let's see. As Jack passes the cashier window, we see an employee hand a piece of paper to a seated man in a green sweater, at 3:24. (If there is entanglement operating in the film, what other scene might this scene reflect that has always bedeviled the audience?) At 3:26, during a second telephone ring that started a second earlier, we hear the first mysterious "sha" sound in the film as Jack walks over the exact spot he will later plunge his axe into the chest, and the heart, of Dick Hallorann. The typing starts immediately after the second ring ends, at 3:27, a variation of 237, as if to suggest that Jack's typing, and the writing of his "play," has now commenced. It starts ringing again at 3:29. Notice too how 4, 6, and 9, are all twins, but at different angles.

The ringing telephone in the distance reminded me of Pavlov's dog, conditioning Jack to act as mechanical in his desire to murder his family as his typewriter in typing the same sentence, over and over again, forever. From this perspective, it is as if the sound we hear from what must be a teletype machine in the back of Suzy's office, and the "sha" sound we hear as Jack enters the "head office" area, constituted Jack sliding the roller of his typewriter back to the left, just like he does after Wendy walks out of the CL after her and Jack's row. Note too how, in the timestamp of 3:21, when we heard the first ringing bell, the number "1" is the lesser twin to the number "7". And in room 237, we hear a heartbeat, as if the ringing telephone and the typing are the electrical and mechanical heart beats of the Overlook itself.

At exactly 3:33, after having just passed through the double doors to the General Manager's office area, Jack glances to his left – 'overlooking' the typing we hear – and the typing abruptly stops. It starts up again at exactly 3:36, as if Jack were again sliding the roller back on his typewriter during the three second interval, or the typist had slipped through a tunnel and, like a cell phone or a radio, lost its signal. And 3:36, of course, reflects doubles.

Although not obvious at first, the sound of typing in the back of Susie's office leads us to take note of the painting we see on the rear wall in Susie's office area as Bill Watson first enters the "head" office. Entitled, "Flock of Loons," it is yet another painting by Norval Morrisseau, otherwise known as "Copper Thunderbird;" a detail that relates to a red Ford Thunderbird outside of the Boulder apartments. That painting hangs in the same area that Jack glances toward as he walks through the double doors to the receptionist area, at the same moment the typing abruptly stops.

Consider this painting. As if to suggest that Jack has just entered through the gates of hell, set against a backdrop that is mostly red, the group of birds in it are mostly yellow, resembling tongues of flame, like the fire so often burning bright as Jack pounds away on his typewriter like a madman. During the interview, Kubrick even reinforces this idea by having the top tips of the wings to the red eagle on the windowsill stick up behind Stuart's head of red hair on occasion, like horns. On the other hand, and more relevant to what we hear as Jack enters the office, the "loons" in that painting, as if to suggest Jack is entering a lunatic asylum like Nicholson was in his previous film and we suspect Holden Caulfield may be in, also happen to resemble the lever-arms of a typewriter rushing together in a phalanx to ravage a virgin page reflected in the white wall beside it. The red backdrop of that painting suggests that page is dipped in blood. In fact, the white wall having a dark wooden wainscoting at the bottom not only calls to mind the idea of Jack's writing table, but even the question, "what's black and white and red all over?" Even the pause in the typing when Jack glanced to his left began to look like it was orchestrated to reflect the idea of Jack the writer stopping to 'overlook' the words he was typing somewhere.

When looked at in this way, the "Flock of Loons" painting appears at rather curious times and places. We see it as Jack's interview commences, just before we hear the story of Charles Grady, which foreshadows Jack's dream and transformation from Jekyll to Hyde. We see it again as Wendy runs to check the snowcat, right after she locked Jack in "the story room." Her exiting the hotel, and Jack being knocked unconscious and locked in the storage room, both reflect Jack's pause in typing and pulling his piece of paper out of the typewriter. And the last time we see that painting is shortly before Jack loses Danny's tracks in the snow in the hedge maze, as if to reflect the idea that the "play" is over because Jack (both Torrance and Nicholson) has run out of words to type and lines to follow. This would even explain why the "Flock of Loons" painting appears to bookend the beginning and end of Jack's story, and the end of the game he is playing.

With regards to twins or reflections, compare the "Flock of Loons" painting to other details. Behind Wendy in Boulder, for example, we see a twin to that painting in a box of Froot Loops cereal. Like Bill sitting next to Jack, so that cereal box sits right next to the Roberts 2% milk carton, as if the two are telegraphing the idea of Jack reading his "fruity"

70

Playgirl magazine, as Holden might refer to it, and becoming a lunatic dressed as Robert Dupea – the character Nicholson played in *Five Easy Pieces*, ten years earlier – who, in a way, is Jack's "second self."

Also, recall that the island we see in the first shot of the film is called Wild Goose Island, so that the "one" who "flew over the cuckoo's nest" is, in fact, the audience. Hence, the "mirroring" Kubrick engages in here is that Jack chasing Danny into the maze is a like Jack going on a "wild goose chase just like Wile E. Coyote chasing the Road Runner in the cartoon Danny is watching, and Elmer Fud hunting the Bugs Bunny Danny is wearing on his jersey – a blue and white jersey, like the spine on the notepad in Stuart's office. And when Danny watches the Road Runner, Wendy is reading a book about a boy who complains about "flits" and "fruits" (transvestites or homosexuals) who is potentially housed in a mental asylum, a cuckoo's nest which houses a "flock of loons."

By strategically placing the "Flock of Loons" painting in the receptionist area so that we see it when Bill simultaneously enters the head office while appearing to exit the side of Wendy's head, Kubrick uses even the smallest of details to communicate subtle meanings. And notice the significance of what we see when we do. On the file cabinet outside of the office, we see a red ball in a box, as if to mirror the "July 4th Ball," with "Jack in the box" of a picture frame; a green elephant figurine sitting next to it – the "elephant in the room," as it were, in contrast to the purple ("Royalty?") elephant on the bottom of the poster board in Danny's bedroom. The light switch under the four scenic pictures to the right of Ullman's office door, which we see when Jack walks into the manager's office later to disable the radio, is absent when

Jack first walks into Stuart's office for his interview. It is as if, because Jack must turn on the lights in the office in the later scene, the hotel itself, as if it were alive, is morphing to the needs of the scene, much like a theater stage or the story as written by an author.

Did the light switch appear in order to provide light in the latter scene the same way the impossible window in Stuart's office was said by some to have been included for the same reason? But if the light switch appears out of a need for light in the later scene, then by the same logic, shouldn't the impossible window then disappear, since it was dark as pitch outside that window? Or would that simply be too jarring a change for people to accept?

And like Jack in the box of a picture frame, so we also see that the walls outside of Ullman's office are black and white, just like the photo Jack ends up inside of like a piece of frozen meat, while the walls inside of Ullman's office are a warm salmon pink, as if Jack entering Stuart's office, both for his interview and when he goes to disable the radio, is like Jack disconnecting from reality to enter the "holy of holies:" the vaginal walls of the woman in room 237.

Other details in the opening scene also began to look as if they were potentially designed to reflect deeper significance. Consider just the colors of the map we see above the radio. Of Colorado, that map is apportioned into sections of colors green, pink, yellow, and light blue. Is it just a coincidence that these colors just happen to be the same colors of the pencils seen sitting on the table to the left of Jack's white or beige Adler typewriter as Jack plays ball with himself in the Colorado Lounge, "A Month Later"? And is it also just a coincidence that Jack's two typewriters reflect half of the black and white, and half of the brown and tan sepia pictures?

On the wooden wicker chair that sits below the wall map of Colorado and between the credenza and the rear door to Stuart's office, sits a box which hugs the left corner of the screen. That box sits on an orange cushion, a color that King associates with "shining" in the novel, because whenever Dick receives a shine from Danny, he smells oranges. That box has a red dot that bounces back and forth like a ping pong ball in and out of the left-hand corner of the fame, as if to represent the part of Jack that he is repressing, which rears its ugly head from the rabbit hole of Jack's subconscious with the change in Jack's personality when Wendy interrupts his first night of typing in the CL. It also mirrors the idea of the red dot we see on a screen called a recording indicator, as if Jack entering Stuart's office means recording is now in progress.

A picture sitting on that chair and behind that box appears to be of a man in the mountains ice fishing with his sled dogs. It hints of the idea of the Donner party, as if it were a painting of the husband of Susan Robertson – the woman who the news reported was on a hunting trip but has been missing for *10* days – engaging in cannibalism of Susan's remains. As Joe Girard pointed out on his website, eyescream237.ca, that painting is by Clarence Gagnon.[20] Painted in 1931 and entitled "Trapper's Camp," - with both Jack and Susan's husband leading their family into a trap, just like Abraham leads his son Isaac, and God leads Adam & Eve, Jesus, and, by extension, all of humanity (the latter of

[20] https://eyescream237.ca/come-together-right-now-over-me-a-guide-to-all-the-shinings-buried-art/

which are expected to praise God their whole life for having been so led) - the next time we see that painting is when Wendy runs upstairs and sees the two men playing together in the upper room. Who is being trapped, we are left to wonder, Jack, the audience, both?

The box that painting leans against appears to have the number "4" written on it, like the numeral 4 we see on Danny's jersey as he eats lunch watching the Road Runner, while the *two* men Wendy later sees just happened to be on the *fourth* floor. And Danny will later stand on a chair to see the twins in the Games Room and hide inside of a metal box right outside the backdoor to Stuart's office. On closer examination, the box has three red dots on it, but two of them are smaller and faded, as if one is Jack in his red jacket, and the other two reflect Delbert and Lloyd.

Above the chair are two black and white pictures. Like the bird painting in the CL that appear to foreshadow Jack chasing Danny down the utility hallway in the lobby with an ax, the lower photograph appears to foreshadow Danny standing outside the hotel looking back up at Wendy as she struggles to crawl out of their bathroom window. In that photo, that hotel is still being built, which places the date of such a photo between 1907 and 1909, even as Danny stands outside the hotel as Jack's plans begin falling apart. Add up the numbers of the year 1908, and we get 18, or $6 + 6 + 6$. And in contrast to Danny looking back up at the bathroom window, as if she is Rapunzel, the photo is during the day.

Then there are the plaques and frames on the wall opposite the radio and the map of Colorado. In a picture frame, we see a rainbow of colors, the same colors of the hexagonal carpet pattern in the hallway outside of room 237. Set against a black background, the rainbow in Stuart's office is in contrast with the Snoopy rainbow sticker seen on the white door of Danny's bedroom, above which sits a sticker of Woodstock who appears to be floating into a blue and white sky holding a similar rainbow balloon, as a red cardinal protrudes from Woodstock's tail. We see what vaguely resembles another red cardinal "A Month Later," right below and blue and white striped butterfly that is the twin to Danny's Apollo sweater, right next to a vanity mirror, with sunlight streaming in through the bedroom window – which, we later discover, is yet another impossible window.

What makes these rainbows more curious is the fact that it may explain, at least in part, why we see an outside window in Stuart's office. This is because, to see a full rainbow, there must be a broad enough angular region of a rainy sky illuminated by direct sunlight. That rainbow also relates to the shadow in the Kensington parking lot and the number on Danny's Bug's Bunny jersey: 42. And this is because a rainbow can only be seen from raindrops that fall anywhere along an angle of 42 degrees between the viewer and their shadow.

Beside the rainbow picture, we see a larger frame, this one with a blue and white page inside of it, with a large white letter "A" stamped in the blue, reminding us of the A-frame ladder we see in the lobby on Closing Day, as if to begin the alphabet soup that Jack will write for us to start consuming through our eyes. A man seen installing the CASHIER sign on Closing Day, who also stands on a smaller A-frame ladder, is also wearing an oversized baseball cap, large enough for the audience to notice even though he is in the background, that is the same color blue and white as the paper in the picture frame on Stuart's wall, and both are the same colors of the spine of the notepad that mysteriously jumps from the radio to inside the brown binder on Stuart's desk.

Above and on either side of the office, we also see shelves where potted plants sit like spectators on the mezzanine level waiting for the show to begin. The plants growing there are curious. They're called pothos, but are also know by other names, including money plant, golden pothos, and devil's ivy. Able to flourish even when neglected for long stretches of time, they're almost impossible to kill. They'll adapt to any room they are placed in and will even thrive in places where there is limited sunlight. Its leaves are either solid green, like the sweaters and shirt Jack wears when he is typing, or they are green with a golden rim, the same colors Jack wears on Closing Day.   And Jack, like a "green man" that reflects the idea of cultivating one's "green thumb," always wears green when he types in black and white.

Outside the impossible window behind Stuart, more plants peer through the window as if looking into a fishbowl, as indifferent to the events about to unfold, and as out of focus, as the faces in the black and white photographs we see littering the walls of the hotel, of "all the best people." Their indifference reflects that of the universe, or even God on high, to the horrors of a man aspiring to the saintly status of the great Abraham. In contrast, those plants mirror the enjoyment of the audience looking into the same room from the opposite side of the looking glass we call a camera, which are reflected back to the audience in the throngs of fuzzy smiling faces. Like the chorus in a Greek play, those photographs, of those above the fray that appear to be watching with amusement from the box seats of their black and white photographs, reflect even the enjoyment of the audience in the seats. Indeed, the faces in those black and white photographs watch the events unfolding in the Overlook in the same way the patrons of Rome watched gladiators fight to the death in the Coliseum, and the Gold Room party attendees watched from the mezzanine their millions provided them, as their profits rose on as a tide of blood spilled across Europe in the theater of World War I.

And then there's the paper tray.

The Phallic Paper Tray

The paper tray on the corner of Stuart's desk, which Kubrick uses in every scene inside Stuart's office, deserves a second look. One theory, touched on in the documentary *Room 237*, was that Kubrick has Stuart walk around to the side of his desk to greet Jack, in part, so that the flashing on the upper level of that paper tray could be used as a phallic representation of Stuart having a "hard-on" for Jack. But is this Jack Torrance or Jack Nicholson agreeing to play the role of Jack Torrance? Presumably, this is why Stuart says, "our people in Denver recommended Jack and for once, I agree with them." For many people, this theory, however amusing, is simply dismissed as wholly ridicules. But is it?

The tray can be seen directly under Suzy's blouse and pointed directly at her vulva. A red book on Stuart's desk is seen just at the end of the tray, like the burning end of a cigarette. And the pink pages of Susie's notebook, which she holds to her chest with both hands clasped together, standout against the brown of her blouse; and all of it appearing to drip with sexual, and perhaps even racial, innuendo. But is any of that innuendo intentional, or am I simply reading into such detail my own racial and even sexual taboos? And to what extent is the flashing also being used to reflect the sexual prowess of the Ull-man to that of Nicholson, as a "dick (Halloran) measuring contest," which is reflected even

77

in the larger "power" necktie Stuart wears, while Jack's necktie seems more like a dog-leash, with one of Jack's screams in the CL even sounding like the bark of the dog we hear outside the Boulder apartment?

Alone, interpreting the flashing on the paper tray as a phallic extension of Stuart's manhood looks farfetched. Yet however farfetched it may look on its own, numerous subtle details in the interview scene strongly support the idea that Kubrick was, on a subliminal level, indeed using the flashing on the paper tray as a phallic symbol. As Jack enters Stuart's office and walks to shake Stuart's hand, for example, if we look closely, we can see two faint orange balls of light follow into the room on Jack's coat tails, 'riding Jack's ass,' as it were. One of those balls of light veers to the left, zeroing in on the paper tray and Stuart's crotch, the other parks just in front of Jack's pelvis. Those balls of light are lens flares, like those seen in the opening scene, and are polygonal, like the hexagon Danny sits on in the 237 hallway.

Seeing those lens flares riding Jack's ass into Stuart's office invites us to reduce our screen to a two-dimensional game board. Behind the ball of light that settles over Jack's crotch we see Stuart's nameplate, white or beige in color (like Jack's first typewriter), slightly smaller, and sitting lower but just as phallic as the black flashing on the paper tray. As Jack steps forward, that nameplate shrinks behind the edge of Jack's coffin-grey sports jacket, like the head of a frightened tortoise retracting into its shell. On the other hand, Ullman - the HNIC, or "head ("N-word") in charge" - stands firm, proudly pulling back his own jacket as if to reveal his black rod-iron manhood, as well as that other phallic symbol for male masculinity in the world of business: the necktie, an officious piece of clothing that stretches from a man's mouth to his penis, which reminds us of lynching and the "CH O KING" signs. Just look at how much larger Stuart's red-power necktie is compared to Jack's green tie. And both ties are knit ties at that, as if the two of them are about to commence knitting together the tall tale we have come to see. In fact, that red tie even makes Stuart Ullman look a bit like Donald Trump.

In the novel, Jack aspired to take Stuart's job. So, is Jack's red jacket an example of a manager in training? Are the "overlookers" watching Jack to see if he has the "belly" for axing people left and right, as is the job of a good manager, regardless of what effect such "firing" has on their ability to "make ends meet"? It's only business after all, even if the result isn't much different than what happened to the Donner party.

Then there are the sexual undertones of the details we see when Jack enters the doorway of Stuart's office. As Jack enters, Stuart scribbles something with his black fountain pen in his secretary's notebook, the cover of which is as brown as Suzy's blouse. Susy stands behind him like a looming shadow. The notebook itself is spread-eagle on Stuart's desk, the pages in it noticeably pink, reflecting, at the very least, Susie's red hair, "and perhaps a bit more." As Stuart scribbles away with his large black fountain pen, his hand directly in front of her vulva, Susie stands directly in front of the four legged totem art on the shelf under the window, holding her left hand on her hip while her right hand appears to be directly on top of the black double-decker paper tray. Her brown blouse also matches the furniture in the room, including the desk and the briefcase she stands directly in front of, which is also spread eagle, opened up like a mouth, as if she were just an inanimate object, a toy to be played with, like Danny's cars or Jack's playmate in 237. The red eagle sitting directly over Ullman's head, frozen in attack position and looking down the length of Stuart's red tie, which is scrolled out like a dragon's tongue or a red carpet into Susie's pink pages, appears to be eyeing Stuart's chicken-scratch, or even mirroring the two men Wendy later sees "playing" together in the upper room.

On the ceiling, the white light fixtures look like longer versions of the two black edges of the paper tray. Both reflect the number "11" turned at a 90-degree angle, like Danny lying in bed and seeing the continuation of the river of blood washing over his eyes.

Told by Stuart to "have a seat," Jack obeys like a dog being told to heel, like pages being dropped into the inbox, while Susy, told to fetch coffee and Bill Watson, walks out of the shot like a curious shadow in the Boulder parking lot walking into an even more curious van.

Notice what happens even as Jack first enters Stuart's office, and how, when considered more closely, it is dripping with sexual innuendo. As Jack knocks on Stuart's door frame, Susie and Stuart (and apparently the red eagle on the windowsill) are all focused intently on what Stuart is scribbling in Susie's pink pages, which are spread eagle on Stuart's desk. Jack knocks – notice the wide-open door – and both look up suddenly, surprised, a bit like Wendy catching two men appearing to have oral sex in the upper room. Stuart quickly removes his glasses, demonstrating he is "far sighted" enough to know Jack is just the man he wants for the hatchet job he needs done, to see who would be brazen enough to interrupt his highness as he dabbled between the pink curtains of one of his underlings.

"Yes?" Stuart responds quickly, thrusting off his glasses in a hurry – a gesture that reflects the idea of two visions or seeing Jack with "second sight" – mouth agape as he awaits a reply.

"I'm Jack Torrance," says Jack.

After hearing Jack's name, Stuart responds by letting out an "Ohhhh!" as if he were having an orgasm, reinforcing the sexual suggestive color of his office, and a verbal twin of the oversized "O" in the "CH O KING" signs we see strategically placed around the hotel.

"Well, *come in Jack*," his invitation a dripping sexual double entendre of Stuart's exclamation, one that not only reflects Jack's Playgirl magazine and foreshadows what Wendy will later see in the upstairs bedroom, but also the comment of Narcissus to Echo of how "we must come together," a line that Echo is then cursed to only repeat, "forever and . . .," you know the rest.

Stuart then hurriedly sheathes his pen back into its holster, a scabbard for his mighty sword, quickly closes the book as if to zip up his fly, fumbling with something caught inside of it as he does (a jam in his zipper, as it were), and hands it to Suzy who cradles it to her chest like a newborn infant, the seed of an illicit union. The modestly of Susy's subsequent posture belies the idea that she had just been caught doing something naughty, with her boss, on his desk, in broad daylight, before a window to the world.

Stuart then jumps to his feet, his left hand appearing to grab Susie's ass as he does, and walks around to the side of his desk, stopping next to his double-decker paper tray and leaning forward to shake Jack's hand. When he does, he assumes a similar posture to the one Jack will take just before disabling the radio, only facing in the opposite direction: like the twins lying dead on the floor in the hallway.

Suzy steps back to let Stuart pass, briefly revealing several red book binders behind her with white labels on their spines, colors that

81

remind us of the Gold Room bathroom. She then steps forward as if to hide them again, as if they constituted the embarrassing evidence of virginity lost, and her illicit encounter "between the sheets" with her boss. All of this seems over the top, of course, until we look more closely at what Kubrick is doing, starting with the paper tray.

Consider the connection of the lens flares over the flashing on the paper tray to the opening sequence. We see the first of Kubrick's lens flares in the opening sequence, just as Barry Nelson's name (who plays Stuart Ullman), which immediately precedes that of Philip Stone (Delbert Grady) and Joe Turkel (Lloyd, the bartender), reaches the exact midpoint of the screen. And we see those flares just as Jack's car enters the tunnel. As it does, the "L" in Nelson's last name even appears to crash into Jack's car just as Jack enters the grey stone tunnel, like a pool cue striking the yellow 1 ball into the side pocket: "Oh, come in Jack." And in the novel, Jack's VW was red.

Curiously enough, at the Stanley Hotel in Este Park, Colorado, there is also a tunnel, in which most of the alleged ghostly activity is said to occur. One of the more frequent sightings of such activity comes in the form of orbs of light. Is it just a coincidence, therefore, that we see lens flares as Jack enters a tunnel at the very same time the names of the two actors who play the two ghosts in the film scroll up the screen?

Contrast that paper tray as a phallic symbol in front of Stuart to other times we see it. When Jack goes to disable the radio, that same paper tray is behind Jack, and is so perfectly perpendicular to the seat of his pants it looks as if both it and Jack are strategically placed side-by-side, reminding us of the "L" in Nelson's name hitting Jack's car into the tunnel pocket like a cue-stick. When Wendy talks to the Forest Ranger later, she places her foot on the desk, wearing a yellow moccasin like the one she wears when she talks to Stuart's female doppelgänger, the doctor, about Danny's episode. Her foot on Stuart's desk looks as if she is kicking that paper tray the same way Mickey Mouse is kicking the football on Danny's sweater. (Even the Goofy figuring is wearing similar yellow shoes to Wendy's moccasins. And while Goofy is an anthropomorphic dog that has a Southern draw and is a good friend of Mickey Mouse, Wendy plays with Danny like a friend and occasionally has a Southern accent as well.) The phallic tray that Wendy appears to be kicking, as such, is "ball less," like the carpet pattern inside room 237, while the Mikey Mouse sweater Danny wears kicks a ball, as if Kubrick is depicting Wendy and Danny to be kicking Stuart in the "cock-n-balls" by escaping the deadly mouse trap Stuart is casting Jack to play in the hotel. And Nicholson, like a mouse in a trap, even only ate cheese sandwiches to get into character: because he hates cheese sandwiches.

When stacked together, these "coincidences" seem increasingly like the kind of precision a man as meticulous as Kubrick might very well be aiming for, especially when we consider the amount of secrecy he required during the filming of *The Shining*, as well as the amount of sexual symbolism he admitted to using in *Dr. Strangelove*. And even if all of this is purely accidental, lens flares and all, it is hard to believe that a man like Kubrick simply overlooked all of it, without as much as a second look.

And there are still other aspects of Jack first meeting Stuart that seem too queerly precise to be accidental. As he and Stuart exchange pleasantries, the red balls of light are triangulated with the red eagle on the windowsill, which is seen directly under Jack's chin. As Stuart and

83

Jack shake hands, their clasped hands line up perfectly with Susie's hands, which she also holds together as she cradles her notebook to her breast like Wendy cradling Danny in the CL. Against her dark blouse, the diagonal edge of the pink pages in the binder, which slash across her chest like an open wound, seems to foreshadow the axe blow Jack will eventually plunge into Dick Hallorann, as Jack becomes a "hack" writer. And behind Susie, a "four" legged totem that is as dark as Dick, Susie's jacket, and even a shadow. Such precision seems intended as a subliminal mix of sex and violence like we see in room 237, the axe as phallic a symbol for Jack as the paper tray and even the fountain pen are for Stuart.

Perhaps nothing confirms Kubrick's sexual innuendos during the scene of Jack and Stuart meeting each other for the first time more than the fact that, when Stuart returns to behind his desk again, the black fountain pen he had been using to dabble between Suzy's pink sheets replaces the paper tray as a symbol of Ullman's black phallus. When Stuart stops behind his desk, the black fountain pen can be seen to align perfectly with the inseam of Stuart's right pant leg; and all with Jack looking up at his master like a dog waiting for a bone, a Nichol -"son" looking up to the Ull -"man," or Roger waiting to fellate Horace Derwent, the owner of the Overlook in the novel. When Stuart placed that black fountain pen back in its holder, recall, it looked as if he were putting his "wick" in the ashtray on the left edge of his desk, next to the paper tray. And when Jack steps forward to tell Stuart he made the trip in three and a half hours – even though Estes Park is only a 40 minute drive from Boulder – we see the ashtray on the right side of the desk strategically situated at Jack's derriere. Jack is crapping cut-glass in his attempt to impress Stuart by putting on airs, in other words; a bit of gas-lighting everyone has to do in an interview – part of the "phoniness" Holden is always complaining about – in order to be hired by someone who will then pay you to allow them to gaslight you for as long as you need the money; in other words, "forever and ever…"

But by far the most compelling piece of evidence for how Kubrick is most definitely using the paper tray as a phallic representation of Stuart's manhood can only be seen in its absence, after we return from Boulder. Look closely at the paper tray when Jack enters Stuart's office. Notice we can see the edge of the red book only to the right of the tray. Directly between the top and bottom trays on Stuart's desk we see what looks like white sheets of paper in the bottom tray, as if subliminally denoting the idea of "sheets of blood," like those pouring out of the elevator, those of a blood-soaked bed, and the ones Jack will later "play" on. Look more closely, however, and we see something else, something that is only evident when we return from Boulder. And it is only evident when we return from Boulder because it is noticeably absent.

Gone from the bottom tray upon our return from Boulder are the white sheets of paper that sat in the lower tray, obscuring our view of the red book behind it. But that's because there were *never* any sheets of paper in the bottom tray to begin with. Look even *more* closely, and what we see is something else: Kubrick appended a white piece of cardboard or paper to the bottom of the flashing on the top shelf of the paper tray. The appendage makes the flashing on the top shelf of the paper tray stand out, so that it appears to reflect Stuart's pecker as he stands next to it. By pulling back his sports jacket, the polygonal lens flare accentuates this effect. When we return from Boulder, the appendage is gone, allowing us to see the red book between those two dark trays. In addition to wondering why it was removed is why did Kubrick put it there in the first place?

We will see a contrast to this on the boxes of pages next to Jack's typewriter in the CL, with the red seen between the dark bars being replaced with gold. As it turns out, even those boxes – of which there are at least three – are not random. And the red book sandwiched between those two shelves reflects in miniature the red and black elevators of blood, turned 90 degrees, like the ones that always sit over Jack's shoulder as he types away: the inverted twin to the red and black door Wendy eventually runs through as she flees from the man from the "party" with his head split open.

In sum, the flashing on the paper tray and the name plate both happen to be situated at crotch level to Stuart and Jack, both pairs of which happen to be highlighted by red polygonal lens flares. That same flashing, which Kubrick uses a white piece of cardboard or paper to accentuate to look like Stuart's phallic member, then appears at the seat of Jack's pants similar to how the "L" in Nelson's last name pokes Jack's yellow Bug into the tunnel during the opening scene. And the fountain pen Stuart was dabbling with in Susie's pink pages ends up perfectly aligned with the inseam of Stuart's right pant leg, and later with Jack's green tie, pointing up to Jack's mouth like the Apollo spaceship on Danny's sweater.

By comparison, after Delbert crashes into Jack in the Gold Room, the woman sitting on the couch smoking a cigarette (who happens to be Kubrick's daughter, Vivian), holds what is called an "opera length cigarette holder," which looks very much like a longer version of Stuart's black fountain pen. And she holds it in such a way as to almost burn a hole in the seat of Jack's pants, much as the flashing on the paper tray will appear to do when Jack disables the radio, and the ashtray sat perpendicular to Jack's derriere in Stuart's office.

And not only do two lens flares ride Jack's coat tail into Stuart's office, but both then settle over the crotches of Stuart and Jack, as well as the flashing on the paper tray, which is black and higher, and Stuart's name plate, which is white and lower. And in this way, Kubrick shows us a visual reflection of the real "white man's burden:" sexual inferiority.

All these errors, and orchestrations, seemed too numerous and meticulous to be intended to reflect the mere merging of multiple realities, each overlapping with these others, like the Hogan and Gibbons twins. Such design clearly suggested something else, something more, was going on. Of all the different continuity errors to be found in Jack's interview, however, it turned out the continuity error that I was looking for, the one which would actually start to make it all make sense, came before Jack even walked into Stuart's office in the first place. In fact, it happens even before Jack makes it to the front desk. Hell, there's even more than one of them. But of all those errors, one served as half of a key that would allow me to start decrypting Kubrick's little game. Half of that key was visual, and the other half audible. And it came in the form of a waiter rushing by Jack in the opposite direction, mere seconds after Jack walked into the hotel. That waiter was, corny as it sounds, the break I'd been waiting for. I just needed to learn how to listen, so I could begin to see.

FOUR

In all chaos there is a cosmos, in all disorder a secret order

Carl Jung

Millions saw the apple fall, but Newton asked why.

Bernard Baruch

T O FIND THE OTHER HALF of Kubrick's key, so we can open the door to his Games Room, we have to jump ahead to Closing Day, and what we see first in the hotel, and hear last. The first time we see Jack in the hotel on Closing Day, he's having a bite to eat and reading a curious magazine, but more about the magazine later. Toward the end of the day, we hear Dick Hallorann explain the nature of the hotel as Danny and he eat chocolate eye-scream in the kitchen. What we fail to realize at that time, however, is how what we hear toward the end of the day is what allows us to understand what we see at the start of the day.

Over his empty goblet, with a slight line of chocolate across his upper lip like the pencil mustache on Oil Can Harry, Danny listens intently as Dick explains how the hotel has something like "shine" to it, which allows certain things to be seen. "Not things anyone can notice," Dick explains, "but things that only people who shine can see." The other

89

half of the visual key seen when the waiter carrying a tray of food rushes past Jack as Jack walks to the front desk for his interview, comes in the next sentence: "*Just like they can see things that haven't happened yet.*" Well, Dick continues, "sometimes they can see things that happened a long time ago." The first half of Dick's comments is why we think Danny sees the river of blood, which Wendy will later see before running from the hotel, and the second half is why we think he sees the Grady twins, even though they're clearly not the Grady sisters Stuart mentioned earlier, who he said were "about eight and ten." And $8 + 10 = 18$, or $6 + 6 + 6$.

This raises questions of who is "they" that can "shine"? And why, and how, can "they" ultimately "see things that haven't happened yet"? Does the hotel make people clairvoyant? More than anything else, the carrot that enables people to see in such a way is a willingness to look at the world not through the stained-glass windows of religiously proscribed judgementalism, but through the lens of curiosity which washes away such judgements. Doing so leaves us to wonder where the waiter who rushed past Jack as he walked to the front desk happened to disappear to, along with the large tray of food he was carrying. He certainly could not have set that tray down on the small table we see between the two chairs, after all, which was the only table in that area. And if we combine what we first see on Closing Day with what we last hear on Closing Day, we find the answer to these questions. That answer was given to Danny by Dick on Closing Day about what "those who shine can see."

From the birds in the CL that foreshadowed Jack chasing Danny with his axe, to the Road Runner cartoons foreshadowing Jack chasing

Danny in the hedge maze, it became clear that Kubrick was not simply mirroring items in the film for the sake of mirroring alone, but was telegraphing images of things that haven't happened yet. But it turns out that Kubrick foretells his audience what is to come using more than just the paintings. He also uses people. And the first place we see this is with the waiter who hurries by Jack with a tray of food, only we never realize he is a ghost from Christmas yet to come. The first place we see this on "second sight" of the film, however, comes in the form of the painting hanging outside of Stuart Ullman's office, called "The Great Mother."

The Great Mother

The author of "The Great Mother" was Canadian artist, Norval Morrisseau. An Ojibway Indian who was also known as "Copper Thunderbird," Morrisseau painted this piece in a year significant to the July 4th date in the final photograph: the bicentennial year of 1976. Yet the painting is noteworthy for numerous other reasons as well.

Consider Morrisseau himself. Like John the Baptist mixed with St. Paul, Morrisseau was living as a nomad on the shores of Lake Superior when he had a vision telling him to begin painting. As "the first Indian to break the tribal rules of setting down Indian legends in picture form for the white man," Morrisseau was "the founder of an art "movement" popularly called Woodland Indian Art."[21] The name Woodland reminds us of Jack chopping through doors and chopping down Dick, and Kim Woodman, one of the artists pictured on the Gold Room sign. Copper being red, the name "Copper Thunderbird" is curious as well, because,

---

[21] https://www.boutiqueboreale.com/us/great-mother-by-norval-morrisseau-card.html

outside of the Boulder apartment complex, we just happen to see a copper red Ford Thunderbird. Coincidence?

The details and colors of the painting are also important, for they appear to foreshadow later events in the film. The woman in the painting, who faces away from Jack (toward screen left) as he enters Stuart's office, vaguely reminds us of Wendy. With wild black hair, which Wendy has after she stops washing her hair over the course of the film, the woman in the painting is also surrounded by the same colors we see Wendy wearing in Boulder: red and blue. When she calls the Forest Service, Wendy later mirrors the Great Mother as she sits on the credenza with her foot on Stuart's desk, like Mickey Mouse kicking the football on Danny's sweater. Even the cigarette she holds as she speaks into the handheld microphone sends up a steady stream of smoke signals. Like the picture of the African American infant seen in the hallway outside of the Torrance Overlook apartment, in "the staff wing of the hotel," the Great Mother's face is brown, reminding us of the brown sports blazer – like the brown blouse worn by Suzi, Stuart's secretary, and Bill Watson – and brown knee-high boots Wendy wears on Closing Day, and even Danny's brown bathrobe. Even Wendy's boots, like the tan moccasins she wears in Boulder, reflect the idea of brown skin and Native Americans. The woman is Wendy's cartoonish twin, and faces a wall of green, like the hedge maze, or Jack in his green shirt, sweaters, and tie, mixed with yellow, like Jack's golden blazer and his VW, even his "second sighted" typewriter.

In addition to the colors of the painting being mostly blue and red and facing a wall of green, the "mother" is also carrying two items. One looks like a large knife, the other a cudgel, reflecting the baseball bat and kitchen knife we will later see Wendy use to crack open Jack's head and cut open his hand.

The Great Mother is also a nod toward ancient Greece and Rome, as if the Overlook Hotel sits at the top of Mount Olympus, and even Danny's bedroom in Boulder. During the Second Punic War (218 to 201 BC), Rome adopted the cult of Cybele, who became known as Magna Mater or "Great Mother," to whom Rome's eventual victory was attributed. Before that, the city of Athens invoked her as a protector, who arrives in a lion-drawn chariot. Her Greek cults included rites to a divine Phrygian castrate shepherd-consort, Attis, who was castrated either by himself or perhaps a spurned lover. Her priesthood was comprised of eunuch castrated mendicants. The carpet pattern seen inside room 237, which resembles a chorus of castrated penises under a triple green halo, allude to the idea of Jack's virtual castration in the arms of a rotting corpse, as if Jack were taking a vow of celibacy for the Overlook. In Greece, Cybele became associated with mountains, fertile nature, and wild animals, which Jack devolves into, especially lions. And in Danny's bedroom in Boulder, we see a lion on the poster board at Wendy's feet, as if she were a lion tamer, as she overlooks the doctor interviewing Danny, a lioness overlooking her cub.

It is not surprising to see the mirroring Kubrick relies on in *The Shining*. He's used this convention in many of his other films as well. In *The Shining*, he just appears to be using it a good deal more than in any of his other films. And that's the thing, there is so much mirroring in *The Shining* it seems excessive. Why? Was it to reflect the story of Narcissus, a mythological character who drowns after falling in love with his own reflection in the water? Or might Kubrick be alluding to the nature of a self-fulfilling prophecy, of how often fiction can become as real as fact?

Even if Kubrick never intended to suggest anything with his excessive mirroring, his frequent use of it throughout the film - especially when considered in light of his casting of Nicholson and Lloyd to play Jack and Danny - portrays the movie screen as a revolving door between fiction and fact. In fact, Jack in the final photograph even alludes to the idea that the screen itself is modernity's "churchyard," where hell itself "breathes out contagion to this world." And two chilling examples of how the "word" of fiction "became flesh" of fact, come from two stories, one written by Edgar Allen Poe, the other by Morgan *Robert*son.

The Entanglements of Fiction & Fact: Poe to Robertson

Quantum physics is the study of the behavior or "mechanics" of the nature of particles on an atomic and subatomic level. It is sometimes referred to as "particle physics." Like an old married couple, sometimes two particles can be so related to each other that one particle cannot be perfectly described without including all the information about the other one. When this happens, the particles are seen as "connected" in such a way that they are not independent of one another. This inseparable relationship, which is like trying to describe the difference between a brown egg and a white egg after making scrambled eggs, is known as "quantum entanglement." In modern sci-fi movies, like Marvel superheroes, entanglement is one of several plot devices in which different time lines merge together, when the destinies of characters become intertwined as if by fate. String theory, recall, is the idea in theoretical physics that reality is made up of infinitesimally small vibrating strings that vibrate at the center of atoms. Hence, entanglement is a bit like the idea that the string within one atom is "married" to the string within another atom, as if the two were actually one. This is true even if those two atoms have divorced and moved to opposite ends of the universe. In *The Shining*, the "string" that entangles events in the film extends between fiction and fact, stretches from the lake to the final photograph, from one ball to another.

Like the paintings in Brazil, the paintings in the Overlook hotel, more than being snapshot previews of what's in store, appeared to be crawling off their canvas and into the physical reality of the hotel itself, like that little girl crawling out of her TV in *The Ring*. The Road Runner cartoons became Jack chasing Danny; the Overlook hotel a rabbit-hole Danny and Wendy fall into, the *Summer of 42* reflecting Danny's Bug's Bunny jersey. Such mirroring reflects an entanglement between fact and fiction like Nicholson and Lloyd playing Jack and Danny Torrance. It also reflects the idea of self-fulfilling prophecies, how fictions can grow to become indistinguishable from sacred "facts," and how a "belief" can grow to become our only "truth" because of how it affects our lives.

Nothing can mold fiction into fact and fact into fiction like the hands of millennia playing our heartstrings like a piano. Aided by our mercurial memories, those able hands rob the graves of earlier mythologies of empires gone by, stitching together various limbs of forgotten literature into the religions of those that follow. Such an idea is even reflected in Mary Shelley's 1818 novel, *Frankenstein; or, The Modern Prometheus*, as if religions are simply old wine poured into new bottles, pieces of dead stories sutured into sacred scripture. Two better examples which reflect this entanglement between fiction and fact, of how "the Word became Flesh," followed Shelly's novel. Like Jack and Shelly, the two men to whom such a miracle of chance occurred were both writers: one being famous for a raven who prophesied about cannibalism, and the other who prophesized about a "ghost ship" and reminds us of the Roberts milk carton.

One example of an entanglement between fiction and fact, like Pinocchio coming to life, comes from a master of horror and the first author of science fiction: Edgar Allan Poe. In 1837, Poe wrote a masterpiece of maritime horror entitled "The Narrative of Arthur Gordon Pym." Like the Donner party in 1846, Poe's story was about a crew lost at sea that was eventually forced to resort to cannibalism. In 1884, that story seemed to crawl from its pages and into reality when the crew of the ill-fated yacht Mignonette, shipwrecked and starving, were forced to treat one of their own like filet mignon. Incredibly, the name of the men who were eaten, in both Poe's narrative and in the story of the Mignonette, was the same: Richard Parker.

A similar metamorphosis happened again in 1898. As if unwittingly forging a form of entanglement between fact and fiction through the black (and white) magic of putting pen to paper, Morgan Robertson wrote *The Wreck of the Titan: Or, Futility*. His story included numerous startling similarities to the sinking of the Titanic on April 15, 1912. Like the Titanic, the Titan hits an iceberg in the North Atlantic and sinks. Both vessels were described as the largest ships afloat at the time, with the sizes and lengths of each being strikingly similar. Both ships were dubbed "unsinkable;" both hit icebergs, on a cold April night, and at the same speed; and both had a dangerous shortage of lifeboats.

Later, Robertson was hailed a clairvoyant, and no doubt could have parlayed this striking coincidence into convincing throngs of people that he had been given the divine gift of prophecy or "second sight," by a deity of one brand or another. Modesty led him to defer such accolades, however, insisting instead only that "I know what I'm writing about, that's all." The year 1912, or course, is an anagram of 1921, while "Robertson" reminds us of both the milk carton behind Wendy in Boulder and Susan Robertson, "who disappeared while on a hunting trip with her husband."

Seeing what Hasn't Happened Yet

Like Poe and Robertson, so Kubrick likewise appears to be using his film to engage in a self-fulfilling prophecy. *The Shining* was released in the United States on May 23, 1980. Because of this, it has been assumed that the events depicted in the film must therefore take place during the winter of 1979 or 1978, or even 1977. The Playgirl magazine Jack is reading in the lobby on Closing Day, for example, is dated January 1978. As it turns out, however, Kubrick may have left behind a clue that clears up this question. That clue plays a dual role of not only allowing the audience to determine when the events in the film are taking place, but also letting the audience know that at least some of the pieces to Kubrick's *Shining* puzzle are not included in the box of the movie screen. The clue comes from the fact that, according to stephenking.fandom.com, Kubrick changes Jack's age, making him older in the film, while Wendy and Danny, like Peter Pan and Holden

Caulfield, never age.[22] If Kubrick indeed changed these details (it being difficult to confirm), then he provided later audiences with the means of determining the date the events in the film are taking place.

Consider first the birth years and ages of Jack, Wendy, and Danny. In both the novel and the film, Wendy is 29, and was born in 1946 and 1950 respectively. Shelly Duval, by comparison, was born on July 7, 1949. Jack Torrance, on the other hand, was 29 in the novel, but 43 in the film, being born in 1946 and 1937, respectively. Jack Nicholson was also born in 1937, on April 22. Like Wendy being ageless in both the novel and the film, Danny remains 5 years old. In the novel, he was born in 1971. In the film, however, Kubrick changes Danny's birth year to 1975. Note that we never learn any of this directly from the film itself. But the fact that Kubrick changes these dates tells us when the events taking place in the film must be occurring. To see this, we must assume birth days for the characters.

Since we have no idea what day of the year Wendy, Jack, or Danny Torrance were actually born, we can start with the assumption that the earliest each of them could have been born was January 1st of their respective birth years. If Wendy was born on Jan. 1st, 1950, then she would be 29 as early as 01/01/1979. If she was born on Dec. 31 of that same year, she would be 29 until Dec 31, 1980, at which point she'd turn 30. If we accept that the events in the film are playing out in real time, then they could not be taking place prior to 1979. But consider Jack and Danny Torrance. If born on Jan. 1st, 1937, Jack Torrance would turn 43

[22] https://stephenking.fandom.com/wiki/Danny_Torrance;
https://stephenking.fandom.com/wiki/Wendy_Torrance

on 01/01/1980. And like Jack, if Danny was born on Jan. 1, 1975, then he would only turn five years old on Jan. 1, 1980.

Notice what Kubrick has done here: while he has allowed Wendy and Danny to remain the same age in both the novel and the film, he has also made it so both Danny and Jack could only reach their respective ages by the time the film was released if the events in the film are in fact occurring in 1980. And if the film was released in May of 1980, and the Overlook hotel is open until October 30th, then the events being depicted in the Overlook hotel are occurring between October and December – *of 1980*. This means, of course, that what the audience is watching is are event that are occurring 5 months, and 7 months, *after the film was released*. Changing Jack's age and the birth years of the characters, as such, was so the entire film would be an example of the audience "seeing something that hasn't happened yet."

Notice what other curious details we discover from this. Stuart tells Jack that the hotel is open from May 15th until October 30th, and Jack is clearly there on a day when the hotel is open, so he is there sometime between these two dates. This means that CLOSING DAY is October 31, Halloween. In 1980, Oct. 31 was the 305th day of the year. There were 61 days remaining until the end of the year and the day of the week was Friday. Interestingly, Daniel Lloyd was born on Oct. 13, 1972. "A MONTH LATER" typically means 30 days later, which would make the first day we see the Torrances alone in the hotel December 1 (because 30 days hath November). December 1, 1980, was the 336th day of the year, with 336 BCE being the year that Alexander the Great takes the throne after his father was assassinated. That means, if we include the first day we see them, then there are 31 days remaining until the end of the year. The day of the week was *Monday*.

Then there are the days on the cue cards. We see five cue cards denoting days of the week, starting with Tuesday, then Thursday, Saturday, Monday, and Wednesday, followed by two cue cards with the time, 8 am and 4 pm, for the following day. As such, the first day the Torrances are alone in the hotel and the last day they are alone in the hotel are symmetrical in that they are only one day removed from the first and last cue cards expressing a day of the week.

The dates associated with the days of the week we see would then be Dec. 2, 4, 6, 8, and 10. And this means that, while the first day without being announced is December 1, the last day without a cue card naming the day would be Thursday, December 11, which is an interesting date indeed.

So, other than the 11 reflecting Danny's Apollo sweater, what makes the date December 11th so interesting about *The Shining*? To best appreciate this, we should first consider the two tribes that Stuart tells Wendy the motifs in the Colorado Lounge are based on: Navaho and Apache.

Neither the Navaho nor the Apache were indigenous to the plains of Colorado. Instead, both Nations lived in and around the state of Arizona. Twenty years earlier, another world-famous horror film had been released that started with an aerial shot like we see with in *The Shining*. In that film, which was shot in black and white, the aerial shot is over a city that ended with two cues given as we fly in through a partially opened hotel window. That film not only depicted the most iconic murder scene in cinema history, it did so inside of a bathroom that looked remarkably similar to the bathroom in the Torrance Overlook apartment. It began with two cues relevant to *The Shining*. Reflecting the home of the Navaho and the Apache, the first said "Phoenix, Arizona." The second, reflecting the last day the Torrances are in the Overlook hotel, said "Friday, December 11." That movie was Alfred Hitchcock's *Psycho*. And as it turns out, the paintings in *Psycho* tells us almost all we need to know to answer some of the riddles posed by *The Shining*. And, like the twin mirrors on the doors to the living room of 237, *Psycho* is also a road sign directing us to look into the theater, not of just our perceptions, but of our own mind.

Waiting to be Seen

All of this indicates that the waiter hurrying past Jack as Jack walks into the hotel is waiting to be seen for who and what he really is: a ghost of Christmas-yet-to-come. While everyone sees that waiter walk by, few notice that there is nowhere for him to set down the tray of food he is carrying in the area we see him walking toward. Even fewer notice that, when Jack walks away from the front desk and begins walking to Stuart's office, that waiter has mysteriously disappeared, along with his tray of food. So where did he and his tray of food go?

Combining what we first see of Jack, and last hear from Dick to Danny, on Closing Day, gives us a lens for seeing an answer. As the camera pans across the lobby of the hotel on Closing Day, Jack sits with a magazine eating a piece of white bread. To his right sits a large tray of food. Later, Dick tells Danny that sometimes we "can see things that haven't happened yet." Combined, the tray of food beside Jack on

Closing Day was brought to Jack by the waiter that rushed by him as he walked to the front desk for his interview.

Of course, the tray of food sitting next to Jack is not the exact same tray of food being carried by the waiter who rushes past Jack on the day of his interview. Similar but not identical, Kubrick illustrates this by showing us Grady twins with each wearing slightly different dresses, and one always having nicely combed hair while the other's is slightly disheveled.

If the waiter we see when Jack walks into the hotel is actually the one that brings Jack the food he is eating on Closing Day, then what does that tell us about everything, and everyone else, in the hotel, both inside and out? As it turns out, piecing together the visual and audible parts of the same whole was the key for cracking Kubrick's long rumored code. Cracking that code finally unlocked the door to Kubrick's games room, so I could finally begin piecing together his puzzle. And of all the pieces, none was more important than the man in a golden jacket standing in front of the elevator as Jack walks into the General Manager's office. That man, who turns to look toward the far elevator dial as Jack enters the office area, is "faceless" as Jack walks by. But we will see his face later, we just don't realize it's him. Only after seeing his face, peering through the wagon wheel of Kubrick's videogame, did the true face of Kubrick's puzzle begin to unmask itself. But I would only understand this after I began finally seeing the truth of who all the people where mulling about the Overlook on Closing Day. To see that, I had to put on my red hunting hat on like Holden Caulfield, and start "hunting wabbits."

FIVE

OPENING THE BOX ON CLOSING DAY

When information overload occurs, pattern recognition is how to determine the
truth.
Marshall McLuhan

Synchronicity is an ever present reality for those who have eyes to see.
Carl Jung

TO START "HUNTING WABBITS" in Kubrick's murder
mystery, I first had to pick a day to inspect, one filled with
plenty of "wabbits" to watch. Like Holden Caulfield, Elmer
Fudd hunts Bugs Bunny while wearing a red hunting hat. And, if you've
read *The Catcher in the Rye*, you know that Holden "hunts people in this
hat." So, the question was easy: where are there the most people to begin
watching their behavior, to see if others were, like the waiter that rushes
past Jack, simply examples of "seeing something that hasn't happened
yet?" And, given the mirroring effects Kubrick relies on so heavily in the
film, there seemed to be no better day to open with than Closing Day.

Closing Day at the Overlook hotel, we learn from the interview, is
October 30th, the eve of All Hallows' Eve. As we can see, the hotel is a
beehive of activity on this day, much as King described the wasp's nest
that came to life suddenly in his novel. (This idea is even captured in the
final photograph of Jack surrounded by WASPs: White Angelo Saxon

Protestants.) More than any other day, Kubrick shows the true nature of his invisible hands, and even makes his opening moves, on this of all days.

When watched closely, and with an intimate awareness of what occurs over the course of the film, the people seen mulling about the hotel on this day suddenly begin to look increasingly suspicious, as if they are all somehow in-on-the-game. With an awareness of things that happen later in the film, things that occur on Closing Day begin to look mighty synchronistic indeed. During the tour of the CL, for example, we see a cleaner move a chair and a table that raises a red flag. It does so, in part, because the table and chair being moved clearly do not belong at the end of the long table where they were parked, a table that acts as the twin to Jack' writing table only turned 90 degrees, nor do we ever see that chair and table parked in the same spot again. Like the waiter rushing past Jack before Jack's interview reflecting the tray Jack is eating off of on Closing Day, so the moving of the chair and table by the cleaner on Closing Day calls to mind the later event that is thought to be a continuity error seen behind Jack in the CL when he begins berating Wendy for distracting him from his writing. Seemingly too blatant to be unintentional, when we see Wendy interrupt him in the CL, a chair and a table disappear behind Jack. And at that same moment, red-jacket Jack appears to awaken and rear his ugly head. Again, is this really just a coincidence, or a synchronicity masquerading as a coincidence?

Consider other details in the CL on this day. We see a man cleaning the glass on the book cabinet directly across from Jack's writing table, between the first two monolith-sized windows, windows which are not only impossible, but are the same size as the large mirrors in the Gold

Room hallway. His attire not only resembles that of a sleeping Jack having a nightmare at his writing table, but he also even bends over after they walk by him, mirroring sleepy Jack's posture. And as Jack sleeps at his table, that same book cabinet can be seen behind him, as if Jack is mirroring the man bending over as he cleans the cabinet, yet turned 90 degrees. He even leans over at the very moment he aligns with the cleaner moving the small table and chair.

Look at what we see also at the other end of the CL. At the base of the grand staircase sits a grand piano, and a man shining it just like Jack's doppelgänger shining the bookshelf. Like one man mopping the floor in the lobby and another installing a CASHIER sign, why shine a bookshelf or wax a piano when the hotel is closing for the next six months, as if it is really opening day? Shouldn't the bookcases and piano be covered with a sheet or something? And why is another man vacuum-cleaning a couch that won't be sat in for the next 6 months, instead of covering it with a sheet as well, like the sheets we see over the couches in the lobby as the camera approaches the final photograph? And why does the vacuum cleaner being used look like a Wet-Dry vacuum, which sucks up dirt and water, which makes me think of the water in the bathtub in room 237? At first glance, these activities are easy to overlook, but with a second look, they look as if they are trying to tell us something, especially considering where that Wet-Dry vac ends up later.

Consider also the man coming down the stairs with a rolled-up rug on his shoulder. Earlier, another man walked through the lobby with a rug on his shoulder; and he just happened to be dressed like Danny on Closing Day: jeans and a blue jacket with a red stripe down the arm. When that man carries his carpet into the lobby, entering from the left frame of the scene, he pauses an unnaturally long period of time behind the first pillar on the left before walking on, as if to reflect Jack hiding behind the pillar at the other end of the lobby for Dick, only ascending the stairwell in unison with Stuart and Jack exiting the lobby. And with the crossfade from the lobby into the CL, that man appears to transition from walking up the stairwell in the lobby to walking up the stairwell in the CL, as if he's on a magic carpet ride to room 237.

Now compare the man carrying the carpet through the lobby to the one we see carrying a carpet, also on his shoulder, coming down the grand staircase in the CL. Is it just a coincidence that we see these two rolled up carpets when there just happens to be two carpets that figure prominently within the film itself: one outside and the other inside of room 237? And while the first carpet carrier heads up the stairs to the second floor with the crossfade, the other is coming down from that same floor. And while the former carries the carpet over his right shoulder, the latter carries the carpet over his left.

These twin rug-carriers look meaningless enough on their own; that is, until we consider the details about the carpets they carry, first up to the second floor, then down. The first carpet we see is as stiff as a board, the second one as limp as a rubber chicken. This difference makes my Spidey-sense tingle because of Danny and Jack. When Danny rides over the carpets in the CL on his tricycle, the sound of his plastic wheels rolling between the hardwood floor and the carpets sound like he is bobbing for apples or shifting back and forth between being asleep and awake, as if he is struggling to wake up, much as we see him locked in a seizure as Jack explores room 237. Danny is also sitting on what looks like a small carpet or blanket with various toys around him when he is watching *Summer of 42*, and both times we see him on the carpet outside of room 237 he is "playing with himself." And again, 42 is the sum of 2 x 3 x 7.

Then there is Jack. Finding a naked woman dripping wet in room 237, who is clearly inviting Jack to "come and play" with her, no doubt gives Jack a "stiffy." Looking into the mirror, however, her turning into an old hag no doubt "kills his wood." As the first rolled up carpet is carried up the stairs toward 237 with the crossfade, and is as stiff as a board, the second rolled up carpet is brought down the grand staircase from the 237 floor as limp as a noodle. Again, is this really just a coincidence?

What also makes those carpets look rather curious is how they even hint at the idea of a magic carpet ride. When Jack first walks into Stuart's office for his interview, we see the mystery "faceless" man standing in front of the elevator I mentioned earlier, the one wearing a golden jacket. He is holding what looks like a stick and a fishing hat. Beneath his feet, a carpet, one we will see again only when we finally see his face. Although hard to notice, it is there when Wendy wheels the breakfast cart toward those elevators "A Month Later." When Jack finds himself standing by those elevators again, after he storms out of the apartment at Wendy's suggestion they leave the hotel to ensure Danny is okay, as he is lured by the sirens song back to the Gold Room, that carpet is conspicuously absent. And when Danny returns from room 237 to the CL, more carpets vanish there as well.

Also, what if there are no coincidences in the film, and everyone operates like that waiter in the lobby in some way? When Wendy runs and finds the lobby filled with cobwebs and skeleton, Dick's corpse is gone. And in a scene that was later cut from the film, Stuart Ullman visited Wendy and Danny in the hospital and informed them that the police didn't find any bodies in the hotel at all. From this perspective, the two rolled up rugs looked like two people carrying two dead bodies – Dick and Jack – like L.B. "Jeff" Jefferies watching his neighbor carrying his dead wife out in suitcases through his *Rear Window*.

◊◊

Curiosity is, according to author William Arthur Ward "the wick in the candle of learning." Thanks to that curiosity, minor details which had always washed right over me before, began to suddenly look like remarkable coincidences. Noticing the second carpet-carrier led me back to the first, which led me to wonder why the first one is not only dressed so like Danny, but how and why he appears to disappear behind the pillar in the left corner of the screen. And how does he manage to do this carrying a long carpet on his shoulder, no less? This led me to notice the ominous patch of floor tile Stuart and Bill are on as they begin their walk to Jack: the same one Dick will be laid out on by Jack's axe. Again, is this pure coincidence? And even if it isn't, so what? Why would it matter? But if it didn't matter, why would Kubrick want it that way?

Other details likewise began lighting up, like electric neon signs shouting, "notice me!" First, for example, we see the camera pan to the right as we see a man in green overalls and blue hat mopping the floor as if he were swabbing the deck of "a ghost ship." Like the waxing, shining, and vacuuming in the CL, he is not only mopping the floor of a hotel that is closing for the winter, he is also simply sliding that mop back and forth in the same spot, as if he were brushing teeth. Is he ensuring the stage will be clean enough for Hallorann to lay down his life on for another? Note too how the emblem Dick's body ends up on and where that man is moping the floor are at a distance similar to the one Wendy and Jack jump over to escape being run over by a green car.

What hides them from view for a couple of seconds is a man in a blue maintenance uniform walking by with two beds on a rack. There was something about those beds that again made my mind tingle, like a thought itch that can only be scratched with curiosity, but I wasn't sure what it was. And then I remembered what it was. And after I did, as odd as it first looked to see such beds being rolled into the hotel on Closing Day, on "second sight," they didn't look so odd after all. Far from it.

Two Rollaway Beds

Of the rollaway beds being wheeled through the lobby on Closing Day, four things struck my eye. First, their colors are similar to the carpet in the hallway outside of 237: orange, red, and black – the same colors of the rainbow picture in Ullman's office. That rainbow is set against a black background, like the black screen we see when Danny blacks-out. In contrast, against a white background, a similar rainbow is seen on Danny's bedroom door just before Danny has his vision and blacks-out in the Boulder bathroom.

Second is how, combined with the walk that Stuart and Bill begin directly on top of the circular emblem where Wendy sees Dick's dead corpse, the two beds are being rolled along a path that forms an upside down cross. Like those beds, Wendy wheels her breakfast cart through the lobby A Month Later. When she does, the Gold Room hallway and the path she walks to the elevators form the same shape. And then we

109

see Jack sleeping in bed, in the same vanity mirror where we eventually see REDRUM spells "MURDER" backwards. And while Jack ends up dead, the panels on the bathroom door where Danny writes "REDRUM" form an upside down cross. In fact, when we see Jack sleeping before falling under the table, where he recounts his dream of murdering Wendy and Danny by cutting them "up into little pieces," even the crossbeams under his table form an upside cross. And on the headboard of Jack's bed, we see three small crosses, strung together like telephone poles.

This then was what made the third thing about those beds look so intentional. The bed on top of the rack is upside down, so that it mirrors the bed below it like the mirroring effect over St. Mary's Lake.

Third, those two beds being stacked in such a way as to mirror each other was curious for yet another reason. They look like two horseshoes that reflect the reason Jack gives for teaching: "making ends meet." Yet they also form an ancient symbol. Discovered on a pillar at Göbekli Tepe in south-east Turkey, the symbol is used by Australian aborigines to represent two people sitting across from each other sharing ideas, like Dick and Danny talking about the shining. It was this kind of interchange of ideas that the schools of philosophy in Greece and Rome were designed to cultivate, and the original synagogues of the ancient Israelites were designed to promote. That all changed, however, with the invention of writing, which gave to a priestly class the power of God through the magic of the written word. And God, of course, is a writer.

Over 12,000 years old, Göbekli Tepe - which is many millennia older than Stonehenge or Egypt's great pyramids - is the world's oldest temple: a manmade cave which some believe marked the beginning of modern civilization, and others saw as an abomination to a God that was greater than the whole sky. Built in the pre-pottery Neolithic period before the invention of writing or the wheel, the temple relates to Wendy carting breakfast from the Gold Room hallway over Dick's grave. In the ancient world, the temples served as the first national banks, and the priestly classes – otherwise known as "the money changers" whose tables Jesus overturned – were in fact the world's first bankers and the coiners of money. "As excavator Klaus Schmidt put it, *"First came the temple, then the city."*[23] Those temples also served as the slaughterhouses for scarifying animals to the gods. And as the lobby scene emerges, Stuart and Bill are standing directly on top of the floor emblem that will serve as the altar upon which Dick's body will later be sacrificed in Danny's stead, for the Overlookers. And that emblem just happens to be directly in front of the CASHIER window.

And we just happen to see something strange indeed, but which we dismiss in the same way we dismiss the absence of the hedge maze in the opening scene: a man in a large blue and white hat standing on an A-frame latter doing something that seems so odd to be doing on Closing Day; but more on that in a moment.

The fourth thing about those two rollaway beds that made my Spidey-senses tingle was both the direction they are being wheeled and their final resting place. To start with, the man is wheeling those two beds in the same direction that Jack motions toward when he tells Stuart

[23] https://en.wikipedia.org/wiki/Göbekli_Tepe
In *Money: The Unauthorized Biography*, Felix Martin points out that "money" was in fact invented using the exact same religious ritual used during Passover and the "Last Supper," the very same ritual still celebrated around the world today during every mass. To write "In God We Trust" on our money is to acknowledge that the "God" in which we trust is, in fact, money.

"My son's discovered the Games Room," where Danny first sees the twins in the hotel. Where do those bed end up? As Danny rides around the 237 hallway, we first see one by the impossible door that would lead into the 237 bathroom. The other is obscured behind a laundry cart by where Danny first began his ride, just beyond a pair of impossible elevators. Later, after the ball rolls up to Danny and he stands and begins walking toward the open door to room 237, we see that the laundry cart is gone, and both fold-up rollaway-beds are sitting at either end of the 237 hallway: one with a white center and the other with a black center, just like the rainbows discussed earlier. In effect, those beds "bookend" the 237 hallway. And room 237 is Jack's "adults only" Games Room.

What these "coincidences" suggest, as a result, is that the man wheeling those beds through the lobby is in fact a stagehand wheeling in props for the "play" we are about to watch unfold inside of Kubrick's Globe Theater. When stage props move and change while the play is in progress, those same stage-hands often remain hidden from the audience, much as they are when various items are removed from the CL. Even more curious is the fact that two such beds should be wheeled into the hotel on Closing Day only to end up like bookends on either end of the 237 hallway, especially given how most if not all of the rooms in that hallway are impossible and that room 237 itself is a rather luxurious room indeed. In fact, all the rooms across the hall from room 237 are clearly impossible, and the two beds are both parked on that side of the hallway. Why, we are left to wonder, weren't they parked down by the boilers, where so many other items and furniture were parked, presumably for lack of having anywhere else to put them?

Note also how Jack says that his "*son's* discovered the games room," with the word "son's" sounding like the verbal twin to the plural "sons." It is as if Jack is saying he has two sons: Danny and Tony, like the two daughters of Charles Grady. As the scene in the lobby then comes to an end, Jack again points in the direction of the Games Room as he says, "I better collect my family," reminding us of Jack having a dream of chopping Danny and Wendy into little pieces, like sentences being assembled from the alphabet soup on his typewriter. In contrast to this, Delbert later mentions that only "one" of his daughter's stole a pack of matches and tried to burn down the hotel, for which he "corrected" them both, and then his wife, for trying to prevent him from "doing (his) duty," as if he were a toy soldier following orders "from the house." And Jack's "sons" comment is then reversed when uses the singular as he says to Delbert, "you chopped your wife and *daughter* up into little pieces," reflecting his own attempt to do the same to Wendy and Danny.

Again, these minor details are easily overlooked, until we become curious enough to not only notice them, but be willing to be intrigued enough to come and play with them. For even a blade of grass, as Walt Whitman pointed out, "is the journeywork of the stars." And as Voltaire said, it is better to judge a man by his questions rather than his answers.

A Clockwork Kubrick

They say "seeing is believing," but it isn't; it's the other way around: "believing" is seeing only what we want to believe and filtering out everything else as a "false" belief. To save myself from feeling overwhelmed by a stormy sea of other possible perspectives, philosophies, and beliefs, I subscribed to one brand of "belief" that I then relied on to act as my only anchor, lens, and lifejacket. Rather than granting me a God's-eye-lens for spotting unvarnished "truth," however, my Catholic religious "beliefs" operated like Ritalin, calming my anxieties about the uncertainties of life and death by stimulating me to focus all my attention on a brand of "beliefs" that promised to save me from the uncertainties that cause such anxieties. And in the same way those beliefs blinded me from admitting that my addiction to "loving" those beliefs was really the result of my fear of living without them, so too those beliefs acted like blinders that kept me from seeing the merits or validity of other perspectives, lest I feel overwhelmed with uncertainty. To save myself from such feelings, I clung to a religion that claimed that it and it alone had been granted access to infallible truth, in order to hide from myself a fear of being a human being who lacks perfect knowledge, especially of the unknown. My religion alleviated this fear by giving me a confidence that there is a God that possess that perfect knowledge, and one lone institutional Church which He uses to inject that truth into the world, and all so a lowly "believer" like myself could calm the fears they feel due to their own lack of such omniscience. But trading my fear of the unknown for faith in a religion that required me to subscribe to and advance its own brand of perspective, rendered me incapable of determining the difference between what is true, regardless of anyone's beliefs, and the truth about the power of a belief to allow us to see only what we want to see, while convincing us there is no other truth but our own brand.

Only by understanding all of this, which took me 42 years to do, could I ween myself from the Ritalin of my own religion enough to begin seeing how simply believing the devil is responsible for Jack's transformation from Dr. Jekyll into Mr. Hyde was blinding me from noticing all the clues that reveal to us what is really going on in, and around, the Overlook. Once I'd matured enough to stop fearing the boogey man we call the unknown, in other words, what looked like everyday things began looking mighty fishy around Kubrick's little fishbowl.

Notice all the activity going on behind Jack, for example, as he reads his magazine in the lobby on Closing Day. Wearing grey overalls, a man walks in carrying a green table and then walks out of the hotel moments later with nothing in his hands. After he enters the hotel, he is followed by a guy who looks like an older version of Danny - which is how Tony was described in the novel - wearing a jacket that is the near "twin" to the jacket Danny will wear when he runs into the maze with Wendy on his heels. It is also like the sweater Danny wears when he does the same thing with Jack hot on his heels. This potential Tony look-a-like is carrying a single green chair, and he walks into the hotel heading toward the Games Room. Where did he get that one, lone, chair, and why was it outside? He walks in right behind two women who say, "Goodbye Mr. Ullman," who we would expect to be walking *out* of the hotel, not into it and toward the elevators. Behind the Tony look-a-like walks another guy carrying two more green chairs. So where did those chairs come from, and why are they taking them toward the Games Room?

At first sight, these details look random. Look again, and it all begins to look incredibly precise. And this is because in the Games Room, just before he sees the twins for the first time in the hotel, Danny climbs atop a chair to retrieve his darts. He then spins around, the camera pivoting between him and the twins. With the change of the camera angle

115

from the twins to Danny and back to the twins again, two chairs and one of the green tables move ever so slightly, as do the ashtrays on the green tables. In fact, even one of the handles on the foosball table shifts a little.

More interesting is that, like the handle on that foosball table, the Grady twins move by a hair to their left as well. To see this, notice the part in the hairline of the twin on the left. With the pivot of the camera back and forth between Danny and the twins, the part in her hairline, which is slightly to the right in the first shot of them, then lines up perfectly with the left edge of the door frame behind her. And like the two women who walk down the stairs outside of the Torrance apartment in the next scene, the twins turn and walk out of the Games Room, yet in the opposite direction. The question is whether this slight shift is designed to suggest that the "Games Room" is the twin to the hedge maze, where Jack and Danny will play hide-and-go-seek. Like the twins in the Games Room, after all, Danny and Wendy likewise play and turn in the center of that maze, while holding hands, as Jack looks down like Zeus in the form of an eagle overlooking his prey.

The chairs and table being carried into the hotel are obviously not the same as those we see move in the Games Room. Still, in a film filled with doubles and twins that are not always identical, to see a table and three chairs being carried into the hotel behind Jack, for no apparent reason, while Danny stands on one chair and then one table and two other chairs appear to move slightly when Danny sees the twins, looks intentional, even when looked at without the assumption that they are. Sure, these may be just coincidences. But with the right "belief" lens, they also begin to look exactly like evidence of "intelligent design" and intentionally orchestrated synchronicities.

116

Then there is the question raised by the moving furniture in the Games Room. To ignore these micro-changes as ultimately meaningless is to reject the idea that *"everything* happens for a reason." So why do the ashtrays, chairs, table, and even the twins and the arm on the foosball table, all move ever so slightly anyway? Behind the scenes photos can be found online that show the twins are standing inside of small square boxes marked out with tape on the floor. Their slight movement to the left between shots, as a result, is not accidental. Are the rest of the items that move in the Games Room not accidental either? But why would a man as meticulous as Kubrick move the twins and the furniture in the Games Room to such a slight degree as to be altogether unnoticeable unless the film could be studied frame by frame, something Kubrick knew computers would eventually allow his audience to do? Is it perhaps because of a rule of twins that Kubrick is bound to obey?

When looked at through a belief that Kubrick is bound by a rule of twins, the strange parade of people we see behind Jack in the lobby suddenly begins to look like parts of a puzzle. Because we see furniture move in the Games Room, we also see people moving furniture through the lobby. Or is it the other way around? Does Kubrick show the audience "stagehands" actually "moving" furniture through the lobby, because the mirrored-twins to that furniture will eventually move, however slightly, in the Games Room? And is it this same rule of mirrored-twins which leads Kubrick to have two women walking *into* the hotel behind Jack, because the Grady twins appear behind Danny and then turn and walk *out* of the Games Room?

Consider also what Jack does when he says his "sons" discovered the "games room" and he should "collect his family." Both times he motions toward not only where the man with the two beds and the Tony–look-a-like just headed carrying a single green chair, but also toward where Danny will be seen riding his trike later, just before encountering the twins again in the hallway outside of their apartment. As if to reflect the large A-frame ladder, which appears to be in the lobby for no good reason, Danny even jumps a floor before seeing the twins "chopped up into little pieces," just like he climbed on the chair in the Games Room. Jack is also motioning in the direction of where we are led to believe they have exited the kitchen on their way to the basement. Not only this, but as we see when Wendy exits the phone closet to call the Forest Ranger, Jack even motions toward the bathrooms seen behind Wendy as she heads to Stuart's office to use the radio.

Is this "intelligently designed" synchronicity? Or is this just my chosen belief-bias coloring my vision with the smell of burnt toast? Whatever it is, such "coincidences" were clearly an invitation to be as insane in how much attention I was willing to pay to Kubrick's details as he was insane in hiding the devil of his game in those details. To see this, just consider the slightest movement of one of the arms on the foosball table, the handles of which are blue and red.

Foosball is a table game resembling soccer in which the ball is moved by manipulating rods to which small figures are attached. (This connection along rods will become important to remember when Jack calls Wendy to tell her he got the job, as it connects Jack to the man at the maze table.) It is also called table soccer. In the lobby, when Jack pitches his tennis ball across the lobby, right over Danny's trike, we see a soccer ball. Related to the rods connecting the players on the tabletop game, the twin to the foosball is "fuzzballs."

There are two kinds of fuzzballs. In 1972, the first kind was at the core of what some physicists theorized to be the true nature of black holes. According to such a theory, at the center of a black hole's "event horizon" – that is, the theoretical boundary around a black hole beyond which no light or other radiation can escape, also known as "the point of no return" – is a ball of strings. Called fuzzballs, this ball of strings had the power to distort space-time and bend light.

Two problems such fuzzballs helped to explain were an "information paradox," where the black hole undergoes zero change regardless of what falls into it, and the "singularity," or a symbiosis that leads to the merging of man with his machines. Both problems are even reflected in Jack being both swallowed into the hotel and captured in the eye of the camera lens, in the final photograph.

The second kind of "fuzzball" is also a bat-and-ball street game related to baseball, usually formed as a "pick-up" game by kids who lack access to regular baseball fields and equipment. Generally played according to the rules of baseball, the one consistent difference between fuzzball and baseball is the use of a tennis ball instead of a baseball. When Jack first enters the hotel for his interview, we see a bag of baseballs associated with tennis, and Jack chucks his tennis ball through the lobby like he's pitching a Ryan Nolan fastball.

Indoor fuzzball is usually played inside of a large net with no base runners, while Jack not only pitches his tennis ball toward a green diamond rug that looks like a fishing net and a baseball field, but we also see Danny inside of a shirt with a basketball net on it while he eats lunch "at home plate." And in small teams, the game is played with "ghost runners," while Wendy calls the Overlook a "ghost ship" and sees a ghost standing where Jack had just passed; the same spot the tennis ball bounces toward after Jack pitches it through the lobby. And if all of this isn't synchronistic enough, the tabletop soccer game, which reminds us of Jack looking down into the hedge maze table as if he is watching Wendy and Danny, was created in 1921. At the very least, something was afoot with that foosball table.

Jack's Play-girls?

Like the foosball table, the people and other details seen behind Jack in the lobby all appear wholly insignificant at first sight. But this changes when we look at these details in light of other events in the film. Like the Playgirl magazine Jack is seen reading in the lobby of the hotel, an awareness of the interconnectedness of things in the Overlook makes all the people mulling about the lobby look a little less queer.

Let's consider some of those details. After the man wheels by with the double beds and we see Bill and Stuart talking about what time the plane leaves – "8:30" or 8 ½, which reflects not only the last two cue cards, but, as we will see, even the man smoking a cigar in the lobby as Jack first enters the Overlook – we first see Jack calmly reading a Playgirl magazine, and we are left to wonder not only why is he reading such a magazine in the lobby of such a ritzy hotel, but why he is so nonchalant about it when his new boss catches him doing so, on the first day of his new job. Can they not see that magazine? And if not, what else does the audience see in the film that the characters in the film may be blind too altogether?

We are also left to wonder if Stuart saying "bye" to two women who are walking *into* the hotel behind Jack is related to the later event of him saying goodbye to the two women (possibly twins) outside of the Torrance apartment (and right after the scene where Danny had climbed on to a chair and seen twins himself) and supposedly *out* of the hotel when he is letting Jack and Wendy *into* their apartment. Like the two men carrying carpets, the first pair of women are walking toward the elevators, while the second pair are walking down the stairs. And in room 237, Jack encounters two women in one, just like the postcard from 1888, after walking up the unnatural stairs in 237, and then back down again as he exists the room.

Even the jersey of the woman walking into the hotel looks intentional. Of the two women walking into the hotel that say, "goodbye Mr. Ullman," the one nearest to Jack and the camera is wearing what appears to be a hockey jersey with a red trim and the number 13 on it. Her jersey reminds us of the blue trimmed shirt Danny wore in Boulder, where all we could see at first was a basketball hoop, Bugs Bunny ears, and the number "4," which turned out to be half of the number 42. Are we supposed to think of that 13 as 1+3? According to Stuart, the season at the hotel runs from May 15th to October 30th, which means Closing Day is Oct. 31: or 13 in a mirror. Coincidentally, Jack Ripper's first victim was Mary Ann Nichols, whose body was discovered on Friday, August 31, and his last victim was Mary Jane Kelly, who was discovered lying on her own bed in the single room where she lived, at 13 Miller's Court. In addition to being considered an unlucky number, with Jesus being number 13 of his 12 apostles, 13 also reflects the number of Jack's final pitch "a-cross" the lobby, as well as his final death blow to Dick.

While all these details, and others, seemed too curiously coincidental to be mere coincidences alone, I had no idea what such "coincidences" were trying to tell me. But then I saw how Kubrick was orchestrating them to "make ends meet."

Making Ends Meet: Inside & Out

What caught my eye in sorting out the myriad details in the lobby behind Jack was what Jack does with his finger while holding a piece of white bread: he points at his luggage and talks about writing. Writing is often about tying together ideas in a seamless web of words. And like the waiter that we see as Jack enters the hotel for his interview tying together with the tray of food Jack is eating from on Closing Day, so what we see on Closing Day both in the lobby and just inside the opening of the hedge maze, right before they are almost run over by a small green car, seemed to be entangled together like motion-twins.

With the crossfade from the bathroom of the Torrance apartment to Stuart, Wendy, Jack and Bill walking past the opening of the hedge maze, Kubrick appears to show us yet again "twin" devils in his details. As if magically transported to somewhere out beyond the hotel from the bathroom that required them to walk back to the hotel itself (the camera now panning left), we see a man just inside the "lobby" of the hedge maze raking gravel. Since the hotel "gets an average of twenty feet of snow over the winter," this is as odd as the guy mopping the floor in the lobby, or even the man shining the piano in the CL, in a hotel that is closing for six months. We would expect to see these activities on Opening Day, not Closing Day. Like the ambiguity of the final photograph, what we see on Closing Day looks more like stagehand's preparing for the opening day of the "play" we are about to watch unfold on the stage of our silver screen.

Recall as well that, next to the man moping in the lobby is a large A-frame ladder, which appears to be there for no good reason, unless it was used to hang the "receptionist" sign, the same way we see another man installing a "CASHIER" sign. This A-frame ladder is parked in a curious place indeed. Not only is it standing where Jack called to tell Wendy he got the job, leaving us to wonder why he couldn't have called from Stuart's office or even the receptionist area, it is also where we see Jack start his walk to the hedge maze table where he will appear to look down into it, as if he were a giant standing on top of a ladder, like Jack and the Bean Stalk.

As they walk past the hedge maze, notice the inset frame of the opening of the hedge maze itself. It is shaped exactly like the vanity mirror in the Torrance apartment, the red outline on the rug in the bathroom of room 237, and even the shapes of the green and gold walls over the bathtub, toilet, and twin mirrors in the 237 bathroom. The outer rim of the hedge maze entrance, on the other hand, is shaped as much like the twin mirrors in the bathroom of 237 as a tombstone. And while the hedge maze is green like Jack's sweater and knit tie, the line on the floor in the 237 bathroom is red, like Jack's jacket, and the jacket on Wendy's copy of the *Catcher in the Rye*; and even the book on Stuart's desk (more on that in a bit). Again, considering the events that follow, all of this looks deliberate, even without the "belief" that it was.

Examine the details seen outside the hotel. Along the wall of the maze directly across from the hotel (seen screen right), two men carry suitcases. One holds a blue and white tennis racket on his shoulder like a baseball bat. Later, a new entrance to the maze will open where they pass that Danny will run into, as if the man with the tennis racket is receiving the serve of Jack's throw through the lobby "A Month Later." When Jack first walked to the reception desk for his interview, a couple dressed in blue and white walked out of the hotel with tennis rackets and a bag filled, not with tennis balls, but baseballs. To the very left of the screen, we see two women leaving the hotel, much as we would have expected the two women who said goodbye to Ullman to have been doing. Behind those two women, we see a man running in the opposite direction, into the hotel. At the very end of the lobby scene as Jack and Stuart walk off to collect Jack's family, we also see a man running toward the lobby elevators. Both scenes reminded me of Wendy and Danny running from the entrance of the hotel to play in the hedge maze "A Month Later."

To clarify, just before the lobby scene crossfades into the scene in the CL, between the pillars on the left of the screen and just behind Stuart, we see, just over the box with the black tape on it that looks like three T's stacked into one, and back towards the "CASHIER" window, a man running to catch up to a woman carrying a shoulder bag as she walks toward the lobby elevators and the "magic carpet" that disappears later. Again, we would expect to see this couple walking out of the hotel, not toward the elevators.

Normally, just seeing two different people running - one inside toward the elevators and one outside toward the entrance of the hotel - would elicit no attention in and of themselves. But if we assume Kubrick is operating in accord with a rule-of-twins, these details begin to stand out. When we look even more closely at the details, we find a shocking amount of evidence to confirm such a rule is in play.

Note what we see directly in front of the entrance to the hotel as it emerges from the left side frame, just as Stuart, Wendy, Jack, and Bill walk past the hedge maze and into the path of an on-coming car. In just that small area of the scene, what we see there is so incredibly synchronized to what we saw previously in the lobby that the chances of it happening purely by accident would be astronomical.

Like the lobby scene, everything we see seems queer. "This is our famous hedge maze," Stuart says, as if he had failed to point it out to them earlier, even though they must have walked past it to get to wherever we now see them returning from. And where are they returning from anyway? The parking lot? And why is he only mentioning the maze as they return to the hotel? Like the opening scene, was it not there when they walked by that area on their way to wherever we now see them returning from? He then mentions that the walls are "13 feet high," which just happens to be the same height as the "iron curtain" known as the Berlin Wall, as if the Hedge Maze is designed to keep people from "ever" leaving, like that song "Hotel California" by the Eagles. Hence, in a film filled with twins, we *hear* the same number we *see* on the hockey jersey of the woman entering the hotel: the unlucky number 13. But there's more; much, much more.

Pay attention to the front of the awning to the hotel as they walk past the edge of the hedge maze. Stacking one chair on top of another, a man in grey overalls picks up both and proceeds inside. Passing him as he does, another man, empty handed and dressed in grey overalls, exits the hotel. Inside the lobby, we saw a man carrying two chairs into the lobby who crosses path with the man who had just carried in the green felt table, as the latter exits the hotel empty handed. As we see the empty-handed man exit the hotel, just as Wendy asks Stuart "when was the Overlook built," we also see three people exiting the front of the awning to the hotel. Those three people – two women and a man – look remarkably similar to the ones exiting the hotel when Jack pointed to his luggage and said, "right there." Like the man exiting the hotel alongside two women in the lobby scene, the man exiting from under the awning is both slightly taller than the two women and wearing a dark colored jacket like Danny's. And like the man in the lobby who overtook the two women as they exited the hotel, so too the man we now see exiting the hotel does so just ahead of the two women. Even their outfits look the same. Like one of the women exiting the hotel from inside the lobby, one of the women seen exiting the hotel outside the hotel is also wearing a tan jacket.

More than looking like mere meaningless coincidences, these micro-details look designed. But why? Why create such precision in a movie so riddled with mistakes and continuity errors? Clearly, Kubrick wanted the scene outside the hotel to operate as a seamless transition from the scene inside the lobby. The jump we are about to see from the path of the green car, as a result, is also a jump across three scenes: the tour of the CL; Danny in the Games Room with the twins and the dartboard with 237 on it; and Wendy and Jack touring their apartment. Does such a seamless jump reflect the idea that the jump from the path of the green car is no accident too? Such precision, after all, looks like the bending of space-time alluded to by the slight shift in the arm of the foosball table. Believing that such synchronicity could be the result of pure coincidence, especially in a Stanley Kubrick film, seemed to require a leap of faith that even the great Evel Knievel would consider insane.

How in the hell, we are left to wonder, could all this fit so perfectly together by accident? And since it would be impossible for such synchronicity to occur purely by accident, how could it be intended for no other purpose than to disorient the audience, especially when noticing it requires being at least as meticulous as Kubrick himself? Hell, we can even consider these three people walking seamlessly across these two scenes as a kind of "tri-cycle" motion twin to the trio of Wendy, Danny, and Dick, seamlessly jumping from one walk-in freezer to another in the kitchen.

Then there is the "black man" in the denim jacket that, for the most part, goes completely unseen by the audience. Right after the leap from the path of the green car, as the four of them walk past the entrance to the hotel on their way to the garage, we see someone behind them exit the hotel. Just as Stuart finishes his sentence that "they had to repel a few Indian *attacks* as they were building it," we see, near the left edge of the frame, a "black" man exit from behind the stone pillar of the awning over the entrance of the hotel. That same man exits in the same direction as Stuart, Wendy, Jack, and Bill walk out from the edge of the hedge maze and are about to me mowed down by that green car. Before the jump, he is seen exiting on the left side of the right-most pillar to the awning of the hotel (when looking at the face of the hotel from the outside). After the jump, he exits the entrance on the right side of that same stone pillar.

Why? Why does Kubrick bother to have this lone African American stand-in exit the entrance to the hotel twice in a row like this, on opposite sides of the stone pillar in each shot, and in such a way as to be barely noticeable at all? Upon his second exit of the hotel, there is also a green chair sitting on the right side of the sand-colored stone pillar as well, that he happens to step out from behind as he exits the shadow of the overhang. (Green and tan?) Considering that Jack the stone pillar and green chair remind us of the green shirt Jack wears as he types on his beige Adler typewriter, and that Jack steps out from behind a large red pillar in the lobby, both when he throws his tennis ball like a baseball and later when he swings his axe into Dick's chest like he is swinging a tomahawk or baseball bat (i.e., when Jack *attacks* Dick), this man – who is not carrying any luggage or boxes, and is the only other black man that we ever see in the Overlook hotel aside from Dick – cannot be wholly irrelevant and altogether meaningless.

Such details only invited me to dig deeper into Kubrick's rabbit hole. And the more I dug, the more I found. That's when I started rifling through Jack's luggage, which he points to and says, "right there." Or did he mean "write their"?

"Right There"

In the lobby, Stuart asks Jack if his luggage has been brought in, to which Jack replies by pointing to an overly large pile of luggage and saying "right there." That pile of luggage is clearly too large to have possibly fit inside the trunk of Jack's VW Beetle, or even the car overall. So, where the hell did it come from? Did Kubrick put it there to be ironic, as part of a joke or a metaphor, or was it perhaps intended to convey some purely symbolic meaning that the viewer is invited to divine for themselves?

It was clear by that point that potentially everything in the film was intended to have multiple meanings. So why would the oddly oversized pile of luggage in the lobby be any different? It would only make sense if it did have some meaning to it that we were being invited to consider. And we know this because of what Jack does next.

How the luggage got there is hinted at by what happens when Jack points to it. With spilt second timing, Jack points to his luggage and says, "right there." In that second, he also points directly at the three people walking out of the hotel – the same three people we see exiting the front of the hotel as Jack and company walk into the path of the oncoming car. As Jack is a writer, this carefully orchestrated alignment implies the pile of luggage represents the characters for the writing project Jack mentioned he was outlining during his interview. In fact, when Jack answers Stuart's question about his luggage, his head is directly in front of the wall sconce behind him, the luggage reflecting his "shining" ideas for his story or "play." What's more, those three people are even the inverted reflection of the three people Jack encounters later: Lloyd, Delbert, and the woman in room 237. And the seamless relationship between these three people exiting the hotel from both inside and outside the hotel, suggests Jack points at them because, like the moving furniture in both the lobby and the Games Room, they are reflections of the story he will "write" while "there," in the Overlook.

That luggage, and those three people, may also help to explain other mysteries. If they constitute the furniture for Jack's "play," do the lamps, rugs, and driftwood vanish in the CL, as well as other items that appear to change, vanish, or move around on their own in the hotel, do so because they reflect changes Jack is making to his manuscript? The CL is where Jack does all his writing, after all, and where he seems more at home than anywhere else in the hotel, even waking up on his writing table as if it were his second bed. Are they therefore "ghosts" mulling about the "ghost ship," not of the Overlook hotel, but of Jack's own mind?

Regardless of how we interpret them, it is a mistake to simply assume that they are, and indeed all of the people seen mulling about the hotel on Closing Day are, just insignificant patrons or employees of the hotel, and nothing more. To do so is to gravely overlook the game Kubrick is inviting his audience to come and play.

Even the way Kubrick aligns items in his shots seem telling. In this case, look closely at the outfits worn by the three people exiting the hotel. When Ullman and Watson first approach Jack in the lobby as he sits reading his Playgirl magazine, the pile of luggage, like the shelves of books seen over Wendy's head in Boulder, is seen directly above and behind Jack's head, as if to also represent a treasure trove of ideas, like thought bubbles in a cartoon. When Watson reaches Jack, he stands directly in front of that luggage, and behind Jack, like a looming shadow. Ullman then says, "Good morning, Jack, I hope you haven't been waiting too long," to which Jack replies, "No problem, in fact *we* had time to grab a bite to eat." It is assumed that by "we" Jack is referring to Wendy, Danny, and himself, rather than speaking only of himself and his alter egos, or even the characters he is dreaming up for his "play." When he says, "no problem," Jack looks to the table beside him, his eyes aligning perfectly with the two plaid suitcases that sit buried at the bottom of the giant pile of luggage; Danny's trike, symbolizing the ideas Jack is riding around and around in his head like Danny in the CL "A Month Later," sitting beside it. When Jack then points to his luggage saying, "Right there," the three people he points to walking out of the hotel are dressed similar to the luggage Jack appeared to look at when he told Stuart "*We*

130

had a chance to grab a bite to eat." And after Delbert gives him "one more chance" to prove himself, Jack ends up eating his words.

Consider the details of the man in the trio exiting the hotel. He is slightly taller than the two women, wearing an outfit that resembles Danny's: white sneakers and blue jeans with a blue jacket. He overtakes and then passes the two women beside him as they all exit the hotel. We will see him again, outside, pulling a cart full of luggage, in the opposite direction.

Then there are the two women beside him. Both wear jackets: one tan, a bit like the sports jacket on Jack, and the other a plaid red and black jacket, just like one of the suitcases, and the jacket worn by Jack's doppelgänger: the man seen later cleaning the cabinet in the CL. Those jackets are not only "twins" to the outfits we see worn by Jack over the course of the film, but they also reflect the colors of the suitcases buried at the bottom of the pile of luggage in the lobby.

Remember that man I told you to remember in the white sneakers and blue jeans with the blue jacket? Outside the hotel, notice what happens just as Wendy asks Ullman "when was the hotel built?" At that moment, Stuart says "Uh . . .," and suddenly we are teleported 90 degrees and the length of a football field down the road. After that jump, a man walks by in the foreground, heading in the opposite direction, pulling a cart of suitcases and cardboard boxes. Not only does the cart he is pulling vaguely remind us of the trike Danny will ride around the CL and the 237 hallway – which is different from the one we see in the lobby – but the man pulling that cart is the very same man seen walking out of the hotel with the two women when Jack pointed at his luggage and said, "right there." It is as if Jack has a Midas touch, his finger fusing that man with the giant pile of luggage, requiring him to pull that cart like Sisyphus, "forever and ever and ever."

As they walk to the garage and the snowcat, look to Jack's left, behind the tree. There, two women walk toward the entrance of the hotel. They look like the same two women who exited the hotel with the man we just saw pulling the cart. In fact, we even see one of those women flip her hair with a turn of her head, in the exact same way one woman did the same thing as they exited the lobby. And now Jack, his head dropping as if he were nodding off, much as it does at the Gold Room bar when Wendy interrupts his trance-like state, walks between them.

Also, look at the cart the man in the blue jacket is now pulling. Just as Stuart, Wendy, Jack, and Bill walked into the path of the oncoming car, that very same cart was filled with wood and being pulled in the opposite direction, by a man in a green jacket. Is it just a coincidence that a fire rages in the CL when Jack types away like a madman on his organ, a phantom of his own opera? Is this why the lamps, and the driftwood, and the (magic?) carpets, all begin disappearing as he does? Even the car that was about to run them over before the mysterious jump, again, was dark green. Does it reflect Jack mowing down Dick? Does the fire reflect Jack's mind burning with the luggage of his ideas?

Like the twin's invitation to Danny, so such incredible precision invited me to "come and play" with Kubrick's film. Again, how could all of this be a meaningless coincident, or merely an attempt to disorient? On the one hand, Jack points to the trio exiting the hotel and says, "write there," while outside the hotel, on the other hand, Jack walks between those same three people at the same moment Stuart is describing when the hotel was "built." Jack, after all, is a writer, who builds his story, out of the luggage of his ideas, and experiences. Of the two women seen in that trio, one wears a red jacket, like Jack's. Also, one is blonde and the other one brunette. And in room 237, Jack encounters two women as well: one blonde, the other brunette. In fact, even the two different old hags we see in room 237 – one kissing Jack and the other, after Jack finds himself kissing an old hag, rising up from the bathtub like a vampire – are brunette and blonde, respectfully.

The more we look, the more we see. At the same moment we see that man again pulling the cart of boxes and luggage, right after the magical leap, Jack is looking toward the hotel, as if he is looking toward where the pile of luggage was sitting inside of the lobby. He therefore never sees the man with the cart of luggage, and only looks back toward Ullman after the man pulling the cart exits the left side of the frame. After he does, Jack looks forward again, his head dropping and springing back up, as if he were catching himself from falling asleep. Again, he does this when Wendy tells him about "a crazy woman in one of the rooms." This happens right when Jack aligns with the stone pillar that the black man is about to walk out from behind. All of this occurs right after the strange yet seamless jump, a jump that implies a kind of "black out" has just occurred, like Danny jumping between the Boulder bathroom and his bed.

So why is there an overly large pile of luggage in the lobby, seen directly over Jack's head as he reads his Playgirl magazine? Is it for the same reason Jack points at that luggage and says "right there" while pointing at two women and a man who looks like he could be Tony walking out of the hotel? Was Kubrick therefore extending his rule of twins to include ambiguous comments, with "right there" being the twin to "write there," or "write their"?

With all of this in mind, and more, suddenly, the two plaid suitcases buried at the bottom of the pile of luggage in the lobby began to stand out as something more than simply suitcases. They looked instead like evidence of a repressed side of Jack that was just dying to get out of the storage room that Jack was pretending to be, and into the story we had all come to see. Jack has his own Tony too. And hadn't we all come to see that other Jack unleash himself, and bathe the screen in blood?

Two Plaid Suitcases

Seen just behind Jack's head and right next to Danny's tricycle on Closing Day, buried at the bottom of the overly large pile of luggage in the lobby, sit two plaid suitcases. As the camera pans across the lobby as the scene emerges, with Stuart and Bill walking toward the camera as Jack sits reading his portentous magazine, those two plaid suitcases appear to cross in one of Jack's ears and out of the other. The colors of those bags appear to be intentional, given what we've seen and will see happen later. One of the bags has red with black stripes and the other has white stripes with what appears to be reds and blues or light black colors. The former resembles the jacket Danny is wearing when he runs to play in the maze with Wendy, the jacket worn by the Tony-look-a-like carrying the lone chair toward the Games Room, and the guy shining the cabinet across from Jack's writing table in the CL. And the colors and patterns of both bags remind us of the shirt and jacket Jack wears when he later chases Danny into the maze, which is perhaps part of the "play" Jack wishes to "write there."

More than just their colors, even their placement looked intended to communicate meaning. Both bags are buried beneath a pile of luggage, with darker bags directly above them like storm clouds gathering, ready to burst into the coming snowstorm. Like twin pieces of luggage to the film itself, they foreshadow Jack pouring out blood from a golden chalice, a golden bough. And in the CL, as they begin their tour, we see sitting on what will serves as Jack's writing table, just such a golden bowl sitting like the Holy Grail of the Last Supper, right where Jack's typewriter will sit. And Jack's first typewriter is beige, while the one we actually see him writing with is grey, like a shadow, reflecting that "shadow" that Carl Jung said inhabits us all, comprised of those shameful parts of ourselves we try to repress, for fear of being rejected for failing to do so.

All the bags look deliberately chosen and organized, too. Above the two dark bags, a tan bag flanked by two green bags, the same colors Jack is wearing: a tan or golden jacket over a green sweater and a light green "collared" shirt. Flanking the plaid bags are a light blue suitcase, on the left, and the light blue back seat of Danny's trike, on the right. That trike is different from the one we see Danny riding around the hotel and parked on top of the emblem when Jack throws his ball. This trike has a white bar under the seat, the other a red bar under the seat, as if it were stained by Danny riding through torrents of blood.

Is it just a coincidence that the gold and green bags happen to match Jack's attire? Along with the "CASHIER" sign being installed on the day the Torrance's move into the hotel, Jack's golden sport's jacket and green sweater remind us of both "the golden fleece" and how money used to be backed by gold. As a noun, "fleece" is the skin of a lamb,

135

which Dick asked Danny if he liked, as if Danny is being led into the mountains to be slaughter like a sacrificial lamb by Jack, just like Isaac had been led by Abraham, so the latter could prove he was worthy of living "forever, and ever, and ever," with the Overlooker. As a verb, it means "to conceal or swindle out of a great deal of money." In mythology, to place Jason rightfully on the throne of Iolcus in Thessaly, King Pelias orders Jason and his crew, the Argonauts, to set out on a quest to find the Golden Fleece. Is Kubrick inviting us to do something similar?

Yet consider the subtle details related to this idea of gold. While Jack wears a golden sports jacket on Closing Day, our very first view of the inside of the hotel when Jack arrives for his interview, as the camera tracks Jack through the lobby, is from the Cashier widow. And the first thing Jack did when he walked into the hotel was look over to where his picture will hang at the end of the film. He is a shining star, in the Gold Room hallway; like stars on Sunset Blvd; a play on the idea of "Going to the Sun" road, that we saw him driving along in his yellow VW, like Apollo riding the chariot of the sun across the sky. Like most people in America, that cashier window is an "impossible window" for a schoolteacher. Yet we only discover this to have been the case when the camera gets a "second sight" of the lobby, as it walks over to Jack reading his Playgirl magazine on Closing Day. And on Closing Day, the camera now watches Jack from the vantage point of the Gold Room hallway, as Stuart and Watson start their walk on the exact spot Dick's body will be laid out like a sacrificial lamb for Wendy and Danny, with a man installing a "CASHIER" sign over a cashier window on one side, which is as decorative as the screen in a confessional, and a laundry cart on the other, which looks like it will be used to cart Dick's corpse from the stage later on.

Other clues that there is something more going on with that pile of luggage than initially meets the eye is the fact that Danny's tricycle is sitting right next to it. As mentioned, that trike is different from the one he rides around the hotel, much like Jack's typewriter, which is the "toy" that we see Jack letting his fingers do the walking on in the CL, also changes colors, from tan or beige to a dark charcoal or black - like the two bags sitting directly over the two plaid bags. As the camera walks to the right, the handlebars of Danny's trike even pass right over Jack's head, resembling rabbit ears like the one's sticking up from under the table on Danny's jersey. Jack then leans forward to talk to Stuart and, when he does, his head aligns with the center of the red and black diamond shape emblem on the floor, which sits directly below the tricycle and in front of the doors to the entrance, and which points both in and out the front door to the hotel.

From a two-dimensional perspective, it is as if Jack is sticking his head up out of a diamond shaped red and black rabbit hole. This may be why Jack wears a golden jacket, because in 1939, Bugs Bunny was called "Happy Rabbit," and was depicted in light blue and white while wearing gold gloves, rather than the white gloves he would come to wear, like the ones we see Delbert Grady wearing. And before that, Bugs was a white rabbit, like the kind Alice played with and the one the behavior psychologist John B. Watson used in 1922 to condition a child to live in fear.[24]

We see still other synchronicities also. Even the chair Jack is sitting in is similar in color and pattern to the tablecloth seen when Wendy and Danny eat lunch in Boulder, and the towel under Danny's bowl when he and Wendy later watch TV again while sitting on the bed. Jack then stands up directly in front of Danny's trike, and when he points at the people walking out of the hotel and says, "right there," they are also directly between Jack and Danny's trike. And while Danny's trike is sitting directly in front of the heater coil behind it, Danny also plays with toy cars called "hot wheels" or "matchbox cars" in the 237 hallway. How interesting it is, as such, that we see heat vents behind Jack as he begins to morph into red-jacket Jack, and a fire is always raging in the CL when he is typing or leering out the window, as if he's in a trance.

Noticing such overlapping precision suggested it was no mere coincidence that the two plaid bags happened to be sandwiched between a periwinkle blue suitcase on the left, and the back of the seat to Danny's trike on the right. Whenever we see Danny riding his tricycle, again, the trapezoidal shape of his back seat mirrors the shape of the dresses worn by the Grady twins, and both are the same color: sky blue. Coincidentally enough, periwinkle blue is not only the same color as the blue in Danny's Apollo 11 sweater, but also the color of the dress in which the mother of

---

[24] More interesting is the fact that Bugs Bunny has been used by psychologists to study how people can develop false memories, where people would be convinced they had seen Bugs Bunny at Disneyland, even though, being a Warner Brothers cartoon, you would never see Bugs Bunny in Disneyland.

someone who, in some ways, reminds us of Jack Torrance was buried in. That someone was Norman Bates in Hitchcock's *Psycho*.

◊◊

As we have seen, assuming that there were no mistakes or coincidences in *The Shining* led me to look at Kubrick's film with new eyes. Only by realizing how my religious "beliefs" were coloring my perceptions like looking at the sun through a stained-glass window, did I discover the incredible level of precision operating behind the mask of Kubrick's continuity errors. And the closer I looked, the more there was to see. Prior to that, I had only ever watched the movie with eyes wide shut, even as I was convinced that the baptismal sacrifice of my foreskin had given me the gift of "second sight" which allowed me to see why the gremlins that stalked my bedroom as a child had to be real, because so was God, and therefore the devil, and therefore my sinful soul. But they were, only because my perception of them, and everything else, was real. What I didn't know at that time was that only a lie requires threats and brides to convince you to "believe" it is "the truth," let alone "the one and only truth." That would be like being taught to believe that the world would plunge into darkness if we stopped believing that the Sun shines its' light because it "loves" us. If the Sun doesn't stop shining its light, regardless of what people think about it, why is a "God" who is said to be so infinitely greater than our puny little Sun so incensed, or even fully disempowered, whenever people fail to spend an hour inside of a particular breed of building every Sunday?

Yet nothing was more revealing than what I saw with a second look at the tour of the CL. There, Kubrick hid a bevy of clues to his puzzle, including one of the most significant clues which came from discovering something which should have been there, but wasn't. And because it wasn't, I began to understand how the piece of paper Jack tears to pieces and throws on the floor resurrected itself and ended up back in his typewriter. But I'm getting ahead of myself again. Before getting into any of that, let me give you the guided tour of the strange happenings in the Colorado Lounge (CL) on Closing Day.

Into the Colorado Lounge

As we crossfade from the lobby into the Colorado Lounge, notice Kubrick's precision. First, recall that when Jack mentioned his "sons discovered the Games Room," he motioned in the same direction they exit the lobby. This is the same direction we later see Danny ride his trike before jumping a floor and seeing the twins "chopped up into little pieces," like Wendy's can of fruit cocktail. And now, we see them exiting the elevators – the only time we ever see anyone exiting elevators – after Stuart pulls back a "scissor" gate.

Consider this scissor gate for a moment. We only see this scissor gate on the elevators they unload from into the CL, elevators that are "twins" to the red and black door Wendy runs through later on, just before she jumps to the darkened Gold Room hallway, the mirror behind her conspicuously absent, and then sees the lobby full of skeletons. We see something similar beside the boilers when Wendy hears Jack screaming from his nightmare. That scissor gate, which appears to be absent from the vision Danny has of the river of blood, is also a three dimensional depiction of the red carpet with the black diamond shape patterns on it, like the Bugs Bunny doll on top of Dick's gravestone is to the picture on Danny's 42 jersey.

So, what, right? Well, notice where we see that red and black carpet. We first see it inside the foyer of the Gold Room bathroom, after Delbert crashes into Jack. At the moment Jack opens that door, he mentions the "fish and goose soirée," reminding us of the pictures of fish in Stuart's office and Wild Goose Island. This line, in fact, relates to Jack' red jacket, and a character Nicholson played in *Five Easy Pieces*, *ten* years earlier. The next two times we see it is first as Wendy rushes out of the hotel to check the snowcat, and then Jack as rushes out of the hotel to chase Danny into the hedge maze. Both times they are rushing out into a winter wonderland, while the bathroom in the Gold Room is called the "Powder Room."

The last two places we see that red and black diamond rug is in the hallway when Wendy sees the river of blood, where it appears to replace the green diamond rug Jack pitched his tennis ball toward, and then hanging on the wall to the right of the final picture of Jack. Given that the carpet is the two-dimensional twin of the elevators, the times and places we see it suggests it alludes to an elevated position, as if the hedge maze is a floor above the hotel, much like room 237 is a floor above the CL where Jack does his writing. As we will see, it also relates to the map of the world we see in Stuart's office.

Notice other queer details as we bleed into the CL. Ullman not only said they should start with a quick look at their apartment, but he also told Bill to take care of the pile of luggage. Bill then walked off in the opposite direction with a curt response: "Fine." Jack then said he wanted

141

to "collect" his family when they exited the lobby. Yet rather than the very next scene being a tour of their apartment, they end up touring the CL instead, with Bill in tow, despite his walking off toward the lobby elevators earlier. And Danny is still absent. Then, when they reach their apartment *after* touring the CL, Bill is absent, and Danny has yet to be "collected." The only consistency from the lobby into the CL is that they are getting "started straight away," as Stuart mentions. It as if they walk screen-left in the CL in order to sow the two scenes together. And what suggests this is the case is both the pile of luggage in the CL and the direction they walk from the lobby.

As they enter the CL, the pile of luggage in the lobby dissolves into four people huddled around another pile of boxes and luggage, and their profile just happens to match the exact same height and width as the pile of luggage in the lobby, and Jack, of course, does all his writing in the CL. The huddle of people around luggage in the CL, as such, is a combination of the pile of luggage and the three people walking out of the hotel, when Jack said, "write their." Note also that as they all walk past that huddle, Jack does something that no one else does.

Again, at a second look, all the details seen in the CL looked like they were chosen to reflect intentional synchronicities. Recall the man carrying the carpet on his shoulder through the lobby, for example, the one dressed like Danny with the blue jacket and red trim, who waits an unnaturally long period of time behind the pillar (like Jack waiting to kill Dick) before ascending the stairs. Combined with the man we then see in green utility overalls carrying another rolled-up carpet down the grand staircase at the other end of the CL, the two appear to depict, among other things, the character arcs of Jack and Danny over the course of the film.

In one arc, Danny grows to become his own man through a trial by fire, with room 237 having an impossible fireplace and being directly above the CL fireplace, and in the other, Jack regresses into a "wild child" until he is frozen like ice-scream. And even the carpet seen in front of the lobby elevators when Jack walks into Ullman's office for his interview – which resembles both the carpet under the bed in the Torrance apartment and the carpet under the bed when Wendy sees the two men in the upper room – disappears later on, as if to suggest that Jack is like a Genie in a bottle floating on a "magic carpet ride," while Danny rides around on the carpets in the CL and the 237 hallway.

As they begin their tour of the CL, we see more synchronicity. Like the Playgirl magazine, Jack does something that no one else appears to do as they disembark from the elevator behind his writing table: he notices a huddle of people around a pile of luggage. Contrast this with the fact that the three people Jack pointed at inadvertently in the lobby when he said "right there" appeared to be invisible even to Jack. Stuart, Wendy, and Bill, on the other hand, all treat that huddle as if they are as invisible as Jack's magazine. (This is the twin, so to speak, of the fact that, besides Jack and Stuart, everyone else treats Bill like he is completely invisible too.) As Jack notices them, they stream into the elevator, as if they are breaking from a football huddle for the next play, perhaps to punt the football. Are they Jack's "stream of consciousness?" Do they "head" to the elevator because ideas for Jack's play are bubbling up from the "shadow" in his subconscious mind and rising to the surface?

Of the four people huddled together, one is a man who, like others, is also dressed like Danny, wearing a blue jacket with red stripes. He stands with *3 Women*: a 1977 American avant-garde drama written, produced, and directed by Robert Altman and starring Shelley Duvall, Sissy Spacek (space X?) and Janice "Rule" (like the "new rule" Jack makes later). Two of the women are dressed in tans, like one of the women who exited the hotel entrance earlier, while the woman standing between them with her back to the camera – "faceless – is dressed in colors Jack will wear for his "killer" performance (with Jack's limp reflecting "break a leg"), only inverted: tan boots, red skirt, and a plaid dark blue jacket with white stripes. That same woman even emerges directly out of the two plaid suitcases in the lobby, as if the ideas those two suitcases contained are coming to life before our eyes. But like Danny with the Grady twins, only Jack can see them for what they are at this point: his own haunting ideas.

Other details surrounding those four people appear to carry some significance as well. As they break their huddle, picking up boxes and suitcases and boarding the elevator, we are left to wonder why the people walking up the stairs behind them aren't doing the same thing, especially since it seems they will have to ascend to a floor above the 237 floor. Notice also what each of them picks up. The woman in the red skirt picks up a single bag in her right hand, a compact plaid red and black bag, and heads for the elevator, while the other two women pick up only boxes, and the man in the blue jacket picks up a box in his right hand and a red and black plaid suitcase in the other, like the one sitting next to Danny's trike in the lobby. Are all the red and black plaids, from the suitcases to the jackets worn by various people in and around the hotel, really just a coincidence, or something more?

If we continue to scrutinize the details of the beginning of the tour of the CL, we see other details connecting to the two plaid suitcases in the lobby. First, note that if we look at the pointer on the dial above the elevator door Jack and company exit, we see that it indicates that they are still on the first floor, the same floor as the lobby; the same floor the elevator is on from which the river of blood pours out of. But this seems impossible. If so, why are so many people heading to the floors above, which indicates we have descended from the lobby? Are the plaid bags seen buried beneath a pile of luggage in the lobby related to the people in the CL because the CL is where Jack unpacks his subconscious mind?

Recall that Wendy hears Jack screaming at his desk in the CL while she is in the boiler room, which we are led to believe is in the basement. While this is expressly stated in the novel, it is only suggested in the film. That she does suggests Jack must be right next door to the boiler room. So, is the CL in the basement? In the novel, the scrapbook was, and always remained, in the basement. Is this then one detail that Kubrick did not change?

Note also that, like the carpet carriers, there are two women climbing the stairs who do not board the elevator, while Jack encounters two women in room 237.

What makes the pointer on the dial above the elevator they unload from so curious is how it relates to the scissor gate and the Gold Room bathroom. As mentioned, the first time we see the red and black diamond pattern rug that resembles the scissor gate is when Jack walks into the bathroom with Delbert Grady. If the pointer above the elevator is on the first floor, which is the same floor as the lobby, then is Kubrick using that pointer to indicate a seamless transition between the lobby scene and the beginning of the tour of the CL scene? If so, that means that when Jack and Stuart walk out of the lobby scene, they end up disembarking from the elevators in the CL because of what Stuart and Jack walk by and toward as they exit the lobby. Recall as well that Jack walks into the Gold Room from the CL, as if the two rooms are both on the first floor, or the same floor, and then mentioned he's having problems with the "old sperm bank upstairs," as if he has now descended into his own subconscious.

Then there's the second half of the explanation. That can only be seen, however, when Wendy exits the phone closet on her way to Stuart's office to radio the Forest Ranger. As she does, behind her are red and black doors, similar to the façade of the elevators in the CL, and the one's Wendy runs through after she sees a ghost that is a hybrid of Delbert Grady and Jack. Those doors just happen to be bathroom doors. Stuart and Jack walk toward those bathroom doors at the end of the lobby scene, and then seamlessly continue to walk in the same direction in the CL scene that follows.

Between the bathroom doors in the lobby hallway and the elevator doors they exit in the CL stood the large A-frame ladder and the man mopping up water. By touring the CL after the lobby, despite Stuart saying they would start with the Torrance apartment, Jack and Stuart appear to walk across the path where that man was mopping the floor, but through the red and black bathroom doors in the lobby, the other side of which are the elevator doors they disembark in the CL. It suggests, in other words, that they are walking around inside of a house of mirrors. And if they were, even the colors could operate like breadcrumbs to be followed.

So, I followed those colors, and they led me straight to two things: Apollo's twin sister Artemis, and Tony. And like breadcrumbs, they even revealed how Kubrick shows us why and how Tony ends up in Danny's mouth.

SIX

TONY & THE COLOR TWINS

We all know that art is not truth.
Art is a lie that makes us realize truth, at least the truth that is given us to understand.

Pablo Picasso

One's destination is never a place, but a new way of seeing things.

Henry Miller

IN 1672, A NEW THEORY OF LIGHT AND COLOR was developed by Sir Isaac Newton. After performing experiments with it, Newton determined that light was comprised of as many as "11" different colors. But "seeing" isn't always "believing." Rather than trust the only sense capable of determining color, he allowed his ears to have the final say in what he was seeing with his own two eyes. Like the gremlins I saw in the shadows of my room, Newton saw the colors of light through the lens of his ears, proving that the world we "believe" in is the world we live in.

Inspired by similarities between the color scale and the seven notes found on the musical scale, Newton forced the round pegs of those 11 different colors into the square holes of seven different categories. When passed through a prism, light diffuses into those seven colors which Newton labeled as red, orange, yellow, green, blue, indigo, and violet.

As if to fashion those abstractions of light into our own image, we personified those colors into a name with the acronym Roy G. Biv. Red, yellow, and blue, which are the primary colors, can be combined to create a gamut of other colors. Orange, green, indigo, and violet, on the other hand, are considered secondary colors.

Like the ball rolling up to Danny, so colors, unlike words, invite us out of our mind and into our senses, as Alan Watts put it, because the music of color can only be heard through our eyes. And to see how *The Shining* is a masterfully orchestrated symphony of colors and light, we must undo Newton's willingness to define colors by the dictates of his ears and learn how to listen to what Kubrick is saying with our eyes through a pantomime of colors.

The tenor of Kubrick's symphony of light can be heard in every detail of every shot of his film. To see this, consider how he carefully orchestrates the colors of costumes. In the first half of *The Shining*, Jack is always wearing something green, while in the second half of the film, he only wears his green shirt when he is typing alone in the CL, and his red jacket the rest of the time. (It should raise a red flag that Jack happens to be wearing his red jacket *inside* the hotel.) In contrast to this, Wendy often wears red and blue in the first half of the film, and earth tone colors like tan, brown, and green, in the second half of the film. She also transitions from wearing a darker blue jumper to a lighter blue bathrobe, while her brown overalls are corduroy like Jack's red jacket.

Such colors and textures suggest that, after Danny enters room 237, Wendy and Jack switch sides on the color scale. On that scale, green is the objective opposite of red, while mixing red and green light gives us the color yellow, like the jacket Jack wears on Closing Day, and the jacket Wendy wears when she calls the Forest Rangers. Even Woodstock on Danny's rainbow sticker, and the rubber ducky in the Boulder Bathroom – which jumps from the bathtub to Danny's windowsill – is yellow.

Reds, greens, and blues dominate throughout the film. Today, these same colors are used in television and computer monitors, including smartphone displays, to produce a wide range of colors.

Blue & White

In *The Shining*, Kubrick uses colors like breadcrumbs. We can see this by following just one of the recurring pairs of colors we see continually popping up together over the course of the film: blue and white. Doing so eventually lead me straight to Tony, and how he ended up in Danny's mouth, as well as how the butterfly is a symbol of our own psyche.

Kubrick's pairing of blue and white comes in two forms in the film: light blue and white and dark blue and white, with each pair being a dissimilar "twin" to the other. Danny's Bug Bunny jersey, for example, contains the first pair of blue and white, his Apollo 11 sweater the second. In fact, the colors of the Apollo 11 sweater are identical to the colors seen in the first bathrobe we see Wendy wearing, and both are identical to the colors worn by the Grady twins and the wallpaper and ceiling outside of the Torrance's Overlook apartment. When Wendy is seen checking the boilers and she hears Jack scream, we see a circular container on the right corner of the desk that is the same colors as Wendy's bathrobe as well: blue, white, and yellow. Wendy's lighter is a darker blue and her cigarettes are white, as are the various boxes of

Frosted Flakes seen with Tony the Tiger on it (and Danny's alter ego is Tony, of course, who lives in his mouth and hides in his stomach) and even the open loaf of white bread.

Danny's Mickey Mouse sweater is also a variation of blue and white, colors that happen to match Hallorann's pajama top. Even the News cast program with Glenn Rinker (Grim Reaper?) begins with a blue screen and a white border around it. Danny's original tricycle, the one seen beside the abnormally large pile of luggage in the lobby, was blue and white, while the one we see him riding around the hotel is blue and red with white handle grips.

Other objects that share these colors include the box of Q-tips seen on the shelf behind Wendy in Boulder, as if to suggest we should listen carefully; the box of Q-tips sits right next to the white ivory bull; just below that bull sits a box decorated in a pattern that resembles piano keys, which are also blue and white; the blue pen in Ullman's silver cup and the white pen on his desk that spins around like a compass, that keeps reversing its reading during the interview; the top edge of the notepad inside of the brown binder on Ullman's desk, which is blue with white dots; and plenty of other various outfits and objects seen throughout the film.

All these details only seemed more interesting, however, when I noticed the couch pillows, the shadow outside of the Boulder apartment complex, the man in the blue plastic jumpsuit with the white stripe, the opening and closing credits, and where there was no blue to be found at all.

Connecting the Dots: From the Notepad to the Butterfly

One of the most important blue and white color combinations needed to connect the dots in Kubrick's coloring book is seen is outside of the hotel on Closing Day. After the jump from where Ullman, Wendy, Jack, and Bill, are nearly flattened like a pancake by a green car, they walk past the main entrance to the hotel on their way to the garage. On the way, they pass directly in front of a pile of luggage, a brown paneled station wagon, and a blue four door AMC Matador sedan with a white roof. To the left side of the station wagon, a man in a blue suit with a white stripe on it – a suit that looks like a "jumpsuit" made from plastic, as if he were a human trash bag or a toy doll – walks past the pile of luggage and heads toward the hotel entrance. As the camera pans to the right, he passes through the windows of the station wagon before exiting the frame.

Again, so what, right?

There is no reason for these details to elicit any special notice from the audience. They only become relevant once we notice a host of other things. Those "other things" consist of the significance of the rear door to the station wagon; what we see as Jack drives to the Overlook; what happens outside of the Boulder apartment building; what happens with the notepad in Stuart's office; what we see when Wendy and the doctor exit Danny's bedroom; and what we see when Wendy brings Jack breakfast in bed. This list is not exhaustive, but the items listed are all entangled with each other in more ways than one.

First, consider Jack's drive to the Overlook in the opening scene. Along the way, he passes a white station wagon parked on the *right shoulder* of the road, just before entering a tunnel. After exiting the tunnel, just as Joe Turkel's name rises through the frame, the road curves slightly to the left and then back to the right. As he snakes along this smaller "S" in the road – the lesser "twin" to the larger backwards "S" we saw him driving along when we first saw his car – we see, hiding just behind a large tree with green and yellow leaves, a car parked in the scenic overlook on the *left shoulder* of the road: a blue two door sedan with a white top, with both doors wide open. Like the green car that almost rolls over Jack and company as they cross the road in front of the hedge maze, the shot ends just before Jack's car is about to cross paths with a dark oncoming car.

That blue and white car parked in the overlook turnout, just beyond the tunnel, resembles the blue and white Matador we see right after the impossible leap from the front of the hedge maze to the front of the Overlook hotel on Closing Day. And not only is Dick driving a Matador after his own "impossible jump" from Miami to Denver, the Matador in front of the hotel is parked right next to a red and brown paneled station wagon.

Is it not curious that, during the opening scene, Jack passes a station wagon and then a blue and white Matador right after emerging from a tunnel, while on Closing Day, Jack is again passing a station wagon and a blue and white Matador right after jumping through a veritable wormhole to escape being run over by a green car? Even the difference between the two doors on the first car, that Kubrick clearly intended for us to see, and the four doors on the Matador in front of the hotel, is curious when we consider that Jack is alone in the opening scene, but with his "other half" – Wendy – on Closing Day. Add to this the seamlessness of Wendy's question and Ullman's answer across the quantum leap, and suddenly we are faced with considering whether the strange jump is just a mistake, or a twin, one that reflects Jack's car passing through the tunnel on its way to the Overlook, or even something more. This is especially true when we consider that Closing Day is really the opening day of Jack's story in the hotel with his family, which is why we see so much of the curious activity we see at the Overlook.

After Jack passes through the tunnel in the opening scene, we cut to the next shot: Jack's car skirting precariously along a steep mountain side that drops off into the shadows of a valley below. Another white station wagon approaches from the other direction, headed for Jack's car. On its roof sits a canoe, which seems a bit out of place considering the rest of Jack's drive is through snow covered mountainsides that increasingly resembles the landscape on the moon.

That canoe reminded me of the fellow Jack passes as he walks into Stuart's office for the first time, the one standing by the elevators with a fishing hat over his hand, and what is vague enough to double as a possible fishing pole. Along with the various photographs and paintings of people fishing in the hotel, such allusion called to mind "tall tales" and paddling "up shit's creek." The fishing references even allude to in the various paintings of lakes we see in the hotel, like the one over the Torrance bed and the one in the foyer of room 237, as well as the fish hanging in Stuart's office and in Hallorann's sunroom in Miami. Yet fishing stands in stark contrast to the idea of skiing, the two reflecting the idea of opposites, an idea mirrored in the opening and closing shots of the film.

Now consider the man in the blue jumpsuit, and why his placement looks anything but random.

After jumping from the murderous path of the green car, we see the man in the all blue outfit walking toward the hotel entrance. With a white stripe down the arm, it has the sheen of a coroner's body bag, and looks like an athletic outfit called a "jumpsuit." With an awareness of other obscure details, that suit suddenly sticks out like a sore thumb.

As Rob Ager has pointed out, as Wendy and the doctor exit Danny's bedroom after Danny's seizure, we see a small painting in the back room of the Torrance apartment. It hangs on a light green wall, a color that reminded me of Jack's Stovington Eagles t-shirt, and over a light blue and white bonnet hair dryer, like Danny's Apollo sweater, that sits over a red velvet chair, like Jack's crush velvet jacket. Of a boy and a girl who are Danny's age or younger, it is framed inside baby-blue matting shaped like an eggshell, reminding me that Danny is Jack "yoke," and of the "sonny" side up egg Wendy brings Jack in bed. Standing profile, the boy wears a blue suit with a white stripe down the side of the arm, while the girl has her back to the world, "faceless," like that man standing by the elevator with a fishing hat.

In the CL, when they first start their tour on Closing Day, recall we see another man wearing a blue jacket with a white stripe, in a football huddle, who then "jumps" on the elevator, with *three* women. Like the paintings of birds in the CL foreshadowing Jack chasing Danny down the utility hallway in the lobby, so the painting in the backroom of the Boulder apartment appears to be a reflected in the man walking into the hotel beside the brown panel station wagon. And both appear to reflect a 3 way magic door, a particularly jumpy notepad, and a rather ominous butterfly, seen beside a mirror as Jack emerges from the tunnel of a good night sleep, A Month Later.

The Notepad, the Sleeper Van, & the Butterfly

Of all of the blue and white items to be found in the film, perhaps three are more telling in their relation to Danny's Bugs Bunny jersey and his Apollo II sweater, than all the rest. The first is a van seen in the Boulder parking lot. The second, and most cryptic of all, is what we see sitting next to the vanity mirror right before Jack wakes up, A Month Later, and right after Wendy jumps from the lobby floor to their apartment floor (presumably via the elevator): a blue butterfly. But before we can relate the blue butterfly to the van parked in the parking lot outside of the Boulder apartment complex, we must address the third most intriguing blue and white item in the film: the notepad in Stuart Ullman's office. What makes this last item so intriguing is what it does before and after the scene in the Boulder apartment. That notepad has a blue spine across the head of it. That spine is studded with white dots. And if we learn to follow Kubrick's breadcrumbs, we discover how to connect the dots to the man we see after the "jump" from the path of the green car, wearing the blue jumpsuit. As it turns out, he happens to pass through a magic door.

Noticing the notepad requires second sight. As Jack first enters Stuart's office, the notepad of note sits on the credenza under the map of Colorado, on the far side of the radio. A blue spine across its header is studded with white dots. Next, we jump back and forth from the Boulder apartment where Wendy and Danny appear to be eating lunch. Upon returning to Stuart's office, the notepad has moved from where it sat. No longer on the credenza beside the radio, it has jumped across the area Stuart walked to shake Jack's hand and landed inside of a dark brown binder on Stuart's desk.

That binder was sitting directly below the brown binder we saw Stuart writing in when Jack first entered his office. Beside it sits a large red book. And just under that red book and beside the brown binder, we see a white book with the word "TRAVEL" written in black letters along the spine. The notepad "travels" from the credenza to inside the binder, while the audience "traveled" back and forth from Boulder.

The white-dotted blue spine of that notepad reminded me of the white stars that wrap around the blue sleeve on Danny's Bugs Bunny shirt, and the red outline around those stars reminded me of the red book on Stuart's desk. So too, the jump of that notepad was like Danny jumping from the bathroom to his bed in the Boulder apartment, the dark color of the binder like Danny's black-out and the tunnel Jack drove thru as he "traveled" to his interview. And after Danny wakes up from his black-out, he's interviewed by the doctor, who then interviews Wendy, who happens to look like a female version of Stuart Ullman; and is dressed in colors that are the same as Susie's outfit, only inside out. And perhaps most oddly of all, Danny is no longer wearing his jeans, as if he had either wet himself or jumped out of his pants, or both, which made me think Danny had abandoned "half of his genes," as he does when he flees the hotel with Wendy later.

The blue and white notepad reminded me also of the blue and white Matadors mentioned earlier. Again, first we see a blue two door sedan right after Jack passes through a tunnel on his drive to the hotel, with both doors wide open as if Kubrick was inviting us to climb inside and take a ride. Then we see an almost identical looking version of the same car sitting in the Overlook parking lot, right after the mysterious jump, but with four doors, and two people inside of it, including a woman wearing a red scarf who climbs into the passenger seat. That four-door matador is parked right next to a brown and red wood panel station wagon, which reminded me of the brown binder and the red book on Stuart's desk. And the notepad reminded me of how much the blue plastic jumpsuit with the white stripe we see worn by the man walking into the darkened entrance to the hotel, right after the jump from the path of the green car, was like the painting in the back room of the Boulder apartment at the end of the hallway Danny had "jumped" across from the bathroom to his bed. And after Dick makes his own impossible jump from Miami to Denver in the middle of a "white out," he is also seen driving a Matador. All of this was only even more curious because of what happens in the parking lot outside of the apartment building in Boulder.

Paying attention to the camera as it crossfades to a view from the far side of the parking lot outside of the Boulder apartment complex, I noticed something move. At first, I thought a fly had landed on my screen. But it wasn't a fly. As the scene fades from Stuart's office to the parking lot, the tallest vehicle in the line of cars in the center of the frame (on the left side of the parking lot) is a light blue van with a white top. That van emerges right out of where Susie had been standing.

Behind Susie, recall, and right below Stuart's impossible window, sat a dark four-legged totem-art sculpture, reminding me of spirits and the Native American art in the CL and the 237 hallway, and also flanking the doors Wendy and Jack exit the hotel through.

Seen in the center row of parked cars facing the fence line, a lamppost, and a lone basketball hoop like the one on Danny's Bugs Bunny shirt, that van is a Volkswagen (meaning "people's car") "Sleeper" van. In the line of cars of which it is parked, it is the fourth or fifth from the camera. The first car facing profile in that row of cars is a golden mustard color with a black vinyl top, but more on that later. The car next to, and on the other side of, the gold and dark vinyl roofed car is a yellow VW Bug, like Jack's, which is offset by the white car just beyond that, between the VW Bug and the VW sleeper van. White, like paper, like notepad paper, or Jack's writing paper. The sleeper van is the same color as the box (of presumably moisturizing cream) seen beside the vanity mirror when Jack wakes up "A Month Later," but also Danny's Apollo II sweater, and the dresses worn by the Grady twins.

That VW sleeper van stood out to me because of how the parking lot outside of the Boulder apartment complex compared to the parking lot outside of the Overlook, both before and after their "giant step forward for mankind." On the screen, the Overlook hotel sits on the left while the hedge maze is on the right. Outside of the Boulder apartments, this is reversed, with the apartment building on the right and the bushes and basketball court on the left. Was this mirroring deliberate or accidental?

In front of the Overlook on Closing Day, as the camera pans left past the entrance to the maze, I noted the cars. The car nearest to the camera is solid blue, and is likely either a Plymouth Barracuda or a Dodge Challenger (is Kubrick issuing a "challenge" to his audience?), from between 1970 to 1974. The green car that pulls out and almost flattens Stuart, Wendy, Jack, and Bill Watson, is a Chevy Vega.

Vega is the brightest "shining" star in the northern constellation of Lyra. It has the Bayer (bear?) designation α Lyrae, which is Latinized to Alpha Lyrae and abbreviated Alpha Lyr or α Lyr. Or to put it more simply, Vega is the biggest star in the constellation of liars, and just before he sees the twins in the Games Room, emblazoned across the back of Danny's blue jacket we see the word "LYERS." Also, our "second sight" of the Gold Room sign outside the Gold Room itself, the decoration that previously sat on top of that sign has been replaced with an instrument called a lyre.

Just beyond the Vega is a white Land Rover, the verbal twin to the word "travel." After the Vega pulls out, which it does just as Ullman passes the edge of hedge maze (the driver obviously being told to pullout upon seeing Barry Nelson), the blue Challenger and the Land Rover mirror the colors of the blue VW sleeper van, only separated, but facing in the same direction (screen left). The green Vega sitting between blue and white, much as Jack walks between the two women and the man dressed like Tony after they "jump" out of the way of the Vega.

Now consider the parking lot in Boulder. There, the car closest to the camera emerges directly in front of Jack's face as the office scene bleeds into the parking lot. It looks like a Chevy Monza, which has two twins: the Buick Skyhawk and the Oldsmobile Starfire. Even this ambiguity seemed intentional to me because Jack is a "Stovington Eagle" while the Chevy Monza was based on the Chevy Vega platform, which would make the two cars veritable "twins" of sorts as well, under their metal skin. The "Starfire" reminded me of the Going to the Sun Road Jack drives along in the opening scene, in a car that looks like the

160

sun. And the Skyhawk is a "twin" of sorts to the large red car parked directly behind it, on the left side of the parking lot.

Parked directly under the basketball hoop, which emerges from the hand-held microphone Wendy speaks through to the Forest Service, the twin to the black Skyhawk is red, like the elevators, and faces in the opposite direction from the Monza. It is a 1970s red Ford Thunderbird; or, like Norval Morrisseau's Indian name, a "copper thunderbird."

At the far end of the row of cars starting with the Skyhawk, another Land Rover, with a green body and white top. Next to that, a dark brown station wagon, like the one parked in front of the Overlook. To me, these cars, these color patterns, even the juxtaposition of scenes, all look intentional, and synchronized.

More evidence for synchronicity can be seen with a man and woman getting into the Dodge Challenger outside of the Overlook hotel, just before the mysterious jump. Both look like the man in the blue jacket and the woman in the plaid red and black jacket of the trio seen exiting the hotel as Jack pointed to his luggage and said, "right there." Just before the jump from the path of the green Chevy Vega, we see a man and a woman climbing into a blue two-door Challenger, which is similar in color to Danny's Apollo sweater, and reminded me of the blue Matador we see in the overlook pull-out just beyond the tunnel Jack passes through on his way to his interview. Both doors of that Matador were wide open. And now, the two climbing into the Challenger before the jump, is replaced by a man in the driver seat of, and a woman climbing into the passenger seat of, a blue and white four-door Matador, after the jump. And two doors vs four door? 42? What's more, the Chevy Vega even appears to be "lying in wait" between the *blue* Challenger and the *white* Land Rover, like Jack "lying"-in-wait for his breakfast in bed, and for Dick in the lobby. Hell, the Vega not only reflects the one Jack walks to Stuart's office, but it also travels a path that mirrors the one Dick will walk to his death in the lobby.

How could this all be mere coincidence, as Kubrick maintained, or designed to simply disorient the viewer? At this point, it was clear that it was a far greater "leap of faith" to simply accept such an explanation, especially in a film by someone as legendarily meticulous as Kubrick, than to wonder if even Kubrick's explanation was part of a smokescreen designed to hide just how meticulous he had really been.

So why is the blue VW "sleeper" van in the parking lot outside of the Boulder apartment complex so significant to anything just discussed? First, again, consider the fact that we see under the red book on Ullman's desk the word "TRAVEL" written along the spine of a white book, perfectly perpendicular to the notepad with the blue spine with white dots, a notepad that has moved from beside the radio to inside of the brown binder next to the TRAVEL book. Second, consider the fact that the Land Rover parked in front of the Overlook is white while the Challenger near it is blue, the Chevy Vega was parked between them, and that the four-door Matador seen after the quantum leap from out of the path of the Vega is, like the VW Sleeper van in the Boulder parking lot, both blue and white: just like what we see next to the vanity mirror in which we see Jack sleeping after we jump "A Month Later." And between the sleeper van and the golden car with the vinyl top is a yellow or white VW Bug, just like Jack's. All these details seem all the more important to notice when we pay particular attention to the front windshield of the "sleeper" van as the scene of the parking lot outside of the Boulder apartment complex begins.

The scene of the parking lot outside the Torrance apartment in Boulder lasts only 8 seconds. From Ullman's office, the crossfade begins at 4:08, and we cut to Wendy and Danny inside the Boulder apartment at 4:16. (Even these timestamps look deliberate.) When the parking lot emerges from Stuart's office, we see the camera creeping across the far end of the lot, like a stalker, and we hear birds singing, children playing, and a dog barking in the distance.

Cut abruptly to Danny and Wendy eating lunch, the sound of Road Runner cartoons playing off-screen, and Wendy engrossed in her red-jacketed copy of *The Catcher in the Rye*.

So short is the parking lot scene that it never occurs to us that it may serve an important purpose, or that anything relevant to the story may take place there. Why, after all, didn't Kubrick just fade directly into Wendy and Danny in the kitchen? Why transition first into the parking lot, and then into the apartment? Sure, this is a technique we are so used to that we simply accept such a transition as part of virtually everything we watch on a screen. But perhaps Kubrick used this transition for another reason as well. Maybe, because he is bound by a rule of twins, Kubrick therefore had to show us how the little boy Danny calls "Tony" ends up in Danny's mouth.

Finding Tony

Kubrick introduces us to Tony even before we meet Danny and Wendy. The trouble is that for most people, Tony is as invisible to us as our own shadow at high noon. Look again, however, and you'll notice him, standing by a lamppost, exactly as he was described by King in the novel. And just like the Grady twins, he is staring at the audience. To see him in Boulder, however, I first had to see something I had overlooked in the Overlook parking lot. More than simply leaping from the path of the green Chevy Vega, Stuart, Wendy, Jack, and Bill had passed through a magic door.

Kubrick's magic door is easy to miss, especially if you're looking at the blue and white Matador parked in front of the hotel. To the left of that Matador is a dark red and wood paneled station wagon. We only see that station wagon immediately after the magical jump from out of the path of the Chevy Vega. At first glance of that station wagon, it looks as random as anything else seen on Closing Day, including the continuity errors. Upon second sight of it, however, it looked not only intentionally placed where it is, but also intentionally parked with its front end facing the hotel and its rear tail gate facing toward the camera. As a result, it is "faceless."

Hazarding a guess, it appears to be a Mercury Colony Park, and likely a model made between 1973 and 1978. Again, note the 3 and the 8, as the one is half of the figure of the other. Even the license plate appears to be either 443 or 448. The word "mercury" has several meanings relevant to *The Shining*. It is a chemical element with an atomic number 80, for example, which is a heavy silver-white (silver screen?) metal that is liquid at ordinary temperatures. It is also a chemical that has been used medicinally, such as for treating syphilis. In the novel, Jack tells Danny to "come and take his medicine," much as the suffering of Christ serves as the sacramental medicine for the stain of original sin.

Most relevantly, is also both a messenger for the Roman gods, with wings on his helmet and shoes, and the closest planet to the sun, and is only slightly larger than the Earth's moon. Like our Moon, the surface of Mercury shows extensive mare-like plains and heavy cratering, reminding us of Danny's Apollo 11 sweater and the fact that the opening shots of hotel resemble the grey rocky dust (pixie?) we would see on the moon. And, like the metal frame on the dartboard in the Games Room and the spoke and wheel pattern on the head of Jack's writing chair in the CL, there is also an impact crater on Mercury that has dark radiating troughs extending out from its' center. Known as "the Spider," its' official name is Apollodorus: the historian from whom we know the most about the myth of Theseus and the Minotaur.

More importantly to the careful placement of the station wagon, Mercury is also the name of an automotive brand. Created in 1938, Mercury is a division of the Ford Motor Company. Marketed as an "entry-level" premium band, it was designed to bridge the price gap between the Ford and Lincoln model lines. This "bridge" is what it appears Jack and others have just walked through when we see this car, from being crushed by the "greenback" (i.e., money) doing blue collar jobs like "shoveling out driveways," to being as cold as ice and the king of a winter castle.

More than just bridging the gap between the Ford and Lincoln model lines of cars, it appears to be no accident that the rear end of that station wagon happens to be facing the camera after the magical jump we have just witnessed. Why? Because the rear door of that make and model Mercury station wagon just happens to be known as a "3 Way Magic Door Gate."

Ford added the Magic Door-gate to its station wagons in 1966. Engineered by Donald N. Frey (Fry?), the "magic door" allowed the rear door of the station wagon to both fold down like a tailgate of a truck, and hinge open to the side like a regular car door, or the rear door of a hearse. This latter motion was initially only possible when the rear window was retracted. Eventually, once Mercury refashioned the door to swing open like a regular door with the window both down and up, the door came to be known as a "magic 3-way door." During the 1970s, various adaptations of this "magic door" would be used on full-size station wagons across Ford, General Motors, and AMC.

Just as important as this magic 3-way door are the people seen on either side of it, near the hotel entrance. As the shot begins with them walking past the station wagon and the blue and white Matador, we see the man in a blue jumpsuit with a white stripe walking toward the hotel entrance, disappearing behind the wagon before emerging in front of it. He then passes through the windows of the blue and white Matador just as the woman with the red scarf climbs into the passenger side and closes the door. When she does, the head of the man in the blue and white jumpsuit is directly above her door.

Coincidentally (?), Jack takes a bite of the piece of white bread he is munching on at the exact moment the heads of two men – both in grey overalls, one walking out of the hotel empty handed and the other walking into the hotel carrying two green chairs wearing a grey hat – are in Jack's mouth, at exactly 20:22 into the film, and 2:03:23 from the end of the film. Around the bags of bread seen in both Boulder and the Overlook kitchen, we see a blue band with golden stars.

Like the Mercury wagon, so the man in the jumpsuit is "faceless" as he walks into the dark yawning mouth of the hotel. And, as soon as he disappears behind the stone pillar to the awning at the mouth of the hotel, the lone luggage-less denim-clad African American emerges from the other side of that pillar, like clockwork. When he does so, we first see his left arm at exactly 23:43 - a timestamp that amounts to 237 - and he emerges fully from behind that pillar at 23:44 (which equals 13) and begins walking toward the camera. (Note how his arm being seen at exactly 23:43 is exactly like Jack's arm when it crossfades into the plant in the sunroom in Miami, right after Jack exits room 237. And when does that happen? At exactly 1:16:12, or 217 + 11 reflected in a mirror.) As the camera pans right, the African American falls outside the frame at 23:45.

Why bother to point all this out? Because of how similar it all is to what happens with what (or who) we see in the Boulder parking lot, as well as what happens in the hallway outside of Danny's bedroom in Boulder after he wakes up from his black-out. Let's start with the hallway outside of Danny's bedroom first.

Like the paintings of birds at the end of the utility hallway in the CL portending Jack chasing Danny down the utility hallway behind the lobby, so the man seen walking into the main entrance of the Overlook in the blue plastic jumpsuit with the white stripe down the arm was also foreshadowed in the image in the painting in the back room of the Torrance apartment in Boulder. Unlike the paintings in the CL, however, this painting was stashed away like an Easter egg in a corner of the film that would've been virtually impossible for the theater audience to ever notice, especially in 1980, let alone recognize as a foreshadowing. That painting was only noticed when, thanks to technological advancements, cinephiles like Rob Ager were able to capture the relevant image and enlarge it enough to see just how significant the details in that painting really were. As mentioned, that painting can be seen in the back room of the Torrance apartment as Wendy and the doctor exit Danny's bedroom after Danny had his vision of the twins and the river of blood before blacking out. And during that black-out, Danny "jumps" out of his pants and across the hallway.

Among other important details of note in that painting are two children who look to be perhaps Danny's age or younger. One, standing profile in the painting, is a little boy, and the other, in which we see her only from behind, is a little girl. Together, the two remind us of Hansel and Gretel, and the fact that Wendy sits with her head in front of the stainless-steel oven when she talks to the doctor, while Danny does the same thing as he talks to Dick. The little girl is wearing a dress that is vaguely similar to the dresses worn by the Grady twins, while the boy is dressed much as the man in the dark blue jumpsuit who passes through the Mercury "magic door," who is also "faceless," is decapitated by the woman climbing into the Matador, and then passes into the dark yawning mouth of Overlook hotel. And like that fellow walking into the hotel, who we see after the magical jump from the path of the *green* Chevy Vega, so we see the painting of the two children in the back room of the Torrance apartment after Danny was nearly run over by the torrent of *red* blood pouring out of the elevator, and then ended up "jumping" across the hall from the bathroom into his bed. And we see two Jacks in the film: green and red. And the color of the wall that painting hangs on is the same as the Stovington Eagles shirt Jack wakes up in bed wearing, inside the vanity mirror, A Month Later.

In the Boulder apartment parking lot, on the other hand, we see more subtle details that are just begging to be noticed, and that appear to tie into the jump from the path of the green Chevy Vega. One of those details is as simple as an altogether inconspicuous car. As the shot of the parking lot outside of the Boulder apartment emerges from Stuart's office, we see rows of cars, on both the left and right sides of the parking lot. At the head of the row of cars near the center of the screen sits a car parked facing away from the apartment building, and toward the basketball court. Like Tony is depicted in the novel, it is parked next to a streetlamp that stands directly in front of it.

This is the mustard yellow car with the dark vinyl top I mentioned earlier. It looks innocent enough, until we look at it more closely. It is unclear what kind of car it is, but it resembles a car that would be significant to *The Shining*. That's because, while it is mostly likely not, it nevertheless resembles a 1970 or '71 Ford Torino.

Torino is the Italian name for the city of Turin, a city made famous by the Shroud of Turin, which is a perfect example of a religious relic acting like the postcard from 1888. First discovered in 1354, the Shroud of Turin it is believed by those for whom faith in their religion is not enough is to be the actual burial cloth of Jesus. On the one hand, it was declared authentic by Geoffroi de Charnay, the dean of the Church of Liery (liar?), France. Like the selling of Indulgences, such a declaration allowed Charnay to begin siphoning extra money out of the pockets his faithful parishioners and into his own. On the other hand, in 1389, Pierre d'Arcis—the bishop of Troyes, France—sent a report to Pope Clement VII claiming an artist had confessed that the shroud was a "cunningly painted" forgery. The bishop further claimed that the dean of the Lirey church knew it was a fake to begin with, and had used it to raise money anyway. In response, Clement declared the shroud wasn't the true burial cloth of Christ. Still, he said the Lirey church *could* continue to display it if *it* acknowledged the cloth was a man-made religious "icon," not a historic "relic." Today, Pope Francis still describes it as an "icon."[25] Yet for those who "believe," such a shroud can never be proven to be anything less than proof of the validity of their religious beliefs, even though a central tenant of that same religious belief is that their faith should need no evidence to begin with.

That such a car even resembles a Torino is curious for other reasons as well. First, the Shroud of Turin mirrors the music we hear in the opening scene, Dies Irae, which is a funeral march played during a Christian mass for the dead. Second, the word "torino" is an Italian word that translates into "little bull," reminding us of both the little bull sitting above Wendy's head and the "big" Minotaur at the center of the labyrinth, who we equate with Jack. And third, the colors of the car – a dark golden mustard body with a dark black vinyl roof – are vaguely similar to the colors in the bed covers and the curtains of room 237. Combined, these three traits provide a creative lens through which to see that car as reflecting the idea of a "golden calf," the very thing Moses slaughtered half of his followers for worshipping after leading them

---

[25] https://www.history.com/news/shroud-turin-facts

around a desert to nowhere for 40 years.[26] He was punishing them, in other words, for the unforgivable sin of having lost faith in the brand of God he was selling them – the same one that required them to wander lost in the desert until an entire generation had died off, and all because Moses had dared to give them all some water without first asking God if it was okay for him to do so. Talk about love.

Just past the (possible) golden Torino, we see something even more intriguing. That something looks like a combination of the African American man who exited the hotel entrance and the man entering the hotel wearing the blue jumpsuit who disappears into the mouth of the Overlook. To see this, first notice that the car that sits on the other side of the golden Torino "twin" is a beige VW Beetle, like the one Jack Nicholson drove in real life in 1971 (although Nicholson's was a convertible) and the one we see (or think we see) Jack Torrance driving to his interview. Beyond the VW, we see two other cars, and then a light blue VW Sleeper van with a white top.

Between the lamp post and the front of the VW Sleeper van, half-in and half-out of the front windshield of the van, stands a shadowy figure. Slightly taller than the van itself, it was that figure that reminded me of the gremlins huddling at the foot of my bed when I was Danny's age, like the people huddled around their luggage in the CL.

Like a spider eyeing an insect caught in its web, the shadowy figure stands perfectly still. Being but a poor shadow, "that struts and frets its

---

[26] Ironically, Moses did this right after he, like Jack, had gone into the mountains by himself and heard a voice directing him to do so, even though that same voice had just written in stone the "commandment" "thou shalt not kill." But of course, rules are made to be broken, especially by God and for God, which, for some, is often a distinction without a difference.

hour upon the stage," and even though it is facing the camera, it is also "faceless." Then, suddenly, almost like the famous 1967 video of Big Foot walking through the forest (at "Bluff" Creek, of all places), the figure turns and walks toward the Torrance apartment building. Passing through the front windows of the van, it disappears suddenly from view, like the man in the blue jumpsuit disappearing into the mouth of the Overlook hotel after walking through the windows of the "magic-door gate."

Incredibly, sitting across the parking lot from that Sleeper van, parked in front of the building and directly under the left set of balconies, is a compact red car with a white stripe on it: colors of the Gold Room bathroom. The colors and pattern of that car are like the car driven by Starsky & Hutch: a 1976 Ford Gran Torino. And on the cover of the Playgirl magazine, we see an article: "The Selling of (Starsky & Hutch's) David Soul," with Jack saying he'd sell his "soul for a goddamn glass of beer," right before Lloyd shows up to grant his wish. What kind of car is it we see sitting in the parking lot? While not entirely clear, the colors, along with the shape of the car itself, look like my nocturnal animals: a 1973 AMC Gremlin. And AMC was one of the manufactures who began installing the "magic 3-way door" to its cars.

Like the shroud of Turn and the image on the postcard, the shadowy figure standing half in and half out of the front windshield of the Sleeper van wears two faces of interpretation. With one face we see an accidental passerby. With the other face, we see something much more interesting. At first sight, some random person walking through the scene like the cars seen passing in the background (which in fact are not random at all either, it turns out), hardly warrants a second look. On second sight, it is a shadow of Kubrick's meticulous design. And only if we accept Kubrick's invitation to play with interpretations of that shadow, can we enter the "kingdom of heaven within ourselves by unlocking the Games Room of our own creativity, and become artists again.

Several reasons favor the latter sight. First, it is "faceless," which is how Danny was described in the novel because he was born with a caul over his face. Second, the fact that it stands half-in and half-out of the front windshield of a "Sleeper" van seemed to be like Nicholson and Lloyd being cast to play Jack and Danny Torrance. And third, more than anything else, what suggests the shadow is a carefully woven thread in Kubrick's loom is where the figure begins relative to where the prior scene ends, and where it ends up relative to where the following scene begins.

Track the shadow from the end of the office scene to the beginning of the lunch scene. It walks from one to the other without notice, like an unconscious impulse sneaking its way across a synapse, an underlying trauma pulling our strings. As the parking lot emerges, the shadow stands behind Susie, in her shadow-brown colored blazer, as if it is her inner daemon, a homunculus living within the pink pages of her own brown binder. Behind Susie, like bars to a cage, stands a four-legged totem; an artistic sculpture which can represent events like birth, death, marriage, people, animals, and spirits. Below that totem are 13 binders: 9 red and 4 black, with white labels on the spines. The former 9 reflect the Gold Room bathroom where Jack talks to his subconscious self, who he refers to as Delbert Grady, with the last four reflecting Jack's "shadow" side. The Sleeper Van shadow is even about the same size as the African American seen exiting the hotel on both sides of the stone pillar on

Closing Day, just after the jarring jump. As Susy walks out of the office, she eclipses Jack's head, which, because he is seated, is at roughly the same level as the shadow that walks into the Sleeper van. And as that shadow walks into the VW Sleeper van, it also walks straight into the lunch scene that follows.

Cutting to the next scene abruptly, the white top of that van becomes Danny's white bread sandwich. Follow the path of the shadowy figure and, like the notepad ending up inside the brown binder on Stuart's desk, that figure ends up walking from Susie and the totem art right into Danny's mouth as he chews his sandwich into tiny pieces. And Tony is "the little boy that lives in my mouth," and hides in Danny's stomach whenever he gets scared; a little boy who "shows me things." This appears to be why Danny is eating at the very moment Tony mentions he doesn't want to go to the hotel: proving that, at that moment, Tony is in Danny's mouth.

Add to this Danny's Bugs Bunny jersey. It is not only blue and white, but the basketball net on it sits right over where Danny would place his hand while saying the pledge of allegiance to the flag, and where Dick will "get the ax" blow from red-jacket Jack. Similar in colors to the bedcover in room 237 and the doors to the Gold Room bathroom, that net even serves as the opposing basketball hoop to the one we see in front of the "copper thunderbird" in the Boulder parking lot: one real, the other a cartoon depiction, just like Jack and Danny in the hedge maze compared to the Road Runner cartoon. And while the shadow turns and hides inside of the Sleeper Van, Tony tells Wendy he doesn't want to go to stay in the hotel for the winter because, as he shows Danny in a vision, he's scared.

The Shadow, a Red Book, & a Clipboard

The shadow beside the blue and white VW Sleeper van is made only all the more intriguing by the stickers on Danny's bedroom door, and two red books, one of which is sitting on Stuart's desk, right next to the binder that swallows the notepad with the blue and white dotted spine.

Sitting on the corner of Stuart's desk is a large red book. Entitled *The Hotel & Motel Red Book*, it serves as the official directory for members of the American Hotel & Motel Association. Released annually by the association, the edition sitting on Ullman's desk is from 1973. Obviously, seeing such a book in Stuart's office is to be expected, just like seeing a baseball in the Torrance apartment in Boulder. And in any other movie, neither item would deserve a second look. But this isn't just any movie – this is *The Shining*, by Stanley Kubrick: a film that appears to have twins "around every corner." And given the fact we just saw a strange *shadow* standing beside a VW *Sleeper* van, right behind Wendy and just above that red book, the most natural twin to *The Hotel & Motel Red Book* is another famous book, written by a man famous for describing the subconscious as our "shadow side," about his attempts to put himself into a twilight sleep. That book is called *The Red Book*.

The Red Book is a detailed record of Carl Jung's attempts to deliberately engage in self-induced trance-like or "hypnogogic states" of mind, from 1913 to 1917. (Incredibly, a year later, the world would engage in a similar act of self-induced trance as fathers the world over sacrificed their sons in the meat grinder of World War I, from 1914 to 1918.) In addition to being the "twin" to the red book on the edge of Stuart's desk, four other things also suggested Kubrick intended it to remind us of Jung's *Red Book*. The first is that Jung's *Red Book* deals with the very same kind of "auto-hypnosis" that the doctor diagnosed Danny as suffering from after his "episode" in Boulder. Like Jack says after returning from room 237, and like the doctor told Wendy, Danny "did it to himself" because he was simply suffering from an episode of autohypnosis. And the fact that Jack, like Wendy's copy of Salinger's novel, wears a red jacket when he meets Lloyd and Delbert, and starts acting more and more like Charles Grady reborn, all suggests that red-jacketed Jack is the "trance like state" of green-Jack the writer. On several occasions, such as when Wendy tells him of the woman in room 237, Jack's head drops and snaps back up as if he is catching himself falling asleep, snapping out of his "trance" with Lloyd.

Second, Jung was famous for his theories about a person's "shadow side," which he claimed was made up of all that person's repressed feelings which dwelled like a shadow in our subconscious. And with the crossfade from Stuart's office to the Boulder parking lot, the shadow by the "Sleeper" van looks like it is walking right out of both that pages of that red book, and Susie, while Susie walks from that sleeper to eclipse Jack and the black "Skyhawk" as she goes to get coffee and Bill Watson, with the latter wearing a blazer as brown as the former.

Third, Jung said that "the shadow is ninety-percent pure gold." By this he meant that much of what we have rejected in our own nature can be a great asset to us if properly developed and integrated. And in the end, where do we ultimately see Jack? In the Gold Room hallway dressed in black, in a black and white photograph: the colors of paper and ink.

And lastly, when Wendy hears Jack scream in the CL during his nightmare, which is the first time we meet Jack in his red jacket, she is holding a clip board as if she were a doctor in a Stanley Milgram experiment designed to teach people to "learn" using electrical shocks, or John B. Watson conducting an experiment with a white rabbit designed to condition a child to have a feeling that is who wholly unnatural them as innocent creatures: fear. And like the boilers and Jack before he boils over, that clipboard just happens to be green.

These reasons and more made everything about the red book on Stuart's desk look intentional. Even more intriguing than just the book's size and color, were the colors of the pages inside of it, and the color of the notepad-eating binder sitting next to it. Inside the red book, there is a light blue section forming a line through the middle of white pages, a bit like a phone book, making the book red, white, and light blue. These colors are also the inverted reflection of the outfits worn by the Grady twins: light blue dresses with a white ribbon through the middle which cuts them in half at the waist, like a magician sawing his assistant in half, with red all over the hallway outside the Torrance apartment. And while Jack's red jacket reminds us of both Jung's *Red Book* and Wendy's copy of *The Catcher in the Rye*, we just saw Bill Watson enter through the dark wooden door at the rear of the office. Combined with the window and the backdoor, it reminded me of the 3-way magic rear door. Even Bill is dressed in a dark brown blazer, as if he were a shadow; the same color as the binder sitting on Stuart's desk. And his tie, slashed with lines, is blood red too.

Then we have a turn of events. Both the brown binder and the red book on Stuart's desk are sitting in straight alignment to each other

177

before we cut to Boulder. Returning from Boulder, both are turned at an angle toward Jack and Bill. Did the binder turn because it swallowed the notepad, and the red book followed suit because it is mirroring the turn of the "shadow" colored binder? As a result, the head of both books cut across each other as they point to Jack and Bill, forming the shape of an "X" in the air, which we see on a crate when Wendy hears Jack scream. Like everything else was proving to be, with a second look, the placement of that X turned out to be no accident.

When compared to Stuart's desk, other items on the desk in the boiler room stand out, too. On the right corner of that desk, the same corner that the red books sits on Stuart's desk, we see a circular container that looks like a sowing box. It is blue and white but also yellow, like the *bath*robe Wendy wears when she feeds Jack his "sonny"- side up egg "yoke." Behind Wendy's head in Boulder, sat a similar box, only that one was square. (A squared-circle?) Blue and white with a piano key design on it, like the piano that mirrors Jack's writing table at the base of the stairway to heaven, it also looks like a sewing box. And, when looked at in the right way, we eventually see sutures over Danny's heart.

What made these items stick out are the boilers. In the novel, the boiler (there's only one in the novel) remind Jack of "a large dozing cat," while we see that blue and white container in the boiler room when we hear Jack, who is dozing at his typewriter, screaming from his nightmare, while wearing his red (book?) jacket and barking like a dog. And when we saw Jack sleeping in the vanity mirror, we again see a light blue and white container, which is possibly facial cream that, along with the vanity mirror, further alludes to the idea of a two-faced Jack.

The thin blue strip of blue pages in Stuart's red book suggested that, perhaps, that book held a secret about all of this. For Jung, the shadow constituted either an unconscious aspect of the personality that the conscious ego does not identify in itself, or the entirety of the unconscious, or everything of which a person is not fully conscious. In short, the shadow is a side of ourselves that we do not know even exists. Like a ghost that lives in the cellar of our subconscious, it is the "soul" that we want someone to save and forgive, but are often too terrified to face, let alone get to know. Until we truly get to "know thyself," however, the shadow that dwells within will be the green "Hulk" we fear, and out of fear, we therefore serve.

If there is any implication of Jung's book, perhaps it is that Bill Watson is not the "Watson" character King describes in his novel; far from it. In the novel, Bill Watson is the building engineer. Gruff and blue-collar, he is nothing like the Bill Watson portrayed in the film by Barry Dennen. Instead, Dennen's Watson is more like the "twin" of the behaviorist John B. Watson.

After conditioning a child to fear a white rabbit in the same way Pavlov conditioned a dog to salivate at the sound of a dinner bell, John B. Watson famously said, "give me a child before the age of seven, and I will give you the man." He said it for the same reason St. Ignatius of Loyola had said the same thing four centuries earlier. Both knew how, by installing fears and insecurities which were wholly unnatural to a child, during the most formative years of a child's brain and mind, they could hook that child to a lifelong dependency of one sort or another. Teaching a child they are born broken and only "God" (as sold by a particular brand of religion defines that term) can fix them is part of that

179

"black magic." Doing so effectively installs the "shadow" into the child's subconscious, leading them to feel a need to repress their true self on the one hand, in order to gain the approval of their Church and their God, and see gremlins and demons prowling about the world on the other,, so they will spend their life praying to be "saved," by their God and their Church (and forking over part of their hard earned income as a salvation tax for the pleasure to do so). And, having no memory of themselves without it, once those fears and insecurities are installed, they become the child's whole identity, the soul of their ego, and it controls their lives thereafter, and they will call it fate.

The "Flock of Loons" painting behind Watson as he enters Stuart's office shuffled these ideas together in my mind. Bill Watson walking into the "head office" out of the side of Wendy's head was like watching the intake of a patient to an insane asylum, like Holden Caulfield or Randal McMurphy (Nicholson's character in *One Flew Over the Cuckoo's Nest*), or even a subject into a Stanley Milgram experiment. And if the window of Stuart's office can be considered the cycloptic eye of the room, the door is like the mouth. And like the shadow in the Boulder parking lot ending up in Danny's mouth, suggesting it is Tony, so Bill walks into the "head office" through the "mouth" of the door to the office, dressed in a shadow brown jacket, while wearing a red tie that matches the book jacket on Wendy's copy of *The Catcher and the Rye*, with lines that cut across it at a 45 degree angle, like the slope of snow Danny slides down as Jack swings his ax; the light in the hallway when Jack exits room 237; and the hole in Dick's chest when he "gets the ax."

Rainbows, Doors, & Dopey

Then there is the connection between the red book on Stuart's desk and the stickers on Danny's bedroom door. Danny wakes up after his "episode" of "auto-hypnosis" with the doctor shining a light in his eyes, a twin to the audience in the theater as the film starts from a black screen. Prior to his black-out he had been watching TV, which is also a form of "auto-hypnosis," as is watching a play, or even going to church on Sundays.

While all the stickers on Danny's bedroom door are relevant, consider just some of them. The Woodstock sticker, for example, reminded me of three things. The first was the red "wood" paneled station wagon with the 3-way magic rear door, and we see it while looking through two doors while looking at the shower curtain as Danny has his face in the "magic" door to the "medicine" cabinet mirror in which he sees the future. Second, the blue and white color of the sky and clouds reminded me of the Sleeper van and the colors of the notepad and the blue jumpsuit with the white stripe. And third, the rainbow colored hot-air balloon reminded me of both the forced hot-air vents seen behind Jack in the CL, and of being "over the rainbow," like Dorothy.

The twin to the rainbow pattern on the hot-air balloon is the rainbow picture in Stuart's office, the colors of which match the hexagon rug outside of room 237. Related to Dorothy and the *Wizard of Oz*, the Minnie Mouse sticker is *below* the rainbow, and depicts Minnie wearing the same ruby red shoes as Dorothy. Minnie Mouse was never depicted wearing such shoes, however, which means this is a deliberate alteration by Kubrick. And like Wendy to Jack, we see Minnie just *before* Danny blacks-out and *after* he watches a violent cartoon about a never ending

181

war between a coyote and a road runner while wearing a jersey with the number "42" on it, and we see her "other half," Mickey, right *after* Danny watches *Summer of 42* – a movie about sexual assault (statutory rape) and World War II – during a "white-out" (blizzard) just *before* we see Jack in his first trance-like state.

Again, this seemed far more like symmetry than mere coincidence. After all, if Kubrick wants his audience to accept that Jack is simply a pawn in a game between God and the devil, a mere puppet who God has commanded to free himself from the clutches of a nemesis whose sole source of power comes from God and God alone, then such an orchestration of this kind of synchronized swimming looks like little more than a colossal waste of time. If we are supposed to accept that Jack is merely a spoke in the wheel of evil running in the Overlook, in other words, why does Kubrick bother to play peek-a-boo with the Dopey sticker on Danny's bedroom door: now you see it, now you don't?

◊◊

Adapted from of an 1812 German fairytale by the brothers Grimm, Dopey is a "magical" character from the 1937 film *Snow White & the Seven Dwarfs*: a fairytale which includes a magic mirror; a sleep-inducing poisoned apple (phone?); a glass coffin; and an Evil Queen warring with seven magical Dwarfs. In it, Snow White is an orphan who lives with her stepmother, the "evil" Queen, whose vanity (which is likely the source of her evil) leads her to constantly ask her magic "mirror, mirror, on the wall," who is the "fairest one of all?" Jealous that the mirror thinks Snow White is prettier than she is, the queen, tormented by her own insecurities, orders her Huntsman to kill Snow White.

Wanting proof, she orders the Huntsman to prove he has completed the bloody deed by bringing back Snow White's heart in a jewelry box. After complying at first, the Huntsman has second thoughts, confessing to Snow White that, because her stepmom is far more in love with her own reflection than her own child, he was ordered to kill her. In effect, the "evil queen" is Abraham's love of his own religious ego, while the Huntsman is a hitman contracted to treat Snow White like Isaac.

Hoping to spare her from becoming a martyr for the Queens vanity, he tells Snow White to run and hide in the woods. She does, but the magic mirror rats him out, informing the "evil" stepmother the Huntsman didn't "have the belly for it." This leads the Queen to come up with plan B.

Plan B is even more idiotic than Plan A. It consists of concocting a poison apple that will put anyone who eats it into a "sleeping death." Rather than killing Snow White, in other words, it puts her into a coma. And this is all because a talking mirror claimed that Snow White was more beautiful than the evil Queen, a Queen who can use magic to turn herself into an old hag but can't use it to make her any more attractive to her own magic mirror, which we presume she must have used her magic to create in the first place. Yet rather than breaking the mirror and making a new one that will give her the answers she craves, she hatches a better plan (and by "better," I mean more stupid). Incensed by her inability to impress her own magic mirror, or even to use her magic to make another mirror, she employs her magic to incapacitate her rival in a beauty contest, a beauty contest Snow White doesn't even know she's in. Never mind that this does nothing to change the fact that Snow White would still be more beautiful, at least to the Queen's own magic mirror. This is like Tonya Harding attacking Nancy Kerrigan, if Kerrigan was a ballerina rather than a figure skater.

Then, like the woman in room 237, the Queen uses another potion to transform herself into an old hag. It apparently never occurred to the Queen she could've just infused the apple she gives to Snow White with the same magical powers she uses to transform herself into an ugly witch. In effect, by turning herself into an old witch, the Queen is merely showing her true face. By turning herself inside out, her previous physical beauty is replaced with the ugly jealously and insecurity that is eating away at her own heart.

Like the serpent with Eve, the Queen then seduces Snow White into eating the apple by convincing her of its magical wish-granting power. And, like all of us, being a sucker for magical wish-granting apples (or just being damned hungry), Snow White follows in Eve's foolish footsteps, takes a bite, and falls asleep (and with that, authoritarian religion was born!). The Queen is eventually defeated by the dwarfs, who then decide to put Snow White into the trophy case of a glass coffin. Playing on the idea of "the kiss of death," they await a Prince to come and awaken her with a kiss; like Jack kissing the woman in room 237.

◊◊

Kubrick appears to allude to this fairytale in more ways than a Dopey sticker on Danny's bedroom door. The Huntsman, for example, is reflected in the husband who took Susan Robertson into the mountains on a hunting trip and Jack acting like Elmer Fudd by "hunting" for Danny in the forest of the hedge maze, while the vanity mirror Jack wakes up in serves as both the "mirror, mirror on the wall," and the "glass coffin" of the final photograph of Jack. Also, when we see Jack sleeping in the vanity mirror, his head is directly over the open jewelry box, like the one the Huntsman was expected to put Snow White's heart in. That jewelry box is the very same colors as the signs to the Gold Room and the doors to the Gold Room bathroom. It is also similar in colors to the curtains and the bedcover in 237. And on the Gold Room sign, we even see that one of the singers is Kim Woodman, and the other is "Danny" Haynes (as in "underwear").

Even the details of Dopey himself appear to relate to other things in the film. Dopey is the youngest of the seven dwarfs, gets his name from his silly antics, and like the Gibbons twins, speaks only in pantomimes. Like Dopey, Danny plays "dopey" when he says "I guess so," acquiescing to Wendy's claim they are all "gonna have good time" at the Overlook, while Dick plays dopey when Wendy asks him how he knew they called Danny "doc." In the fairytale, not only was he a friend of Doc's, but, like Minnie's ruby red shoes, Dopey was also never depicted in the colors seen in the sticker: yellow and red. Those colors reflect the sun and Danny's favorite food: French fries and catchup. Hell, they even reflect the colors of egg-yokes and bacon, the rubber duck in Boulder that jumps from the bathtub to Danny's windowsill, and even the yellow jacket and red scarf we see Wendy in when she radios the Forest Service.

Panning Down a "Barrie" Deep Rabbit Hole

The Dopey sticker is only one sticker that we could follow into a rabbit hole of mirrors in *The Shining*, but it is certainly not the only one. In fact, all the stickers on Danny's bedroom door become equally relevant in one way, shape, or form, once we consider the name of the

Boulder apartment complex in which we find the Torrance apartment. That apartment complex serves as an example of how some of the pieces needed to assemble Kubrick's puzzle are not included directly in the film but are instead only alluded to, directing the audience of the need to sometimes extend its search for clues to outside of the box of their movie screen.

As Juli Kearns astutely points out in her "mind searing" analysis of *The Shining*,[27] the Torrance apartment complex is called the Kensington. In late November or early December of 1906, novelist J. M. Barrie published the story for which he is most remembered today: *Peter Pan in Kensington Gardens*. In 1904, Barrie had written a "play" that depicted Peter Pan as the first Holden Caulfield: *Peter Pan, or The Boy Who Wouldn't Grow Up*.

Kubrick litters his film with veiled references to these two stories. The earliest drafts of Barrie's play were called "Peter's Never Never Never Land." Like Wild Goose Island seen in the opening shot of the film, "Neverland" was a fictional island that served as home for Peter Pan, Tinker Bell, Captain Hook, the Lost Boys, and other mythical beings and creatures. Although not all people who come to Neverland cease to age, its best-known resident - Peter Pan - famously refuses to grow up. Thus, the term is often used as a metaphor for eternal childhood (and childishness – like red jacketed Jack), as well as immortality (Jack in the 1921 photo) and escapism (Jack in the Gold Room and out of the pantry, and Danny from the bathroom and the hedge maze).

---

[27] https://idyllopuspress.com/idyllopus/film/shining_toc.htm

Like the Dopey sticker, so Kubrick appears to reference the *Peter Pan* fairytale in more ways than one, doing so sometimes visually, sometimes verbally. Jack saying "Wendy, darling" as they climb the grand staircase that mirrors his typewriter is an example. In *Peter Pan*, Wendy's full name is *Wendy* Moira Angela *Darling*. And like Sleeping Beauty, Wendy Darling is often depicted in blue and white.

Kubrick even appears to draw the Grady twins, which are not present in King's novel, from *Peter Pan*. Among the Lost Boys living in Neverland there are also twins, who are known only as "First" and "Second" twin. As Lost Boys, these twins are prohibited from knowing anything that Peter does not. As a result, they must focus their attention on knowing about Peter, not themselves.[28] They eventually grow up to work in an office: a modern-day maze of cubicles that reflects the idea of both living in a box and being like Schrodinger's cat; that is, not knowing whether you are dead or alive.

Like Nicholson and Lloyd playing Jack and Danny, so all these parallels within the story of Peter Pan were only half the story. The other half was how J. M. Barrie himself was even more disturbing than his story.

The Hypnotism of J. M. Barrie

J.M. Barrie's story of Peter Pan was not the only thing that seemed to be reflected in various ways in *The Shining*. Even Barrie's own life

---

[28] This serves as a metaphor for how the Catholic Church strictly forbade the spread of knowledge outside of its ecclesiastical purview, including a prohibition on reading or owning your own copy of the Bible in the years immediately following the invention of the printing press. Those who were found in possession of their own Bible were often subject to imprisonment, or torture, or even death.

looked a little like he was slowly transforming into Jack Torrance for the love of power.

Compare the man to the movie. He was born James Matthew Barrie on May of 1860, while *The Shining* was released in the U.S. in May of 1980: numbers that looks like anagrams of each other.

More interesting than flipping numbers like flapjacks is the question of whether it really is just a coincidence that Kubrick has Jack Nicholson play Jack Torrance, only to end up having Jack being interviewed by two men named Barry: Barry Nelson (Stuart Ullman) and Barry Dennen (Bill Watson). Perhaps this also is just a coincidence. But as we consider other curious connections to J.M. Barrie, it becomes harder and harder to completely dismiss the idea that Kubrick's decision to cast Nelson and Dennen was wholly unrelated to *Peter Pan*.

Consider Barrie's inspiration for the *Peter Pan*. It came from five children belonging to Sylvia Llewelyn Davies. Davies was the daughter of George du Maurier, a cartoonist for *Punch* magazine and author of the famed *Peter Ibbetson* (1891) and *Trilby* (1894) novels, both of which turned on psychic phenomena and post-hypnotic suggestion. More specifically, *Trilby* is the story that gave the world "a sobriquet for sinister, hypnotic seducers: Svengali." In a story that fitted into the gothic horror genre that was undergoing a revival in the 1890s, Svengali was an evil musical genius who transforms a poor artist's model named Trilby O'Ferrall, into a diva, using hypnotism.

The Svengali motif goes back to the Greek myth of Pygmalion, a king and sculptor from Cyprus who fell in love with a statue he had carved, like an ancient tale of Pinocchio. Pygmalion is relevant to the blue butterfly, as we will see, because most of what we know about him comes from Ovid's narrative poem *Metamorphoses.*

What makes Barrie's use of post-hypnotic suggestion stand out is how Stuart says something during Jack's interview that reminded me of Svengali. He does this when he says the word "isolation." Twice during the interview Stuart says this word, and both times he does so in a peculiar way. First, he uses the word "isolation" in isolation of any other words, pausing just before and after saying it, as if he is trying to implant a hypnotic suggestion. While less acute, there is a similar suggestion in his second use of the word. It's only after he says these words that Stuart then proceeds to tell Jack the story of Charles Grady, a story Jack will strive to duplicate. And between those two "isolations," Jack pauses briefly and looks directly at the camera, at exactly 7:32: 8 seconds after the first use of the word "isolation," and 16 seconds before the second.

The word "isolation" also relates to Jack's Adler typewriter, and Alfred Adler. But for the time he demands Wendy "don't come in," he always uses that typewriter in isolation. It is also the name of Austrian psychotherapist Alfred Adler. A contemporary of Jung and Freud, Adler emphasized the importance of feelings of inferiority, leading him to coin the term "inferiority complex." Such a complex leads people to seek isolation. And Jack not only isolates himself in the Overlook hotel, but he also then isolates himself inside the CL, opting for his typewriter rather than take a walk with Wendy after she brings him breakfast in bed. He then puts his inferiority complex on full display when he explodes at Wendy's suggestion they leave the hotel to take care of Danny, confessing his fears of being only good enough to work at a carwash or "shovel out driveways."

189

Even Barrie's own life becomes a kind of parody of *The Shining*, starting with a death that may have been murder. In his book, *Neverland: J. M. Barrie, the Du Mauriers, and the Dark Side of Peter Pan*, Piers Dudgeon tells the tragic tale of the relationship between J. M. Barrie and the Du Maurier family. Driven by a need to fill the vacuum left by his own sexual impotence, Dudgeon tells how Barrie develops a fascination and eventual obsession with the Du Mauriers. This obsession, according to Dudgeon, traces back to the loss of Barrie's brother, David, who died in a skating accident. Although other Barrie biographers have discussed this event, it was Dudgeon who, after sifting through the facts of David's death, began to suspect that Barrie may have played a role in it. And he's not alone in this suspicion. With Barrie's death in 1937, however, we may never know the truth either way.

After his stint as a potential murderer, Barrie began to dabble in the art of stalking. Living in London many years after the death of his brother, Barrie would walk his dog – a St. Bernard like the one found in *Peter Ibbetson* – not far from his house in (of all places) Kensington Gardens. There, he eventually meets a young boy named George Llewelyn Davies, who just happened to be the son of Sylvia Llewelyn, who is in turn the daughter of George Du Maurier. For some, this was no coincidence.

At the time, coincidentally enough, little George was wearing a red Tam o'shanter, which is a Scottish cap, like the red hunting cap Holden Caulfield wears as he walks through Central Park. Like Holden, there were rumors that Barrie was possibly homosexual or even a pedophile, but such rumors have never been substantiated. But then, neither do we know for sure if Holden was ever molested either.

Enamored by Du Mauriers strange Svengali-like powers, powers which Barrie sought to learn and emulate, he identifies Arthur and Sylvia Llewelyn Davies as parents of particularly "darling" children. After doing so, Barrie proceeds to insinuate himself, along with his wife, onto the guest list for a New Year's Eve party that the Davies will attend. The date of the New Year's Eve party was 1897.

An anagram of 1897 is 1978: the same year as the edition of the Playgirl magazine Jack is reading in the lobby. Like those Jack sees in the lobby after he Hulk's out on Wendy for asking to take Danny to see a doctor, pictured on the cover of that magazine is a vanity mirror bedecked with pink and purple party favors, like those we see in the lobby as Jack is lured back into the Gold Room. Reflected in that mirror is a man undressing from a tuxedo, and a note that says "December 1977, Saturday, Party!" In the bottom right-hand corner of the cover of that magazine, a banner reads "Happy New Year!"

Even the article on the cover of the Playgirl magazine titled "Incest: Why Parents Sleep with Their Children" seems relevant. George du Maurier had a son named Gerald, who happened to also be Barrie's favorite actor. Like the biblical character Lot after fleeing Sodom, Gerald was rumored to have had an incestuous relationship with one of his own daughters (Lot had incest with both of his daughters, while the writer of the story blames the daughters, which is like God blaming Adam & Eve, rather than the serpent, or even Himself).

And the kicker to all of this may be Danny's sweater, on which we see Mickey Mouse kicking a football. Not only is that sweater similar in colors to the outfits worn by Sleeping Beauty and Wendy Darling and even the "Sleeper" VW, but George Du Maurier's nickname was "Kicky."

In sum, the harrowing story that Dudgeon lays out in his book is one of greed and psychological abuse, with Barrie eventually applying the lessons he learned from George du Maurier about mind control to ingratiate himself to, and then captivate, George's son and daughter, Gerald and Sylvia, along with Sylvia's five children. It was those five children that Barrie said he "rubbed violently together" to create the Darling family in his immortal *Peter Pan*.

So obsessed was Barrie with the Du Mauriers, in fact, that he even went so far as to alter Sylvia's will after her death so he could become the sole legal guardian of her boys. In the process, he pushed several members of the family to have nervous breakdowns and even commit suicide. All this this led D. H. Lawrence to write that "J. M Barrie has a fatal touch for those he loves. They die."

Digressing into the relationship between *The Shining* and the strange life of J. M. Barrie helps to illustrate how, the more we put Kubrick's masterpiece of horror under a microscope, the more we discover an ever-sprawling web of connections. That ball of thread, you'll recall, is referred to as a "fuzzball," that physicists theorized in 1972 exists at the center of a black hole. Hell, even the date 1921, if we flip the 9, swap the 21, and reinterpret the last 1 as its larger "twin," 7, can be seen to reflect both 1972 and 1672: the year that Newton developed his New Theory of Light and Color. And it was that theory of light, and color, which eventually led me to unmask Apollo's twin.

SEVEN

CHASING BUTTERFLIES

The world is full of magic things,
patiently waiting for our senses to grow sharper.

W. B. Yeats

Because we think in a fragmentary way, we see fragments. And this *way* of
seeing leads us to make actual fragments of the world.

Susan Griffin, *A Chorus of Stones*

TO FIND HIS TWIN, we have to know a little more about Apollo. Considered to be the national divinity of Greece, he was also responsible for protecting the young. Perhaps this is why Danny lived to tell of his adventures in room 237 and the Overlook.

As mentioned already, Apollo also has a twin sister: Artemis. Less well known, however, is that, according to some traditions, he also has a half-sister. And it is that half-sister that just happens to make an appearance in Kubrick's film that relates directly to Danny wearing his Apollo 11 sweater. She is in disguise, of course, because *The Shining* is a masquerade ball, and the Gatsby of this ball is none other than the "great" Stanley Kubrick.

With the walking shadow beside the VW "Sleeper" Van in the Boulder parking lot and the blue notepad sitting next to the red book on

Stuart's desk, Kubrick not only alludes to Jung's theory of the unconscious parts of a person's personality, but he also begins leaving a trail of breadcrumbs that lead us to discover Apollo's half-sister hiding among the many varied flowers of his film. But to see her, and more importantly to notice why her appearance is so significant, we must watch the scene in which she shows up, with our eyes wide shut.

What does that mean? It means that when Apollo's half-sister shows up, she also comes with a pair of continuity errors, darkened doorways, and a mysterious jump. These telltale signs can only be perceived, however, not just from paying attention to what we see, but also from what we hear. More specifically, her appearance comes in what we should see and hear, but don't. And in more ways than one, the two scenes in which Apollo and his half-sister strut and fret their hour upon Kubrick's stage, even appear to be holding hands, just like the Grady twins, and Wendy and Danny in the hedge maze. The difference is that they are doing so through a mirror.

To follow the breadcrumbs that lead to Apollo's half-sister, and to understand why she appears in the disguise she does, when she does and where she does, we have to follow two kinds of breadcrumbs at the same time. The first kind of breadcrumb comes in the form of the mistakes or continuity errors in the film, starting with the notepad in Stuart's office. If everything has a "twin" in the film, then this would include every error. The second kind of breadcrumb comes from tracking how Kubrick uses twin pairs of blue-and-white color combinations throughout the film: one pair being slightly different than the other, just like the Grady twins. Kubrick does this same thing with the black and white pictures in the hotel, for example, with some being black and white and others being sepia color, and thus browner and off-white. So too, Kubrick uses two pairs of blue and white, where the blue is lighter in color than the other pair of blue and white, in which the blue is a darker or "navy" blue, because the hotel is like a "ghost ship." The difference is seen between the notepad, the jumpsuit, and the AMC Matador, which are darker blue and white, and the VW Sleeper van and the dresses worn by the twins, which are a lighter blue and white. The significance of these colors can be seen in Danny's Apollo 11 sweater, which is the latter, and his Bugs Bunny jersey, which is the former.

What is harder to notice, however, is how Kubrick first aligns these two pairs with holding hands, A Month Later, and then combines them in the twin to that scene in the vanity mirror. And by doing so, he not only reflects the jump from path of the green Chevy Vega on Closing Day, but also the relationship he is constructing like Hansel and Gretel between Apollo and his half-sister: Aphrodite.

Aphrodite is an ancient Greek goddess associated with love, lust, beauty, pleasure, passion and procreation. Like the Grady twins, even Aphrodite is herself a twin of sorts, with two versions of the goddess appearing across three different stories, much like Goldilocks and Snow White falling asleep across three of the dwarf's beds. In one myth she is the daughter of the Earth Goddess Gaia and the Sky God, Uranus. In a second myth, Hesiod's *Theogony*, she is miraculously born from the water of Paphos on the island of Cyprus, after the Titan Cronus killed and castrated his own father, Uranus. Cronus, mind you, is the father of Zeus, and thus the grandfather of Apollo. And in a third myth, Homer's *Iliad*, she is a daughter of Zeus and Dione, a minor deity. In the first two legends she is Apollo's great-great aunt or aunt, so there are either two or one generation(s) between them. In the last legend, Apollo and Aphrodite are half-siblings, just like Apollo and Artemis.

In his *Symposium*, Plato asserts that the two origins of Aphrodite belong to separate entities: Aphrodite Ourania (a transcendent, "Heavenly" Aphrodite) and Aphrodite Pandemos (Aphrodite common to "all the people," like "Volkswagen" meaning "the people's car"). Among other names, she was also known as Cytherea (*Lady of Cythera*) and Cypris (*Lady of Cyprus*, like the king and sculptor, Pygmalion, who is the basis for Svengali), because both locations claimed to be her birthplace. In Laconia, Aphrodite was worshipped as a warrior goddess, but all things being fair in war *and* love, she was also the patron goddess of prostitutes. Across the Greek world, she was known by various names, including "Mother," "Black One," "Dark One," and "Killer of Men."

While there is almost no interaction between them in myths, both Apollo and Aphrodite are patrons of artists, and relate to beauty, inspiration, and artistic abilities. What connects these two together in *The Shining* is Danny's light blue and white Apollo sweater on the one hand, and the darker blue butterfly with the white stripe on the other. But to see the connection, I had to also tiptoe through a tulip field of Kubrick's carefully orchestrated details. So, with all of this in mind, let's proceed.

Blood Red Apollo

Even the subtle details that are so easily overlooked in the Kensington parking lot in Boulder appear to be carefully placed chess pieces on Kubrick's cinematic chess board. As the initial scene of Jack's first encounter in Stuart's office ends, as if we are taking an intermission of Jack's interview, the scene crossfades into the parking lot outside of the Kensington apartments in Boulder as Susie exits the room.

With the crossfade to the parking lot, the black Chevy Monza/Buick Skyhawk on the right of the screen ends up parked directly in front of Jack's face, the color of which reflects the phallic rim to the paper tray on Stuart's desk. Like Turin, Monza is a city in northern Italy. Curiously enough, the Skyhawk is based on the Chevrolet Vega – the same car that nearly runs over Jack and Wendy in the Overlook parking lot – with the two cars sharing the same wheelbase (2460 mm) and width (1660 mm). Like the Chevy Vega, we see a green car parked outside the Kensington apartment complex that faces toward the three-story apartment complex and away from the basketball court. That car appears to be, or at least strongly resembles, an early 1970s Mercury Capri, a car marketed as part of a line of affordable, compact, sporty cars known as the "pony line." As previously mentioned, the light blue car parked next to the Vega in front of the Overlook appears to be a Plymouth Barracuda, which was the first pony car to be released (even though it is named after a fish) or a Dodge Challenger, which is the Barracuda's automotive twin. And in the Boulder apartment, we see the Alex Colville painting of a dark horse or "pony" racing toward an oncoming train, the former perhaps reflecting Dick and the latter Jack's train of thought.

Perhaps the most curious of all details in the crossfade from Stuart's office into the Kensington parking lot are three things: the relationship between Susie and the shadowy "Bigfoot"- like character standing beside the blue and white Sleeper Van; the green car that might be a Mercury Capri; and the dark car with the light roof that emerges right at the top of Stuart's red tie.

When the crossfade begins, Susie is standing where the shadow in the parking lot is standing, as if the shadow in the parking lot is a homunculus living inside of Susie, like Mighty Angelo the circus flea from the cartoon playing in Durkin's garage, living on the dog in the country, while Susie is effectively Stuart's lapdog. That shadow, as mentioned, ends up walking out of the pages of the red book on Stuart's desk, between the double decker paper trays, and into Danny's mouth in the very next scene, via the light-blue and white VW Sleeper Van.

Before that shadow turns and starts walk, exactly 4:12 in the film, a flash of light occurs in the window of the Capri that looks anything but natural. And two seconds later, the shadow turns and walks toward that "shining" light.

Most interesting of all, however, is what emerges at the very top of Stuart's red tie, which reminds us of the red trapezoid below the "O" in the "CH O KING" sign. With the crossfade into the parking lot, Stuart has a seat at his desk. As he does, a dark car emerges out of Stuart's head. Like the Gold Room bathroom, that car is blood red in color, with a white top. Although it probably isn't, the car strongly resembles a 1974 Buick Apollo. And both Stuart and Danny are dressed in red, white, and blue.

Looking for Aphrodite

In 1915 - yet another year that can be rearranged to reflect 1921 - Franz Kafka published his best known work entitled *The Metamorphosis*. His story took its name from a story by the same name by the Roman poet Ovid, in which Ovid tells various myths, one of which just happens to be the myth of Theseus and the Minotaur. An allegorical novella, Kafka's tale tells the story of a salesman named Gregor Samsa, who one morning awakens to discover he has been transformed into a giant insect, like Jack being reduced to a yellow beetle crawling up a mountain in the opening scene. It was this story that came to mind when I noticed Kubrick pairing his twin pairs of blues and whites and, by doing so, coupling Apollo with Aphrodite like Hansel and Gretel wandering through the forest. And Kubrick does this with the careful placement of a blue butterfly.

First, let's recap a few relevant details. Recall that after Danny blacks out in the bathroom, he ends up in his bed. Then, when Wendy and the doctor exit Danny's bedroom, we see a small painting in the background of two children who look like stand-ins for Hansel and Gretel: a small boy facing profile and a small girl facing away from the viewer, "faceless." Recall as well that after Jack and Wendy mysteriously jump out of the path of the green Chevy Vega, we see the man in the blue plastic-looking "jump" suit walking into the hotel through the glass of the Mercury Station wagon with the 3-way magic rear door. And on Danny's Bug's Bunny jersey, he has a white armband of stars around his blue sleeve.

These events appear to be "motion twins" to the notepad seen beside the radio in Stuart's office, the one with the blue spine with white dots, jumping from the credenza to inside the brown binder beside the "red book" on Stuart's desk. They also appear to reflect, thanks to the arm band of white stars on Danny's blue sleeve, Danny jumping from the bathroom mirror to his own bed.

It's here that things, especially the continuity errors, start to get interesting.

"A Month Later," the Torrance's honeymoon period in the Overlook is still in full swing with Wendy bringing Jack breakfast in bed "around 11:30." It starts with Wendy wheeling the breakfast cart to Jack in bed through the lobby. Cut to Danny wheeling around in a circle in the CL, where Jack does his writing, with both reflecting Jack attempting to devour Danny in the hedge maze for dinner.

At the cut, Wendy is standing where Bill Watson says "8:30." Leave the minute hand on 30 minutes past the hour, and flip the face of the clock upside down, and that hour hand moves from the 8 position to the 11: the same time that Jack wakes up in the mirror.

When we cut to a shot of Jack sleeping in bed as Wendy walks into the apartment with the silver breakfast tray, the camera pulls back from watching Jack, with arms folded in guarded secrecy like double locked doors, sleeping in the vanity mirror. Again, note that Jack's head is directly over the jewelry box, which is not only open, but is the same colors as the bathroom doors in the Gold Room, and the bedcovers and the curtain to room 237. As the camera pulls back, we see a vase to the right of the mirror.

The vase, like the cigarette in the ashtray during Jack's interview, comes and goes. At the mouth of that vase sprout a bed of green leaves. Just above that nest of green sits a small red object which, although out of focus, might be a rose or a small plastic cardinal. Above the red object, several plastic butterflies appear to be escaping the vase itself, like caterpillars escaping their cocoon; genies released from a bottle; Danny escaping the bathroom and hedge maze, and Wendy escaping the hotel.

And while that vase is first absent when Danny sees Jack sitting on the bed, when he goes to retrieve his fire engine, it is back when the camera jumps to looking at Danny from the bathroom door. And when we see it, the cardinal is then facing to the left, toward the mirror, rather than the right, away from the mirror.

At the base of the vase, a circular tub of perhaps facial cream is the same colors as the Sleeper Van. And like the shadow figure half-in and out of the front windshield of that Van, so the facial-cream container now sits half-in and half-out of the vanity mirror. We only see half of Jack's body in the mirror as well. Notice too that in the mirror, the container is blue with a white stripe while the side that faces the camera is mostly white with a light blue square and top, as if the mirror has reversed the design, like the time, like the woman in 237; like the Jack's two faces.

The tallest item sticking out of the vase is a blue butterfly with white spots and stripes on either wing. Kubrick relates that blue butterfly to the twins and Wendy and Danny in three ways. First, we see it when Wendy walks into the room with her breakfast tray. When she does, her right hand aligns perfectly with that blue butterfly. We see it again when Wendy uses her right hand to pour a cup of coffee for Jack, which we never see him drink. As she pours the coffee, her right hand appears to hold hands with the right hand of Jack's reflection (his actual left hand) in the mirror.

Lastly, we see a reflection of the butterfly in the glass of the door in the hallway closet, the closet that opens on the other side of the wall into Danny's bedroom. There, we can faintly see Jack's head align with, and then emerge from behind, the blue and white butterfly. As it does, and just before that blue and white butterfly exits the right frame, Jack

201

opens his mouth and sticks out his tongue, as if to let the butterfly out of the cocoon of his own head, like a genii being let out of the bottle, as if he was releasing his own red-jacketed version of Tony out of his mouth. And the mirrored reflection of Jack opening his mouth to release that butterfly is Danny walking into the mouth of room 237 wearing his Apollo 11 sweater.

That butterfly is known as a Morpho Cypris. A Neotropical breed of butterfly, it is indigenous to Panama, Costa Rica, Nicaragua, Colombia, Venezuela, Trinidad and Tobago, and Ecuador. Like *Summer of 42* during a blizzard, it stands in contrast to the Colorado Rockies like black to white. We see Jack waking up inside the mirror, and the butterfly outside of it. Like Kafka's story, it reflects the metamorphosis of Jack from a Jekyll to a Hyde, and as an insect, it reflects the ability to notice colors.

The most important thing about that blue butterfly comes not from Kubrick's *Shining*, but Hesiod's *Theogony*. In it, we discover that Apollo's half-sister, Aphrodite, was miraculously born on the island of Cyprus. Cypris, in other words, is another name for Aphrodite, with the word "morpho" representing change. That blue butterfly, in short, is Aphrodite's "second self." But it is also Kubrick's cryptic message.

With those colors, once we learn to listen to them as Lame Deer invited us to do, Kubrick is trying to tell us something. On it, we see both a white stripe down each wing, like the man in the blue jumpsuit and the picture of the boy in the backroom of the Boulder apartment, and a line of white spots, like the notepad that jumps/"travels" from beside the radio to inside the brown binder on Stuart's desk, and the armband of stars around Danny's Bugs Bunny jersey with the number 42 on it.

Below the blue butterfly in the vase next to the vanity mirror in which we see Jack awaken, we see a fuzzy red item which appears to be yet another symbol associated with Aphrodite: a rose. Being as fuzzy as the faces in the black and white photographs in the hotel, however, gives it the same qualities as that postcard from 1888. In addition to a rose, it also resembles a cardinal, like the one on Danny's bedroom door, seen right next to the rainbow balloon sticker of Woodstock floating away into the clouds as Danny spoke to Tony in the "magic mirror, mirror" on the medicine cabinet. There is an old saying that "cardinals appear when angels are near," because the cardinal is a symbol of the presence of light in the middle of darkness and warmth in the coldest of winters. Like Iris and Hermie, two quintessential messengers in Greek mythology, the cardinal is also considered to be a messenger from the gods. And in *Summer of 42*, the main character is a boy, about Tony's age, who is infatuated with an older woman, like Danny encounters in room 237. And while 2 x 3 x 7 = 42, the name of the main character in *Summer of 42* is also Hermie.

As all of this illustrated, Kubrick was using color twins as breadcrumbs in his cinematic hedge maze. Specifically, he was using the pairing of blue and white as color twins to triangulate Apollo and Aphrodite, and he was pairing those color twins with both mirrors and the Playgirl magazine. Danny disappears as he walks into the twin full-length mirrors that lead to the "living" room of 237, for example, while wearing a blue and white Apollo 11 sweater with a Roman numeral that is the twin to a Gemini symbol. When Danny emerges from room 237, he has become mute, and then awakening transformed as Tony, much as Jack awakens at his writing table in his red jacket. Disguised as a blue

203

butterfly with white stripes, Apollo's twin sister, Aphrodite, appears beside the vanity mirror as Jack awakens "around 11:30." Like a cocoon, so the mirror reflects the transformation of the woman in the 237 bathroom, while the "11" reflects the twin of Danny's Gemini symbol on Danny's Apollo sweater, and the ":30" reflecting half of a whole hour. And when we cut from Wendy walking through the lobby with her breakfast cart, we do so when she is standing in the exact spot that Bill Watson – Stuart's "other half" – tells Stuart his plane leaves at "8:30:" a time that not only reflects the last two cue cards in the film, when the murderous designs of the film begin to "take off" (much like the opening shot of the film itself), but also reflects the hour hand of a clock on 11 when flipped upside down. And while the figure 8 is the symbol for infinity, it also reflects two number 3s but down the middle and sutured together into a whole.

◊◊

What the blue butterfly also illustrated, in addition to the fact that Kubrick was using King's novel of a ghostly masquerade ball to design a film filled with images that were begging to be unmasked, was that Kubrick was also "transforming" the movie screen into a number of different symbols, including a piece of anamorphic art: art that could only be seen for what it was designed to reflect when looked at from the right angle.

Consider the transformative symbolism of Kubrick pairing that butterfly with the mirror. Later, we see Danny paired with Jack's reflection in that same vanity mirror, a mirror which we see Jack awaken inside of "a month later," symbolizing the cycles of the moon, reflected in Danny's Apollo sweater. Looking into the mirror in the 237 bathroom transforms the seductress of Jack's wet dream into a dead corpse, one being sentient and the other lasting forever and ever and ever. Such an idea reflects Jesus rising from the tomb, but in reverse, with his human life being a temporary fleshly prison, destined to return to dust; a fate from which we are "saved" through the sacred injustice of murdering an innocent man, born of a virgin, as if the sacrifices of vestal virgins in previous religions were flawed because they relied on women. Even the mirrors in the 237 bathroom, in fact, are in the shape of tombstones. And what ultimately is Jack, like so many Christians, saved from? His own life, stained with the sin of his own fleshly sexual desires, and his own "free will" to exercise those desires even within the privacy of his own dreams.

The reason Kubrick's film had failed to be unmasked for over 42 years as such, was because to see its true face, the audience needed to adjust the dial on its perspective. To see it for what it really was, in other words, I needed to undergo a paradigm shift. Like Yeats, Kubrick had created a world full of magic things. And while I was wandering around the mind-maze of my Roman Catholicism for 42 years, Kubrick's film was patiently waiting for me to develop the sensitivity needed, and for my senses to grow sharp enough, to see what had been staring back at me from the screen the whole time.

EIGHT

PARADIGM SHIFT

If art reflects life, it does so with special mirrors.
Bertolt Brecht

My goal is to create a unique perceptual experience for the viewers.
Michael Murphy, Anamorphic Artist

UNLOCKING THE DOOR to Kubrick's Games Room requires following the advice of that heretical theologian, Peter Abelard. "The key to wisdom comes from constant and frequent questioning," wrote Abelard, "for only by doubting are we led to question, and by questioning we arrive at the truth." Doing this reflexively with Kubrick's film was the result of first applying such a philosophy to the same sacred and cherished brand of religious faith as Abelard, for which he was condemned as a heretic. When C. S. Lewis said that "hell is a place where the doors are locked from the inside," it never occurred to me that the key to unlocking those doors was the same one needed to escape the hedge maze that had grown up inside my head with the seeds of self- doubt that I'd been *cult*ivating in my whole life for my brand of religious beliefs. That key came in the form of "axing" questions, because only by asking questions can we ever use our divine abilities, let alone exercise our free will, to look at dusty old questions in a whole new light.

With the paradigm shift in my own perception of *The Shining*, from being a simple movie to being a spiraling web of synchronicities, two aspects of the film emerged. The first was how Kubrick was using an artistic technique known as "anamorphic," which traditionally used inanimate objects to form a single picture. Kubrick, however, was using it for *motion* pictures. Second, such techniques enabled Kubrick to convert the playing (killing) field within his film from the three-dimensional space inhabited by his audience, to a two dimensional space, like that of a chess board. In fact, this is the same thing that happens to Jack, as he freezes in a three-dimensional maze and ends up in a two dimensional photograph. That chess board was comprised of black and white squares, on which the pieces all moved in accord with a set of unseen rule of twins; puppets being animated by an invisible hand.

So, what exactly is anamorphic art? An anamorphic image is an image that can only be interpreted when viewed from a particular angle or through a transforming optical device, like a mirror. Like the scientific term for the blue butterfly, the name of this technique is derived from the Greek word "anamorphosis," meaning "to transform." Common practical examples of such images include the writing seen on the lower front end of an ambulance, which is designed to appear the right way around in the rear-view mirrors of vehicles, and road surface markings which are predistorted for oblique viewing by motorists.

The earliest known example of this technique is believed to be an artistic piece by Leonardo da Vinci entitled *Leonardo's Eye*. Perhaps prophetically, this piece of art was included in his *Codex Atlanticus*, sometime between 1483 and 1518, or between the finding of the "new world" by Columbus and, as a consequence, the Protestant Reformation: two paradigm shifts that forever changed our view of ourselves, God, religion, everything.

In 2015, as if paying homage to both Da Vinci and Martin Luther pointing out the desperate need for religious reform, Michael Murphy used braided ropes and 1,252 painted wooden balls to create a 3D anamorphic sculpture of an eye called *Perceptual Shift*. Like only seeing a rainbow when viewing sun-tinted water droplets from a 42-degree angle, which may have been the first clue Kubrick was providing his audience that his film could be decoded if looked at from the right angle, Murphy's sculpture only looks like an eye when viewed from one particular vantage point. When viewed from any other angle, the sculpture becomes distorted and looks like just a group of black balls hanging from the ceiling on strings of different lengths. Designed to dominate both the viewer's physical and mental space, such a sculpture forces the brain to piece together the various balls that form the image of an eyeball, as the viewer slowly modifies their perspective by walking to the position necessary for all the balls to fall into alignment. And Kubrick's *Shining*, it turns out, works the same way.

Clearly, such art can be viewed from at least 360 different degrees of perspective. Some pieces of anamorphic art are even designed to reflect different images from different angles, so that something that may look like a horse from one angle looks like a butterfly from another, and a motorcycle from a third. The "truth" of such art is that what it reflects depends on who is looking at it, and from what perspective. Unlike six blind men offering their perspective on what an elephant looks like,

Kubrick's film, like ideas of that infinite abstraction we call "God," was designed to allow people to see an infinite number of different faces looking back at them from the wagon wheel of a movie reel, depending on how they looked at it.

We see this loud and clear in Stuart's office. There, Kubrick uses lens flares to shine a light on how he aligns objects like pieces of anamorphic art. He does this not only with Jack and Stuart's private parts, but also the piece of white paper or cardboard appended to the bottom edge of the top shelf of the paper tray on Stuart's desk, and even Stuart's name plate. By doing so, Kubrick, like Tyler Durden splicing single frames of porn into family films, provides a subliminal message to his audience, just for the fun of it. Like an usher with a dim flashlight showing a patron to their seat in a dark theater, Kubrick uses those lens flares to guide the viewer's subconscious mind toward seeing Stuart and Jack's first meeting as two primates that not only sublimate their sexual instincts for making love into making money instead, but with their neckties operating as a leash to ensure they do.

Noticing those lens flares led me to wonder if Kubrick had possibly designed his entire movie to operate like Michael Murphy's sculpture, of *Leonardo's Eye*, directing us to look at scenes from a certain perspective. If he did, he did so without the aid of a computer programme, like Murphy relied on, or access to CGI produced special effects. And even more incredibly, it appeared he had done so without ever letting a single person in on the kind of art he was trying to create with *The Shining*.

That Kubrick choreographed every detail, in every shot, of every scene, seemed too impossible to believe. To do it, he had to balance the movement of both characters and camera angles in relation to the

209

arrangement of items across the span of every scene. And he appeared to do all of this without any help, including computer aids, or even letting anyone in on his game plan. He aligned items on Ullman's desk to create subliminal allusions that were at least as ambiguous as the postcard image or a Rorschach inkblot; images that the audience could argue over endlessly because they were as obvious to some as they were easily deniable to others. Once seen, however, the intentionality was impossible to overlook. From the "L" in Barry Nelson's last name appearing to strike Jack's car as he drives into the tunnel on his way to the Overlook like a pool cue striking the one ball into Stuart's side pocket, to the lens flares that act like red balls of light that zero in on Stuart and Jack's "yarbles," as if they were starting a game of billiards across the desk, such precision suggested that even the smallest details may in fact be altogether deliberate, and designed to reveal a shadow-story operating behind the "false-face" of King's narrative.

This left me to wonder: were the countless changing details seen from shot-to-shot throughout the film, *all* operating in patterns that revealed an underlying logic, a logic which was designed to hide the true face of Kubrick's precision behind a smokescreen of myriad inconsistencies and continuity errors? Why else would Kubrick have felt the need to engage not only in such secrecy in the making of the film, but also the grueling number of retakes he required, even for the simplest of scenes? He did more than 60 takes of perhaps the simplest scene in the film, for example, where all the camera does is slowly zoom in on Dick Halloran as he lay on his bed watching TV in Miami. What kind of a maniac does that, and why?

On the other hand, maybe all this really was simply the result of my own confirmation biases working with my pareidolia to confirm a belief I had chosen to accept was "true." Maybe everything in the film only appeared to me to have a twin, because I had chosen to simply "believe" that there was not a single coincidence in the entire film that was not intended by Kubrick, not even the mistakes. This, as such, was the religious belief I had decided to put all my faith in. Maybe all I was seeing, therefore, was simply the fruit of my own confirmation bias, which is the very thing my Catholicism relied on to insulate my own brand of "beliefs" from over-exposure to the sunlight of my own skepticism. Maybe there really was no "solution" to Kubrick's puzzle, no answer to whom or what was responsible for it all, which seemed to be the consensus of the vast majority. Indeed, maybe I was simply being lured into an optical illusion by a magician who had turned the movie screen into a motion picture that operated like a drawing by M.C. Escher; and all in order to blind me with the lens of my own confirmation bias and a brain that could never stop looking for meaning. Was I seeing the "true" reality of the film, in other words, or like those gremlins in my room all those years ago, was I simply projecting my "beliefs" into the film, and thus only seeing what I had chosen to believe in the first place, and then bending every detail I could find to fit the narrative I had simply chosen to believe was an "infallible" and ultimate "truth"?

As these thoughts bubbled to the surface of my brain, a tide of questions and doubts began bleeding into my mind: What if *The Shining* really was simply the visual equivalent of the Siren's song, a celluloid maze designed to put "toys of desperation, without more motive, into every brain," as Horatio warned Hamlet of the specter of his father's ghost, and all to simply "draw us into madness," just like Jack? In the same way looking down into the sea from a high cliff can make a person think about jumping, so Kubrick's labyrinth called audiences to not only "come and play," but worse, to Abandon All Hope Ye Who Enter Here. But some people entered anyway, because they simply couldn't resist. And neither could I. If Kubrick's labyrinth was a leviathan, I was Jonah who couldn't wait to jump in with both feet. But with all the insane synchronicities that appeared to be pouring out of my screen at that point, it became increasing difficult to decide exactly how or where to proceed to next in such a maze, let alone know if there was any end to it all.

So, because Kubrick had invited Danny into room 237 by rolling a ball to him in the hallway, I thought that maybe the best thing to do at that point was to just follow the bouncing ball.

The Ball Game

Curiosity can be a curse, hence its' reputation the world over for executing so many cats, whose only crime was being as curious as a child. Yet we can only ever discover any kind of "truth," about the world let alone ourselves, by following curiosity wherever it leads. All curiosities can therefore be understood to lead to a discovery of one truth or another, as if every human mind is drawn to such a light the way seeds are drawn out of the soil toward the sun. It is this irresistible pull of our curiosity that lured Hamlet to follow the ghost of his father, even though that ghost, as Horatio warned, may only be luring Hamlet into madness and right off a cliff.

Like Hamlet's ghost, my own curiosity had either lured me to the cliffs of insanity or the ghost of Stanley Kubrick was confessing it had a

212

story to tell. Either way, my curiosity was a fish that had been caught in a sprawling web of repeating patterns and precision. Those patterns made it increasingly clear that Kubrick was mirroring perhaps every single detail in the film, starting with the opening shot. Or was I simply a fool, the very kind of which Kubrick wanted to bait, so he could lure them to the cliffs of insanity with the ghost of their own pareidolia masquerading as synchronicity?

Like Neo being told by his computer to "follow the white rabbit," so the two lens flares that ride Jack's coattails into Stuart's office invited me to doubt my self-doubts, reject my Catholic Conditioning to fear God as much as my own skepticism about my Catholicism, and to follow my instincts and intuition with as much "faith" as I had been taught to follow my Catholicism. Those instincts were telling me that even the smallest of details were meaningful clues that Kubrick was not only inviting us to notice, but daring us to play with, and follow.

Consider those two balls of light. Like headlights, they led me to notice that Kubrick had subliminally cast the initial interaction between Jack and Stuart as being a competition for social status between Stuart as the "Ull-man" (i.e., the "Ultra-man") that Jack aspired to be, and Jack as the "ullboy" that he eventually devolves into, which Wendy finds buried in the weeds of Jack's manuscript of mechanical repetition that made him more machine than man: the very thing his job required of him.

Obviously, the film being a piece of art, no one was required to accept such a single interpretation of it. Kubrick's subtle use of lens flares, however, was certainly inviting us to do so if we so dared. Those flares meant it was possible to see how Stuart was to Jack what Jack was to Danny, with the former trying to trap Jack in what ultimately becomes his "dead-end job," and Danny escaping such a fate – life like a Jack-in-the-box – through his willingness to cultivate his self-reliance by venturing into the forbidden zone of knowing his true self, with the hedge maze reflecting what Immanuel Kant called the "hell of self-discovery that leads to Godliness," so he can both unify the two sides of himself – Danny and Tony -- then trust himself when he takes a 'second look' at things.

Yet Jack and Danny swapping roles of father and son were far from the only pair of contrasting reflections that could be found in the film. Instead, the more I looked, the more such a contrast could be seen in practically everything, including in the differences we find between the novel and the film.[29] From changing Jack's VW Beatle from red in color to yellow and Wendy Torrance from a strong blonde to a meek brunette, to the old corpse in room 217 first being a young woman in room 237, Kubrick appears to have built the maze of his video game out of a hall of mirrors. And within that maze, the mirrors reflect both twins and inverted twins; both the Grady twins and the woman in room 237. The former could be seen in Kubrick's precision, while the latter were reflected in the various continuity errors and spatial inconsistencies. And both were rolled up together into a ball and rolled out to the audience to play with, from the box of a theater screen, in the form of Jack's VW Beetle, to Jack in the box of a picture-framed photo of the Overlook Ball.

---

[29] A great deal of work was done to catalogue all of the differences between the novel and the film online by johnny53, and can be found here:
http://jonnys53.blogspot.com/2007/12/differences-between-novel-and-movie.html

By bookending his film about a writer-gone-mad between these two different balls, Kubrick appeared to be inviting his audience to follow the bouncing ball. After all, the first thing we see is Jack inside of a car that looks like a tennis ball, then Danny wearing a shirt with a rabbit "under the table" and a basketball hoop in colors similar to those of the bedcovers in room 237. And the first time we see Jack's typewriter, which is similar in color to Jack's car, Jack is bouncing a tennis ball off a mural of "twins" standing between stalks of maize as Wendy and Danny run to "play" in the maze, as if it were a field of dreams. And Jack not only appears to be knocking on the head of the buffalo with each throw of his ball, "bashing its' brains in" with each hurl, like Dorothy knocking on the doors to the Emerald Palace, but directly behind the mural over the fireplace sit the twin doors to room 237. All of this, as such, was inviting me to follow the bouncing ball.

NINE

Follow the Bouncing Ball

What we call chaos is just patterns we haven't recognized.
What we call random is just patterns we can't decipher.

Chuck Palahniuk

There is only one way to see things,
until someone shows us how to look at them with different eyes

Pablo Picasso

A S THE CAMERA SWOOPS DOWN on Jack's yellow VW Beetle climbing up a mountain road, we see two yellow lines beside the car. Like a golden string seen over the Gold Room sign being unspooled from a July 4th "Ball" of thread, Kubrick is laying out a thread for us to follow both in, and back out, of his maze, just like the one Ariadne gave Theseus to navigate the labyrinth and slay the Minotaur. That thread draws us into a maze, one with a three-dimensional reality on one end and a two dimensional reality on the other. Inside that maze is a man who becomes a Minotaur, as he forces his brain, which you'll recall has the power to think in 11 dimensions, into a two-dimensional box of sacred beliefs. That thread can lead us to the answers we need to escape Kubrick's maze, but only if we know how to ask the right questions. So, let's start with asking questions about the beating heart of this maze: room 237.

Who or what rolls the ball over to Danny outside of room 237? Did it come from someone, or some*thing*, inside of that room? And is there any way it could be the same ball Jack was throwing against the wall with the mural of the red and blue figures standing in the maize, above the fireplace, in the Colorado Lounge? We see that mural as Wendy and Danny, who are often wearing red and blue, run into the hedge maze. And right before we jump into room 237, we see first Dick in bed, dressed in blue pajamas, then Danny in bed, in a red one-suit pajama, and then we see Jack wearing his red jacket. And in Boulder, when we see Danny eating that shadow off his home plate, as Juli Kearns pointed out, Wendy is wearing a blue single piece suit over not one, but *two* "union" suits.

So, are the colors trying to tell us something more about Kubrick's ball game, and perhaps even where the ball that rolls up to Danny in the 237 hallway actually came from? Like Jack going from one ball to another, is Danny being lured into room 237 wearing an 11, as if to reflect the number of dimensions with which his own mind is designed to "shine" with understanding, and walking toward mirrors that reflect a two dimensional image of himself, like a Narcissus in love with a black and white photo of himself, because his 11 dimensional mind is being sucked into two dimensional black and white thinking, reflected in the black and white photographs in the hotel? And if so, is it Jack who is inviting Danny to make the change, the same way he had to, in order to prove he's an adult?

218

It seemed impossible that the ball that rolls up to Danny in the 237 hallway could be the same one Jack was throwing days earlier in the CL. But like so many other things in the film, it also seemed like there was a pattern to everything, and therefore a way for us to find where that ball actually came from. If it was the same ball Jack was throwing the CL, for example, it would have to turn 90 degrees for it to land in front of Danny. Well, we do see a pattern that reflect this. The last time Jack throws his ball in the lobby, it soars right over Danny's trike and Bugs Bunny doll, then bounces at a 90-degree angle toward where Wendy will later see the man with the cracked head offering his opinion about the "party." In fact, when Danny later runs from Jack into the hedge maze, it not only looks like he is on the moon, but the new opening to the maze he runs into is also at a 90-degree angle of difference from the one he ran into with Wendy earlier on.

Another curious detail that suggests the ball that rolls up to Danny came from Jack can be found in the last time Jack throws his ball in the CL, just as Wendy and Danny exit the hotel while appearing to be exiting the mouth of the fireplace. After the last throw we see Jack heave at the mural of the figures in the maize, we never hear that ball hit the wall. Instead, it was like the ball passed through a hidden window, or even an "impossible window," like the one we see in Stuart's office, and into that hallway. And the fact that Jack starts off inside of a car that looks like a ball, even though we never see his face, and then ends up in a picture of a July 4th "Ball," with a date that adds up to 24, left me to wonder if the ball that rolls up to Danny was an invitation to the audience from Kubrick to follow the bouncing ball. So, like a curios cat, I did.

In the same way Kubrick was inviting us to play mahjong with his color twins, it also seemed he was inviting us to piece together the various balls he litters throughout his film. Doing so was the only way to see if they too operated like breadcrumbs through Kubrick's maze. Jack driving in a car that looks like a giant tennis ball, for example, appeared to have its lesser twin in the ball rolling up to Danny in the hallway outside of room 237. And this invited me to engage in that old assignment from high school English class: compare and contrast. While the Apollo II rocket went to the moon, Apollo was also the god of the sun, who rode his fiery chariot across the sky, like Jack rides his yellow VW Bug along the Going to the Sun Road and ends at a hotel that looks like it could be on the moon. This same duality could be seen in Jack in the final photograph, in a posture that embodied both Jesus Christ and Baphomet. As if playing charades with his images, such doubling suggested Kubrick wasn't just inviting us to "come and play;" he was also throwing out a pitch and saying, "Let's play ball!"

Although something I would normally dismiss as ridicules, considering Kubrick's *Shining* to also be a ball game of sorts, led me to notice something interesting about the very moment the ball first rolls up to Danny outside of room 237. When it comes to a full stop in front of him, Danny's left hand, along with the two cars he is pulling across the hexagon he sits in, align perfectly across the top of the center of that hexagon, cutting off the top triangle of the hexagon itself. As a result, the center of the hexagon Danny sits on has the shape of home plate in a baseball diamond. And this reminded me of where Jack is standing when he winds up and pitches his ball through the lobby: directly over Danny's Bugs Bunny doll.

Alone, such a detail is easy to overlook, and appears to be purely coincidental. But when considered with other details already explored, choreographing Danny's actions to make the center of the hexagon below him resemble "home plate" looks just as intentional as the red and black diamond that Jack is standing on in the lobby when he winds up and pitches his tennis ball. And that diamond is the twin to the black and white diamond Jack walks over when he first walks into the Overlook for his interview.

On his red and black diamond mound, Jack even does a full pitcher's windup by spiking the ball like a football and then circling all the way around it, much as Danny and Wendy get turned around in the hedge maze. The ball then sails right over Danny's tricycle, in which a stuffed Bugs Bunny doll sits, as if the Bugs Bunny on Danny's jersey in Boulder had crawled off his shirt and into the hotel. The Bugs Bunny doll not only sits on the very spot Dick will be laid to rest, but the 42 on Danny's jersey leads us back to room 237, because 2 x 3 x 7 = 42. And the Bugs Bunny doll faces away from the front of the tricycle, just like the bloodied corpses of the Grady twins face away from each other, and Danny, and even the audience.

Compare all of this to the very center of the hexagon Danny is sitting on in the 237 hallway: it is also a diamond pattern, only with the edges or "wings" clipped off, much as the rug pattern inside room 237 is of a chorus of castrated phalluses. Even the small island we see when the film opens, along with its reflection in the lake, forms the shape of a diamond. And like Danny, the audience, which is sitting in their seats enjoying the ride, sees this right before we see Jack's car rolling like a ball, uphill, to the Overlook: a hotel shaped like half a hexagon.

Other details about the emblem Jack throws his tennis ball over equally stand out. Danny's trike is not only parked on top of where Dick will be laid to rest, but that emblem also looks like both a giant serving plate and a rounded hexagon. It even contains the same colors we see on Danny's plate, at home, in Boulder. In fact, the colors of that emblem and Danny's "home" plate are even similar to the colors of the 1980 uniforms worn by the National Football League's Washington Redskins (currently the "Commanders"). And while noticing such colors seems like a stretch, it nevertheless reminds us of Danny's Mickey Mouse sweater, and the fact we see a guy loading an unnaturally large pile of luggage into a freight elevator outside of the kitchen on Closing Day, wearing a jacket with the very same colors as the Miami Dolphins. And not only does Dick bounce like a super ball from Miami to Denver to save Wendy and Danny, dolphins have also been known to save people from sharks.

Also, Danny's trike sits directly between a gollywog doll and a Winnie the pooh doll: cartoon twins of Dick and Wendy, just like the Road Runner cartoon is a "cuckoo" bird that reflects the movie Nicholson had previously "starred" in, and Jack chasing Danny in the hedge maze. And all of this sits just below the CASHIER window, which is the "twin" to the box-office window.

Yet Kubrick's synchronicity is not just seen. If we count Jack's throws, we also *hear* Kubrick's synchronicity. He pitches the ball to the wall twelve times. The number of thundering "booms" we hear when the ball hits the wall, however, is the same as we see on Danny's Apollo sweater: 11. As mentioned already, we never hear the twelfth "boom" of the ball hitting the wall as we crossfade to Wendy and Danny running to the hedge maze, as if they were exiting both the entrance to the hotel and the fireplace below the mural of the twins in the maize, who are one floor higher: just like when Danny encounters the Grady twins outside of his apartment. And not only do the twin doors to room 237 sit directly behind the mural over the fireplace, which makes Jack's "booms" sound like Dorothy knocking on the doors to the Emerald Palace, but like the sound we hear in room 237, the sound of Jack catching the ball after those "booms" give it the familiar double-thump of a heartbeat.

Jack's ball throws in the CL at the mural of figures between the maize are later doubled with the same number of swings at bat. After Jack escapes the pantry, he "hacks" his way into their apartment. After he does, he strikes the bathroom door with his axe - twelve times. Like the twelfth and final throw of his ball in the CL, the twelfth and final blow of the axe finally passes all the way through the bathroom door. Fully clearing the panel from bathroom door with that 12th blow, the axe appears to strike Wendy in the chest as she cowers "around the corner" from the door. And of course, 12 throws and 12 blows equal 24.

When we cut to an outside shot of the bathroom door as Jack listens to Dick pulling up in the snowcat, we see that now *two* panels are cleared from the door, even though Jack had only cleared one. The two missing panels form a figure 11, or II, directing us back to Danny in the 237 hallway. That missing panel suggests there is at least one missing axe blow, or more. And that missing axe blow, which will eventually end up opening Dick's chest, is lucky number 13.

Jack's 13th throw of his tennis ball from one side of the lobby is mirrored in the 13th swing of his axe on the other side of the lobby, each reflecting two halves of Jack: one green, one red; one pitching, one at bat. (Is this why Jack enters the lobby from the opposite end we see Wendy do so with breakfast?) After throwing his tennis ball against the mural over the fire place, Jack then meanders into the lobby, starting at the corner of the reception desk where a couple walked out of the hotel with tennis rackets when Jack walked in for his interview, and a large A-frame ladder sat on Closing Day. After he does, he pitches his ball a thirteenth time, a number that was reflected on the hockey jersey worn by the woman who oddly walked into the hotel on Closing Day, even as we would expect her to be walking out of the hotel. She even proceeded to walk in the same direction that Jack will throw his tennis ball for the 13th time. And the last walk Dick will ever take follows along the same path as that woman and Jack's 13th pitch, and Wendy wheeling breakfast to Jack as he "lies-in-wait" in bed, much as he lies in wait around the corner for Dick.

Paying attention to such details revealed that Kubrick doesn't just throw curve balls at his audience. He throws fastballs too, around every corner.

Books & Baseballs

Kubrick throws his audience their first curve ball with Danny in the Boulder apartment. After watching the yellow car that looks like a giant tennis ball and two red balls of light and watching Jack step up to the plate to be the bread winner of the family, we cut to Danny, at home, over a plate, chomping as much on his white-bread sandwich as the shadow from the Kensington parking lot. On the ironing board directly behind Danny's head, a baseball: the opening pitch. Like the moon, it sits on the far side of Danny's head, the shining sun of a TV screen "shining" the colors of a rainbow into his eyes. His red, white, and blue jersey reflects America and the angle a person needs to stand in relation to their shadow to see that rainbow: 42. Hell, even the shape and color of the Overlook Hotel itself resembles what we can imagine the seating of a baseball stadium might look like, if it were on the moon.

Although a perfectly normal object to see in the apartment of a five-year-old boy, that baseball moves in a queer fashion. When we cut to inside the Torrance apartment in Boulder, Danny and Wendy are first seen in a single shot. He eats his sandwich with his eyes glued to a TV, while she has her face stuck in a red-jacketed book with matching front and back covers. At first, the baseball is seen on the right side of Danny's head, just to the right of a stack of books. (Is it a mere coincidence that it is sitting on, of all things, an ironing board?) Then, when we cut to a close-up shot of Danny, the baseball and the stack of books shifting with the cut to the left side of Danny's head. With this cut, Kubrick has just thrown the audience a fast ball that passed "in one ear and out of the other."

Naturally, we attribute this change of the baseball, from one side of Danny's head to the other, to be the mere result of the shift in the camera angle. But when we consider that the counterpart to a baseball is a baseball bat, which Wendy will later use to flatten out Jack when she strikes him on the left side of his head at the top of the stairs in the CL, the shift of the baseball from the left to the right side of Danny's head looks more like a foreshadowing of the later event rather than just a meaningless, purely coincidental change. "We are seeing, in other words, a reflection of something that hasn't happened yet."

And like the mirroring of Wendy's book jacket, while we see the baseball as Wendy tells Danny she's looking forward to *going to* live in the Overlook hotel, just before we see a doctor examining Danny's head and right after Danny's black-out, she is telling Jack they should *leave* the hotel and take Danny to see a doctor just before Jack "catches" a bat to the head, and is knocked out of the ballpark of his own skull.

After he's knocked out (i.e., put to bed) with the baseball bat, Jack tumbles down the stairs like that old nursery rhyme about a pale of water and a girl named Jill. And when Danny wakes up in bed, we see a baseball mitt right in front of a chalk board that covers the face of a golden tiger on a green poster. While this reminds us of Tony the tiger, that poster is the same colors Jack wears on Closing Day.

The baseball behind Danny's head is sitting right next to a stack of books, while the first time we see Wendy she is engrossed in her copy of *The Catcher in the Rye*: a book with a title that sounds like it could be as much about a kid playing baseball in a field somewhere, as a catcher on a baseball team with a drinking problem.

The baseball and books behind Danny's head led me to notice what sits directly over Wendy's head: twin salt and pepper shakers. Normally, those items sitting would sit on the table. By placing them directly over Wendy's head like two little guardian angels, Kubrick appears to not only allude to the idea of "twins" but also opposites: pepper and salt, black and white. It also suggests that Wendy, despite being a "scream machine," has a mind seasoned with the wealth of books we see not only on the shelf above her head, like an overflowing thought bubble or a crown of wisdom that can only come from the benefit of different perspectives, but overflowing their apartment, like that blood from the elevator. And what's black and white and read all over? Spinach for the soul, that's what.

How Reading Fiction is Spinach for Our Synapses

The ball behind Danny's head invites us to consider the bookshelf above Danny and Wendy's head in Boulder. That bookshelf is also a twin to the impossible window behind Stuart Ullman. Books, after all, operate like an impossible window that allows us to peer into the deepest contents of another person's mind, to experience the world through another person's eyes, even long after that person is dead and gone. "The reading of all good books is like a conversation with the finest minds of past centuries," wrote Rene Descartes, while Joseph Addison wrote "reading is to the mind what exercise is to the body." Books, as such, operate as a lens which enables us to see other ways of looking at reality, ways which may be radically different from our own. They "are a uniquely portable magic," according to Stephen King. Yet they also operate as unique mirrors, as Carlos Ruiz Zafón described them, because "you only see in them what you already have inside you." And perhaps most appropriately of all, according to Neil Gaiman, "a book is a dream you hold in your hands."

The "impossible window" into the minds of others represented by the shelves of books above Wendy's head in Boulder is not only the twin to the impossible window in Stuart's office, but it also teaches us emotional intelligence. Like Popeye eating spinach, as author of *The Goldfinch*, Donna Tartt, pointed out, reading fiction can transform us from the inside out. In an interview with *Chatlaine* in 2013, Tartt explained how, "in films, we are voyeurs, but in novels, we have the experience of being someone else: knowing another person's soul from the inside."[30] The former fosters a degree of detachment and, by extension, indifference, while the latter, as Tartt puts it, is "a kind of long morality problem," that a reader navigates like a maze of options. Unlike film, novels cultivate a perspective that looks beyond merely the surface narrative, or "false face," that may serve as window dressing to a story. If a film leads us to judge a book by its cover, a novel invites us to ignore that cover, and venture on a journey into a person's soul.

The effects of such a journey on our own brain were discovered at Emory University, where researchers found an increase in the neuroplasticity of the brain correlated to reading fiction. Reading not only helps to create heightened connectivity in the brain, but it may also increase the ability of the brain to form new connections and pathways and change how the circuits of our brain are wired.

In 2016, psychologist at the Princeton Social Neuroscience Lab, Diana Tamir, demonstrated how this happens.[31] Using brain scans, Tamir showed how reading fiction and social cognition both recruit a part of our brain called "the default network," which is "known to support our capacity to simulate hypothetical scenes, spaces and mental states." Doing so increases a person's ability to empathize with what other people are thinking and feeling. In her studies, she found that if students read an emotionally compelling story, not only did their empathy levels rise immediately afterwards, but if they felt emotionally transported by the story, they scored even higher on empathy a week

---

[30] https://www.chatelaine.com/living/books/interview-with-donna-tartt-author-of-the-goldfinch/

[31] https://www.ncbi.nlm.nih.gov/pmc/articles/PMC4733342/

later than they did right after reading the story. While this can happen with stories that are non-fiction, fiction provides a penetrative lens that other forms of writing, like journalism, often lack. Unlike non-fiction, fiction gives the reader access to the character's interior world in a way that is far more intimate than anything we might see in journalism or even film. This was why Shakespeare has Hamlet give a soliloquy about whether it is better "to be or not to be," so that the audience can understand the questions that he is wrestling with internally, and the process by which he tries to resolve them.

More than that, novels also allow us to do two things that are hard to do anywhere else. The first is that it takes an investment of time and attention that commits us to getting to know our subjects. And second, with that investment, we slowly get a view of a character's life over many years, allowing us to better appreciate and empathize with their perspective, regardless of how much we may happen to disagree with it.

Now, compare all of this to, say, the Bible. If reading fiction can increase empathy and the number of synaptic connections in the brain, reading non-fiction, or even reading a fictional story as if it must be interpreted as non-fiction, can have the exact opposite effect. Like writing the same sentence over and over again, reading the same story the same way, over and over again, like a monkey turning a screw on an assembly line in order to defend the company it works for, can deaden our soul and drive you mad.

As such, the books blanketing the apartment suggest Wendy is a bookworm, the twin to the idea of the rabbit-hole alluded to by the Bugs Bunny's ears on Danny's jersey sticking up from under the table. Danny is even dressed like Uncle Sam in red, white, and blue. And while Danny watches cartoons, Ullman looks like a cartoon character or even a game show host like Pat say-Jack. And the rabbit hole they are about to fall into is riddled with wormholes that appear to run between scenes, scenes which are all connected to each other like reflections in a mirror.

Like the salt and pepper shakers, Wendy eventually shakes Danny as she tries to wake him from his "bad dream:" which is the twin to Jack's bad dream. And next to the salt and pepper shakers we see a white bull, which Ariadne's mother mated with to create the Minotaur. It sits like the red eagle on the windowsill behind Stuart, and reflects our ability to see into the minds of the mythmakers who created such a story, as a warning for future generations, like ours. And in the same way Danny is watching game film of Jack, as if he's preparing to outsmart him in the hedge maze, so Wendy is reading about a lunatic in a red jacketed novel, who hunts people in a red hat, so she can follow the thread that will allow her to escape the Minotaur, the maze, the cuckoo's nest she signed up to be a part of.

Kubrick's Curve Ball

Then there is the ball that Kubrick slips past his audience inside a tennis match, "two love." If Jack's car is Kubrick's way of throwing out the opening pitch to start his game, the first curve ball he throws the audience does not come in the form of Jack's car or even the baseball we see slide in one of Danny's ears and out the other, like so many of the meanings of the myths that were written to warn future generations of the dangers of their unwillingness to question. Instead, it comes disguised as a curve ball, passing right before our eyes as Jack curves toward the camera to reach the reception desk. As he does, he passes a couple exiting the hotel with tennis rackets. And in the smallest of details associated with the couple walking off to play a tennis match, Kubrick begins showing us his long list of hidden Easter eggs.

Notice what we see if we pay close attention to that man and woman walking out of the hotel. Both are seen carrying a pair of tennis rackets, while the woman nearest to the camera carries a red fishnet bag of balls. From the aerial shot of the hotel seen seconds earlier, we saw snow on the ground outside the hotel. And like the missing hedge maze, we saw no tennis courts around the hotel in which they can play. Stranger still, however, is the fact that the woman is wearing high heel shoes, rendering it impossible for her to play tennis anyway. And perhaps most curiously of all, the bag of balls she is carrying is full of not tennis balls, but baseballs.

However odd such details may at first appear, upon a second sight of the film, the more we consider those details, the more all of them seem rather prescient. Notice the colors of the tennis rackets and the outfits worn by the couple, for example. The man is clothed in blue and white, with a short sleeve shirt, all of which are like Danny's Bug's Bunny jersey. The woman is wearing a black and white sun visor, with a white short-sleeve shirt and black pants, a beige sweater tied around her waist. Not only should she probably be wearing that sweater, since we do not see the snow melting around the parking lot outside, but the colors of her pants and sweater are similar to the colors of the bedcover and curtains in room 237.

Look closely at their tennis rackets. Her tennis racket cover is blue and white. But whatever overlays his tennis racket, which looks more like a Lilly pad than a racket cover, is green. The crest of his racket itself, which extends past that green Lilly pad like a halo, is red. Is this just a coincidence that these are the same colors Jack wears throughout the film?

Then there's the fact the woman is wearing high heels. Is it just a coincidence that she happens to be stepping out from behind the pillar at the corner of the receptionist desk where the large A-frame ladder will stand on Closing Day, the very spot Jack begins his walk through the lobby to overlook the hedge-maze table, as if he were at the top of a beanstalk?

Consider also the bag of baseballs she carries, rather than tennis balls. How coincidental is it that those balls, along with those heels, remind us of the many pitches Jack makes toward the mural in the CL, and the many times Wendy will try to knock Jack's head out of the park - "swing-and-a-miss" - as they walk in tandem up the grand staircase in the CL? And, at the very moment Jack eclipses the couple with the tennis rackets and the pillar behind which the large A-frame ladder will be parked, he says the word "Hi" to the receptionist.

Such precision look again like the foreshadowing of how "high" Jack will be when he looks down into the model of the hedge maze, and when he tumbles down the stairs like a character in a nursery rhyme, after Wendy cracks open his head with a homerun hit so she can get the hell out of Dodge.

Also, compare those baseballs to Danny's strange kung fu grip of the 237 doorknob. Both appear to reflect Jack's pitch through the lobby, and Wendy's homerun hit at the top of the stairs. When Danny first tries to open the door to room 237, he grabs the doorknob with a strange grip. When he does, his fingers form the shape of rabbit ears with his index and middle finger, just like Danny's handlebars formed over Jack's head as the camera panned right as Jack sat reading his Playgirl magazine. More interesting, however, is how it also happens to reflect something else, something King mentions in his novel.

To test Danny's "shine," Hallorann tells Danny to "give me a blast, think at me," like a psychic version of Ronnie from the *Jersey Shore* saying, "come at me bro!" After Danny does so, Hallorann asks him, "what did it feel like to you?" to which Danny responds, "like I was Nolan Ryan throwing a fast ball." And it just so happens that the strange grip Danny applies to the doorknob of room 237 is the same grip a pitcher uses to throw a fast ball.

◊◊

Back in Boulder, another ballgame that Kubrick appears to add to the mix of ballgames in his film is basketball. Next to the baseball behind Danny's head as he eats his sandwich and watches cartoons, we see a laundry basket, a golden laundry basket, which reminded me of the various green and yellow laundry machines we see as Wendy rushes out of the boiler room to wake Jack from his nightmare in the CL. Like the stories by Poe and Morgan Robertson, so Jack's nightmare will eventually come to life when Jack chases Danny like Wile E. Coyote chasing the Road Runner in the cartoon Danny watches. And the contents of those washing machines end up inside of that basket, much as the stories we tell ourselves clothe our ideas.

Like light passed through a prism and reflected in a mirror, the baseball and the laundry basket are two sides of "basket-ball." And both in the Kensington parking lot opposite the VW Sleeper van and in the upper right-hand corner of Danny's Bugs Bunny jersey, we see a basketball hoop. And the one on Danny's 42 jersey is brown and gold:

233

the same colors we see on the doors to room 237, and the Gold Room bathroom, and the jewelry box at the base of the vanity mirror below Jack's sleepy head.

Like the Bugs Bunny doll in the lobby compared to the one on Danny's shirt, so the basketball hoop on Danny's shirt is the cartoon twin of the one we see in the parking lot. Like Danny talking to his reflection in the mirror, one is two dimensional, the other three. And the shadow by the sleeper van walks from one toward the other just before it disappears into the "sleeper" and Danny's mouth, even as Tony wakes up screaming "red rum" later. Is that why Jack opens his mouth and sticks out his tongue in the vanity mirror, as if he is letting the genii out of the bottle, mirroring the idea of that shadow walking into Danny's mouth from the Kensington parking lot in Boulder?

Both Bugs Bunny and the basketball hoop are reflected in what we see when Jack throws his tennis ball down the lobby on the first day we see the Torrances alone in the Overlook hotel, a month later. When Jack pitches that tennis ball toward the driftwood in the lobby, the ball soars directly over the circular emblem on the floor in front of the Cashier window, a marble stone that will eventually serve as both an altar and an "Indian" headstone for Dick. Sitting on top of that circular emblem is the tricycle Danny will ride around in a loop in both the CL and around the 237 hallway; as if to reflect the circle it now sits on. And sitting in the driver seat of that tricycle is a stuffed Bugs Bunny doll, facing backwards, watching Jack. Given all of this, is it just a coincidence that that circular emblem just happens to also vaguely resemble both a giant basketball and what it would look like to stand on top of a giant A-frame ladder looking down through an oversized basketball hoop?

Gollywog & Mickey Mouse, Hatchet Wounds & Football

The more I paid attention, the more Kubrick provided Easter eggs galore, each strategically positioned in every frame of the film to help us stitch together a film that, like a jigsaw puzzle, was "chopped up into little pieces." When he throws his tennis ball down the length of the lobby and over the emblem where Danny's trike sits and Dick's body will land, for example, Jack is standing directly in front of a cartoon twin to Dick Hallorann in the form of a black ragdoll lying on the floor.

Called a "gollywog doll," as if to suggest the hotel they are in is really a dollhouse to be played with by Overlookers, it was a children's toy that was originally inspired by blackface minstrels. As if to ease children into a culture of racism through the Trojan horse of harmless toys and entertainment, the gollywog was written into life in the nineteenth century by the American born English cartoonist, Florence Kate Upton.

It began its life in the pages of children's books. As a toy, the gollywog helped to normalize racist iconography with children much in the same way the Road Runner cartoons helped normalize Danny to ideas of cannibalism. (It's a "dog eat dog world" out there, after all, and Danny better damn well get used to it.) Usually depicted as a type of rag doll with its pitch-black skin being fashioned from minstrel cloth, it was designed with exaggerated red lips, bone white teeth, and wild savage-like hair. Like the minstrel, the doll has long been associated with the racism that was so prevalent in America and England during both the century in which the doll was born and in 1921 (and in some places, unfortunately, even in 2021).

One theory of the origin of the name "gollywog" is that it comes from the acronym used for Egyptian laborers that worked for the British soldiers who colonized Egypt during the second half of the nineteenth century. Like America colonizing Hawaii and the Philippines, so the colonization of Egypt was just part of the "white man's burden" to civilize the "darker" more savage races of the world. Those workers, who were like Great Britain's version of the Hebrews of the Old Testament, wore armbands with the insignia W.O.G.S. on it: an acronym that stood for "Working on Government Service."

By employing W.O.G.S., the British Empire could rely on socialism to enrich itself from its colonies but did so far enough away that the citizens of the British Empire would be none the wiser. British troops spoke of these laborers as "ghouls:" an Arabic word for a desert ghost.[32] And of course, the Overlook Hotel is a "ghost ship" in a desert of snow and ice, in which Dick will be turned into a ghost with the swing of a stick and the flick of a pen; and all in accord with the will of the Overlookers.

Considering where we see it laying on the floor in the lobby, if noticed at all, the gollywog doll is a dollhouse version of Dick Halloran. Reflecting the racism the doll embodied, Delbert Grady later refers to Dick as "a nigger cook," a phrase that accurately reflected the racism so endemic in the upper echelons of "enlightened" American and British society during the 1920s. In that decade, in fact, eugenics based on race was being embraced culturally, championed by Christian Titians of industry like John D. Rockefeller and Henry Ford, and the Ku Klux Klan

---

[32] http://www.historyofdolls.com/history-of-famous-dolls/history-of-golliwog/

was so powerful it succeeded in engineering the elections of officials from coast to coast, including the mayors of Portland, Maine, and Portland, Oregon.

Even the placement of the gollywog doll, and other various details surrounding it, appears to be carefully planned out. Like the bloodied bodies of the twins in the hallway, for example, the golliwog doll is face down while, a few feet from that doll, Dick's corpse will eventually lay face up. And right beside the pillar Jack will later step from behind to "redrum" Dick, we see a Winnie the Pooh doll, while "Winnie" is the nickname Dick asked Wendy about as they entered the kitchen: "Mrs. Torrance . . . Are you a Winnie or a Freddy?" That same Winnie the Pooh doll is sitting on the couch to the left of the fire engine as Wendy and Danny watch their second episode of Road Runner cartoons in the Overlook apartment. Even more telling is the fact that, just past the Winnie the Pooh doll, we see a soccer ball: a ball the rest of the world refers to by a different name. And because they do, it seemed especially relevant to the gollywog doll's two-dimensional twin.

Finding the Gollywog Twin

In a film that operates like a game of mahjong filled with different variations of twins, the gollywog, Bugs Bunny, and Winnie the Pooh dolls are not only toy twins to Dick, Danny, and Wendy, respectively, but each doll also appears to have a "twin" as well. The twin of the Bugs Bunny doll sitting on Danny's trike, for example, is the Bugs Bunny image we see on Danny's jersey in Boulder, while the Winnie the Pooh doll has two appearances in the film: first on the floor in the lobby and then on the couch next to the fire engine and the baseball bat. Winnie the

Pooh first faces away from the camera in the lobby, and toward the camera in the apartment: just like the bodies of the Grady twins. And Bugs Bunny's face, which we see on the doll in the lobby, in Boulder is hidden from view under the table and then under the bottom of the frame. Both, as such, have appearances as facing us and "faceless," just like the blood Grady twins.

Given Kubrick's use of triangulation, the gollywog doll should either appear more than once or it must have a twin. And if the basketball hoop and Bugs Bunny are any guide, one should be two dimensional and the other three. And since the doll itself is a three-dimensional thing, the "twin" should be a two dimensional image. That twin may be obvious, but it wasn't to me, not at first anyway. As it turned out, it had to do with where we see that soccer ball in the lobby, and why we see it where we do, when we do.

So where is the gollywog twin, and why does it matter? In one respect, a possible candidate for that twin is the shadow standing by the VW Sleeper van in the Kensington parking lot. It might also be the Minnie Mouse sticker on Danny's bedroom door. But there is another option that, thanks to the soccer ball, is a dead ringer. And it matters because it not only indicates Kubrick is, in fact, operating according to a rule of twins, it also tells us something about what really happens to Danny in room 237, and who unlocks the door to that room in the first place.

Why should we wonder if that gollywog doll has a twin in the film anyway? Well, Kubrick appears to be following patterns, and because he does, those patterns suggest that the film is operating according to a set of rules, like the movement of pieces on a chessboard. As such, the gollywog doll should either make two appearances in the film, like Winnie the Pooh and Bugs Bunny, or at least have some kind of twin lurking about somewhere in the film. Finding that twin becomes important because it helps us understand the crime scene we are investigating, and thus the true face of Kubrick's game.

By giving Winnie the Pooh and Bugs Bunny two showings in the film, Kubrick triangulates Wendy and Danny with two cartoon images. We even see something similar with Jack, as Kubrick triangulates Jack with two viewings of the Road Runner cartoons. We even have three sightings of the "Flock of Loons" painting ferchrisake! He even equates Jack with Zeus taking the form of an eagle and kidnapping Ganymede to be his cupbearer, "and perhaps a bit more," with both the green Stovington Eagle he awakes inside of, and the red ceramic eagle on the windowsill in Stuart's office.

Kubrick even triangulates three sleeping Jacks: one Jack in the vanity mirror in his green t-shirt, and the other two sleeping in his red jacket. One red-Jack awakens at his writing table and the other in the "story room;" a connection that hardly seems like a coincidence.

Kubrick does this also with Stuart Ullman and Dick Halloran. Stuart's two twins are a female doppelgänger, in the form of the doctor who interviews Danny then Wendy in Boulder, and a male doppelgänger, in the form of the man stacking dishes in the hallway as Stuart, Bill, Wendy, and Jack make their way to the boiler room on Closing Day. (No wonder Stuart doesn't flinch when that man walks through the backdoor into Stuart's office.) He does a similar triangulation of actual characters in the film with Dick Halloran, by giving us both Larry Durkin, and the often-overlooked African American who exits the hotel on Closing Day, who steps out from behind the stone pillar to the awing at the mouth of the hotel, and a green chair. (Because we see another green chair in the mirror in room 237, is it any wonder that Kubrick cast "Tony" Burton to play Larry Durkin?)

But consider how Kubrick does something similar with the Grady twins and the colors light-blue and white.

When Danny finally enters room 237, his Apollo 11 sweater not only reflects the Gemini sign for twins, but it is also the same colors of light blue and white as the dresses worn by the Grady twins. The yellow stars (pink in the Blu Ray release) on that sweater not only makes it the same colors as the first bathrobe we see Wendy wearing when she brings Jack is "sonny" side up egg yolk, they are also the same color as the chair he climbed on top of to retrieve his darts before turning around and seeing the twins in the Games Room. And on the dartboard behind Danny when he sees the twins, we see the numbers 2, 3, and 7, written both *forward and backward*.

Also, Danny has two flashes of the twins, first while looking into the mirror in the Kensington bathroom and then again while standing in front of the "twin" yet mismatched golden door knobs to room 237, in which he can also see his own reflection. In the Kensington bathroom, he stands on a step stool, in the Games Room he stands on a chair, and in front of the 237 doorknobs he is not only on the second floor, relative to the CL, but he had also just risen out of the seat of his tricycle. He even stands up from the floor when he finally enters 237.

A third triangulation of Danny with the twins occurs when Danny encounters the twins in the hallway outside of their apartment. In this encounter with the twins, Danny is sitting in his tricycle again, "playing with himself" as it were, just like the Bugs Bunny doll sits in the trike backwards in the lobby when Jack throws his ball for the 13th time. Then, the twins first invite Danny to "come and play" (like Stuart saying to Jack, "Oh, *come in* Jack), and then say "forever and ever and ever" after we see them switch from playmates to bloodied corpses. Look closely, however, and it appears their corpses are still breathing. They are, that is, the living dead. This switch mirrors the switch of the playmate Jack encounters in the 237 bathroom, who first invites him to play and "cum," only to imply "forever and ever and ever" in death, in the mirror, even as she's still breathing as she laughs and laughs.

Notice too that it is only when Danny encounters the twins bloodied bodies that he is wearing a red jacket, like Jack when he has his nightmare, kisses the woman in 237, and kills Dick. And, again, just before encountering the bloodied twins, Danny rides a "Z" shape pattern that jumps from the lobby floor to their apartment floor, the same pattern of the mirrored light fixture on the ceiling in the bathroom in 237. That fixture is shaped like a lightning bolt, the triplet of which we see at the top of the pillar in the lobby: *Z Z Z*. Those Zs remind us of sleeping cartoon characters. And in the overhead view, we see something very similar in the hedge maze.

Other slight yet seemingly intentional differences: When we see the twins in the hallway, the one on the right stands slightly forward from the one on the left, mirroring not only the doors to the living room of 237, but also to Danny at the front doors to 237: once locked out, then walking in. And while Danny stands on a golden chair that faces him in the Games Room where we see 237 on the dartboard, we see a dark chair turned facedown when we see the bloody twins. The difference in colors

241

of those chairs is the same as the difference in the colors of Jack's two typewriters, which mirrors the grand piano and staircase at the other end of the CL.

All this triangulation indicates there should also be a triangulation of the gollywog doll with Dick Hallorann. But the gollywog doll makes only one appearance in the entire movie. Yet the other dolls we see in the lobby when Jack pitches his ball, all appear to be reflections.

The placement of the dolls even reflects Dick, Danny, and Wendy, in the same order they toured the kitchen, only reversing that order after they exit the C3 walk-in freezer. As if walking into the mirror, that position is reversed when we see the timeclock and the mirror across from the C3 door. Those dolls, in other words, are body doubles, while the "dead meat" in the walk-in freezer was a foreshadowing of Dick walking into the hotel from the cold and ending up as dead meat, laid out between the gollywog and the Bugs Bunny doll sitting backwards on Danny's trike; like a piece of bacon and egg-*yoke*.

The dolls on the floor in the lobby appear to operate as body-doubles. But that means the same would be true of the gollywog doll, and even the soccer ball, between which we see Bugs Bunny and Winnie the Pooh. The skin of a soccer ball is black and white in color. And its markings are comprised of 32 polygons: 12 black pentagons and 20 white hexagons. And Danny sits inside of a hexagon outside of room 237 that is like the emblem on which his tricycle sits with Bug's Bunny facing backwards.

So, what does all of this tell us about the gollywog? With its black skin reminding us of both the shadow in the Kensington parking lot and the black tuxedo worn by Delbert Grady, and its red and white overalls reminding us of the colors of the Gold Room bathroom, face down, it has a vague resemblance to another world famous cartoon character. Like the successor to the gollywog doll, it likewise first appeared in children's stories, and was famous for wearing red overalls. We see it when Danny goes to retrieve his fire engine from his room, only to find Jack staring as blankly out the window as Danny had been while watching Road Runner cartoons in Boulder.

Danny creeps into the apartment like a little boy attempting to avoid awakening a red dragon or a fairytale giant at the top of a beanstalk. As he does, we see the face of his two-tone sweater, colored in blue and light-blue or white, with a picture of Mickey Mouse on the breastplate, as Danny tries to be as quiet as a mouse. Coincidentally, like Jack's sports jacket, Bugs Bunny is typically colored in grey with a white breastplate, but sometimes his grey hair appears like a light blue, a bit like the dresses worn by the Grady twins. And Danny's Mickey Mouse sweater mimics the costume of Bugs Bunny, as if to suggest Danny, upon finding Jack staring blankly out the window, is like a mouse in a maze that is descending even further down a rabbit hole.

Danny even mimics the posture of Mickey Mouse on the sweater after he climbs to the top of the stairs. Standing with his arms and shoulders pulled slightly back, he leans back as if to catch his balance from recoiling at the sight of Jack, before freezing in place like topiary or an ice sculpture. What made all these details stand out is how they all tie together with each cross-thatching to the others, like a lattice; like a spider's web; like the lines on the green and red diamond pattern rugs.

Born in a Disney short film in 1928, Mickey Mouse's first starring role was as an airplane pilot in the animated silent film, *Plane Crazy*.

And not only is the Mickey Mouse from that era a veritable twin to the minstrel characters that inspired the gollywog doll, albeit with a whiter face and bigger ears, it just so happens that we see Dick on an airplane just after we see Jack disable the radio in Ullman's office, confirming he has gone 'plain crazy.'

Also, on Danny's sweater, Mickey is depicted as kicking a football. In the lobby, Jack starts to throw the tennis ball like a baseball while standing in-line with the gollywog doll, then passes in front of Danny's trike with a Bugs Bunny doll on it, and finishes with aligning with the Winnie the Pooh doll and the "football." And when the tennis ball rolls up to Danny in the 237 hallway, it does so as if someone had rolled it to him, like a goalie rolling a ball out to a teammate during the World Cup.

Then, where the football on Danny's sweater sat really jumped out at me, because of what it foreshadows. It sits in the same place on Danny's chest as the basketball hoop sat on Danny's Bugs Bunny jersey while in the lobby, a Bugs Bunny doll sits backwards on Danny's trike, which happens to sit on an emblem that resembles an oversized basketball and what it would look like overlooking an oversized basketball hoop while standing on top of a very tall A-frame ladder. And both the football and that basketball hoop sit over Danny's heart, where he would hold his hand to say the pledge of allegiance.

Other details in the scene of Danny sitting on Jack's lap also appear to be revealing. Danny and Jack happen to be color twins in the scene, with both wearing dark blues and red clothing. With Danny, we see the red in the collar of his plaid flannel shirt, while with Jack we see red around the collar of his sock. Like the brown outfits worn by Susy and

Bill Watson during the interview and Wendy on Closing Day, so clothes can be seen as artificial skin. Danny, as such, often wears colors that reflect the colors of clothes worn by both Wendy and Jack. The blue sweater with red plaid shirt Danny wears when he sits on Jack's lap are the same color as the jacket Danny wore on Closing Day, with the red stripe and letters that said "FLYERS," and are the same colors we first see Wendy wearing. In fact, in Boulder, the red we see of Wendy's union suit is around the collar and shoulders, like Danny's flannel, and the red we see the next time she dressed all in blue is her red boots, like Jack's flannel socks, and Dorothy's red ruby slippers. And now, as Danny sits on Jack's knee like a kid telling Santa Claus what he wants for Christmas, we see the football on his sweater angling toward the bathroom window that Danny will later 'fly' out of, sliding down the snow embankment like Santa sliding down the chimney, or that poster in the Games Room of that fellow skiing down the mountain.

With all these details came a rising tide of questions. Are all these things really just meaningless or purely accidental coincidences? Is it really just a coincidence that we see a soccer ball near a Winnie the Pooh doll lying on the floor right beside the pillar Jack will later step out from behind to kill Dick, when a soccer ball is the twin to a football on Danny's sweater and Wendy is Jack's "other half? Or that Jack hits Dick in the chest by swinging his axe like a baseball bat, as if he were knocking the ball he had pitched earlier "out of the park," when the Mercury Station wagon with the magic 3-way door was a Colony Park, and Danny, who watches game films of Jack in the guise of Road Runner cartoons, later "flies" from the hotel from the upper floor window like a high-fly ball, while behind Larry Durkin is a cartoon about "Angelo the Mighty *Flea*"?

Why, too, was Kubrick so specific in these details, if they ultimately didn't mean anything at all? Why ensure that Jack's final pitch and final axe swing both happen to be at opposite ends of the lobby, as if he is playing midnight baseball with his own reflection, and both where the last of unlucky 13? And is it really just a coincidence too that Jack just happens to strike Dick in the chest with an ax in roughly the same spot we see both the basketball hoop on Danny's Bugs Bunny jersey *and* the football on Danny's Mickey Mouse sweater, when the emblem Dick and Danny's trike are on look like an overlook of a giant basketball net, and the baseball diamond Jack was standing on when he throws that ball is also shaped like a football, while the football on Danny's Mickey Mouse sweater, complete with laces, looks a lot like an axe wound that has been sutured together with stiches? Hell, even Jack picking up Danny and dropping him down on his left knee is a kind of twin to Mickey dropkicking the football with his right leg! And Dick's body, when Wendy eventually sees it laid to rest on the circular emblem, looks like he is sliding down a giant drain hole, feet first, like Danny sliding down the embankment of snow from the bathroom window and stirring his finger around the bathroom drain when Tony tells him Jack got the job and was about to call Wendy.

Like that guy said in *The Princess Bride*, that all of this could be utterly   meaningless   and   purely   coincidental   was   simply "Inc*onceivable!*"

With the opening scene of the film, Kubrick introduces his audience to the experience of seeing both twins and inverted twins, by rolling a tennis ball out to the audience in the form of Jack inside of a yellow VW Beetle. Like the tennis ball being a miniature version of Jack's car, when Danny walks through the double doors to room 237, he does so as if he is walking into the mirrors on the back of the double doors that lead into the "living" room of 237. In those mirrors, just above a "shining" lamp shade, we see a painting of a boy, overlooking a river, just like the audience is watching a river of dancing spectral lights, through the mirrored lens of a camera.

Like so many other paintings in the film, the painting behind the lamp inside the foyer of room 237 is by Alex Colville. Painted in 1958, it is entitled, "Dog, Boy, and St. John River." Does the fact that we do not see the dog in that painting having anything to do with Wendy seeing a man in a dog costume later? Like Danny walking into room 237, that painting mirrors the camera soaring like an eagle in opening shot of the film, the boy reflecting the audience overlooking St. Mary's Lake. We see a similar painting over the Torrance bed, minus the boy and the dog. And while the camera walks forward into the mirror of the lake in the opening scene like Jack in the vanity mirror and Danny into room 237, in King's novel, Jack (like Jack Nicholson as well) is named "John," while the symbol of St. John the Evangelist in Christian iconography is an eagle.

And Jack wakes up as if he were Zeus himself hungry for Ganymede, in a "vanity mirror, like Narcissus, wearing a Stovington Eagles shirt: a name that happens to remind us of a "stove," like the one in Hansel and Gretel, and Jack having his head "stove-in" by Wendy. And like anamorphic art, Wendy's head is directly in front of a stainless-steel stove as she's interviewed by the doctor, and Danny's head is in front of the same thing as he is interviewed by Dick. And when Dick is cut down like a pig led to slaughter, Danny is inside of a "stainless" steel cabinet that looks like he is inside of a stove.

Danny inside of his Mickey Mouse sweater kicking a football brings us to the second time we see Kubrick roll a ball out to us in the form of Jack's yellow VW Bug: Closing Day. And the first time we see Jack in the hotel on that day, he is reading a Playgirl magazine. And the dog we do not see in the Alex Colville painting inside the foyer of room 237, a room Danny was lured into with a yellow tennis ball, Wendy sees later engaged in an act that looks like it had crawled out of the pages of Jack's Playgirl magazine and into one of the upper rooms of the hotel.

But notice the only reason Wendy even sees those men in that upper room: she does so after running upstairs while looking for Danny. She does this, even though she had just put Danny out the window, which the foreshadowed by the football on Danny's sweater as he asks Jack if he would ever hurt "mommy or me," and Wendy had watched Danny "run and hide," as she instructed him to do, toward the hedge maze where they'd played earlier. So why the hell does Wendy, right after exiting the bathroom where Jack was definitely trying to hurt Wendy and Danny, and knowing that both Danny and whoever just showed up in a snowcat are downstairs, start running upstairs, calling Danny's name, as if she fully expects to find him up there? Shouldn't she have run downstairs, not up?

As it turns out, the football on Danny's sweater has a "mighty" secret to tell indeed, and it was that secret that, in part, sent Wendy flying up the stairs looking for Danny, where she found those men playing hide the sausage. And part of that secret is who the dog-suited man was playing with in that upper room: the guy standing at the elevator in the golden jacket with the fishing hat over his hand, who we first see as Jack walks into Stuart's office for his interview.

At the elevator, that "faceless" man looks away from us and toward the other elevator. When Jack comes back to the lobby and finds it strewn with party favors and music luring him back to the Gold Room party, after his visit to room 237, we see the needle on that elevator is on the fourth floor. And after Wendy puts Danny out the bathroom window, which allows us to see their apartment is on the second floor of the hotel, she then runs up two more floors: to the fourth floor. And when we finally see his face in that room, he looks directly into the camera to see whose watching.

And the other part of the secret the ball on Danny's sweater has to tell, is why that door is wide open in the first place, and what room number they are in.

◊◊

All of this brings us to Jack's Playgirl magazine.

On the cover of Jack's Playgirl magazine, we see a woman who is the veritable "twin" to the young woman in the bathtub in 237; a man undressing from a tuxedo like the one Jack will wear in the final photograph and the fellow in the upper room; and another vanity mirror, like the one Jack wakes up in "A Month Later," and the two Danny walks toward (or into) in room 237. While the edition to that magazine is January 1978, a note taped to the vanity mirror on the cover says, "31 December 1977, Saturday," and in handwritten cursive across the bottom of that note, "*Party!*" Like the Donner party and the one Jack attends in the Gold Room, this reminds us of both the dead man's party in a lobby full of skeletons, and the man in the tuxedo with the cracked skull who reminds us of Tony the Tiger by asking Wendy, "Great party, isn't it?" Even the sum of the numbers "1977" add up to 24, while Danny watches Road Runner cartoons and talks to Tony, while inside of a 42 jersey, which is darker blue and white, and he enters room 237 wearing a lighter blue and white sweater, and, again, 2 x 3 x 7 = 42.

Consider also how the month of December has two faces. Being formed from the Latin root decem- which means "ten," it is also the twelfth month of the year. In 750 BCE (73+2), the ancient Romans established their first calendar, which was only ten months long. It began in March and ended in December, after which came a nameless time of year that reflected the wasteland of winter. And the month in the final photograph –July – is named after Julius Caesar.

That magazine invites us to consider its cryptic meaning in still other ways. Like the opening shots of the film drawing us into the mirrored reflection of St. Mary's Lake, the 'camera walks' us into the vanity mirror as Jack awakens 'A Month Later, in the same way it does as Danny walks into the "living" room of 237 and, at the same time, the twin full length mirrors on the backs of those doors. And both invite us into the mirror we see on the cover of the Playgirl magazine, and the pictures inside.

Like the images in that magazine and even the film itself, "It's just like pictures in a book, Danny," Tony reminds Danny when he sees the twins inviting him to come and play, "It isn't real." And if it "isn't real," then those pictures shouldn't be able to hurt anyone. Right?

As a Catholic, I was raised to believe that such pictures could, indeed, hurt us very much, by hurting my chances to be saved from eternal tortures, tortures my parents assured me their God was threatening to inflict upon me for so much as looking at such pictures. But, as I asked at the very opening of this book, how and when did we become so terrified of so many things, especially ourselves, let alone pictures in a magazine? We weren't born this way. So, what happened?

To understand that, we have to look into a long history that such a magazine is inviting us to return to and remember. Doing so not only helps us to understand Jack from the inside out, but it is also the necessary first step for unmasking what is really going on in room 237, and how what happens there leads directly to Jack both escaping the pantry and ending up in a black and white photograph dated 1921.

TEN

THE PLAYGIRL MAGAZINE

It is not that something different is seen, but that one sees differently.
It is as though the spatial act of seeing were changed by a new dimension.

Carl Jung

The present is the past rolled up for action,
while the past is the present rolled out for understanding.

Will Durant

HOW DOES THE PLAYGIRL MAGAZINE we see Jack reading in the lobby of the Overlook on Closing Day invite us to see *The Shining* in a whole new light? How, in other words, does the film invite us to consider how much our religious "beliefs" hide from us a vast history related to the sexuality symbolized by that magazine? And might that magazine, as a symbol of both a history hidden from view and the psychological harm done through shame, provide a perfect way of explaining the supernatural evil we blame for Jack's murderous rampage by the psychological, as Kubrick hoped we'd one day be able to do, much as we did with replacing our religious understanding of "witches" with scientific understanding of the brain? As it turns out, nothing provides a better lens for understanding both Jack, and even ourselves, than Kubrick's clever yet cryptic placement of that Playgirl magazine.

◊◊

Like the face on the postcard from 1888, Stanley Kubrick and Stephen King had very different views about what we mean by "evil," and what the source and cause of that evil really is. While Kubrick saw evil as exclusively human in origin, King, as already mentioned, was more "interested in what's under the surface of a man's exterior, and the dark, private thoughts he keeps bottled to himself, until the supernatural forces them out." The question is which perspective is scarier for us to consider: evil that comes from within ourselves, which eats at our table and sleeps in our bed, or evil that comes from outside ourselves, from a "supernatural" source like "Satan" that we can blame for the worst we do, and only defend against by repeating prayers and sacred rituals?

An even scarier perspective comes from conjoining these two perspectives. What if the very prayers and rituals we perform to save us from supernatural evil are in fact the very things that have always been relied on to conjure forth the darker demons of our nature, much as that book by Robert Chambers about "The King in Yellow" drove people mad just be reading it? Indeed, every person who was ever tortured, either physically or psychologically, because they were labeled by "believers" as a witch or a heretic, can easily see how the true source of all evil is always fear masquerading as a love for whatever promises to save such people from what they fear most. And far scarier than homosexuality to such "believers" is the fear of eternal torture for their failure to fear homosexuality as a mighty sin against their brand of "God," even though this is like believing that sneezing the wrong way threatens to blow out the light of the sun.

Unmasking the ugly truth operating behind the love we have for a beautiful lie is by far the heaviest cross a person can bear. Of his own religion, Catholic theologian Blaise Pascal was forced to bear such a cross when he concluded that "people never do evil so fully and gaily, as when they do it through a false principle of conscience." The question is whether my Catholic religion had installed just such a "false principle of conscience" by teaching me to believe in things like witches and devils and hell, or that I was a sinner who, born destined and deserving of hell, needed the very savior that only my brand of religion happened to sell. Was it not just such a "false principle of conscience" that colored my perspective as a child, leading me to see impish Oompa Loompas prowling about the chocolate factory of my own cerebral cortex? And had I been an adult living in Salem during the witch trials or in Germany after 1945, who might I have then attacked as responsible for unleashing such inky-demons into my bed chamber? What "dark forces" are first installed and then unleashed on the world, in other words, by teaching people to believe their own desire for sexual pleasure, if not practiced according to men who have chosen to live their life as eunuchs for a disembodied intelligence they are incapable of demonstrating exists at all, is enough to win us all an eternity of physical pain? Worse, we are taught such eternal physical pain can only be avoided by accepting the emotional pain that comes from "believing" that indulging such desires outside of the rules proscribed by a class of priestly eunuchs constitutes the very sins that caused Jesus so much pain and suffering on a cross, and even continue to do so today, and all because this was the only way God could think to forgive us for such sexual "sins," in order to save us from the hell He alone created and maintains, "forever, and ever, and ever."

As a modern-day Faust making a deal with the devil in Stuart Ullman, it is these very ideas that Stuart may be relying on to trigger Jack's descent into murderous rage. Why, after all, do Stuart and Bill Watson appear not to notice, or care, about the Playgirl magazine Jack is reading? Perhaps it is because they both intuited the latent homosexual desires Jack is keeping "bottled" up inside of himself during the interview, desires which they hope the "isolation" of the Overlook will force Jack to pour out of himself, and externalize toward his family, in the form of the self-loathing he has for those parts of a sexuality he has been conditioned his whole life to believe he should feel deeply ashamed of.

As far-fetched as this perspective may sound, there is plenty of research and evidence that shows it is at least one way of explaining what has long been attributed to supernatural evil, and always by religions that often make a killing by convincing people such a "belief" is infallibly true, by the psychological. Symbolized by the butterfly and Aphrodite and even Apollo, the transformation from a gentle Jekyll to a hellish Hyde can happen when the tendency of a repressed wish or feeling on an unconscious level becomes expressed at a conscious level in a contrasting form.

Described by Sigmund Freud as "reaction formation," consider just three real world examples of how the sadism a person is conditioned to experience within themselves can produce a mask of a moralizing without. One example is Ted Haggard. A firebrand Christian minister who led a campaign against same sex marriage, the true source of Hydish attacks was unmasked in 2006, when Haggard was discovered to have been 'hiding' his own homosexuality, and carrying on a three year relationship with a male prostitute. A better example of how the things we hide can turn us into Mr. Hyde for our unquestioned "beliefs" is FBI Director J. Edgar Hoover, a man famous for his fetishistic bisexuality. In 1951, Hoover launched the bureau's "sex deviates" program. A modern-day witch hunt, it became known as "the war on gays," which cost thousands of people their livelihood, terrorized countless more, including those who simply feared being accused of being gay even if they weren't, and lasted until at least the 1970s. Lastly, we even find an example on the silver screen in 1960s that reflects a reality that surpassed what fantasy would permit.

The archetypical cinema trope of how sexual desires can turn Dr. Jekyll into a Mr. Hyde for a religion by causing deep emotional suffering within that leads to violence without is, of course, Norman Bates. From Hitchcock's *Psycho*, Norman was based on the serial killer Ed Gein, a man who, like St. Augustine, had also been taught by his mother to see his own sexual desires as the root of all that is evil in the world. More than the devil, it was the suffering such ideas sowed in the souls of such men, and fear of eternal punishment for failing to adequately abhor such desires, that led them to transfer their emotional fears into the physical suffering of so many innocent victims. For many serial killers, in fact, prostitutes are not only easier to victimize, but are even seen by such killers to in some way deserve their fate.

◊◊

The Playgirl magazine we see Jack reading on Closing Day is therefore possibly the most surprising and revealing detail in the whole film. With this simple prop, Kubrick not only invites us to explore one of the most important yet complicated parts of being human, along with a whole history of ideas around both sex and concepts of gods and religions, he also provides a powerful mnemonic device for recalling that history. And by acting as such a device, it not only provides a lens for interpreting why Jack is reading such a magazine in the first place, and why the man in the golden jacket standing in front of the elevators when Jack walks into Stuart's office ends up in an upstairs room with a man in a dog suit, but also how the Overlook Hotel is designed to operate as Kubrick's memory palace.

So, what's a "memory palace," and how does it relate to *The Shining*? Such a palace relates to *The Shining* in two ways. It was born from an event that was remarkably similar to something that happened at the Stanley Hotel in 1909, directly below the very room Stephen King stayed in when he first started writing his novel: room 217. And it serves as the opening scene in a favorite movie found in Wendy's novel, *The Catcher in the Rye*.

Also known as the "memory journey," a memory palace is a mnemonic method that uses visualizations of a familiar spatial environment to enhance the recall of information. Used by story tellers in Ancient Greece and Rome to remember and recite all 27,000 lines of Homer's *Iliad* and *Odyssey*, the method was born as a result of a dinner party that turned into a "last supper" for the attendees after the ceiling of their banquet hall collapsed on top of them. The only survivor of the tragic event was Simonides, who, as fate would have it, had been fortuitously summoned outside by the sons of Zeus. To account for the dead, Simonides recalled the names of all the attendees by remembering the seating arrangements during the banquet. Fortunately, when the same thing occurred directly below room 217 in the Stanley Hotel in 1909, no one was killed as a result.

In *The Catcher in the Rye*, on the other hand, we see such a palace being relied on in a favorite movie. Holden Caulfield, the protagonist of the novel, has a ten-year-old sister named Phoebe. Her favorite movie just happens to be Alfred Hitchcock's, *The 39 Steps*. About a man falsely accused of murder trying to prevent a ring of spies from stealing military secrets, the film starts with the main character, Richard Hannay (played by Robert Donat), sitting in a London music hall theater watching "Mr. Memory" demonstrate his powers of recall, which he does by relying on a memory palace.

Like *The 39 Steps*, Kubrick's *Shining* invites us to remember by seeing with new eyes how a simple image can call a whole history of ideas to mind, and how that history can shed some light on how our beliefs can divide our mind against itself. Like a cross embodying the whole history of Christianity, so the Playgirl magazine opens the pages of a whole history revolving around sex and gods, and even sin and suffering, much of which is so often caused unnecessarily by our brands of religious beliefs.

Take Apollo and Aphrodite, for example. Like Mount Olympus, Jack has come to live with his family for the winter in a mountain top resort for "all the best people." Both being children of Zeus, Aphrodite is the patron saint of lesbians while Apollo was the patron saint of same sex love. And, as if on eagle's s wings as we fly over St. Mary's Lake in the opening scene, Zeus incarnated in the form of an eagle to kidnap a small boy named Ganymede, to act as both his cupbearer and his concubine.

Then there is the idea of incest hinted at by the Playgirl magazine. As film analyst Rob Ager pointed out, there is an article on the cover of the edition of the Playgirl magazine Jack is reading entitled "Incest: Why Parent's Sleep with their Children." Being the giant pervert that he was, Zeus slept with more than one of his own daughters. Not only did Zeus marry his sister Hera, but he would later incarnate in the form of a snake to mate with his daughter (by another wife, Rhea) Persephone, which resulted in the birth of Dionysus, the god of fertility, wine, and pleasure. One of his special powers of Dionysus was his ability to drive mortals insane. And Aphrodite, of her own volition, also had an affair with her father, Zeus. In retaliation, his jealous wife, Hera, laid her hands upon the belly of Aphrodite and cursed their offspring with malformity. Their child was the ugly god Priapus: a dwarfish man with a giant ever erect penis.

As it turns out, ideas about incest, as they relate to Zeus or Jack, are only half the story. The other half reveals who it was that rolled the ball up to Danny in the 237 hallway, who let Jack out of the storage room, and who or what is really inside of room 237.

And to understand how the Playgirl magazine reveals what is really going on in room 237, and even the Overlook hotel overall, we must accept Kubrick's invitation to "come and play" with a whole history of ideas that will help us better understand Jack's insanity by better understanding the roots of our own ideas, from both the inside out and the outside in. And to do that, we have to jump into the rabbit hole of history and remember what we have long forgotten.

◊◊

What happens in the mind of a child when we teach that child to associate the sexual urges they experience with the onset of puberty, with feelings of shame and a fear of being rejected or burned alive, like a witch or a heretic, only for all eternity? And how is this made worse when those same children are also forced to value attachment over their own authenticity, and relentlessly attacked with hyper-sexual images from without, while awash in raging hormones from within? And, worst of all, they are forced to grapple with such issues not only before they've learned how to use their own mind to control their brain, but are forced to do so long before their own brains are decades away from fully developing that part of the brain that would enable them to use the higher faculties of the mind needed to help them regulate such desires? And, with regards to Jack, how might the repression or suppression of such desires, especially ones that are taboo, affect that child into adulthood?

While the intent is obviously to seed the child's mind with ideas that will help them to be more sexually responsible, such tactics may feel to an innocent child like a crown of thorns has been placed on their head. And by nurturing a child to associate sin, death, and suffering, with what nature has made to be a source of one of life's greatest pleasures and the key to life itself, the mind of such a child can be turned into a house divided against itself. Such a cocktail of sex and "sin" can cause feelings of sexual arousal to trigger emotional pain from thoughts of shame and rejection. Like Jack after his experience in room 237, planting the seeds of such "shame" can then snowball into acts of extreme violence toward the object of one's desires, just like we saw with Norman Bates, and even the great St. Augustine's condemnation of sex overall, due to his addiction to the prostitutes of Rome.

According to studies, the relationship between repressed sexual desires, violence, and shame, which provides at least one way of interpreting the Playgirl magazine as being the potential clue about the origins of Jack's psychopathy, may operate like a feedback loop. According to renowned Harvard psychiatrist and violence expert, James Gilligan, the relationship between sexual shame and violence is practically symbiotic. Best known for his series of books entitled, *Violence: Reflection of a National Epidemic*, Gilligan's insights about the motivations for, and the causes behind, violent behavior, come from working in the American prison system for 25 years. During that time, a common thread that ran through all the domestic abuse cases he studied was one he described as "humiliated fury."

Humiliated fury occurs when individuals transform high-intensity shame into anger because the latter offers some relief from the unbearable pain of the former. Like an explosive mix of anger and hostility known as "narcissistic rage," which arises from threats to a narcissists' fractured sense of self, humiliated fury is a trait exhibited more often in narcissists than in others. Both forms of hostility are typically expressed more in men, who see the expression of anger as exerting dominance, than in women, who view such hostility as a loss of control.[33]

---

[33] https://pubmed.ncbi.nlm.nih.gov/15183371/

Other than Jack's murderous intent being triggered by repressed desires for sexual taboos, humiliated fury can also grow out of poverty. "Poverty is essentially a form of structural shaming," Gilligan explains, "as those who lack resources are invariably humiliated at every stage of their lives." Recall that Jack berates Wendy for asking him to break his contract with the Overlook before he threatens to "bash her brains in." Before that, after showing fatherly concern for Danny upon his return from room 237, Jack flies into a rage at Wendy's suggestion they leave the hotel. What appears to trigger Jack? Jack's fear that if they leave, he'll end up "shoveling out driveways" or working in a carwash.

What is at issue here is Jack's relative poverty, not his absolute poverty. Inferiority is a relative concept. As Gilligan points out in *Preventing Violence*, "When everyone is poor together, there is no shame in being poor. As Marx said, it is not living in a hovel that causes people to feel ashamed, it is living in a hovel next to a palace. And as he also said, shame is the emotion of revolution, i.e., of violence"[34] Having tasted the good life, Jack's fear of being cast down among the "sodomites," to wash cars and shovel out driveways, only adds fuel to his shame and thus his humiliated fury. Unable to revolt against the system, however, which is like a fish revolting against the water it swims in, Jack revolts against the family that is the cause of his financial burdens instead.

For Gilligan, "all violence begins with shame," with the two creating a feedback loop that can operate in a downward spiral, just like the one we see Jack being sucked into. Like Jack, a person can get so lost in a

---

[34] Gilligan, James; *Preventing Violence*, ch. 5 (2001).

spiral of being ashamed of their shame, that shame itself becomes the dominant force in their life. And, until we become conscious of how that shame operates within our unconscious on an emotional level, as Jung pointed out, we often mistake it for fate or special providence. In truth, however, anger becomes one way of soothing the pain of shame. Violence, as a result, can be a projection of one's own pain onto others through anger, or even onto oneself through suicide (which may help to explain why Jack never uses his ax to chop his way out of the hedge maze).

From the perspective that he is attempting to deaden his pain from the shame of his own sexual desires or financial difficulties, it is easy to see how Jack would prefer martyrdom for the Overlook over "working in a carwash" or "shoveling out driveways." At the very least, such a death allows Jack to feel some amount of power and autonomy over his own life rather than being seen as weak and incompetent, as Delbert Grady intimated in the pantry. Through this process, feelings of being as fragile and pathetic as a human being are replaced with feeling as powerful as a god.

Consider also the relationship between suicide and martyrdom, and how it is as unclear which Jack is ultimately engaging in as it is to tell the difference between Jack and Abraham. Both are acts of suicide, but the former can result from being too critical of oneself and too sensitive of the criticisms of others, while the latter can result from being too critical of other people's beliefs and refusing to be critical enough of one's own. Like reflections in a mirror, both lack a sense of proportion for how woefully imperfect one's knowledge of anything always is, especially of oneself. Yet with hell and heaven hanging in the balance, religions selling such ideas tend to offer only threats of pain to discourage one just as much as they promise eternal pleasures to encourage the other. The problem is that, given the inherently fickle and fallible nature of human perception on the one hand, and on the other, the inability to fully know just how much trauma or fear may be exerting control over our imperfect perceptions from our unconscious, we always lack an ability to clearly distinguish a difference between the two. Suicide is a form of martyrdom for oneself, from beliefs that are considered flawed or wrong, as such, just as much as martyrdom is a form of suicide for one's soul, in the service of some brand of "belief" that is considered infallible or right. Yet both seek only to avoid pain of one sort or another and obtain peace or pleasure. And Jack, in this respect, is simply the Halloween costume of Abraham.

Like our consideration of the Hogan and Gibbons twins, seeking to explain the supernatural with the psychological leads us to wonder if the Playgirl magazine is a sign that Jack's descent into madness is less the result of evil, as was the case in the novel, and more because of cultural conditioning. Is it natural for human beings in general to have a hostile response to homosexuality or to equate it with weakness, as traditional Catholic interpretations of the story of Sodom and Gomorrah led me to believe, or are such responses the result of nurturing that is not only contradicted by both biology and most cultures throughout history, but also leads us to respond to different sexual appetites with a level of fear and violence that are far more unnatural to us as homo sapiens than having different sexual desires? As Frans de Waal pointed out in his book, *Different: Gender Through the Eyes of a Primatologist*, homo sapiens are the only species that treats members of its own species differently based on differences of sexual behavior or physical appearance. The question is why: are we born this way, or must we be taught to think this way? And if the latter, does such a perspective use shame to make us better through conformity to religious dogmas, or make us worse by giving us reasons to live in "fear and trembling"[35] of each other, while pretending that such a fear makes us more worthy of God's love?

From a young age, long before a child even knows what it is, Christianity uses shame and guilt like a hammer and chisel to shape one's sexuality to conform to a sacred mold. Cultures like Ancient Greece and Rome, however, which thrived under a diversity of sexual expressions from Zeus to the great Achilles and Alexander the Great, demonstrated that what is most unnatural us is fear and judgement, especially of different sexual proclivities, with is like being afraid and judgmental of someone who likes the taste of liver (unless they eat it "with some fava beans and a nice Chianti").

Demonstrating this unnaturalness, and how such tactics actually cause more harm than good, two studies compared the occurrence of shame-related anger in North American cultural contexts (where shame is devalued and anger is valued) to its occurrence in Japanese contexts (where shame is valued and anger is devalued).[36] Across the two studies, and in line with previous research on humiliated fury, shame predicted anger for U.S. participants but not Japanese participants. Instead, it was

---

[35] In Philippians 2:12, St. Paul says we must "work out your own salvation with *fear and trembling*," even though this is a direct contradiction to Jesus saying "be not afraid," in Luke 12:32.

[36] https://pubmed.ncbi.nlm.nih.gov/29283312/

only in U.S.-origin vignettes that Japanese respondents reported shame-related anger. The findings suggest that, rather than being something natural to us as homo sapiens, shame-related anger is a culturally conditioned phenomenon.

As such studies help to illustrate, the seeds of shame we sow in attempts to subdue our sexual desires can operate like the flapping of butterfly wings that become a hurricane of violence "humiliated fury." As Sigmund Freud pointed out, such shame tactics only serve to increase, not decrease, one's focus on sex. Known as a "rebound effect," prohibitions against sexual expression actually end up adding fuel to the fire of one's sexual desires, like a child moving out from under the watchful eye of their own parent's when they go away to college. The dopamine rush our brain rewards us with for our courage to test taboos becomes almost too strong to resist. And in room 237, notice that the "impossible windows" in the room are closed with curtains that just happen to match the bedcovers, much as the curtains are all closed in the lobby when Jack finally sinks his phallic ax into a bit of fresh meat. And the Playgirl magazine operates as one of the greatest taboos of all, especially for a family man like Jack.

Then there is the shame of feeling or appearing weak. Culturally, American men are taught to despise feelings of weakness more than even death itself. Between the two, it is manlier to embrace martyrdom than say mea culpa. As a central part of that culture, Christianity has equated weakness with femininity, and associated homosexuals, who have often been treated no differently than heretics or witches, with both. As recent as the 1950's, for example, Christian conceptions of homosexuality led to the castration of at least ten boys in the Netherlands. One report of the incident stated that "surgical removal of testicles was regarded as a treatment for homosexuality and also as a punishment for those who accused clergy of sexual abuse."[37]

While obviously not the case for the vast majority of Christians, this example nevertheless demonstrates how, much like teaching people to believe in witches, religious condemnations of homosexuality as "evil" can cause a climate of fear that leads to horrific effects. Such a response by a priestly class reflects a "belief" central to Christianity that it is more natural to behave like a eunuch for an immaterial intelligence than to have sexual desires that run outside the lines drawn by such eunuchs. And so strong is such a fear that it can even recast acts of mutilation into moral requirements for ones' salvation. The only difference between such priests and the demons children are taught to fear stalk their souls, is that the former are real, and the latter are used to create an emotional dependence upon them.

This example only invites us more to wonder which perspective leads people to engage in more "evil:" Jack's potentially repressed homosexuality itself, or the fear that leads to such repression, which comes from teaching that homosexuality is a "sin" and that all those who practice or accept it as normal deserve to be treated no better than witches from the fifteenth to eighteenth century? Like those persecutions, we can also ask who was worse: those accused of being witches, or those who did the accusing and burned those they accused of being witches? Fueled by Christianity, fear of both witches and the eternal fires of hell led to

---

[37] http://thenewcivilrightsmovement.com/catholic-church-castrated-homosexual-boys-and-those-who-accused-priests-of-abuse/news/2012/03/20/36836

the murder of as many as 60,000 people between 1427 and 1782. And like 9/11, those murders were used to terrorize millions more into submission to Christian authoritarians "on a mission from God," to define who was a sinner, and who was a saint.

Nor was such terrorism simply an embarrassing problem from the past. According to historian Wolfgang Behringer, who works as a professor specializing in the early modern age at Saarland University, such slaughter for sacred beliefs still occurs today, in Africa, Southeast Asia, and Latin America. "In the 20th century alone, more people accused of witchcraft were brutally murdered than during the three centuries when witch hunts were practiced in Europe." As Behringer further points out, "between 1960 and 2000, about 40,000 people alleged of practicing witchcraft were murdered in Tanzania alone."[38]

Like the gremlins I was taught to fear in my room as a child, and like that postcard from 1888, I had to reconsider who the real "witches" really were: those accused of being witches, much as homosexuals and transgendered people are treated today, or those who claim to drink blood in the worship of a man who rose from the dead like Nosferatu, who attack those they fear and accuse of being witches, or just damned "sinners"? And which is Jack Torrance really acting more like: the former or the latter?

To remove from my own eye the cross shaped plank of my own beliefs, I had to consider all of this, in order to see both history, and Jack, in a whole new light. Only then could I see how Jack and Danny were

---

[38] https://www.dw.com/en/witch-hunts-a-global-problem-in-the-21st-century/a-54495289

tied together by not just their trauma and their ability to shine, but by their environment, in the Overlook, and how it operated like a maze of mirrors in a gallery of echoes. To see the madness that was being reflected back to them, we have to look into the past to understand how three ideas embodied in the Playgirl magazine are being used to cut up Jack's mind into little pieces.

The Trinity of Forbidden Desires

What symbolic meaning was Kubrick inviting us to play with by having Jack read a Playgirl magazine on Closing Day? Does it symbolize sexual abuse of Danny by Jack, as film analyst Rob Ager theorized,[39] or "perhaps a bit more"? And if so, is Jack engaging in such pedophilia because he suffers from his own repressed homosexual desires, or because he is just trying to fit into a culture at the Overlook that reflects the "royalty" of ancient history? While Ager does a good job of arguing for the former, there is a long history of "royalty" and "all the best people" engaging in the latter.

On its' face, the Playgirl magazine therefore invites us to consider the history of essentially three ideas: incest (because of an article on the cover entitled "Incest: Why Parents Sleep with Their Children"), homosexuality, and pedophilia/pederasty. Let's start with incest.

INCEST

Among "royalty," since Wendy asked Stuart if that was the Overlook's clientele, incest was accepted and practiced at least as

---

[39] On YouTube or CollativeLearning.com, see "THE SHINING: Danny's ordeal and the bear costumed man – film analysis Rob Ager"

far back as ancient Egypt, and more recently among members of royal families like the Habsburgs, from the 16th to 18th century: the same centuries when witch hunts were so fashionable. In fact, the ability to engage in the very kinds of behaviors of which the masses were prohibited by priestly excoriation was precisely what having power is all about, from incest and rape to feeding people to the lions and convincing (or compelling) the masses that slaughtering each other is "God's will" and thus the highest moral imperative imaginable.

Nor were the perceived virtues of incest merely the product of an antiquated past. As recent as 1974, for example, Freedman and Kaplan's *Comprehensive Textbook of Psychiatry* even claimed that incest may have health benefits: "Such incestuous activity diminishes the subject's chance of psychosis and allows for a better adjustment to the external world. . . . The vast majority of them were none the worse for the experience."[40] Like Thomas Aquinas condemning homosexuality and denouncing women as the devil's doorway while supporting pederasty, such a "scientific" perspective was clearly one based more on a "belief" than on actual understanding.

More than being just a desire to engage in what is socially taboo, however, incest was also practiced out of a desire to keep the family genes, well, "all in the family" (cue Edith and Archie Bunker playing the piano). As scientific discoveries mixed with ideas of spiritual superiority, reaching their zenith in Nazi Germany, "all the best people" had begun to "believe" that, like their spiritually superior religious beliefs, they

---

[40] Van der Kolk, Bessel, *The Body Keeps the Score*, Viking Press, 2014, p. 190.

must also therefore be biologically superior as well. Racism and religion, in this respect, are merely two sides of a mirror of moral superiority.

The royal families that practiced incest were merely aping a religion that illustrated God's own divine preference for it. According to the Bible, in fact, incest was God's preferred method for getting the ball rolling in the whole human race, at least initially. We see this with both Adam & Eve and their sons and daughters (Genesis 4; 5:4); Abraham marrying his half-sister, Sarah (Genesis 20:12); Lot impregnating his daughters (Genesis 19), Moses' father, Amram, marrying his aunt Jochebed (Exodus 6:20); and David's son, Amnon, getting it on with his half-sister, Tamar (2 Samuel 13). Such stories reflect the status of royalty, including among the gods and heroes of Greece, in which such practices were well known.

In sum, incest was the "sin" that God forbade, as it says in Deuteronomy and Leviticus 18:7–18 and 20:11–21, even though He required the first humans to engage in it in order to comply with His command to "be fruitful and multiply." And while the first humans were commanded to engage in incest to propagate the whole human race, it was also a "sin" so displeasing to that same God that He threatened to torture people who would only exist as a result of it, for all eternity for taking any pleasure in engaging in doing so, as He had biologically designed them to do. And it is into this hall of insanity that Jack is being indoctrinated, and we wonder why he's losing his mind.

HOMSEXUALITY

Then there is the other more obvious element symbolized in the Playgirl magazine: homosexuality. To understand how this relates to *The Shining*, we must see how homosexuality was understood by Native Americans, African slaves, and the ancient eras of Greece and Babylon.

With all the Native American art in the Overlook hotel, seeing a connection between *The Shining* and Native American culture is easiest of all. Seeing a connection between the Playgirl magazine and Native American sexuality, however, is more difficult. The latter hides an interesting history that reflects the use of violence against those who failed to conform to religious ideals about what sex was, and how it could be practiced. As a result, non-conformists were often treated like witches or heretics, and brutalized by Christian missionaries as if they were the new Sanhedrin punishing Jesus himself for his disobedience to their authority.

The *Berdache*

In the sixteenth century, among Native American tribes, Jesuits labeled transvestite men who dressed and behaved like women, both socially and sexually, as "*berdache*." For European Christians, any gender variation outside of the male-female binary was as terrifying to their souls as "witches" and the devil himself. Even sexual positions that deviated from the "missionary" position were defined by the Roman Church as perverted and "deviant." In fact, so worried by the threat those different sexual positions had to both salvation and the moral fabric of society, the church even passed laws and employed a "sex police" that could execute couples that dared to allow the wife to be on top during sex. According to these holy men, who like Vestal virgins had chosen the pleasure of penance over the pleasures of their own penis, the intent of sex was first and foremost for keeping God happy, and making babies, not for the pleasure of those who had been commanded to do the latter, even if it angered the former. This was like a five-star rated chef insisting his food is first and foremost for nourishing one's body, not for the pleasure of our taste buds. (Thanks a lot, St. Augustine.) (Dick.)

Terrified by the prospect that sexual and gender non-conformists were inviting God to treat the world overall like Sodom and Gomorrah, and anyone who tolerated such non-conformists could expect to be treated no better than God treated the sinners He sought to smite with his wrath, the term *berdache* was intended to convey judgment and condemnation. In effect, it was a term cast like a stone with one's tongue, to shame both the individuals who occupied such roles, as well as the cultures that accepted them. The hope was that by doing so, God wouldn't firebomb whole cities again; because even though He promised not to flood the planet again, He made no such promises about using a flame-thrower or nuclear weapons.

In the arts and other areas of life, the *berdache* were instrumental parts of a culture that suffered from a phobia of the female gender. Like the theater in ancient Greece and during the English Renaissance, and even Japanese kabuki theatre, which treated the female gender overall like the Rosa Parks of male dominated societies, the *berdache* performed the vital roles of female in male ritual ceremonies. Without them, ironically enough, the gods who desired to be honored with such ceremonies could not be appeased.

Yet the role of the *berdache* was not limited to the ritual ceremonies or theater plays. Like the priest, it was a permanent position. In fact, like John the Baptist, Paul on the road to Damascus, or even Jesus Christ,

273

those who devoted themselves to such a role often did so after having a sacred vision. And because they did, like the Pharisees who orchestrated the crowd in the courtyard to scream "crucify him" (because Jesus threatened their power and privilege), so the Jesuits, who encouraged their faithful flocks to cast their moral condemnations at the *berdache*, did so because the *berdache* held the privileged position of spiritual authority among their tribes – a position that the Jesuits wished to covet for themselves. Simply put, the Jesuits, who wore robes that were like a woman's dress, wanted to take the jobs of the *berdache*, who performed the same role while wearing the same kind of dresses.

In addition to a host of other elements, there is also a spiritual component to the homosexuality alluded to by the Playgirl magazine that dovetails into the Native American art seen in the lobby and the CL. In his book, *The Hidden Spirituality of Men*, theologian Mathew Fox pointed out that Native American tribes understood homosexuality as providing a powerful lens that facilitated a greater appreciation and understanding of the dualistic nature of human experience. From without, much like women and minorities in some cultures, homosexuals provided a perspective of society from outside the binary lens of heteronormative perception offered by religions that define sex as being, as St. Augustine argued throughout his life, the root of all of the sins of the flesh.[41] From within, the power of the *berdache* lay in their flexible

---

[41] Naturally, St. Augustine never cared to address the most obvious questions about his faith, like why a "perfect" and wholly immaterial God would feel the desire, let alone the need, to create a wholly flawed and imperfect material reality, and then populate it with spiritual beings (us) who He had imprisoned inside of sinful "fallen" flesh, the strongest desire of which was for sexual pleasure so we would "be fruitful and multiply," but against which we were commanded to struggle and resist our whole lives, and always in accord

perspective on gender, a perspective which enabled them to operate as a nexus of understanding between men and women, or between Mars and Venus. Such a lens, which amounted to being able to see the female elements in every man and the male elements within every woman, was why women keep "falling in love with gay men (not knowing they were gay)," Fox explains, "because gay men understood women so much better" than heterosexual men, "and they project a more attractive interest in life, the arts, and their own bodies."[42]

More than being just a nexus through which men and women could better relate to one another by better relating to that other half that dwelled within themselves, homosexuals also functioned in many Native American cultures as the conduit between human and spiritual worlds. As a result, they held "special spiritual powers: of healing, of leading some ceremonies, and of seeing into the future," much as Danny does. And because they did, as Fox further points out, "much of the animus against the Indians exhibited by the original Spanish conquistadors was an animus against homosexuality, which was quite open among the Mayans."

Like the Pharisees toward Jesus, Spanish missionaries masked their lust for power over Native Americans behind the false-face of "God's love." With the authority of a religion that began as a heretical cult in Rome, came the power to judge those natives like a God. More importantly, that authority came with the power to impose upon those deemed by that religion to be sinners and saints in this life what God

---

with ever changing perspectives on sex and sexuality, in order to save ourselves from being tortured forever for failing to do so. What a great plan.

[42] Fox, Matthew, T*he Hidden Spirituality of Men*; New World Library (2008), p. 123-4.

alone had previously held the authority to bestow in the next. And as Christianity swept through those cultures like a spiritual corona virus, ideas about sex were laid to waste and a lust for ideals, defined by a new class of spiritual rules who saw abstinence as the greatest of virtues, rose in its wake. While sex had always been understood as the greatest gift given to humanity from the gods, which even the gods themselves regularly sought to partake in it with humans as often as possible, Christianity transformed it from a celebration of life (reflected in the young seductress in room 237) into a mechanical process for pleasing an immaterial intelligence that was said to be infinitely greater than our own, making babies, and the doorway to hell and spiritual death (the old hag), for anyone who engaged in it just for the pleasure of it. Even the ancient motif of a God procreating with human wives to produce divine children, with Zeus himself fathering around 100 children, including Apollo and Hercules, was rewritten to reflect Christianity's fear of sex as a gateway sin, which is why Mary had to remain "ever virgin."

And lastly, like Jack's posture in the final photograph, the role of transvested homosexuals as spiritual mediums and religious leaders among Native American communities allowed them to serve as a visible symbol of the spiritual harmony of opposites, the personified embodiment of the yin and the yang.

This same pattern can be seen in how homosexuality relates to the brown outfits worn by many of the employees of the Overlook, as well as the paintings of African American infants in the "staff wing of the hotel." Again, such pictures allude to the idea of "the white man's burden" to "civilize" both Native Americans and African slaves, by teaching them who to judge, and to even judge themselves, as sinner and saint, according to whatever brand of the Christian religion held sway in "them thar hills."

The *Jin Bandaa*

Like the *berdache*, the first Portuguese to visit Angola found transvested "sodomites" were an apparently respected caste of *jin bandaa* or *quimbanda* (medicine men).[43] In addition to caring for and performing funeral rituals, this caste performed the roles of spirit mediums and religious leaders.

The homosexuality found among these tribes was the result of the fact that their culture fostered a large degree of homosociality, just like the priesthood or a prison. In their culture, men and women tended to live most of their lives in largely separate spheres, with both typically having their own huts, fields, institutions, rituals, games, and so on.[44] This separation was especially pronounced in pastoral, hunting, or military societies. Unlike Europeans, the homosexual "play" that might result in these cultures was, much like in the gymnasiums of Ancient Sparta, "often regarded as appropriate "training" for heterosexual marriage, preferable to heterosexual mixing that could result in illegitimate pregnancies and political complications."

Stolen from their homes in the sixteenth century and sent to work in European colonies, the *jin bandaa* were tortured and burned at the stake by Portuguese and Spanish Inquisitors. By the turn of the nineteenth century, the spread of colonialism and capitalism led Christian law

---

[43] Haggerty, George E., *Gay Histories and Cultures: An Encyclopedia*, Garland Publishing, Inc., New York and London, 2000, p. 17.
[44] Ibid. p. 18.

makers to redefine the customary homosexual "play" practiced by such tribes as "unnatural acts" (as if a vow of celibacy to appease a totally immaterial "being" isn't the most "unnatural act" of all) punishable by death, a hundred lashes, or five years in prison.

Like reaction formation, according to Carl Jung, the loathing of sexual non-conformists may be a form of self-loathing. Much like our physical brains and ourselves in the first months of development as a fetus, our unconscious is in fact transgendered. Like the left hemisphere of our brain being more digitally inclined while the right hemisphere is more analogue, so too our "shadow-side" is comprised of what Jung called the anima and animus: two terms that are directly related to the man sitting in the foreground smoking a cigar as we see Jack first walk into the lobby.

The animus, according to Jung, constituted the unconscious masculine side of a woman, while the anima was the unconscious feminine side of a man. These qualities were not inherent to everyone's personal unconscious, however, but constituted two sides of the collective unconscious.

This "collective unconscious" was comprised of mental concepts that are so common and pervasive within a culture that we never really think about them. Examples include our ideals, instincts, or archetypes, that latter of which includes The Great Mother and the Tree of Life. As sociologist and social psychologist Erving Goffman pointed out in his book, *Gender Advertisements* (1976), the ideals, instincts, and archetypes we rely on to delineate our binary codes of behavior are largely designed for us. And they are so invisible to us, and seem so natural to us, that they constitute the cultural oxygen we breathe.

Transcendence, from this perspective, could only come from elevating one's own personal psyche above the clouds of the larger collective unconscious, in order to become conscious of the anima or animus operating within a given society. Jack reading his Playgirl magazine after he has ascended into the clouds, as such, looks as if maybe he is striving to "fit in" to an ancient culture of "beliefs," one whose sacred ideals are praised as reflecting the absolute and immutable virtues of the Gods; virtues and ideals which are said to last "forever, and ever, and ever." In truth, however, such "ideals" never last, because we are always changing our minds about them.

Unbeknownst to him, however, what repressed desires might Jack be unwittingly unleashing by striving to fit it?

For Jung, the *berdache* of Native America, the *jin bandaa* of Africa, and the traditional understandings of homosexuals in Greece and Rome, were all more enlightened than the European belief systems which replaced them centuries later, which saw such people as no better than witches. And while Inquisitors and conquistadors, who coveted the positions held by the *berdache* and the *jun bandaa* mostly for the power and privilege such positions provided, bled them from society by the sword, Christian theologians used the pen to recast them as inveterate sinners responsible for the suffering of Christ, the loss of souls, and the death of societies and even whole empires. The story of Sodom and Gomorrah was likewise recast from a story detailing the sin of inhospitality - a core cultural understanding in Homer's *Iliad* and *Odyssey*, which was reflected in Mary and Joseph having to lodge for the night in a barn - into one of sexual perversion in which the guilty and the innocent were punished indiscriminately with nuclear destruction.

279

Christianity turned the tides on all of this. In the process, theologians from Augustine to Thomas Aquinas praised only those ideas of Greece and Rome that served to fortify their own prejudices, even as they rejected the rich cultural pluralism and tolerance that had been required to give birth to such ideas in the first place. But this was to praise selected fruits and flowers of a garden while condemning the soil in which they grew. And St. Thomas Aquinas, who supported the practice of pederasty between men and boys, saw no contradiction in his condemnation of homosexuality among consenting adults. Like Jack in the Overlook, Aquinas had a miraculous ability to see only what he wanted to "believe." And such moral relativism is what could even be said to start driving Jack to be as homicidal for the Overlook as Augustine eventually became for his Catholicism.

Babylon & Greece

Another ancient culture in which "all the best people" would've expected to see Jack reading a Playgirl magazine on his first day on the job jumped out at me from the shelves in Stuart's office. Combined with the color of the room, those shelves resembled the labia minora: two small folds of skin that extend backward on each side of the opening into the vagina. From this perspective, the back of the room first Jack, then Wendy, walks through, may even be why Dick Hallorann told Larry Durkin that the Torrance's "turned out to be completely unreliable assholes."

Recall that the vines hanging from those shelves are known as "Devil's ivy" and "the money plant." Those vines, and those shelves, hinted at the Hanging Gardens of Babylon (yes, of course this is a stretch, but that's the point!), a place in which both homosexuality and anal sex were seen as perfectly normal. Even the Great Mother painting just outside of Stuart's office, of a woman wearing blue platefoolmail, armor, hinted at the blue bricked gateway into the inner city of Babylon. Called the Ishtar Gate, it was named after the ancient Mesopotamian goddess, Ishtar, who was associated with love, sensuality, fertility and war, giving her the extraordinary ability to both create life, and to take it away. And while the blue platemail reflected the blue outfits we see Wendy wearing in the beginning of the film, the contrast of love and war are reflected in the woman in room 237.

On the other hand, the red eagle on Stuart's impossible windowsill invites us to peer into the mythology of Greece, which was also steeped in homosexual relations of various sorts. That eagle, along with the one Jack wakes up wearing, call to mind the first King of kings, the supreme God of all the gods, and the father of both Apollo and Aphrodite: Zeus. Combined with the Woodstock sticker on Danny's bedroom door, those eagles allude to the legend of Ganymede.

To see the relationship between Zeus, those two eagles, Woodstock, and Jack's Playgirl magazine, it is important to understand some context. According to Plato's *Symposium*, homosexuality was held by many people in Greece to be in some ways, a bit like the *berdache* and the *jin bandaa*, superior to heterosexuality. This was because, as Plato points out, Greek mythology claimed there were originally three kinds of complete human beings (or Adam's and Eve's). All three were spherical creatures. Of the three, some consisted of a man and a man, others of a woman and a woman, and finally the heterosexual kind made up of a man and a woman. As punishment from the gods, these spherical humans were eventually sliced in half (mitosis?), so that now, each half runs around in search of its other half. As Plato further explains, the heterosexual half was spoken of with scorn:

> Then all men who are cutting of the old common sex which was called manwoman are fond of women, and adulterers generally come of that sex, and all women who are made for men, and adulteresses. . . . but those which are a cutting of the male pursue the male . . . and these are the best of boys and lads because they are naturally bravest . . . Here is great proof: when they grow up, such as these alone are men in public affairs . . . [They] do not trouble about marriage and getting a family, but that law and custom compels them.[45]

This view that heterosexual relations were more problematic than homosexual unions was reflected in the story of Adam & Eve and later, in St. Augustine's claim that it would have been better that God had created as Adam's companion another man, rather than a woman. (That he was criticizing God, and even suggesting God had made a mistake, was a far more crucifiable offense than anything Jesus Christ had ever even been falsely accused of.)

On the other hand, the bravery that same-sex relations could produce was detailed in Plutarch's accounting of an elite corps of homosexuals knowns as "The Lovers Battalion" from Thebes. Also known as the "holy troop," it remained undefeated until the battle of Chaironeia in 338 B.C.E. The basis of its superiority was believed to be the fact that it operated on the principle that "it is good to put a lover side by side with his beloved." Not only is one most concerned about their beloved when

---

[45] Ranke-Heinemann, Uta, *Eunuchs for the Kingdom of Heaven*, Germany, Doubleday, 1988, p. 321.

danger arrives, so the reasoning went, but lovers especially want to distinguish themselves in the eyes of their beloved.

Among the aristocracy of Athens, and in part because of the renowned bravery of The Lovers Battalion, such relations were idealized and even encouraged. From great Theseus leaving his wife for Pirithous, king of the Lapiths of Larissa, to Alexander the Great's close emotional attachment to his childhood friend, Hephaestion, which was compared to that of Achilles and Patroclus, such relationships merely reflected the power of Zeus and Apollo.

In Sparta, where the practice was said to have begun with young boys training naked in the gymnasiums, it slowly began to lose its luster. But even as it did, Greeks overall never saw such a practice as something that would lead the gods to treat Athens and Sparta like Sodom and Gomorrah. It would take the rewriting of ancient history to convince lovers of a particular brand of "God" that Sodom and Gomorrah deserved exactly what they got, not for failing to welcome strangers as was the highest duty for such cultures, but for daring to exercise their own God-given "free will" to love who they freely choose.[46]

THE CHRISTIAN PARADIGM SHIFT

Christianity changed our perspective on sexuality on the whole, and on homosexuality most of all. It convinced us that our sexual desires, however natural to our flesh, were unnatural to our soul's desire for salvation from eternal hell. To save our soul from the latter,

---

[46] Presumably, this is because if God had made robots instead of people with "free will," He could not justify torturing them for all eternity for how they used that free will to make Him so eternally angry, and still come out smelling like roses.

Christianity taught us that sexual desires needed to be pruned and regimented like military recruits in boot camp. As a result, such desires were seen as permissible only if they were subdued and practiced in accord with religiously defined parameters. Anything outside of those parameters was grounds for eternal torments without the opportunity for parole or appeal. Sex, from this sacred perspective, was for making babies, and the pleasure of that came from the act was simply an inducement to that end, but certainly not to be enjoyed for its own sake. Homosexuality, as a result, was recast from something enjoyed by heroes and Gods, from Achilles to Zeus, to being something for which whole cities could be razed to the ground, with all who lived in those cities, who were not homosexuals, being punished for their tolerance of those who were.

I was reminded of all of this by how much the cashier window in the Overlook resembles the screen in a confessional. Men who saw their flesh as subordinate to their ideals ended up sublimating their natural desires with the power they acquired through the sexual voyeurism provided by the confessional. And the more the salacious details pricked and tempted their libidos from the latter, the more such men used their power to castigate their congregations about the sinfulness of the former. Fueled by a vow of celibacy, which was far more unnatural than the homosexuality they abhorred, such men flexed their spiritual power by proscribing rules and dogmas about who could have sex, how, when, where, and why, and threatening anyone who failed to conform to their dictates with eternal pain. What those who proscribed such draconian dogmas overlooked, however, was the irony that came from the fact that if there was only one "right way" to have sex, celibacy, which honored that belief by rejecting the practice altogether, amounted to a form of sexual atheism. Indeed, practicing celibacy for an immaterial "God" is like showing your gratitude to the corporation that awarded you a free lifetime supply of Viagra by acting like a eunuch.

From these perspectives, the Playgirl magazine we see Jack reading allows us to interpret the events of the film as being simply a result of Jack, like a modern-day Augustine, trying to murder a side of himself he may have been conditioned to loath as part of a sinful nature he was born with. Rather than molesting Danny, perhaps Jack is trying either to murder that side of himself that he has learned to identify with sin, or he is tired of having to work all the time to hide his own homosexual desires, because "all work and no play makes Jack a dull boy."

Like the Hogan and the Gibbons twins, so imagining Jack's murderous rampage to be triggered by a self-loathing for his own repressed homosexuality also has a real-world counterpart that even reflects Danny's Mickey Mouse sweater: American footballer Aaron Hernandez. Before his career ended abruptly after his arrest and conviction for the murder of Odin Lloyd in June of 2013, Hernandez played for three years in the National Football League as a tight end for the New England Patriots. In a TV interview that aired in January of 2020, Aaron Hernandez's brother, Johnathan, divulged that, just before committing suicide in prison, Aaron had tearfully told his mother that he was gay.[47]

---

[47] https://nypost.com/2020/01/29/aaron-hernandez-tearfully-told-mom-he-was-gay-before-prison-suicide-brother-says/

This raises a question for Hernandez's family. To what extent might the muscles, the tattoos, and even the violence, both on the gridiron and in the killing of Lloyd, have been fueled, at least in part, by a desperate need of a man trying his best to hide that very part of himself he not only loathed, but also considered to be part of a feared and shameful "them?"

Coincidentally, Caitlyn Jenner confessed to something similar. According to her, more than anything else, what drove her to win a gold medal in the decathlon during 1974 Olympics was her attempt to use her masculinity as "Bruce" to drive out and ultimately destroy the feelings that her gender was incompatible with her sexual anatomy. From a Christian perspective, such "feelings" should be considered "evil," even though from other perspectives, it is the teaching that such feelings are "evil" that is the real evil we should fear.

Among Native American's, such a feeling is honored as reflecting someone who was revered as a "two spirit" person, someone blessed with an ability to see with both a masculine and feminine perspective at the same time. Such people could even be considered to have, like Danny, "second sight." With the rise of the vilification of sex and sexuality, however, such people have, like Hernandez and Jenner, often been culturally conditioned to feel like June and Jennifer Gibbons: as if one half of themselves must die so the other can live a "normal life," unburdened by the curse of such "second sight."

From this perspective, Jack is simply trying to teach Danny about how society requires him to treat any ideas about sex or gender that fall outside of the parameters defined by religion or society - especially if he finds himself feeling like Hernandez or Jenner - just like God treated Sodom and Gomorrah. (Clearly, since it's in the Bible, such a burnt-earth response to coloring outside the lines of sexuality drawn by a priestly class of eunuchs is the morally appropriate response.) And he is teaching him this, like so many others do, despite the fact that such "intersexed people" – some of whom are born with both male and female genitalia – are in fact proof that, to truly be made in the image and likeness of a lone divine Creator (like the Earth itself, or the Universe as a whole), each of us, like our earliest of ancestors, would have to also be somewhat intersexual. Hell, for the first couple of months of gestation in our mother's womb, we are!

Even the virgin birth of Jesus, since the Y chromosome needed to produce a male child must come from a flesh and blood male father, suggests that one reason that contributed to Jesus's crucifixion was because he was, as the "new Adam," intersexual. In a theory referred to as "The Microbial Eve," scientists have offered a perspective of our most distant biological ancestors that indicates the story of God creating Eve from the rib of Adam is actually just the fig leaf of a metaphor for explaining mitosis and meiosis. According to such a theory, "all life on Earth evolved from a single-celled organism that lived roughly 3.5 billion years ago."[48] So, it turns out that Adam and Eve were also Adam and Steve. Who knew?!

The irony of this is that the transgendered community overall is so often treated by religious leaders today in the very same way Jesus Christ was treated by the leaders of his own brand of religion in his own day, and perhaps even for the very same reason.

---

[48] https://www.nationalgeographic.com/adventure/article/100513-science-evolution-darwin-single-ancestor

PEDERASTY

All of this leads us to the idea of pederasty, a practice exercised by the most royal "royalty" of Greece: the gods. While not exercised everywhere in Greece by humans, Plato indicates that at least one place where pederasty was popular was Crete: the very same city where King Minos was sacrificing children to the Minotaur in the Myth of Theseus.

The most celebrated model of man-boy relationship is the paiderasteia of the ancient Greeks, whose culture was thoroughly permeated by the institution. From the godly Alexander the Great who had Hellenized the known world, to the great Thomas Aquinas who helped to convert that world to Catholicism, such a practice was seen as normal and even useful (which may help to shed some light on the prevalence of such a practice within the Catholic Church today).

The pederastic element in Hellenic culture was part of the whole system of paideia. The paideia constituted the education that was intended to make a boy a good soldier, a good father, a good citizen, and a good statesman; and all to endow him with the combination of qualities which Greek civilization cherished and admired in the adult. Plutarch's "Life of Lycurgus" mentions edicts of that archetypal lawgiver to the effect that a man was obligated to form such a union, and that a boy was disgraced if he could not find an honorable lover who would be responsible for his conduct on the battlefield. To this end, although the Greeks practiced several varieties of pederasty, a particularly admired form was practiced by the military culture of Sparta.

Ganymede

So natural was "homosexuality" – a term invented to describe same-sex attraction in the 19ᵗʰ century – to Greek culture that one of Greece's most famous myths, regarding its greatest "royalty," has to do with pederasty: the abduction and rape of Ganymede by Zeus.

As a young man from Troy, Ganymede's beauty was said to be unparalleled. So striking was his beauty, in fact, that Zeus, unable to resist his desires any longer, finally abducted the boy and brought him to Olympus to serve as both cupbearer to the gods and his personal lover. Like Jack's Stovington shirt and Woodstock being carried into the clouds, according to legend, Zeus swooped down in the form of a giant eagle and carried Ganymede to Olympus. As Homer puts it:

> "Zeus carried off golden-haired (like Danny's) Ganymedes because of his beauty, to be amongst the Deathless Ones (Gold Room party attendees?) and pour drink for the gods in the house of Zeus—a wonder to see–, honoured by all the immortals as he draws the red nectar (red rum?) from the golden bowl."

Zeus also offered to make Ganymede an immortal, blessed with eternal youth, serving in the banquets of the gods, forever, like Jack appears to be doing in the final photograph (he is dressed like Delbert Grady, after all). What's more, on Closing Day, when Stuart, Wendy, Jack, and Bill, first walk through the CL, sitting right where Jack's typewriter will eventually sit for the rest of the movie, we see a large "golden bowl," which we will never see again. And from that bowl, Jack outpours his "Redrum" across our screen, poured out as sacrificial wine for the gods to drink as they enjoy the blood sport they have come to feast their eyes upon.

The myth of Ganymede has a still darker side. Although none of the sources mention Ganymede's age, it is assumed that he was quite young, probably adolescent. Some even think he may have been an infant. In fact, the ancient sources explicitly imply that he was young, definitely an adolescent, but perhaps even younger than that. While today the age of consent is a legal indicator separating pederasty from valid sexual relationships, in antiquity, no such demarcation line existed.

Nor do we need to go back to ancient Greek mythology to see how the gods seemed to have a proclivity for pederasty. Even in the Catholic Church, such behavior has long been defended and practiced. In addition to the great St. Thomas Aquinas supporting pederasty, in 1531, Martin Luther upbraided Pope Leo X[49] for having vetoed a measure that cardinals should restrict the number of boys they kept for their pleasure, "otherwise it would have been spread throughout the world how openly and shamelessly the Pope and the cardinals in Rome practice sodomy."[50]

Nor was Leo the only one. Guided by Aquinas's divine perspective on the legitimacy of pederasty, Pope Benedict IX was famous for debauching young boys in the Lateran Palace, leading Saint Peter Damian to describe him as "a demon from hell in the disguise of a priest." Pope Julius II (1503-13), who commissioned Michelangelo to paint the Sistine Chapel ceiling, caught syphilis from Rome's male prostitutes. Pope Boniface VIII (1294-1303), known as a pedophile who massacred the entire population of Palestrina, even famously declared that "pedophilia" was no more a sin "than rubbing one hand against the other." And Pope Julius III, who was elected in 1550 and oversaw the

---

[49] Leo X also famous for admitting about Christianity: "How well we know what a profitable superstition this fable of Christ has been for us and our predecessors."
[50] *Derek Wilson (2007). Out of the Storm: The Life and Legacy of Martin Luther. London: Hutchinson.* This allegation was made in the pamphlet *Warnunge D. Martini Luther/ An seine lieben Deudschen*, Wittenberg, 1531

second session of the council of Trent (1552-1554) that reaffirmed the celibacy of priests, entered a sexual liaison with a 15-year-old boy he had picked up off the streets of Parma. In fact, in 1555, before his death, Julius even made the boy a bishop. And with allusions to the article about incest in Jack's Playgirl magazine, "pope" means "papa" in that dead language: Latin.

Incredibly, the same Catholic Church that condemns homosexuals and pedophiles as sinners, much as it condemned women as "witches" in league with Lucifer, treat those within its own ranks that engage in such activities as people suffering not from sin, but from a psychological disorder. Such is the privilege of spiritual rank that it empowers those who claim to have access to infallible truth when it comes to all matters of faith and morals to know that certain sexual acts engaged in between consenting adults, which harm no one but the feelings of an infinitely superior God, are the result of supernatural evil, while the acts of rape which harm countless children, can all be explained by the psychological.

◊◊

By reading a Playgirl magazine in the lobby on his first day on the job at the Overlook, Jack opens this history for us to play with, a history that has largely remained hidden from our eyes behind a curtain of sacred beliefs: the same curtain that was torn open in the temple after Jesus gave up the ghost, as if to show the world the true nature of the religious wizards of his own day. In the absence of such a history, it is easy to interpret the magazine as a symbol for child abuse alone. With an awareness of such a history, however, new perspectives open to us, perspectives that offer a host of other interpretations and, by extension, understandings. It allows us to see why Jack's new boss ignores the Playgirl magazine as if it is a "completely normal" thing for Jack to be reading.

If we can think of the Overlook like Mount Olympus, Jack settling into the Overlook with his "tribe" can even reflect the idea of 1921 B.C.E., when wandering tribes first began settling in Greece. And whenever anyone moves to a new country or culture, especially for gainful employment, to assimilate into the new culture, a person will adopt its norms, its mores, and certainly its religions, as their own. Rather than reflecting merely incest or latent homosexual tendencies, the Playgirl magazine may be simply Jack's attempt to assimilate into a culture of "royalty" where homosexuality, pederasty, and even incest, are seen to be as "perfectly normal" as Charles Grady, much as they were among the "royalty" of ancient Greece and Babylon. And as Joe Girard pointed out, there is even a picture of the tower of Babylon in the Torrance apartment.

Even in room 237, we find more references to Greek mythology in general, and Aphrodite more specifically. Like the woman rising out of the water in the bathtub, Aphrodite is described in Hesiod's *Theogony* as being miraculously *born from the water* of Paphos on the island of Cyprus, after the Titan Cronus killed and castrated his own father, Uranus. And with the woman turning into an old hag, Jack is symbolically castrated. Even the rug pattern inside of room 237, as already mentioned, resembles a chorus of castrated penises, all of which are crowned in green laurels and pointing in unison toward the bathroom. In the same way, the Chorus in Greek theater was used to direct the audiences' attention and emotions.

We see even more allusions to Aphrodite with Danny and Jack. The son of Aphrodite was Eros, who often carried a bow and arrow or a lyre, while on Closing Day, we see Danny throwing red darts in the Games Room before seeing the Grady twins, and the word we see emblazoned across his back is "LYERS." And like Jack locked in the story room after Wendy knocked him down the stairs, Zeus eventually marries off Aphrodite to Hephaestus, who was a cripple. And finally, yet another symbol for Aphrodite is the mirror itself.

ELEVEN

THE BOOK OF REVELATIONS

"In a world full of people who seem to know everything, passionately, based on little (often slanted) information, where certainty is often mistaken for power, what a relief it is to be in the company of someone confident enough to stay unsure (that is, perpetually curious)."

George Saunders

The only true voyage of discovery, the only fountain of Eternal Youth, would be not to visit other lands but to possess new eyes.

Marcel Proust

DID YOU EVER LIE DOWN IN THE GRASS, gaze up into the sky, and see faces and other familiar shapes or objects in the clouds? If you did, you were experiencing a phenomenon referred to as "pareidolia," which is the tendency to perceive a specific image in a random or ambiguous visual pattern. The twin of this ability is "apophenia," which occurs when we then attribute meaning onto the patterns we perceive. Often, these two subconscious habits are influenced by our cultural formatting and the "beliefs" that color our perceptions. And, because we often come to depend on them for our identity, meaning, purpose, security and sense of social status and

294

community, those beliefs can then become immune to our willingness to question, even as they operate in our unconscious to magnify our fear or skepticism of everyone else's beliefs. A Christian may see the face of Jesus in a piece of burnt toast and think it means they need to go to Church, for instance, even as they deny that a person in China, who might see the face of Confucius in that same burnt toast and think it means they should sit in a garden and contemplate the nature of existence itself, is simply having the exact same culturally conditioned experience. Seeing is not believing as much as we only see what we believe. "There is no world save the one we make with our minds," George Saunders wrote, "and the mind's predisposition determines the type of world we see."

As a child, my pareidolia had been colored by the lens of my Catholicism. And the meaning I then attributed to the shadows that clawed at my bedcovers in the middle of the night, much like the meaning I attributed to everything and anything, merely reflected the biases my Catholic beliefs had injected into my subconscious imagination through the Trojan horse of my own trusting parents. Accepting such a "belief" as infallible truth, my prayerful attempts to save myself from such demons only operated to reinforce my belief that such demons were real, and that only my brand of "God" could save me from then, and then only if I was willing to obey my Catholic overlookers and sell my brand of religion. My Catholicism turned me into the little match girl, in other words, who would only be fed the bread of eternal life if I sold the matches of my Catholic religion as my Heavenly father required. And if I failed at this endeavor, I could be burned at the stake for all eternity.

Because my Catholicism was the only paradigmatic lens though which I had been wholly conditioned to see and interpret all my experiences, feelings, and indeed everything, it was inevitable that I would eventually become terrified by the images my own pareidolia and apophenia had been conditioned to create and interpret out of thin air painted in shadows and light. And from the torture chamber that my own mind had been turned into through the baptismal waterboarding of such "beliefs," I had been desperately trying to heal, and awake, and escape, my whole life.

And that's when Kubrick, on "all hallows eve," invited me to "come and play" with the matches of my own curiosity, by rolling out a ball that only "those who shine" could see. And by illuminating my own "shine" by being as curious as a child and choosing to play with the images that danced before me, Kubrick taught me that "the only thing that was ever wrong with me," as Glennon Doyle put it so aptly, "was the belief that there was something wrong with me."

Having lived under the tyranny of such a belief for decades, and convinced I was "free" because I had accepted such "truth" all the while, I knew I needed to turn the tables. Aware of the confirmation biases my "beliefs" had seeded in my subconscious about my sinful nature, I knew I needed to reclaim the "wonder twin" powers of my pareidolia and apophenia from my Catholic colonizers. To do that, I would need to resurrect my creative potential from the temple of obedience to a religion, so I could rebirth my inner child to be as creative as every child can be. After all, the synchronicities and incredible precision I had discovered lurking about in Kubrick's film appeared to be a clear invitation to not only come out and play, but also to "dare to strike out and find new ground." And I could only do that by being daring enough to truly know thyself.

Reclaiming the "wonder twin" powers of my own pareidolia and apophenia allowed me to finally see what was really happening between the Hatfield's and McCoy's that the two hemispheres of my brain had been turned into by my religion. Only then could call a truce and, like those soldiers who crawled out of their foxholes to play football on Christmas during World War I, "come and play" with Kubrick's *Shining* video-ball game. Less interested in finding ultimate answers than for the sake of play itself, such a cinematic sandbox was actually a boot camp for training your mind to challenge its most sacred and cherished beliefs. And as it turned out, play for the sake of play, freed from the cudgel blows of judgement about ability or worthiness, is where we find all the answers we're looking for, both about the film and the one playing with it. Because it is only through play that we can ever know who we really are.

According to Aristotle, "the most important relationship we can all have is the one you have with yourself." And we must strive to know that, as Soren Kierkegaard argued, "before knowing anything else." According to Thales of Miletus, the pre-Socratic philosopher who paved the way for scientific skepticism, this is the hardest thing of all to do. For Aristotle, the most terrifying journey a person could make was one of self-discovery, because "knowing yourself is the beginning of all wisdom." And this is so terrifying for the same reason it leads to wisdom: because we fear truth to the same degree we cling to our beloved "beliefs." Facing the truths to be found in the former, however, is the only way to safeguard against, and overcome a dependence on, the falsehoods being smuggled into our souls under a banner of "truth, love, and salvation" by the latter. And when Jesus said, "the kingdom of God is within you," he was actually inviting us to know ourselves because, as Immanuel Kant explained so aptly, "it is only through the descent into the Hell of self-discovery that we can achieve godliness." Or as Jung put it, "only by making the unconscious conscious" can we free ourselves from what we mistakenly call fate.

The anxiety caused by modern living, which is exceedingly more precarious than living outside of the social superstructures we call "civilization" that we are born to depend on for everything, "makes us want to judge, be sure, have a stance, definitively decide." Having a fixed, rigid system of belief, as George Saunders observed, "can be a great relief" from such anxieties. Yet, on the one hand, those anxieties are as manmade as the civilizations that cause them, just like it manufactures are wants and desires to fuel and economy. And on the other, clinging to such beliefs to relieve such anxieties is to pillory our infinite capacity for creativity and imagination, with the shackles of a single sacred perspective, while fearing in ourselves that which alone makes us most like any form of infinitely creative intelligence we may call "God." It is, in short, to cramp an 11-dimensional mind into the two-dimensional box of a sacred "belief," a "belief," that claims to be sacred, because it is as unchanging as a photograph, and as straight and inflexible as a cross.

Yet it is only the creative capacity inherent to our biological design that allows us to see both faces in that postcard from 1888, while a dependence upon a sacred "belief" to save us from such a biological capacity requires us to acknowledge only one face on that postcard and

298

to deny the existence of the other. Such a "belief," as such, not only requires us to deny ourselves the way Peter denies Jesus, but in doing so, it bars us from every knowing ourselves. And by preventing us from ever knowing ourselves, we are permanently barred from ever "entering the kingdom of God" that Jesus said was "within" ourselves, by a "belief" that we are too sinful to enter such a kingdom, unless we prove ourselves worthy of forgiveness and love through our obedience and servitude.

To free myself from such shackles I had to learn how to play with the matches of my own curiosity and creativity in order to, like both the little match girl and even Jack in the novel, burn the maze of cherished "beliefs" I had been indoctrinated into from birth, to the ground. To do that, I had to "know thyself" enough to understand the true source of my fears and anxiety about those shadowy gremlins, so I could begin to parse out the difference between what I wanted or needed to believe was true, even if it wasn't, and what was true, at least for me, even if I didn't' want to believe it. More importantly, I had to determine whether beliefs that offered me some relief from the anxieties of the uncertainties of modern life were worth the price of sacrificing my own creativity, a creativity which I could only grow to fulfill its potential by seeing such uncertainties, not as something to be feared and safeguarded against or proof that my own intelligence was flawed because it failed to be as omniscient as a God, but as opportunities to think as far outside of the box of my sacred beliefs, as I was creative and courageous enough to go.

All of this required me to consider the criteria I used to determine what I was willing to believe was true, and what beliefs about truth I needed to question in order to see the truth operating behind the mask of my cherished religious "beliefs." And for you, dear reader, it is now up to you to decide if what you've read here has convinced you, or swayed your opinion in anyway, that Kubrick died with a *Shining* secret, only the edge of which the pages in this book has pulled back the curtain on to reveal. Rest assured, there is far more to unmask about the film, such as the room number those two men are in that Wendy sees, and why Jack's Mickey Mouse sweater is the key to understanding who frees Jack from the storage room, and also how the hotel itself can be pieces together, despite claims to the contrary.

Either way, what should be crystal clear by now is how the movie begs us to consider what criteria we use to determine what is true and what is false, and who gets to decide on such criteria, and who doesn't? And while it may look as if we've taken a dive deep into the entrails of Kubrick's video maze, the truth is that we've barely skimmed the surface of the rabbit hole Kubrick is inviting us into by rolling out Jack's little yellow car like a tennis ball to an audience sitting in their seats, playing with their beliefs about what they think they see.

Everything I have presented here, however, is far more than needed to finish putting *The Shining* puzzle together, in order to decipher what is really going on in the movie, and who or what is really looking back at us from the final photograph. But being like chess, a game that invites us to engage not in acting like a pope but like children playing in baseball in a field of rye, the only infallible truth I can assure the reader about this game more than anything else in the universe is this ...

Check.

Your move.

About the Author

Raised in a house where religion was more important than life itself, P. Michael Heffron is more of a survivor of his Roman Catholic upbringing and education than a product of it. Terrified by the prospect of being burned alive for all eternity, he saw no greater sin than to knowingly bring children into a world in which the ultimate point of being alive seemed to boil down to whether a person would end up, after death, with the reward of an eternity of pleasures for their obedience to both a religion that was full of contradictions and impossible to make sense of, and an institutional Church that was no better than any other institution on the planet (despite having an arsenal of supernatural sacraments, sole access to infallible truth, and claiming to be protected from sin and error by the spirit of God himself), or be boiled alive for all eternity for failing to abandon a need to make complete sense of such a religion and simply "believe" it to be "infallibly" true anyway. Trying to find some way to know that he, and any potential children he might one day have, could rest assured of avoiding the eternal tortures due anyone for the original sin of simply being born, he became convinced that the "work" of faith necessary for salvation came only from using the intelligence he'd been born with, not to find reasons for why he must always cling desperately to a "faith" in a brand of religion, but to free himself instead from the fears his religion had assured him he needed to both believe in, and therefore be saved from, which only his brand of religion could do, even though it was his brand of religion that had installed the fears he wanted to be saved from in the first place. And after 42 years of being lost in the wilderness of those worries, he finally found his way home by accidently sitting down and playing a game of chess one dark and stormy Halloween night, with the ghost of Stanley Kubrick. And checkmated his ass.

For anyone who may wish to know more, he can be reached at: pmichaelheffron@gmail.com

Made in the USA
Middletown, DE
18 July 2023